Presented to Crosby Hall
March 10, 1974.

This book was written at Crosby
Hall, 1972-1973.

Sister Mary Edith.
Willow, Ph.D.

AN ANALYSIS OF THE ENGLISH POEMS

OF ST. THOMAS MORE

BIBLIOTHECA

HUMANISTICA & REFORMATORICA

VOLUME VIII

THOMAS MORE
(Detail of a sculpture by L. Cubitt Bevis outside Chelsea Old Church, London)

AN ANALYSIS
OF THE ENGLISH POEMS
OF ST. THOMAS MORE

By

SISTER MARY EDITH WILLOW, Ph. D.
Sister of the Holy Family of Nazareth

NIEUWKOOP

B. DE GRAAF

1974

ISBN 90 6004 316 2

Printed in the Netherlands by **N.V.** Drukkerij Trio • The Hague

TABLE OF CONTENTS

5

CHAPTER I

INTRODUCTION

THOMAS MORE, A NEGLECTED TUDOR POET

Thomas More, the renowned author of *Utopia*, is not universally known as a versatile humanist who attempted to write poetry and who attained facility and success in this art. The purpose of this study is to probe into a new facet of Morean scholarship and to reveal the skill More manifested in the field of English prosody. The writer will limit herself only to the twelve English poems that Thomas More wrote, since the subject matter and the length of these poems justify a study of this nature.

The English poems that are printed in William Rastell's 1557 edition of *The Workes of Sir Thomas More Knyght* range from 7 lines to 433 lines; altogether they comprise 1,342 lines of poetry. They are distinguished by an adroit use of rhythm and a rich use of imagery. The rhyme royal stanza, which was used extensively in the first decades of the fifteenth century, is the form More uses for all but one poem. This exception is the humorous ballad, 'A meri iest how a sergeant would learne to playe the frere', which is composed of dimeter and trimeter verses. Having written 234 rhyme royal stanzas in all, Thomas More became adept in the manipulation of this poetic form. It is no wonder that his biographers refer to this stanza as his favourite one, and yet sometimes they fail to see or are reluctant to admit his dexterity with it.

The writer was drawn to this work by the very fact that no specific and detailed study of this kind had been made before. Yet the substantial and quantitative bulk of the twelve English poems More wrote seemed to justify a study of this nature. William Ratell's black-letter edition contains thirty pages of poetry written by More: sixteen pages are in the section entitled 'These fowre thinges' and fourteen pages in *The Life of John Picus Erle of Myrandula*, while the two short ballads written in the Tower appear at the end of this edition.

Another factor contributing to the choice of this topic was Thomas More's skillful translation into Latin of 102 Greek epigrams. In addition to these translations, about 160 Latin epigrams are his original compositions. Although some resemble the poems in the *Greek Anthology*, they are original in detail and interpretation. One can surely carry over the skill in writing poetry from one language to another; and hence, if More is considered a good versifier in the Latin language, there is little reason for his inferiority in the vernacular, as some critics, such as Saintsbury, Garnett, and Gosse would have one think. Thomas More's poetry has not been looked into carefully by the majority of Morean scholars; consequently, it has not been appreciated impartially and criticized objectively. The purpose of this book is to present Thomas More in the role of a Tudor poet who, although not the most outstanding poet of the age, is nevertheless a good poet whose poems deserve to be found in present-day anthologies of that period.

William Nelson puts his finger on the neglected areas of past studies when he says:

> Despite the intensive study of Thomas More during the last decade, a study stimulated by his canonization, by the fourth centenary of his martyrdom, and by the enthusiastic and scholarly work of A. W. Reed, R. W. Chambers, and other writers, there remain significant aspects of his life that have received comparatively little attention. In a stimulating paper published eight years ago, Marie Delcourt demonstrated that the 'English' tradition of More's biography, the tradition created by More's kinsfolk and followers, represented a conscious attempt to emphasize his saintly qualities and those of his works which supported his claim to canonization. For this reason, these biographers gave little weight to More's humanist activities . . .[1]

Although no comparable study of Thomas More's English poems exists, a recent one of a related nature had further encouraged the writer to choose this topic and added more meaning and value to More's poetry. In his doctoral dissertation, *The Fortuna Concept in the English Writings of Sir Thomas More* (1953), William Stewart, of Johannes Gutenberg University, Mainz, analyzes the English poems in reference only to their relationship to the Fortuna concept.

Three provocative and leading statements by Tudor scholars, supported, encouraged, and gave impetus and direction to the nature and scope of this research study:

1. Fitzroy Pyle from Trinity College, Dublin, says in his enlightening article on 'Sir Thomas More's Verse Rhythms':

> Scanty though it is, the poetry of St. Thomas More deserves to be held in esteem if it were only for the interest of its rhythms. This is an aspect of his verse to which little consideration has as yet been given, largely, no doubt, because of the uncertainty of the metrics of his day . . .[2]

2. In his recent book, *English Literature in the Sixteenth Century, Excluding Drama*, Clive Staples Lewis asserts:

> All Barclay's works are outweighed in value by the few poems which Thomas More wrote in his youth . . . they succeed not by anticipating any new conception of poetry but by momentarily restoring the medieval kind to something of its former value.[3]

3. J. S. Phillinore in his lengthy and scholarly article, 'Blessed Thomas More and the Arrest of Humanism in England', makes this interesting remark: 'Great lawyers are not great poets, yet More was no mean master of English verse, as a stanza can show'.[4] He then quotes the following stanza as an example of More's poetic skill:

But and thou wilt needs medle with her treasure,
Trust not therein, and spende it liberally.
Beare the not proude, nor take not out of measure.
Build not thine house on height up in the sky;
None falleth far but he that climbeth high.
Remember Nature sent thee hither bare:
The gifts of Fortune, count them borrowed ware.[5]

A study of this kind can be approached in two ways: (1) by the method of literary analysis, the writer being mindful of the fact that a work of art cannot be comprehended or analyzed effectively without reference to specific norms and values; (2) by the method of literary history in which the writer fits the work of art being analyzed into the context of the literary output of the period and the milieu of the age, and judges it according to existing literary standards.

A combination of both methods with special emphasis on the first – literary analysis, implying for the most part, rhetorical analysis – is used in this book. The essential worth of Thomas More's poetry lies in its medieval features and in his craftsmanship in metrics, and thus, necessitates a related study of the nature and characteristics of medieval poetry and of the prosody of early sixteenth-century England. The writer hopes to reinstate More as a Tudor poet, a distinction which he enjoyed during his lifetime. 'Even his enemies', says R. W. Chambers, 'would scoff at him as a "poet",'[6] and allude to his writing as 'painted poetry'.[7] Sir John Harrington calls him 'plasant Sir Thomas'[8] and, referring to his epigrams in *The Metamorphosis of Ajax*, says that they 'fly over all Europe for their wit and conceit'.[9] Gabriel Harvey compares More to Tully in his *Marginalia* and praises 'theire speciall grace and fylicity . . . Both to be reckonid in the number of those, whom we terme very good . . .'.[10] Perhaps the highest commendation Thomas More received in this capacity was the keen observation Thomas Percy exhibited when he made the following reference to Thomas More's tale of 'A meri iest' and saw in it a close affinity with the famous ballad, 'The Nut Brown Maid':

> The editor of the Prolusions [*Select Pieces of Ancient Poetry*, ed. Capell, London, 1860] thinks that it cannot be older than the year 1500, because, in Sir Thomas More's tale of *The Serjeant*, &c., which was written about that time, there appears a sameness of rythmus and orthography, and a very near affinity of words and phrases with those of this ballad.[11]

If further scholarship could solve the anonymity of this renowned ballad and More could be proved to be its author, what a tremendous boon his reputation as a Tudor poet would receive! Francis Gummere, who made a detailed study of the 'popular ballad',[12] convincingly states that 'The Nut Brown Maid [is] in itself sufficient in form and music and theme 'to make the fortune' of any century . . .'.[13]

Since only six poems are included in Rastell's 'These fowre thinges' – the title he uses for More's English poems – and the remaining six are in other sections of his edition, the following titles are given for the reader's orientation:

1. 'A meri iest how a sergeant would learne to playe the frere'
2. 'Nyne pageauntes'
3. 'A ruful lamentacion of the deth of quene Elisabeth . . .'

'Certain meters' written for the *Boke of Fortune* includes the following three separate poems which nevertheless form one unit:

4. 'The wordes of fortune to the people'
5. 'Thomas More to them that trust in fortune'
6. 'Thomas More to them that seke fortune'

The four poems forming a unit in the *Life of John Picus Erle of Myrandula* have the following titles:

7. 'Twelue rules of John Picus Earle of Myrandula, partely exciting, partely directing a man in spiritual bataile'
8. 'The twelue weapons haue we more at length declared as foloweth'
9. 'The twelue propertees we haue at length more openly expressed in Balade, as it foloweth'
10. 'A praier of Picus Myrandula unto God'

The two short ballettes written in the Tower:

11. 'Lewis the lost louer'
12. 'Dauy the dicer'.

The first poem, 'A meri iest how a sergeant would learne to play the frere', is cast in the form of a humorous ballad and adumbrates Cowper's popular tale of 'John Gilpin'.[14] James Mackintosh highly praises this poem and says that it exhibits More's 'natural disposition to pleasantry'.[15] He commends the 'dancing mirth in the metre'[16] and says 'that in a rude period the structure of verse may be regarded as some presumption of a genius for poetry'.[17]

The second poem printed in Rastell's black-letter edition consists of nine rhyme royal stanzas which provide the texts for allegorical paintings on the stages of man's life. As A. W. Reed mentions in his 'Philological Notes' appended to the Campbell edition of More's *English Works*, this theme was not an uncommon one, but five or six panels only were usually used for this representation.[18] Although the conventional number for a series of panels representing allegorical subjects may have been five or six, 'there can be no doubt', says Israel Gollancz, 'that the "Nine" had previously figured in pageants, tapestry, and decorative embellishments'.[19] Thomas More's execution on painted cloth was in nine panels, and to Petrarch's 'successive triumphs and overthrow of Love, Chastity, Death, Fame, and Time and Eternity'[20] he added the panels depicting the *child*, the *youth*, and the *poet*. One can perceive in this arrangement the influence of humanism with its stress on the individuality of man, for More makes a human being the center of his allegorical representations. He significantly begins with a child and ends with the poet. Perhaps better than any other critic who has commented on this poem, Dr. P. S. Allen shows the relationship of the personified abstractions to man as the pivotal attraction in

10

this representation when he says in the following statement: '. . . a series of Pageants shows man as a child, hunter, lover, aged counsellor, with Death, Fame, Time, and Eternity disputing their rights over him'.[21]

A pronounced influence of Boccaccio's *De Casibus Virorum Illustrium* is seen in the third poem, 'A ruful lamentacion', written in honour of Henry VII's wife, Queen Elizabeth, who died in childbed in the year 1503. This English humanist, like his contemporaries, most probably attempted to imitate Italian models, since at this time Italian culture was being transplanted into England with great avidity and success. The twelve rhyme royal stanzas portray a deliberate experiment with the use of a refrain, which adds charm and lyrical quality to the poem. Echoes of the tragical soliloquies of Lydgate's *Fall of Princes* give this elegy haunting and somber characteristics. Cayley speaks of it admiringly, and he calls it 'a curious specimen of the poetry and language of that age'.[22] By 'curious' he means 'ingenious' or 'skillful' (OED).

The fourth of 'These fowre thinges' entitled 'Certain meters' consists of three distinct poems in which (1) Fortune speaks to the people, (2) Thomas More speaks to those who trust in Fortune, (3) Thomas More speaks to those who seek Fortune. In the writer's opinion these rhyme royal stanzas portray the pinnacle of More's success with the medium of poetry. She agrees with Arthur Cayley, whose biography of More is best for the study of his poetry, that

> Sir Thomas, although not to be numbered with Sannazaro, Fracastro, Vida, and others of his time, is allowed to have been no indifferent poet; and a more assiduous application to the muses would probably have made him a superior one.[23]

The seven-line stanzas comprising 'Certain meters' appended to the *Boke of Fortune* conform to the criteria of good poetry for the following reasons: (1) the sound structure is composed of pleasing rhythm, varied assonance, and meaningful rhyme; (2) the meaning structure presents an interesting theme based on a contemporary incident and superstitions that have a singular fascination for the people of that age; (3) the imagery in this poem is adumbrative of Spenser's excellent personifications; (4) the pertinent allusions to Biblical, mythological, and historical personages give the verses a distinct flavour and help to elucidate the poet's point of view; (5) the convictions mirrored in these lines betray deep emotion and strong control over one's innate desire to become didactic with the intention of swaying the reader's will. The two short rhyme royal poems written in the Tower, namely, 'Lewys the lost louer' and 'Dauy the dicer', reveal a return to a pastime that Thomas More enjoyed in his youth and an adeptness with a medium in which he found facility and satisfaction.

The theme for the next group of poems revolves around the *Life of John Picus Erle of Myrandula*. The four poems which comprise this group are entitled: 'Twelue rules', 'The twelue weapons', 'The twelue propertees or condicions of a louer', and 'A praier of Picus Myrandula unto God'. More's preoccupation with rhythm, imagery, and emotion is apparent in these verses. Religious thought and sentiment, which often annoys the modern reader, fortunately does

11

not digress into boring didactism. The fact that 137 stanzas are written in the rhyme royal form causes one to speculate whether this was More's or the favourite meter of the age. Theodore Maynard informs us in his doctoral dissertation on *The Connection Between the Ballade, Chaucer's Modification of It, Rime Royal, and the Spenserian Stanza* that 'the trend in English verse at the time was in the direction of enormous shapeless poems. And rime royal became the accepted medium for them'.[24] Apparently, from More's use of the word 'Balade',[25] he, as well as his contemporaries, used the term synonymously with the rhyme royal stanza. Chaucer experimented with the seven-line stanza and set it free from some of the restrictions of the *ballade*, but later poets confused the two, i.e., the *ballade* and the *ballade royal*. It was in the sixteenth century that the term rime royal was first used, and Maynard clearly points out that 'James I of Scotland's use of that stanza had nothing whatever to do with its being named rime royal'.[26] As its name signifies, it is a noble form of verse and is employed for the expression of serious and lofty subject matter.

Thomas More uses *ballette*[27] synonymously for a short poem consisting of one rhyme royal stanza in 'Dauy the dicer' and 'Lewys the lost louer'. On the other hand, he calls 'The twelue propertees', which consists of twenty-six rhyme royal stanzas, a *balade*,[28] thus distinguishing it from the short poems. Contrary to Chaucer's conception, this poem has no refrain and is much too long to be placed in this category. However, 'A ruful lamentacion' has certain ballade characteristics, the most pronounced of which is the haunting refrain, 'and lo now here I ly', yet Thomas More does not call this poem a *ballade*. Evidently, he experimented here with a new form and Maynard sees in it 'a perhaps unconscious incipience of the Spenserian stanza'.[29] Thomas More, whose originality in the coinage of new words was outstanding, whose freshness of imagery added much beauty to his poems, and whose rhythmical cadence corresponded to his 'sensitive ear'[30] for music, may well have attempted this form with initiative and deliberation. Maynard, who does not consider More 'a very skillful poet',[31] assumes that he meant to write the entire poem with alexandrines in the twelve refrains and that 'the substitution of a decasyllabic line may be supposed to have been an oversight'.[32] It was apparently no 'oversight' on More's part, for the majority of the refrains are in decasyllabic lines, while the sixth, seventh, eighth, tenth, and eleventh stanzas end with a hexameter verse. Why the enterprising poet employed seven five-stress refrains and five refrains ending with an alexandrine is a tantalizing feature of his prosodic technique; nevertheless, one can make a plausible inference that meter in his hands was a flexible medium and that he exhibited a tendency to experiment with it. Fitzroy Pyle, a Morean scholar who examined his poetry more impartially perhaps than anyone else did in the past, gives a fair and objective summary of More's metrical skill:

> That More was not unaffected by the forces making for chaos is shown by the drift into four-accent verse in the 'Twelue rules'. That he was not always consciously concerned about metrical uniformity we see, for instance, from the refrain-lines of the 'Ruful lamentacion'. But proofs

of his being possessed of a fine feeling for rhythm are to be found in every one of his poems; and in spite of, and because of, his not coming to metre intellectually, he composed rhythm incomparably superior to those of the more 'regular' versifiers of the next generation ... More's line of approach was not that of intellect but of artistic intuition, and though this was fortunate for the quality of his own verse, it meant that – even if he had written more – he could not be recognized as a metrical prophet. The times needed something cut and dried, and that an artist could not give.[33]

Pyle finds vigorous rhythm in the 'Meri iest of how a sergeant would learne to playe the frere', 'cumulative rhythmical effect that is remarkably impressive' and refrain variations that 'obviously ... have been designed with artistic intent' in 'A ruful lamentacion', a 'vigorous example of trisyllabic substitution in "Certain meters" for the *Boke of Fortune*, and rhythm ... admirably adapted to the matter'[34] in the three poems annexed to the *Life of John Picus Erle of Myrandula*. His greatest praise is reserved for the last poem, 'A praier of Picus Myrandula unto God', and, describing its conclusion which 'rises by successive enjambent up to a magnificent crescendo and then dies away with a beautiful headless line',[35] he gives it a place among the best literary pieces. Unlike Maynard, Pyle does not see in More a 'tendency to use syllabic variations wantonly', but concedes that 'he often employs them very artistically'.[36]

Clive Staple Lewis, who together with Fitzroy Pyle made a thorough study of the prosody of the Tudor Age, speaks with an unbiased attitude when he says of Thomas More's English poems:

All Barclay's works are outweighed in value by the few poems which Thomas More wrote in his youth ... the lamentation on the death of Queen Elizabeth (1503) is of real value, and the next piece, the verses for the *Book of Fortune*, is perhaps better ... Few things even about More are more impressive than the merit of these two poems. They are quite off his own beat: they owe nothing to his humour or to his classical scholarship ...[37]

Although the statement that More's English poems 'owe nothing to his humour or to his classical scholarship'[38] appears to be a sweeping verbalization, it is encouraging to know that a Tudor scholar who peremptorily dismisses Hawes and Barclay as inferior poets has such words of praise to bestow on More's English poems.

What was More's theory of poetry and what canons he believed it should follow is a question one may pertinently ask at this point. The first criterion for this English humanist was that poetry should come from the heart; sincerity and depth of emotion should bring it into existence. In a beautiful and emotive Latin poem written to his children in 1517 while on a journey to Calais, More alludes to the necessity of emotion as a primary factor in poetry:

... From these verses you may gather an indication of your father's feelings for you – how much more than his own eyes he loves you ...

Poetry often springs from a heart which has no feelings; these verses a
father's love provides – along with a father's natural anxiety.[39]

Secondly, More believed that a good poem should be characterized by facility
of rhythm and felicity of expression. Not he himself, but Beatus Rhenanus gives
testimony to the qualities More possessed as a poet. In a letter written to
Willibald Pirckheimer (1518) in which Beatus urges this learned councilor to
read More's epigrams, Beatus says:

> How pleasantly his poetry flows! How utterly unforced is his work! How
> adroit it all is! Here is nothing harsh, nothing rough, nothing obscure . . .
> Furthermore, he seasons all his work with a certain very delightful
> humor so that I have never seen anything more charming. I could believe
> that the Muses conferred upon him all there is anywhere of mirth, charm,
> and wit.[40]

Thirdly, More, who was reputed 'the wittiest of moralists and the most moral
of wits',[41] believed that poetry should amuse and instruct and should avoid
didactic and moralistic overtones. In translating the Greek epigrams he deliberately omitted those concerned with the 'dull religiosity of the northern
humanists',[42] just as he banished the licentiousness of the Italian poets from
his writing. The four English poems which enrich the *Life of John Picus, Erle
of Myrandula* are written on a religious subject, but are embellished with
artistic treatment which gives the poems a certain captivating elegance.

The fourth criterion that More held as a reputable standard for good poetry
was that sound should not overpower the sense in a poem. Consequently, for
him the meaning structure was always more important than the sound structure,
and he would not hesitate to sacrifice the latter for the former. Even in translating, Thomas More was not a slavish adherent to form, and he made deliberate
changes in his text if they made the meaning more clear and emphatic. At times,
he blends the two to produce a perfect work of art as he does very charmingly
in 'A ruful lamentacion of the deth of quene Elisabeth'.

The fifth norm for the writing of poetry is exhibited by More in a remarkable
degree, namely, the wit and brevity for which Beatus praises him so highly.
'He (More) provokes laughter', Beatus says, 'but in every case without pain;
he ridicules, but without abuse'.[43] His rhyme royal stanzas comprising the
'Certain meters' for the *Boke of Fortune* are units of perfect craftsmanship
adorned with wit and characterized by brevity. Speaking to those who trust in
Fortune's power, Thomas More says:

> Recken you neuer of her fauoure sure;
> Ye may in clowds as easily trace an hare,
> Or in drye lande cause fishes to endure,
> And make the burnyng fyre his heate to spare,
> And all thys worlde in compace to forfare,
> As her to make by craft or engine stable,
> That of her nature is euer variable.[44]

14

Lastly, Thomas More embellished his poems with rhetorical schemes and tropes, and for him, as well as for his contemporaries, 'Rhetoric [was] an adjunct of the poet'.[45] His twelve English poems are excellent patterns in rhetorical style, and extensive use of *prosopopoeia, anaphora, hyperbaton*, and *accumulation* adorns his verses. Donald Lemen Clark, who made a scholarly study of *Rhetoric and Poetry in the Renaissance*, says:

> In a word, the whole traditional division of rhetoric is transferred to poetry, and at the same time both rhetoric and poetic are limited to the single part which they have in common – diction.[46]

Not only did rhetoric and style mean the same thing to Tudor poets; they also had the same functions – *docere, delectare, et movere* – i.e., to teach, to please, and to move. Thomas More's poetry could well subscribe to the medieval criteria for good poetry which were carried over into the Renaissance period, 'The belief that poetry was composed of two parts: a profitable subject matter (doctrine) and style (eloquentia)'.[47]

In his *Memoirs of Sir Thomas More*, Cayley quotes an anecdote which shows More's critical acumen in appreciating good poetry:

> More and the man who asked him about the publication of his writing: More said it would be better if you put it into verse (probably wanting to dissuade him). The man versified the book, brought it again the next day and More said,
>
> Now it is somewhat, for now it is rhyme;
> before it was neither rhyme nor reason.[48]

The writer, having summarized Thomas More's theory of poetry from the internal evidence of his English and Latin poems, discusses next the method she proposes to use for each chapter. Although literary analysis is used consistently in the chapters devoted to an explication of the poems, i.e., Chapters Two through Six, a brief discussion of the occasion of the poem and the influence of other poems upon it forces her to trespass into the realm of literary history. The theme, form, sound and meaning structure of each poem gives direction to the following pertinent treatment it receives.

The second chapter considers 'A meri iest how a sergeant would learne to playe the frere'. Rastell placed this poem first in his 'Fowre Thinges', yet it may not necessarily be the first poem Thomas More wrote. A study of its nature and context reveals that it probably belongs to a later period, perhaps in the year 1509 when More's association with the Mercers was well established. It would hardly be conceivable that as a 'beardless boy',[49] this young humanist would give sound and fearless advice to the masters of the leading crafts of early sixteenth-century London.

Nevertheless, by placing it first, William Rastell, a clever and witty printer, probably realized that 'A meri iest' would appeal to the average Londoner on account of its mercantile flavor and narrative technique. At the beginning of this chapter the London companies and the feasts peculiar to them are briefly described, for one of them may have furnished the occasion for the recitation of this ballad.

Since it is a narrative poem, its narrative technique is analyzed according to exposition, plot development, characterization, and setting. Sound and meaning structure play an important part in the analysis of this poem, as well as in the rest of the eleven poems.

The 'Nyne pageauntes' is, in the writer's estimation, the first English poem Thomas More wrote, but there may have been several other poems of anonymous authorship which research has not yet proven to have come from his creative pen. The reason for this assumption is that these nine stanzas on 'A goodly hangyng of fyne paynted clothe'[50] appear to be a form of experimentation with a classical theme, and hence, represent More's early attempts at writing poetry. The subject matter is indicative of his studies at Oxford and it was here, as Hutton tells us, that Thomas More 'was learning . . . that sense of form and style which he never lost'.[51]

The verses on the 'Nyne pageauntes' are analyzed in the third chapter according to the norms of medieval rhetoric, such as: style embellished by schemes and tropes, syntactical arrangement, paratactic and hypotactic structure, and perspicuity, force, and eloquence of diction. Since the framework of voice and address plays a very important part in these verses, it is discussed in the light of this technique. To place the poem in its respective milieu, its incipient development from the medieval mystery play and its extension of the 'dance of death'[52] motif, which figures so prominently as an adornment and reminder on tapestries and the walls of churches, necessitate a brief explanation. In order to understand more fully the nature of the 'Nyne pageauntes', to trace their development to the present form, and to realize the underlying techniques they exhibit, a study of the term *pageant* gives the poem more depth and meaning. The obvious pattern of similarity with Petrarch's 'Trionfi' is brought out in the successive overthrow-and-triumph technique which More employs with ingenuity.

The fourth chapter discusses 'A ruful lamentacion . . . of the death of quene Elisabeth' according to the norms for the sound and meaning structure in an elegiac poem. Its parallelism with Lydgate's *Fall of Princes* and Sackville's *Mirror for Magistrates* is pointed out briefly. The analysis is based on the voice and address framework, since this particular poem presents an admirable study therein. The refrain in each stanza enhances the effectiveness of the rhythm, which, in turn, is another pivotal theme for discussion. Meaning structure, in this poem perhaps more than in any other, is tied up with historical data and consequently deserves to be discussed here, since it gives the poem its unique interest and significance.

'Certain meters' written for the *Boke of Fortune* comprise the subject matter for the fifth chapter of this dissertation. The writer considers these verses the most accomplished and artistic of all. The method used in the discussion of the

16

three poems on the tantalizing subject of Fortune is a combination of literary history and literary analysis. The first part explains the Fortuna cult and traces its development from the pagan tradition to the Renaissance tradition. The meaning structure is correlated adroitly with allusions to the Bible, to classical and historical personages, and to current beliefs and convictions concerning the prediction of one's future by means of astrological horoscopes or the playing of the dice game in the popular *Boke of Fortune* manual. Since the poems reflect More's most successful attempt in poetical craftsmanship, a number of pages are devoted to the analysis of their sound structure and the description of the personification and imagery that are so outstanding in them.

In the sixth chapter the poems that are annexed to the *Life of John Picus Erle of Myrandula* are treated from the point of view of sound structure, since the meaning structure is obvious and needs little or no elucidation. The three main divisions of medieval rhetoric, which are: (1) arrangement or organization, (2) amplification and abbreviation, and (3) style and its ornaments, afford a neat and organized plan of analysis for these lengthy poems. The fourteen pages of verse consist of seventy-three rhyme royal stanzas in which style and form receive as much consideration and treatment as the religious thought and sentiment inherent in the meaning structure of the poems. The historical facts which throw some light on the circumstances of composition and the occasion for which the poem was written are given preliminary discussion. R. W. Chambers makes an excellent observation when he traces Thomas More's dedication of the *Life of John Picus Erle of Myrandula* to the tradition of addressing treatises on perfection to cloistered women. Although he is a bit vacillating about this suggestion, a study of the four poems, the life of the Italian humanist, and the introductory letter above all, give his conjecture more validity than he assumed at the time. 'I am not suggesting', he says, 'that when young Thomas More wrote his book "unto his right entierly beloued sister in Christ, Joyeuce Leigh" ... he had necessarily in mind any single one of the five treatises addressed to cloistered women which I have just mentioned. But', he adds with certainty, 'he was following a tradition'.[53]

Walter Hilton's *Scale of Perfection*, addressed to his 'Ghostly Sister in Jesus Christ',[54] enjoyed the popularity of five editions during More's lifetime and was printed by Wynkyn de Worde and Julian Notary, who also printed More's works. Up till the fifteenth century the *Ancren Riwle* was still one of the most popular religious treatises addressed to nuns in the vernacular, and Thomas More's dedication of the *Life of John Picus Erle of Myrandula* to a cloistered Poor Clare Sister was evidently following this precedent. Not only was his translation from the Latin into English an activity indicative of humanistic interest, but his dedication elevated the prestige of women and was probably the beginning of Thomas More's interest in the education of the female sex, whose rights and privileges he firmly believed in and staunchly defended.

The writer wishes to bring to light the fact that Thomas More was no mere dilettante in the art of poetry. Having published more than two hundred Latin epigrams ranging from two lines of verse to 223 lines of verse, he acquired facility of rhythm for which his contemporaries highly praised him. He carried these accomplishments over into the realm of the vernacular and produced English poetry that Samuel Johnson did not scorn to include in the *History of the English Language* prefixed to the *Dictionary* as 'models of pure and elegant style'.[55] As a matter of fact, it is highly significant that Johnson devotes only two pages to Chaucer's poetry, two and a half to Skelton's verse, not even one full page to Barclay's works, and five large folio pages to More's English poems.

Sir James Mackintosh, recognizing More's initiative and versatility with the vernacular, highly praises his contribution to the development of English vocabulary:

> ... he is to be considered as our earliest prose writer, and as the first Englishman who wrote the history of his country in its present language ... A very small part of his vocabulary has been super-annuated. The number of terms which require any explanation is inconsiderable; and in that respect the stability of the language is remarkable. He is indeed in his words more English than the great writers of a century after him, who loaded their native tongue with expressions of Greek and Latin derivation.[56]

P. S. Allen further observes that in the *Oxford English Dictionary* More's use of many words is cited as the earliest authority.[57] J. Delcourt calls More 'a creator or an importer of words ...'[58] and points out many words that this English humanist coined or 'half-coined'.[59] He cites the following ones as examples: *to paddle, to pule, to fimble, to shuffle,* and *to taunt.* Delcourt maintains that these words have not been found in any texts previous to More's writing. 'It may seem strange', he adds with a convincing tone, that 'the word *fact*, a word so simple and so frequent that it might almost have figured among the native or quasinative terms ... should have to be added to the number, but then it is a fact'.[60]

The writer does not propose to prove that Thomas More is a great Tudor poet; she merely wishes to entice others to read his poems and to give them a fair chance. His correlation of medieval subject matter and treatment exhibits pronounced humanistic and Renaissance overtones which caused C. S. Lewis to say admiringly of these English poems: 'they succeed ... by momentarily restoring the medieval kind to something of its former value'.[61]

1 William Nelson, 'Thomas More, Grammarian and Orator,' *PMLA*, LVII (June 1943), 338.
2. *London Times Literary Supplement* (January 30, 1937), 76.
3. Clive Staples Lewis, *English Literature in the Sixteenth Century, Excluding Drama* (Oxford, 1954), p. 133.
4. *Dublin Review*, 153 (July 1913), 20.
5. 'To Those that Trust in Fortune,' as quoted by Phillimore, *ibid.*
6. Elsie Vaughan Hitchcock, ed., *The Life and Death of Sir Thomas Moore, Knight, Sometymes Lord High Chancellor of England*, with an Introduction 'On the Continuity of

English Prose from Alfred to More and His School,' by R. W. Chambers (London, 1932), Introduction, p.clvii.

7. *Ibid.*
8. Sir John Harrington, *The Metamorphosis of Ajax* (London, 1596), p. 39.
9. *Ibid.*, p. 38.
10. Gabriel Harvey, *Marginalia*, ed. G. G. Moore Smith (Stratford-Upon-Avon, 1913), pp. 113–114.
11. Thomas Percy, *Reliques of Ancient English Poetry* (London, 1886), II, 32.
12. 'Ballads,' A. W. Ward and A. R. Waller, *CHEL* (Cambridge, England, 1907–1927), II, 395.
13. *Ibid.*, II, 429.
14. For further discussion see William Hayley's *Life and Posthumous Writings of William Cowper* (London, 1806), II, 61.
15. *The Life of Sir Thomas More* (London, 1844), p. 17.
16. *Ibid.*
17. *Ibid.*
18. William Edward Campbell, ed., *The English Works of Sir Thomas More*, (London 1927–1931), I, 195. This edition will be designated henceforth as *Works I or II*. Lines of the poem will be indicated by the marginal letter and the number of the lines. For the Method used, see 'Philological Notes,' *Works*, *I*, 194–197, and 'The Collations,' *ibid.*, I, 231–235.
19. Israel Gollancz, ed., *The Parlement of the Thre Ages, an Alliterative Poem of the XIV Century* (London, 1897), Introduction, p. xviii.
20. *Ibid.*, p. 203.
21. Percy Stafford and Helen Mary Allen, eds., *Sir Thomas More: Selections from his English Works* (Oxford, 1924), Introduction, p. vii.
22. Arthur Cayley, the Younger, ed., *Memoirs of Sir Thomas More* (London, 1808), p. 18.
23. *Ibid.*, p. 203.
24. Catholic University of America (Washington, D.C., 1934), p. 97.
25. *Works*, I, 'The twelue propertees,' I, 28, A, 2.
26. Maynard, p. 92.
27. *Workes*, ed. Rastell, p. 1432.
28. *Works*, ed. Campbell, 'The twelue propertees,' I, 28.
29. Maynard, p. 120.
30. Pyle, p. 76.
31. Maynard, p. 120.
32. *Ibid.*
33. Pyle, p. 76.
34. *Ibid.*
35. *Ibid.*
36. *Ibid.*
37. Lewis, p. 133.
38. *Ibid.*
39. Leicester Bradner and Charles Arthur Lynch, eds., *The Latin Epigrams of Thomas More* (Chicago, 1953), p. 230.
40. *Ibid.*, p. 126.
41. David Harrison, *Tudor England* (London, 1953), I, 43, citing R. W. Dixon in the *History of the Church of England*, i, 9.
42. Bradner and Lynch, Introduction, p. xxvii.
43. *Ibid.*, p. 126.
44. *Works*, I, 'Thomas More to them that trust in fortune,' Fourteenth page, D. 2–8.
45. John Hoskins, *Directions for Speech and Style*, ed. Hoyt Hopewell Hudson (Princeton, 1935), p. 55.
46. (New York, 1922), p. 54.
47. *Ibid.*, p. 73.
48. Cayley, p. 247.
49. Raymond Wilson Chambers, *Thomas More* (New York, 1935), p. 87.
50. *Works*, I, 'Nyne pageauntes,' C. ii^v D. 2–3. The pages on which the poems are given are unnumbered. Hence the signature having a mark similar to *C* is used with ^{r} signifying recto and ^{v} signifying verso. Lines of the poem are designated by the marginal letter and the numbers of the lines.

51. William Holden Hutton, *Sir Thomas More* (London, 1895), p. 12.
52. Alfred Woltmann, *Holbein and His Time*, trans. F. E. Bunnett (London, 1872), *passim*.
53. Hitchcock, ed., *Introduction* by R. W. Chambers, p. cxxiii.
54. *Ibid.*
55. *A Dictionary of the English Language* (London, 1755), p. 9.
56. Allen citing Mackintosh, Introduction, p. vii.
57. *Ibid.*
58. J. Delcourt, 'Some Aspects of More's English,' *Essays and Studies*, XXI (Oxford, 1936), 11–28.
59. *Ibid.*
60. *Ibid.*
61. Lewis, p. 133.

CHAPTER II

A HUMOROUS AND DIDACTIC BALLAD

'A MERI IEST HOW A SERGEANT WOULD LEARNE TO PLAYE THE FRERE'

In the Introduction to the *English Works of Sir Thomas More*, A. W. Reed suggests that this poem, 'A meri iest how a sergeant would learne to play the frere' may have been 'associated with the Sergeants' Feast held on 13th November 1503, in the Archbishop's palace at Lambeth, John More being one of the newly-elected Sergeants-at-law'.[1] Upon a close examination of this feast, however, one becomes impressed with the dignity and solemnity of the affair, which in many ways resembled the ceremony of the coronation of a king. William Herbert, in his *Antiquities of the Inns of Court and Chancery*, gives a description of one of these feasts:

> Their dynner was not epicuryous, nor verrey sumptuous, but yet moderately, discretely, and sufficiently ordered, with a wyse temperaunce, without greate excesse or superfluyte, as it was most conuinyent, and to learned lawyers, and sobre and experte cownselors, was most decent and requisyte.[2]

Since Thomas More was not only youthful and fun-loving but also tactful and prudent, he suited his jests to the occasion and directed his effusions of wit and satire to those who would profit from them. Considering, then, the nature of the feast and the audience for whom the 'Mery Iest' was intended, this humorous ballad was most probably not recited at the Sergeants' Feast. On the other hand, plausible arguments can be found for associating it with the feast of the Lord Mayor's Pageant or with the feasts of the twelve livery companies of London.

In the fifteenth century the livery companies enjoyed great prestige and the Lord Mayor was often chosen from their ranks. Similar to the medieval craft guilds, the livery companies were industrial, mercantile, and charitable corporations. They had their patron saint, chaplain, coat of arms, pageants, and entertainments. On the 'Gild Day', the day of the saint to whom the guild was dedicated, the members heard Mass, distributed alms, and then went to their decorated hall to enjoy the anniversary banquet.[3]

The reference to St. Katherine in the poem, besides being used for the sake of euphony and rhyme, may be an allusion to the name of the patron saint of the company which sponsored this feast. Thus, St. Peter was chosen by the Fishmongers, St. Anthony by the Grocers, St. John the Baptist by the Merchant Taylors, the Virgin Mary by the Drapers, St. Dunstan by the Goldsmiths, St. Martin by the Vintners, and St. Katherine by the Haberdashers.

The Haberdashers originally were a branch of the Mercers, dealing like them,

21

in merceries or small wares. They were divided into two fraternities and were dedicated separately to St. Catherine and St. Nicholas since their trade consisted of two distinct branches: 1) haberdashers of hats, also called hurers or cappers; 2) haberdashers of small wares, also called milliners, 'an appelation derived from their dealing in merchandise, chiefly imported from the city of Milan, in Italy, such as ouches, broches, agglets, spurs, capes, glasses, etc.'.[4] The Haberdashers by the name of the Faternity of St. Katherine are mentioned in the Bishop of London Registry, and a small vellum book of ordinances has a good illumination of St. Katherine, the company's patron saint.[5]

More's interest in these companies and their feasts can be substantiated by the fact that both he and his father were members of the Mercers' Company. In the list of aldermen of the city of London for Farringdon Ward Without, one finds More's name with the designation 'Mercer' after it for the nominations of July 31, 1503.[6] This fact is corroborated by Russell Ames, who quotes the citation of John Watney in this regard: 'I should be very glad to be able to claim Sir Thomas More as a member of the Mercers' Company, and think that ... I may do so with confidence'.[7] Roper states that before More entered the service of King Henry VIII, at the request of the English merchants who held him in high esteem for his learning, wisdom, and discretion, he was twice made an ambassador in their cause.[8]

From the internal evidence of the last four lines, one can infer that the poem was an introduction to a feast. It was also addressed to a large group composed of masters of various crafts whom More exhorts to pursue one business venture only. If the king, the queen, or other noble and distinguished individuals were present at this feast, More would have surely recognised their presence and directed his envoy to them. Instead, he alludes to the masters present and, having entertained them with his merry ballad, he invites them to the ensuing feast in these words:

> Now masters all,
> Here now I shall,
>   Ende there as I began,
> In any wyse,
> I would auyse,
>   And counsayle euery man,
> His owne craft use,
> All newe refuse,
>   And lyghtly let them gone:
> Play not the frere,
> Now make good chere,
>   And welcome euery chone.[9]

The poem contains practical advice to the masters, wardens, and apprentices of the various livery companies, which apparently were represented at this merry feast. Like his predecessor, Chaucer, who combined the *sententia* with the *exemplum* in the beginning of the *Legend of Good Women*, Thomas More uses the same combination in the opening lines of this ballad:

> Wyse men alway,
> Affyrme and say,
> > That best is for a man:
> Diligently,
> For to apply,
> > The business that he can.[10]

More, the aspiring merchant and poet, substantiates his own philosophy with the assertion of 'Wyse men'. By doing so he shows himself to be both humble and prudent: humble, because he does not consider himself an authority worth listening to, and prudent, because he proves his point with the sound thinking of philosophers. The *sententia*, inherent in More's introductory verses, has overtones of Plato's Republic. Both advocate the pursuance of one task only in order to strive for perfection in one's craft, which will result in a greater stability of society and will bring personal happiness and staisfaction. Thomas More not only informs his listeners of the dangers and pitfalls of leaving one craft in order to pursue another one without the necessary preparation and practice, but he also enlightens them regarding the results such a procedure inevitably brings about. The end, he maintains, is indubitably failure for the individual and for society.

The assertion that it is most profitable to keep to one task only is the foundation on which the whole poem is built. With characteristic friendliness, humour, and good will, he clothes his counsel in the disguise of a 'Mery Iest'. Nevertheless, he does not conceal his intention in writing the ballad, for the moral is apparent at the beginning, in the middle, and at the end. In spite of persuasive didacticism the poem is not moralistic and repelling, but light and facetious. The narrative form creates interest and empathy in the audience while the vigorous and true-to-life dialogue gives it verisimilitude and colour.

Clive S. Lewis commends the medieval treatment given this poem and sees in it 'nine successive variations on the proverb *ex sutore medicus*'.[11] The wholesome and practical *sententia* enunciated in the proverb are confirmed by the wise men, who clearly see the peril in the rise of a shoemaker to a physician's profession. The nine variations are described in the introduction to the poem and comprise the following crafts:

1.	The *hosier*	strives to become a				*shoemaker.*
2.	The *smythe*	,,	,,	,,	,,	*painter.*
3.	The *draper*	,,	,,	,,	,,	*clerk.*
4.	The *butler*	,,	,,	,,	,,	*cutler.*
5.	An *old trot*[12]	,,	,,	,,	,,	*physician.*

23

6.	The *man-of-lawe*	„	„	„	„	*merchant.*
7.	The *merchant*	„	„	„	„	*lawyer.*
8.	The *hatter*	„	„	„	„	*philosopher.*
9.	The *pedlar*	„	„	„	„	*theologian.*

If one is inclined to judge the author's philosophy of life by the nature of his writing, then it seems apparent that More's life was not in strict accordance with his theory on this matter. Did not his interests include history, oratory, theology, science, poetry, rhetoric, and drama, although he was engaged principally in the legal profession? How, then, could he pursue all these vocations and avocations successfully? At the end of the introductory section to the poem, he stresses this incompatibility in the following words:

> Whan a hatter
> Wyll go smatter,
>   In philosophy,
> Or a pedlar,
> Waxe a medlar,
>   In theology,
> All that ensue,
> Suche craftes new,
>   They driue so farre a cast,
> That euermore,
> They do therfore,
>   Beshrewe themselfe at last.[13]

More's versatility and his diversified interests followed the pattern of the humanistic trends of his day. In the sixteenth century a humanist was vitally interested in many things and endeavoured to do these many things well. More's contemporary, Linacre, was both a renowned scholar and a physician of note. John Colet, who was eleven years More's senior and whom More had chosen for his spiritual director, was a 'Mercer, priest, and social critic'.[14] Ames points to John Rastell as an example of 'the splendid many-sided genius – the middle class man at his historical best, individualism in its most productive phase'.[15] More's versatile brother-in-law was a lawyer and a judge, a maker of pageants, a playwright, the chief of army transport, a trench engineer, a printer, an architect, a colonizer, a member of a parliament, a pamphleteer, and a political and religious rebel.[16]

As a matter of fact, it was customary in those days for a man of learning to try his hand at verse, and this practice was considered a necessary accomplishment conducive to the perfection of the whole man. In this regard More, then, can be classified with the humanists, who exhibited a multiplicity of interests and an eagerness to attempt the successful execution of various enterprises. Already, at the age of twenty-three, in the year 1501, he gave a series of lectures on St. Augustine's *City of God*, a favourite work of the humanists, and thus, added to his interest in poetry and language an interest in history, philosophy, and theology. Since Thomas More was a humanist by inclination and study, there is little disparity, then, between his theory and practice in the embracing of a multiplicity of interests.

If this ballad was recited at the feast of one of the livery companies, then it is apparent that More's audience did not strictly represent the realm of scholars, but people drawn from the mercantile trades for whom it was necessary to strive for perfection in the mastery of their particular craft.

The incipient idea for the poem is based on what appears to be a true incident which occurred a short time before the ballad was written:

> This thing was tryed
> And verefyed
> Here by a sergeaunt late.[17]

Like a skillful journalist, More builds on the present and achieves interest by concentrating on a contemporary incident. This technique enables him to prove his point forcefully and effectively. The nature of the incident as well as the name of the sergeant involved is obliterated by the lapse of years and the dearth of historical data on this subject. An incident, however, which took place in September of 1507 may have given More the idea and the pattern for this ballad, while the 'sergeaunt late' alluded to in the verses above may be a verbal disguise for the Italian impostor, John Damian. Since Thomas More's 'Mery Iest' is so analogous to William Dunbar's 'Ane Ballat of the Fenzeit Freir of Tungland' that either one may have been the precedent for the other, a brief summary of this exciting contemporary incident will be helpful to a better understanding and appreciation of More's poem. The facts comprising this incident are faithfully recorded in the *History of Scotland*:

> By his skill as a surgeon and apothecary this imposter [John Damian] first gained the good-will of James IV and then abused his confidence by pretending to multiply gold. Having failed in this attempt, he made wings and tried to fly in order to escape to Turkey.[18]

Shortly after the scandal of John Damian, who disguised himself as the Abbot of Tungland, Dunbar wrote the above-named ballad describing this incident, which vehemently aroused the people's curiosity and interest. In More's poem the sergeant disguises himself as an Austin friar and suffers severely and unexpectedly for his lack of integrity in this regard. The beatings the feigned friar in More's ballad receives at the hands of the merchant and the maid are similar to the ones the false Abbot of Tungland suffers from the birds and fowls that look upon this strange phenomenon in the sky – a man with molten wings – as a creature who is trying to usurp their power. The treatment both false friars receive is described in such an analogous style that one is almost convinced Thomas More was acquainted with this poem and even patterned his ballad

25

on it. It may have been the other way around, but since Dunbar is More's senior by eighteen years, it appears more plausible that his ballad should have been the prototype for More's account of this contemporary incident.

Having aroused the interest of his audience in an event that had recently taken place, More proceeds to describe the officer in his narrative who played such an obnoxious dual role:

> That thriftly was,
> Or he coulde pas,
>   Rapped about the pate,
> Whyle that he would
> See how he could,
>   In goddes name play the frere . . .[19]

With keen psychological insight More gains the confidence and good will of his listeners and has their attention in the palm of his hand. He continues in this tantalizing manner:

> Now if you wyll,
> Knowe how it fyll,
> Take hede and ye shall here.[20]

In the introduction to the poem, More speaks to the audience in his own voice and prepares their heart and mind for the reception of the tale that will ensue. Then, beginning in a narrative vein, he employs the 'once upon a time' technique. He continues to speak in the role of the narrator, but steps out of it whenever a need arises for the characters to talk for themselves. Thus, in turn, he assumes the voice of the crafty sergeant, the young spendthrift, and the wary maiden. No doubt, this method of oral presentation added immeasurably to the hilarious enjoyment of his Tudor listeners, and gave him an opportunity to give vent to his effervescent love of drollery and to exercise his dramatic ability.

Thomas More is not the participant or the observer in this narrative but the omniscient author, who has full knowledge of the machinations of the plot and the actions of all the characters involved in the story. He holds their destiny in his hands and knows from the start how the tale will end. Yet, in his employment of this method the poet avoids becoming tedious and loquacious, for his passages of analysis are short, and he permits the listeners to draw their own conclusions. Since this humorous ballad was meant presumably to be narrated or perhaps even sung, the appeal was to the ear rather than to the eye. Scintillating dialogue and swift-moving action enliven the poem and give it dramatic features; an element of suspense is sustained until the climax is reached. Then with a well-planned and forceful dénouement More enters the scene again as the author omniscient, but at all times avoids boring his listeners with a long soliloquy or a tedious moral. He makes his objective in telling the

26

story in a brief, appealing, and meaningful manner, and thus fully achieves his purpose in narrating this entertaining story for profit and pleasure.

According to Carl H. Grabo, this method of employing the omniscient author is usually the swiftest and the least awkward of all methods of narration, for the author gives us the story with as little delay as possible. The method is justified for the reader or the listener in so far as the analysis proves interesting and enlightening. One makes no question of the author's assumption of insight, but may justly criticise the result for its truth to human nature.[21]

The first seventy-two lines comprising the introduction are characterized by succinctness of thought and economy of expression. The method of enumerating various crafts which More uses in the context of these introductory verses enables him to obtain the interest of a heterogeneous audience who represent the following companies: Hosiers, Drapers, Goldsmiths, Clothworkers, Haberdashers, Mercers, Grocers, and Merchant Taylors. In clear, strong language he reminds them of the chaos and confusion that arise from not keeping to one line of business:

> He that hath lafte,
> The hosiers crafte,
>   And falleth to making shone,
> The smythe that shall,
> To painting fall,
>   His thrift is well nigh done.[22]

To bring out his point even more efficaciously, More uses plain diction and simple antithesis not only in the idea presented but also in the use of adjectives which describe the particular trade:

> A *black* draper,
> With *whyte* paper,
>   To go to writying schole,
> An *olde* butler,
> Becum a cutler,
>   I wene shall proue a fole.[23]

Technically, each craft is built up in a separate unit and contains the elements of contrast and anti-climax. This structural technique reminds one of the placing of stone upon stone to make a lofty edifice and consequently, achieves an effect of beauty, design, and proportion. Women were probably present in the audience, for More disparagingly alludes to an 'old trot' as an old woman who can do 'nothyng but kysse the cup' (an expression used for taking a sip of liquor), and who, instead of helping others with her 'phisick,' weakens them mentally and physically:

An old trot,
That can god wot,
    Nothyng but kysse the cup,
With her physick,
Will kepe one sicke,
    Til she have soused hym up.[24]

He finds success well-nigh impossible for the man-of-law who

. . . neuer sawe,
    The wayes to bye and sell,
Wenyng to ryse,
By merchaundise,

and he prays that 'god spede hym well'.[25] After ending the verse with the lawyer
who covets the merchant's profession, he reverses the picture and presents a
merchant who aspires to success as a lawyer, and who falls 'in sute',

Tyll he dispute,
    His money cleane away.[26]

More employs a little good-natured satire in the following lines:

Pletyng the lawe,
For euery strawe,
    Shall proue a thrifty man,
With bate and strife,
But by my life,
    I cannot tell you whan.[27]

Good rhythm, apt diction, and delightful tone quality can be found in his
concluding verses which epitomize the various crafts alluded to:

Whan a hatter
Wyll go smatter,
    In philosophy,
Or a pedlar,
Waxe a medlar,
    In theology,
All that ensue,
Suche craftes new,
    They driue so farre a cast,
That euermore,
They do therefore,
    Beshrewe themselfe at last.[28]

The philosophy of keeping to one task only, was such a prominent feature of the London livery companies in the fourteenth century that the charter from Edward III gave them complete control of their trade. No one who had cloth to sell could sell it except to a draper. The dyers, weavers, and fullers (the business of the last-mentioned craft was to scour, cleanse, or thicken the cloth) were to keep strictly to the respective and distinguishing features of their trade and they were in no way to meddle with the making, buying, or selling of cloth or drapery on pain of forfeiture.[29] To facilitate the necessity of pursuing one task only, persons engaged in the same trade lived in the same quarter of the city.[30] The uniformity of their occupation and the equality of their social status would make it foolish indeed

> To enterpryse,
> An other faculte,[31]

for, surely,

> . . . he that wyll,
> And can no skyll,
>   Is neuer lyke to the.[32]

After a comprehensive and well-integrated introduction, More, conscious of the fact that he is telling a story, presents the exposition to his humorous narrative in a logical and forceful manner. At the very outset he reveals the fact that a rich, prosperous man died and left his inheritance to his son:

> It happed so,
> Not long ago,
>   A thrifty man there dyed,
> An hundred pounds,
> Of nobles rounde,
>   That he had layed aside:
> His sonne he wolde,
> Should haue this golde . . .[33]

The wealthy man is described as a 'thrifty' individual, and More apparently used this adjective in the sense of *thriving, prosperous, well-to-do, fortunate.*[34] The reference to *nobles rounde* is to an old English coin first minted by Edward III which had the value of ten shillings.

The narrator is eager to give his audience an early insight into the ultimate reason for the disguise of the sergeant. With apparent impatience but with the precision of thought of a law practitioner, he uses the following lines as his starting point for the development of the plot:

> For to beginne with all:
> But to suffise,
> His chylde, well thrise,
>   That money was to smal.[35]

In the last three lines of the above verses one finds an implied characterization of the carefree man, and the weakness of his character is analogous to the tragic flaw of a heroic protagonist but on a much smaller scale. The selfishness hinted at here becomes the cause of the merchant's future anxiety and unhappiness as, in fugitive fashion, he spends his time avoiding his debtors and ultimately, the demands of the law.

According to the meaning of the word *thrise* in the *New English Dictionary*, the most plausible explanation perhaps would be the hyperbolic allusion to *many times* or *three times in succession* or on *three different occasions*. At any rate the epithet describing the money as *well thrise* presumably means that even three times as much money would still not be a sufficient inheritance for this prodigal youth. Obviously, since his father was an industrious and ambitious man, he expected his son to use his wit and energy to accumulate more money and thereby to achieve fame and wealth. Here More interrupts the narrative and, speaking in his own voice again, as he did in the introduction, he gives advice to his audience. He does not offer his own judgment as the criterion for belief but substantiates it with the opinion of others:

> Yet or this day
> I have hard say,
>   That many a man certesse,
> Hath with good cast,
> Be ryche at last,
>   That hath begonne with lesse.[36]

The young man's dissoluteness was brought about gradually. First, he put the gold in a pot, but not finding this solution satisfacotry, he then hid it in a cup, and 'supped it fayre up. In his owne brest . . .'[37] More, who later became so adept in the use of subtle irony, tells his listeners that 'it was a joy'[38] to see how this man employed his money. The merchant prudently considers the fact that his ship, laden with treasure, may not come into port safely if he invests his money in merchandise, or that some crafty men may beguile him and thus diminish his substance, which is the very joy of his life. Not outdone by others in craftiness of design, he finally hits upon a good idea:

> First fayre and wele,
> Therof much dele,
>   He dygged it in a pot,
> But then him thought,
> That way was nought,
>   And there he left it not.[39]

The gold is, indeed, a joy to behold and a treasure worth hoarding, but it becomes the cause of the young man's worry and unrest. The best solution to the

30

problem, in his estimation, would be to spend the money for his own comfort and pleasure, and thus derive the most benefit from it himself, unmolested by those whose greedy eyes were continually upon it. His own breast finally becomes the pot, the cup, the hiding place where his precious gold becomes safe and secure:

> In his own brest,
> He thought it best,
>   His money to enclose,
> Then wist he well,
> Whateuer fell,
>   He coulde it neuer lose.[40]

He seeks the company of jolly men and lives merrily for many days with 'lusty sporte'.[41] Men looking upon his prosperity and ease consider him Fortune's favourite child; for money, pleasure, and friends are all at his disposal night and day. Certainly this way of life is by no means conducive to working for one's living as his father had done, in order to acquire wealth, honour, and prestige. Even the ministers of the law are just as ready to wait upon this fortunate and rich young man as they are upon the mayor. But with a masterly stroke of irony and keen insight into human nature, More, the narrator, informs his audience that the dissolute young man

> Hated such pompe and pride,
> And would not go,
> Companied so,
> But drewe himself a side . . .[42]

Covetousness inevitably led to extravagance, for the young man 'supped up' not only his own money but also the money of other men who freely gave him the sums he asked for, while trusting his character and integrity. But alas, he

> Neuer payd it,
> Up he laid it,
>   In like maner wyse.
> Yet on the gere,
> That he would were,
>   He rought not what he spent,
> So it were nyce,
> As for the price,
>   Could him not miscontent.[43]

In the course of time he accumulated so many debts that even the sight of an officer of the law put fear into his heart. Consequently, to avoid the presence of this unwelcome official he 'drewe himself a side, to Saint Katherine's'[44] where he chose to abide. More gives probable reasons for this withdrawal as he lets the audience decide the issue for themselves:

> For devocion,
> Or promocion,
> There would he nedes abyde.[45]

The allusion to St. Katherine's is most probably a reference to a place named after this popular and well-loved saint. A curious sixteenth century poem entitled 'Cocke Lorelles bote' by an anonymous author contains proverbial allusions to old London, among which is a reference to St. Katherine's place. A pertinent excerpt from the poem follows, since it helps to elucidate the meaning structure of Thomas More's ballad:

> There came such a winde from wynchester
> That blewe these women ouer the ryuer
> In wherye as I wyll you tell
> Some at *Saynt Kateryns* stroke a grounde
> And many in holborne were founde
> Some at saynt Gyles I trowe
> Also in ave maria aly and at westmenster
> And some in shordyche drive theder
> With grete lamentacyon.[46]

The poem is written in the same stanza form which More uses, namely, the *aabccb* rhyme scheme. It also enumerates various crafts such as: 'Laylers, taverners, drapers, ale brewers, mercers, boke prynters, myllers and botyll makers . . .'.[47] Like the 'Mery Iest' it too belongs to the typical medieval Latin type and contains long catalogues, subtle satire, and concreteness of detail. This particular locality may have been named St. Katherine's on account of the stately and ancient abbey in East London, originally founded by Queen Eleanore as a religious house under a definite obligation to pray for the souls of her two children. After Henry III's death, Queen Eleanore refounded the hospital adjoining the Abbey and stipulated that six poor scholars were to be fed, clothed, and provided for. On November 16 of every year twelve pence were given to the poor scholars and the same amount to twenty-four poor persons; on November 20, the anniversary of the King's death, a thousand poor men yearly received one halfpenny each. A point of great importance was that the people who received this charity at the good Queen's hands were obliged to live in this particular precinct in order to be its recipients. Perhaps the line, 'There would he nedes abyde',[48] has a specific reference to the name of some place where the young man went to escape his many debtors. Yet, here too, he spends the little money he has left or what he manages to borrow from others in frivolous pastimes and foolish pleasures, until he becomes totally penniless.

His debtors catch up with him

> To aske theyr det,
> But none could get,
>   The valour of a peny.[49]

He argues with them, and asks them for more time:

> With visage stout,
> He bare it out,
>   Euen unto the hard hedge,
> A month or twaine
> Till he was faine,
>   To laye his gowne to pledge.[50]

Instead of looking for work and obtaining his money honestly, he ponders what he should do next and where he should go to avoid his pursuers. By now, being quite adept at feigning other roles and disguising his real intentions, he hides in his friend's house under the pretence of sickness:

> Than after this,
> To a frende of his,
>   He went and there abode,
> Where as he lay,
> So sick alway,
>   He myght not come abroade.[51]

Money ill-spent had been the cause of his mental torment and the deterioration of his character. How much better it would have been for him to engage in some physical work or to learn some craft and thus preserve his mental equanimity, physical well-being, and enthusiasm for life! Instead he is pursued by his enemy and haunted by those generous individuals who once trusted him enough to lend him the money he so quickly and foolishly hoarded 'in his owne brest'.[52]

This incident brings us to the second development in the plot and introduces a new character in the person of the officer, who henceforth becomes a main character in the narrative. A merchant, who desires to have his money returned to him and who has been pursuing the culprit to no avail, finally goes to this officer for advice:

> And he answerede,
> Be not aferde,

> Take an accion therefore,
> I you beheste,
> I shall hym reste,
> And than care for no more.[53]

Upon seeing the hesitancy of the merchant to give credence to these words, for the merchant knows only too well the hypocrisy and craftiness of the young man, the officer boastfully assures him that the arrest will take place soon. With confidence in his own power and with egotism savouring of pride, he says:

> Be not afrayed,
>   It shall be brought about.
> In many a game,
> Lyke to the same,
>   Haue I been well in ure,
> And for your sake,
> Let me be bake,
> But yf I do this cure.[54]

He says nothing more to the merchant but, with a determination to assert his dignity and to prove that he can be successful in this venture, he leaves his company. The self-confident officer goes immediately to the Austin friars, whom he presumably knows, and remains with them for a whole day, devising his disguise and method of attack. He puts on the long black habit with the broad sleeves and the white scapulary with the black leather belt – the distinguishing habit of these friars – and even practises imitating their mannerisms to appear more like them in reality. More's treatment and description of the friars never degenerates into malicious satire, and the narration is such that it could be heard or read by the friars themselves without offending them. The officer takes great pride in his successful disguise:

> So was he dight,
> That no man might,
>   Hym for a frere deny.
> He dopped and dooked,[55]
> He spake and looked
>   So religiously.[56]

The sergeant takes great pride in his ostentatious attire and religious demeanour and, inflated with self-confidence, he goes the following day to the young man's hiding place to claim the money for the anxious merchant. More steps out of the role he had been playing just now and again speaks in his own voice, for he obviously wishes to regain the complete interest of his Tudor audience and to inform them that the climax will soon be reached:

34

Then forth a pace,
Unto the place,
   He goeth in goddes name,
To do this dede,
But now take hede,
   For here begynneth the game.[57]

The narrative proceeds with heightened interest as the storyteller's tone keeps pace with the increasing intensity of both the actions that follow and the clear, functional diction employed. More has obtained the undivided attention of his listeners and a sympathetic rapport has been established between himself and them. One can almost hear his voice change its tempo and tone quality and see the varied expressions on his face, as he leans towards them and says at first, almost in a whisper:

He drew hym ny,
And softely,
   Streight at the dore he knocked.[58]

He increases his velocity and pitch and continues in a narrative tone:

And a damsell,
That hard hym well,
   There came and it unlocked.[59]

One is amused to think how More must have changed his voice to assume the part of the maid, the merchant, and the disguised sergeant. His actions must have been as humorous as his facial expressions, and one is inclined to think that Thomas More himself enjoyed the recitation and dramatization of this ballad as much as his fun-loving Tudor audience did. The very fact that it was probably narrated or sung at a merry feast points to its appropriateness for such an occasion. Its message and its method of expression imply the presence of many listeners who represented the leading crafts in London during the early sixteenth century. The advice contained in the epilogue, namely, the exhortation to follow one craft only and the ensuing invitation to a merry feast, substantiate the fact that the ballad may have been sung or recited orally. The poem does not lend itself to singing as well as it does to narration, and it can be inferred that More alone dramatized the various parts.

What added to the effectiveness of his gesticulations, if he was the sole interpretor of the poem, was the fact that he was well acquainted with the life and observances of the monks in the Charterhouse. As a youth he lived with the Carthusians for four years (1499–1503) without taking any vows. Harpsfield further tells us that the young More had entertained serious thoughts at this time of becoming a Franciscan friar.[60] However, far form ridiculing them and exposing their frailty and shortcomings, the poem satirizes the individual sergeant who disguises himself as a friar and not the friars of sixteenth century London. This is precisely why More emphasizes the moral of the poem so much because it is the action and not the person that he pungently but good-naturedly satirizes.

The development of the plot proceeds energetically and rapidly, as it is sustained and enlivened by the witty, vigorous dialogue which plays such a big part in it. The conversation between the maid and the sergeant disguised as a friar is facetious and enjoyable; that of the 'friar' and the 'sick' man is full of witty innuendoes and subtle hypocrisy on the part of the two men who are feigning a certain state of life, on the one hand, and physical infirmity on the other. This duplicity in thought and word accelerates the unfolding of the plot, for each one craves justice for himself. One can imagine the audience sitting on the edge of their chairs in eager anticipation of what will follow after the maiden leaves the sergeant and the sick man together. A mischievous twinkle appears in the narrator's eyes, a foreboding look comes upon his face as he raises his hands and says with deliberately slow pace and with strongly accented words:

> Whan there was none,
> But they alone,
> The frere with euyll grace,
> Says, I rest the,
> Come on with me,
> And out he took his mace.[61]

Spurred on by dialogue replete with onomatopoetic devices and characterized by swiftness of action, the poem reaches its climax when the young man is arrested by the crafty sergeant's designs. But it becomes readily apparent that the 'sick' man is no longer physically indisposed as he aggressively throws off his feigning demeanor and says in an angry voice:

> . . . horson thefe,
> With a mischefe,
> Who hath taught the thy good.
> And with his fist,
> Upon the lyst,[62]
> He gave hym such a blow,
> That backward downe,
> Almost in a sowne,
> The frere is ouerthrow.[63]

The sergeant is then thrown headlong down the stairs by the maid and the wife who, upon hearing the noises of the rumbling and tugging, immediately come to their friend's aid and join their forces to his. If women were present at this feast, they must have enjoyed thoroughly the successful part the two women played in punishing this guilty male culprit. Not only does the disguise of the sergeant fall off from him when he is thrown down the stairs, but also his pride and confidence in his own scheming:

> Up they hym lift,
> And with yll thrift,
> > Hedlyng along the stayre,
> Down they hym threwe,
> And sayd adewe,
> > Commaunde us to the mayre.[64]

The swift-moving climax is immediately followed by the dénouement, which is brief and pertinent. The sergeant, fearful and chagrined, rises slowly and painfully from his awkward position and makes his escape as he says to himself:

> Quod he now lost,
> Is all this cost,
> > We be neuer the nere.
> Ill mote he the,[65]
> That caused me
> > To make myself a frere.[66]

The moral, light in tone and brief in content, clinches the poem effectively. One should stick to one business only and not feign knowledge and perfection in another state, for this inevitably brings about failure of the enterprise, chagrin over the outcome, and frustration of one's plans. By the following twelve-line epilogue, More admirably links the end of the poem with its beginning and presents the narration as a unified and coherent whole:

> Now masters all,
> Here now I shall,
> > Ende there as I began,
> In any wyse,
> I would auyse,
> > And consayle euery man,
> His own craft use,
> All newe refuse,
> > And lyghtly let them gone.
> Play not the frere,
> Now make good chere,
> > And welcome euery chone.[67]

Although pithy and unpretentious, the above epilogue performs a four-fold function:

1. It is addressed to the 'masters all' and it gives the readers an insight into the nature of this sixteenth century feast.
2. It is unifying re-statement of the opening theme.
3. It contains an invitation to the ensuing merry feast.
4. It is built on the framework of the 'Merry Jests' which ended their tales with a moral.

In keeping with the narrative technique More set out to follow in this poem, the setting, which will now be discussed, serves primarily to develop the plot and to bring out transitions in time and place. Since he begins his narrative with the clear and forceful enunciation of an idea which becomes the predominant theme of the poem, he leads his audience to the philosophers, the 'Wyse men'[68] of the past, in order to make an assertion which will have the stamp of experience and veracity on it.

Having captured the interest of his audience with a contemporary incident still fresh in their minds, he begins his story in an arresting and tantalizing manner. One can almost hear the people rustle about in their seats to assume a comfortable position as More, the entertaining story-teller says:

> It happed so,
> Not long ago,
> A thrifty man there dyed . . .[69]

The elements of time and place rapidly flash before one in the following verses as one sees and observes the various ways in which the newly-made rich son employs his money. He hides it in a pot, then puts it in a cup, and finally stores it up safely in his own breast by spending it all. The rapidity of the action increases the listener's interest while the concomitant shifting of scenes is done quickly and efficiently.

The next setting is conditioned by the uneasy state of the young spendthrift, who obviously thought it expedient to leave his present environment, especially the courteous sergeant-of-law, who was eager to wait upon him 'as sone as on the mayre'.[70]

> . . . drewe himself a side,
> To saint Katherine.[71]

Here he is pursued by his many debtors and must again contrive a new hiding place, for going to work and learning a trade are the things furthest from his mind. The transition of time and place is rapid and keeps appropriate pace with the theme and tempo of the poem. The culprit now feigns illness at his friend's home, which becomes the immediate setting for the climax that will soon follow:

He went and there abode,
Where as he lay,
So sick alway,
He myght not come abrode.[72]

The inclusion of stairs in this scene is an indication of foresight on the part of the author, and the two-story house is indeed an appropriate place for the 'luggyng', 'tuggyng', and 'waltring'[73] that takes place there. When the disguised sergeant insists on seeing the sick young man, one becomes aware of the stairs in the house for the first time:

Quod she I wyll,
Stonde ye here styll,
Tyll I *come down again*.[74]

The wary maiden goes upstairs to tell her master about this strange and inopportune visitor, and he in turn

. . . mistrustying,
No maner thyng,
Sayd mayden go thy way,
And fetche him hyder,
That we togyder
May talk.[75]

A tense feeling of suspense is experienced by both men during the interval of the maid's climbing up and down the stairs. She ascends them slowly and thoughtfully to deliver the message to the man who had recently become so skeptical of all visitors; she descends them obediently to bring the answer to the crafty sergeant who had played this game before:

In many a game,
Lyke to the same,
Have I been well in *ure*.[76]

Consequently, the stairs serve as a protection between the culprit and the sergeant, while the time spent in the maid's ascending and descending of them enables each party to plan his method of attack. Perhaps when the young man selected this house as his hide-out, he foresaw the important role stairs would play in his scheme of defense. Certainly, he was crafty enough to invite the 'friar' upstairs because, if need be, he would make his descent so much the faster. The maiden does not have any premonition of trouble as she obeys the injunction to bring the visitor up:

> ... Adowne she gothe,
> *Up* she hym brought,
> No harme she thought,
>   But it made some folke wrothe.[77]

The following verses are replete with excitement and suspense, and the sergeant's hyporitical words of cheer precipitate the climax. Both he and the crafty merchant simultaneously beguile each other with mellifluous words which clothe an evil intent:

> Syr quod the frere,
> Be of good chere,
> Yet shall it after this,
> For Christes sake,
> Loke that you take,
>   No thought within your brest:
> God may tourne all,
> And so he shall,
>   I trust unto the best.
> But I would now,
> Comen with you,
>   In counsayle yf you please,
> *Or* ellys nat,
> Of matters that,
>   Shall set your heart at ease.[78]

For a moment the man accepts this counsel in good faith and orders the maiden to go downstairs. Turning to the friar with a ray of hope in his heart, he says:

> Now say on gentle frere,
> Of this tydyng,
> That ye me bryng,
> I long full sore to here.[79]

The two men are now alone and the sergeant does not waste any time, nor does he utter any more words of comfort and assurance, but takes out his mace and boldly arrests the sick man. The latter immediately gives up his pretense at sickness and vigorously attacks his opponent. The sergeant is thrown headlong down the very stairs which he so confidently ascended a short while ago. The setting in this humorous ballad is functional, for it is bound up with the characters and is at the same time essential to the preconditioning of the plot.

Apropos of characterization, Cleanth Brook's tenet that 'the most significant way of presenting character is through action' is adhered to in this ballad. 'When the writer thinks of a character', Brooks further states, 'he cannot think of him simply as a static personality or a psychological description but as

40

a complex of potentialities for action'.[80] It is true that characterization is inextricably woven with the actions that make up the plot of the story, but it is perhaps even more significant that the interpretation of character is so closely bound with dialogue that one cannot separate the two. The words a person utters himself or the statements of others about him describe character in an effective and reliable manner. When Thomas More as the author-omniscient introduces the character, he gives us our first insight into his motives and mode of behaviour. His two main characters, the sergeant and the rich man, are fully drawn, while the minor ones, including the father who bequeathed his gold to his son, the merchant, the maid, and the debtors, are in complete harmony with the plot development of the narrative.

The delineation of the young man who squandered his newly-acquired inheritance so quickly is characterized by a mild innuendo in the first part of the ballad:

> But to suffice
> His chylde well thrise,
> That money was to smal.[81]

From the above description of the thrifty man's son one can infer that he was not satisfied with the 'hundred pounde of nobles rounde'[82] that his father had laid aside for him. In view of this fact one wonders whether More is stating a positive fact or whether he is being ironical when he says in the next six verses:

> But this yonge manne,
> So well beganne,
> His money to imploy,
> That certainly,
> His policy,
> To see it was a joy.[83]

The young man is distrustful of people and their interest in him, as well as of industries and their possible collapse; therefore, he exercises great ingenuity in concealing his wealth. As a result, he spends more time and energy scheming ways of hoarding the money than he would by working physically to increase it:

> Men with some wile,
> Myght hym begyle,
> And minish his substance,
> For to put out,
> All manner dout,
> He made a good puruay,
> For every whyt,
> By his own wyt,
> And toke an other way.[84]

He hides the gold in a pot, encloses it in a cup, and not satisfied with either hiding place, he finally 'sup[s] it fayre up In his own brest'.[85] His mind is now temporarily at peace for the money is well 'enclosed'[86] and he is no longer under the nervous tension of running the risk of losing it in one form or another. From a smug miser the greedy spendthrift becomes an irresponsbile wastrel as he unscrupulously borrows money from other men and spends it lavishly on dress, food, and 'lusty sport'.[87]

The young merchant is further delineated as a resourceful and aggressive person who is not outdone in cunning or strength. The following verses portray his mingled emotions of fear and anger when he is taken by surprise and arrested by the sergeant. Nevertheless, he quickly subdues his fear and gives vent to his anger with words and blows:

> This marchaunt there,
> For wrath and fere,
>   He waxyng welnigh wood,
> Says horson thefe,
> With a mischefe,
>   Who hath taught the thy good.
> And with his fist,
> Upon the lyst,
>   He gauve hym such a blow,
> That backward downe,
> Almost in a sowne,
>   The frere is overthrow.[88]

The merchant's fear is now occasioned by a different motive, for he is afraid that he had mortally wounded the sergeant, who was not prepared for this sudden attack. To assure himself that he did not commit such a vile deed he endeavors to bring him to life with heavy 'rappes and clappes'.[89] The sergeant angrily rises, and the two continue fighting:

> With many a sadde stroke
> They roll and rumble,
> They turne and tumble,
>   As pigs do in a poke.[90]

Due retribution is meted out to the disguised friar, but one is a little disappointed that the young merchant who squandered his inheritance, incurred innumerable debts, and never worked hard in his life, was so successful in evading just punishment by the law. However, one can infer from the context of the poem, particularly from the description of the culprit's state of mind and his constant running away from society and ultimately from himself, that he was bereft of peace of mind, the satisfaction of physical labor, and the comradeship of his fellow men.

The sergeant is also described through the medium of dialogue, and the words he utters pronounce sentence about him. He is egotistic and boastful, scheming and obsequious. He lacks foresight and prudence, and thus becomes an easy prey to his enemy. The very first time he opens his mouth to speak, his abrupt and decisive answer reveals an over-confident attitude toward settling the merchant's problem quickly and effectively:

> It happed than,
> A marchant man,
>> That he ought money to,
> Of an officere,
> Than gan enquere,
>> What him was best to do.
> And he answerde,
> Be not aferde,
>> Take an accion therefore,
> I you beheste,
> I shall hym reste,
>> And than care for no more.[91]

The worried merchant is not appeased by the sergeant's peremptory statements. He has a strong presumption that the arrest of the clever scoundrel will not be accomplished with the ease and assurance the sergeant boasts of. The officer immediately senses his distrust and, deeply hurt with it, even more boastfully acknowledges his ability to restore the merchant's money:

> Be not afrayd,
>> It shall be brought about.
>
> . . . .
> And for your sake,
> Let me be bake,
>> But yf I do this cure.[92]

His shallowness of mind and heart is further portrayed when he dons the garb of the Austin friars without imbibing the spirit that ought to accompany it. With vanity and self-satisfaction he looks at himself in the mirror and is almost certain

> That no man might,
> Hym for a frere deny,
> He dopped and dooked,
> He spake and looked,
>> So religiously.[93]

In this disguise, which one is made to understand he had assumed more than once, he goes to the specified house and, exulting beforehand in the success of this ingenious venture, he asks to see the young man under the pretense of giving him spiritual counsel.

The sergeant's complacency and lack of foresight precipitate his downfall and ruin. He does not wait for the opportune moment, nor does he plan a possible rebuttal in case his plan should fall through, but upon being left alone with the merchant, he immediately takes out his mace and arrests him. But alas! he has come to grips with someone superior to himself in physical strength and mental scheming. Quickly and painfully he learns his lesson as he rumbles and tumbles down the stairs to the accompaniment of the hilarious laughter of the three individuals at the top of them:

> Hedlyng a long the stayre,
>   Downe they hym threwe,
>   And sayd adewe,
> Commande us to the mayre.[94]

The characterization of the sergeant is consistent to the very end; for, in his shallowness and lack of integrity of character, he blames the merchant for having indirectly inveigled him to set this trap:

> The frere arose,
> But I suppose,
>   Amased was his hed.
> He shoke his eares,
> And from grete feares,
>   He thought hym well a fled.
> Quod he now lost,
> Is all this cost,
>   We be neuer the nere.
> Ill mote he the,
> That caused me,
>   To make myself a frere.[95]

The maid does not play a large part in this narrative poem; nevertheless we become aware of the strong points in her character – her prudence, foresight, and agility – through the responses she gives to the sergeant. When the latter states the purpose of his visit and asks to see the man who 'lodgeth here',[96] intuitively she recognizes some evil design for she quickly retorts:

> Well syr quod she,
> And yf he do what than.[97]

44

The sergeant's intrigue takes on the form and colour of irony when he suavely says in his meekest tones:

> Quod he maystresse,
> No harm doutelesse:
> It longeth for our order,
> To hurt no man,
> But as we can,
>   Every wight to forder.[98]

The damsel exhibits foresight and prudence when she does not take the friar upstairs but tells him to wait until she returns.

> Stonde ye here styll,
>   Tyll I come downe agayn.[99]

She faithfully reports the message to the man upstairs, who has found refuge in her father's home, and she meticulously describes the appearance of the friar and the nature of the colloquy downstairs. The maid also exhibits the virtue of obedience, for she does exactly as she is told; and even her first premonition of an evil design on the part of the visiting friar disappears when the merchant tells her to leave their presence so that they may talk together. However, as soon as she and her mother hear the rolling and rumbling upstairs, they immediately go there to give assistance to the merchant:

> And whan they spye;
> The captaynes lye,
>   Both waltring on the place,
> The freres hood,
> They pulled a good,
> Adowne about his face.[100]

The damsel does not hesitate to punish the sergeant for this intrigue, for,

> Whyle he was blynde,
> The wench behynde,
>   Lent hym leyd on the flore,
> Many a joule,
> About the noule,
>   With a great batyldore.[101]

The mother joins her daughter in administering retribution for this foul deed:

> The wyfe came yet,
> And with her fete,
>   She holpe to kepe him downe,
> And with her rocke,
> Many a knocke,
>   She gave hym on the crowne.[102]

One an imagine what rollicking laughter and hilarious outcries their actions evoked in a Tudor audience that enjoyed such exhibition of female mastery over the culprit. The fact that feminine strength is mainly used to overthrow the guilty sergeant makes the dénouement light and facetious and takes away from it the sting of bitter reproach and sardonic irony. As a consequence, the poem is a fitting invitation to a merry feast and ends on a note of humour and hilarity.

'A meri iest how a sergeant would learne to playe the frere' is cast in the form of a ballad, which in the fifteenth and sixteenth centuries was 'a deliberate narrative, long and easy of pace, free of repetitions, bare of refrain, abounding in details, and covering considerable stretches of time'.[103] More than thirty ballads of this type recount the lively adventures of Robin Hood with the sheriff of Nottingham, and attribute a great part of his success to his unfailing and sincere devotion to Our Lady. More's ballad is similar to these Gest poems in its introductory appeal to the audience:

> Now yf you wyll,
> Knowe how it fyll,
>   Take hede and you shall here.[104]

The disguise technique is also apparent in the Robin Hood ballads which so closely resemble 'A meri iest'. In both poems the balladist indulges in proverbial comment and regards action as conduct which reveals one's personality and character traits.[105] It is interesting to note that the music of some of the Robin Hood songs seems to have been church music. Miss Pound, who made a detailed study of the origin of the ballad, affirms that 'there should be nothing surprising in the singing of ballads to music of ecclesiastical type . . .'.[106] Like the hymns of the Middle Ages, the ballad's stanzaic structure is not uniform. Some old ballad texts are in couplets; others are in quatrains, and many have variants of both forms. Pound goes on to say that 'the early Tudor period was one of great musical impulse . . . and that the earliest approaches to the song manner of ballads which remain to us are ecclesiastical'.[207] The refrain does not appear until the sixteenth century in most of the ballad-like verse, through refrains are frequently seen in other lyric poetry.[108]

The versification in 'A meri iest how a sergeant would learne to playe the frere' is admirably suited to the theme and the occasion. The rhythm of the

46

poem has a horse-trot quality which fortunately does not degrade it, but adds to the humour in oral delivery as well as in its subject matter. More's interest in the *Meri Iest* type of subject matter and form may be traced to the *Jeux d'esprit* literature so popular in his day. It is the assumption of William Carew Hazlitt that the *Summa Praedicantium* of Johannes de Bromyard and the *Joci ac Sales of Luscinius* (1524) were the types of books Desiderius Erasmus of Rotterdam might have sent across the sea to amuse his Chelsea correspondent. He further presents some interesting and substantial proof that Thomas More may have been the author of the anonymous *Hundred Merry Tales* which came from the press of John Rastell in 1526.[109]

The word *Gesta* had undergone different meanings and, at the time of the introduction of printing in England, it took the literary form of a ballad. It combined the narrative and historical data inherent in the *Gesta* with the function of the *jester* or *joculator*, whose purpose was to amuse and entertain.[110] Several poems of this nature appeared in More's lifetime: 'A Meri Geste How the Plowman Lerned His Pater Noster' and 'A Mery Iest of the Mylner of Abyngton'. Although he followed a popular precedent, More never became a slavish imitator in subject matter or technique, for the treatment of his friar is facetious but dignified, frivolous but not disrespectful. Then, too, his introduction to the poem is more fully developed than that of his contemporaries, who seem to plunge immediately into the unfolding of the plot.

The narrative is fully and skillfully developed in four hundred and thirty lines of dimeter and trimeter verses. In William Rastell's 1557 edition the stanzas in this ballad are divided into twelve-line units, rhyming: aab / ccb / dde / ffg. Thus, we have the following stanzaic structure:

	Number of feet
Wyse men / al way /	2
Af fyrme / and say /	2
That best / is for / a man /	3
Di li / gent ly /	2
For to / ap ply /	2
The bu / si ness / that he can /	3
And in / no wyse /	2
To en / ter pryse /	2
An o / ther fa / cul te /	3
For he / that wyll /	2
And can / no skyll /	2
Is ne / uer like / to the /.[111]	3

Upon comparing Rastell's edition of the poem with Julian Notary's separate publication of it in 1516, one readily sees the superiority and efficiency of Rastell's work. The following rendition is an example of Notary's confused and inefficient publication of 'A meri iest':

Wyse men alwaye
Afferme & say / yt best is
For a dylygently   (man

For to apply / ye besynes
Yt he and in no wyse   (can[112]

There is a strong possibility that More may have intended six-line stanzas with internal rhyme which was a popular form of versification in the early sixteenth century. It is quite significant that the anonymous ballad of 'The Nutbrowne Mayde' is almost identical in rhythm and stanzaic structure with More's ballad. A comparison of the two poems will serve to illustrate this point. The words designating the internal rhyme are underlined:

'A meri iest'

	Number of feet
This thing / was *tryed* / And ve / re *fyed* /	4
Here by / a ser / geaunt late /	3
That thrift / ly *was* / Or he / coulde *pas* /	4
Rap ped / a bout / the pate /	3
Whyle that / he *would* / See how / he *could* /	4
In god / des name / play the frere /	3
Now if / you *wyll* / Knowe how / it *fyll* /	4
Take hede / and you / shall here / [113]	3

The same meter and line arrangement are found in the introductory stanzas of 'The Nutbrowne Mayde':

	Number of feet
Be it right / or *wrong* / These men / a *mong* /	4
On wo / men do / com plaine /	3
Af fer / myng *this* / How that / it *is* /	4
A la / bour spent / in vaine /	3
To loue / them *wele* / For neuer / a *dele* /	4
They loue / a man / a gayne /	3
For lete / a *man* / Do what / he *can* /	4
Ther fa / vour to / at tayne /	3
Yet uf / *a newe* / To them / *pur sue* /	4
Ther furst / tre lo / uer than /	3
La boureth / for *nought* / And from / her *thought* /	4
He is / a ba / nished man / [114]	3

The rhythm in More's ballad, besides having a songlike quality, is vigorous and flexible. It is full of onomatopoetic overtones and is charged with the assonance

48

which makes it particularly suitable for oral delivery. Like the American twentieth-century poet, Robert Frost, Thomas More chooses his words carefully not only to represent the idea clearly, but also to add rhythm and virility to its sound pattern. Thus, in the following lines the strong vowels o, e, a, y and the diphthong ou, with their Anglo-Saxon qualities of grit and determination accentuate the rhythm and give it a matter-of-fact tone:

	Stressed Vowels		
Down went / the mayd /	ou	e	a
The mer / chaunt sayd /	e		a
Now say / on gen / tle frere /	a	e	e
Of thys / ty dyng /	y		y
That ye / me bryng /	e		y
I long / full sore / to here /	o	o	e
Whan there / was none /		e	o
But they / a lone /		a	o
The frere / with e / uyll grace /	e	e	a
Sayd I / rest the /	a	e	e
Come on / with me /	o		e
And out / he toke / his mace /	ou	o	a

Obviously, the pronunciation of these vowels in More's day differed slightly from our pronunciation of them in the twentieth century. J. Delcourt makes some excellent observations on the contribution Thomas More's English poems make for a better understanding of the pronunciation, syntax, and diction of the sixteenth century.[116] He describes the numerous changes that followed the great vowel shift of the Middle Ages and the resulting inconsistency in the sounds of words. A sound, for example, common to two words has remained in one word but has been altered in the other or has been substituted for a new sound as in the case of *enclose* : *lose*.[117] Delcourt makes the concluding inference from his study of More's writing that 'English had at one period given up its medieval system of sounds and reached a new one, the earlier tradition could easily be appealed to, while the door was open to new developments, or to influences from outside the main current'.[118]

Thomas More dexterously handles his meter to achieve a harmonious fusion of rhythm and emotion. The smoothness and evenness of the following lines admirably support the disguised sergeant's intentions:

Line 1 For Chris / tes sake /

2 Loke that / you take /

49

3 No thought / wi thin / your brest /

4 God may / tourne all /

5 And so / he shall /

6 I trust / un to / the best /

7 But I / would now /

8 Co men / with you /

9 In coun / sayle yf / you please /

10 Or el / lys nat /

11 Of mat / ters that /

12 Shal set / your heart / at ease /[119]

But when the velocity of the rhythm increases with the heightening of interest and proximity to the climax, the poet employs words strong in emotional impact and vigorous in connotative qualities. The rhythm appropriately takes on the same tempo and pitch, and rushes like a swift waterfall from the precipice of a mountain ridge to its climactic conclusion. The inversions in lines two, three, four, and eight prevent the verses from having a mere jingling, horse-trot meter. The trochees in lines two and eight followed by an iambic foot. 'Loke that /you take' and 'Co men / with you' partake of the nature of an entreaty while the one in line four, 'God may / tourne all' is followed by a spondee, which gives the verse vigor and determination.

The multiple caesuras in the ballad give it a conversational tone and make it easy to narrate and pleasant to listen to. Like a skillful technician, More puts these pauses in places of great dramatic interest and thereby creates suspense in his listeners. The caesuras in the following verses give them an almost staccato effect. The double bars indicate a regular pause; the triple bars, a heavy pause:

Sayd // mayden // go thy way /
And fetche him hyder /
That we togyder /
May talk /// adowne she gothe /
Up she hym brought //
No harme // she thought //
But it made some folke wrothe / [120]

The units of thought structure in the ballad range from three to twelve lines. The syntax is clear and the inversions used do not detract from the thought; rather, they give colour and dramatic impact to the rhythm of the line. The punctuation marks consist of the comma, the colon, and the period. The commas, which may have been inserted by the printer, smoothly carry the reader or the listener to the climactic end of the statement, analogous to the conclusion of a periodic sentence:

> Than forth a pace,
> Unto the place,
>   He goeth in goddes name,
> To do this dede,
> But now take hede,
>   For here begynneth the game.[121]

The colon is employed to show a shift in dialogue or to bring another person into the same unit of thought structure for the purpose of completing, contrasting, or describing the idea more fully. The following two examples illustrate this function:

> He drew hym ny,
> And softely,
>   Streyght at the dore he knocked:
> And a damsell,
> That hard hym well,
>   There came and it unlocked.
> The frere sayd,
> God spede fayre mayd,
>   Here lodgeth such a man,
> It is told me:
> Well syr quod she,
>   And yf he do what than.[122]

In keeping with his poetical theory that sense should not be sacrificed for fidelity and precision of the rhyme scheme, one finds that meaning holds a prominent place in More's poetry. Even in this humorous ballad his rhymes are not naive or superfluous. They are, in almost all cases, subordinated to the thought inherent in each successive verse unit, and they are a natural outcome of the syntactical pattern rather than an extraneous appendage to the metrical system employed therein. He, together with his contemporary, William Dunbar, adapted the medieval lyrical stanza to a narrative verse form. The latter is more consistent in his adaptation; More, on the other hand, uses it as a precedent but never follows it slavishly. Thus his rhyme scheme is devoid of a refrain, so characteristic of the ballad stanzaic structure, and it is set according to the following pattern: aab, ccb, dde, ffe. As seen in the following stanza, More's rhymes serve as the key ideas of the verse pattern and form a pleasing synthesis of meaning and emotion:

> So long aboue,   a
> They heue and shoue,   a
>   Togider that at last,   b
> The mayd and wyfe,   c

To break the strife,   c
   Hyed them upward fast.   b
And whan they spye,   d
The captaynes lye,   d
   Both waltring on the place,   e
The freres hood,   f
They pulled a good,   f
   Adowne about his face.[123]   e

More achieves variety by the direct inclusion of feminine rhymes to offset the virility of the strong masculine rhymes and to give the poem a light, facetious touch. The conclusion to the introduction of the ballad contains some delightful feminine rhymes which stamp the verses with buoyant and subtle meaning:

Whan an *hatter*
Wyll go *smatter*,
   In philosophy,
Or a *pedlar*,
Waxe a *medlar*,
   In theology.
All that ensue
Such craftes new,
   They driue so farre a cast,
That euermore
They do therefore,
   Beshrewe themselfe at last.[124]

A well-integrated consonant pattern strengthens the mood of the poem and gives it colour, euphony, and unity. In the verses that follow, the initial *th* diphthongs, the initial *w* consonants, the initial and final *t* consonants, and the two *fr* blends accelerate the tempo of the lines and impart to them a sense of excitement:

*Th*ey layd his mace,
Abou*t* his face,
   That he *w*as *w*ood for payne:
*The fr*yre *fr*appe,
Gote many a swappe,
   *T*yll he was full nygh slayne.
Up *th*ey hym lif*t*,
And *w*ith yll *th*rift,
   Hedlyng a long *th*e stayre,
Downe *th*ey hym *th*rewe,
And sayd adewe,
   Commaunde us *to the* mayre.[125]

52

It is interesting to note how an almost identical pattern of consonants with a slight change in the initial, medial, and final positions alters the mood of the respective verses. The following twelve lines exemplify how the exciting and turbulent atmosphere noted in the consonant pattern above takes on an air of gaiety and frivolity. These lines have just been quoted, but since they are so pertinent to this elucidation, it is hoped that the repetition is justifiable. The main difference occasioning this alteration in mood is the position of the *wh* (hw) and *w* consonants as opposed to the position of the initial *th* diphthong in the preceding verses. The *fr* blend with its grating sound gives way to the limpid, languishing *dl* blend; and the medial *t* is doubled as in the words, ha*tt*er, sma*tt*er. As a result, the lines are immediately invested with humour and drollery, and the rhythm is likewise affected with these qualities:

> *Wh*an an ha*tt*er
> *W*yll go sma*tt*er,
>   In philosophy,
> Or a pe*d*lar,
> *W*axe a me*d*lar,
>   In *th*eology,
> All *th*at ensue,
> Suche cra*ft*es new,
>   *Th*ey driue so farre a cas*t*,
> *Th*at euermore,
> *Th*ey do *th*erefore,
>   Beshrewe *th*emselfe a*t* las*t*.[126]

The diction More uses in 'A meri iest' is clear in its connotations, functional in its purpose, and suited to the type of poem he has chosen to entertain his Tudor audience. The words and phrases he employs savor of colloquial usage and have the imprint of reality upon them. His verbs carry the weight of the sentence and are dynamic in tone quality and vigorous in their portrayal of empathetic experiences: *shove, spye, roll* and *rumble, luggyng, play, welcome,* and *beshrewe*. As a matter of fact, almost every verse in each of the successive twelve-line units has a verb in it; this technique gives the narration greater unity and emphasis and adapts it effectively to oral delivery. In the following unit of verse a total of ten verbs in the indicative, infinitive, and imperative moods is used in twelve succeeding lines:

> It *happed* than,
> A marchant man,
>   That he *ought* money to,
> Of an officere,
> Than *gan enquere*,
>   What him *was* best to do.

> And he *answerde,*
> *Be* not aferde,
>> *Take* an accion therefore,
> I you *beheste,*
> I *shall* hym *reste,*
>> And than *care* for no more.[127]

The nouns in this ballad are, for the most part, monosyllables which readily fall into Dante's classification of diction. According to the author of *Divina Commedia*, words are classified as childish, feminine, manly, combed, shaggy, etc. Ha makes the observation that particular types of words are necessary for the realization of specific poetic forms or desired rhetorical or grammatical effects.[128] Apropos of this theory, Thomas More's poetic diction in 'A meri iest' follows a logical grammatical pattern, and his words may likewise be classified as feminine and masculine. The feminine nouns are clear, direct, and concise while the masculine ones are characterized by strength and vehemence of action. In the first group we would classify such nouns as: *mayd, wyfe, pate, chylde, joy, fole, thing, tyde, howre, cup, damsell,* and *mirth.* They give the poem its light touch, take the sting out of the satire, and make the narration an appropriate introduction to the ensuing merry feast. The nouns classified in the second category lend themselves readily to onomatopoetic overtones and give the poem the flavor of excitement and vigor of expression. The following nouns may belong to this group: *wight, batyldore, marchaunt, stroke, thefe, mischefe, strife, clouche, knocke, rappes,* and *clappes.*

In moments of intense emotion the characters speak in monosyllables. This method is both congruous and effective, particularly for oral interpretation. One normally does not give vent to an outburst of polysyllabic words under the stress of pain, anger, excitement, or fear. The following lines illustrate this theory quite well, for of the thirty-four words used in a particularly exciting passage, twenty-seven are monosyllables while the remaining seven are disyllables or polysyllables. For graphic illustration the monosyllables are underlined once and the polysyllables twice:

> *The* FRERES *hood,*
> *They pulled a good.*
>> ADOWNE ABOUT *his face.*
> *Whyle he was blynde,*
> *The wench* BEHYNDE,
>> *Lent him leyd on the flore,*
> MANY *a joule,*
> ABOUT *the noule,*
>> *With a great* BATYLDORE.[129]

More's further use of trisyllabic and polysyllabic words animates and enriches: his ballad; yet it does not make it ornate and erudite, for it fits in admirably with the subject matter and tone quality of the poem. For example, the words, *philosophy, diligently, covetously, certainly, enterpryse, religiously, marchaundise* and *miscontent* are words that may have been recently coined or amalgamated into the English language, and hence his use of them helped to give these words permanence and stability. Indeed, according to Professor Baugh, More's contribution along these lines is positive and noteworthy. In the *History of the English Language*, Baugh gives More credit for enlarging the English vocabulary and enriching it with newly-coined words:

> Another writer who introduced a large number of new words was Elyot's older contemporary, Sir Thomas More. To More we owe the words absurdity, acceptance, anticipate . . . monosyllable, necessitate, obstruction, paradox, pretext, and others . . . What More and Elyot were doing was being done by numerous others, and it is necessary to recognize the importance of individuals as 'makers of English' in the sixteenth and early seventeenth century.[130]

Of the 1,537 words Thomas More uses in the ballad of 'A meri iest how a sergeant would learne to playe the frere', A. W. Reed explicates fortythree in his 'Philological Notes' with reference to the facsimile text of Rastell's 1557 edition of More's *Works*.[131] This list of words can, in turn, be classified according to the following headings:

Unintelligible for modern readers (explication necessary)	*Probable meanings that can be arrived at from the context.*
1. B. 7. *to the*: to thrive	H. 7. *beganne*: he can
2. F. 8. *thriftly*: well and soundly	D. 3. *degre*: status
3. E. 17. *hard hedge*: the very edge or limit	D. 11. *go*: gone
4. G. 9. *beheste*: promise	D. 12. *bode*: bidden
5. A. 4. *lyst*: ear	G. 10. *rest*: arrest
6. E. 14. *frappe*: tight bound, tied up	G. 5. *as for the price*: modern usage
7. E. 4. *batyldore*: a bat for beating clothes in washing	E. 3. *noule*: noddle, head
8. B. 4. *faculte*: business or craft	E. 2. *houle*: strike or knock
9. A. 6. *whyt*: circumstance	A. 5. *puruay*: provision or plan
10. E. 8. *rocke*: distaff	E. 2. *smatter*: chatter, prate
11. D. 13. *with bate and strike*: with debate and strife	B. 6. *can no skill*: has no special knowledge
12. C. 9. *waltering*: rolling	D. 10. *pletyng the law*: pleading the law

13. A. 11. *toted and he peered*: looked	B. 2. *the business that he can*: the business that he knows
14. C. 14. *may*: maiden	B. 8. *and with tuggyng*: pulling with force
15. A. 10. *He dygged it in a pot*: (a misprint for dyght – put)	
16. H. 5. *Haue I bene wel in ure*: I have had much experience.	F. 1. *Hedlyng along the stayre*: headlong.

Figurative and proverbial meanings:

- H. 12. *wood*: mad
- E. 7. *for promocion*: 'Promoters were informers to escape arrest'
- D. 9. *to wayte*: to attend or to lie in wait
- C. 4. *an olde trot*: an old woman
- F. 1. *driue too far a cast*: 'to cast beyond ourselves'
- C. 9. *soused hym up*: soaked him thoroughly
- A. 15. *dawde*: awakened, aroused
- A. 5. *dopped and dooked*: nodded and bowed
- C. 14. *Some man is borne | To haue a lucky howre*: good fortune comes one's way.

Excluding the remaining three explications: G. 2., H. 2., and E. 12., which are repetitions of the interpretations cited above, the total number of words unintelligible to the modern reader, according to A. W. Reed, would be forty. If this list is broken down, however, fifteen words can be interpreted readily from the context, while only twenty-five would necessitate the use of a glossary for a complete understanding of the poem.

In Tudor rhetoric onomatopoeia is defined as 'forming, as the name of a thing, a word which imitates it'.[132] More's skillful use of this figure of speech gives the ballad a distinctive auditory appeal which makes the narrative much more dramatic and effective. Fifty of the most exciting lines in the narrative[133] realistically describe the struggle between the sergeant and the merchant with the aid of this stylistic device. When the merchant perceives that the solicitous friar has not come to him with good tidings of a spiritual nature but has foully deceived him with his disguise, he becomes very angry and his words take the form of blows:

> And with his fist,
> Upon the lyst
> He *gaue* hym such a *blow*,
> That backward downe,
> Almost in a sowne,
> The frere is *overthrowe*.[134]

Fearing that he has slain the friar, who did not expect these rebuffs, he resuscitates him in the following manner:

> Tyll with good *rappes*,
> And hevy *clappes*,
>   He dawde hym up againe.[135]

The friar comes to his senses quickly, orients himself regarding his present situation, and endeavors to overthrow his opponent physically since he had failed to do so through intrigue:

> The frere toke harte,
> And up he starte,
>   And well he layde about,
> And so there goth,
> Between them both,
>   Many a *lusty cloute*.
> They *rent* and *tere*,
> Each others here,
>   And clave togyder fast,
> Tyll with *luggyng*,
> And with *tuggyng*,
>   They fell downe bothe at last.[136]

The onomatopoeia in the above verses takes the form of 'muscular imitation'[137] and even the length of the words *luggyng* and *tuggyng* plus the medial position of the guttural *g's* gives them the impression of slow, painful movement, violence, and discomfort.

On the other hand, the long rounded *o* and the short *u* add vigor and directness to the onomatopoetic words in the following lines:

> Than on the grounde,
> Togyder rounde,
>   With many a sadde *stroke*,
> They *roll* and *rumble*,
> They *turne* and *tumble*,
>   As pygges do in a poke.[138]

The simile in the last line 'As pygges do in a poke' strikes a humourous note, and thus, prevents the fighting from becoming too gruesome for public entertainment. It also performs the function of a relief scene in drama and enables the struggle to continue until the dénouement is reached and poetic justice is achieved. The alliteration of the *p's* suggests onomatopoetic overtones in keeping with the rest of the consonant sounds, while the medial *g's* in the word *pygges* associate it with the *luggyng* and *tuggyng* in the above lines. More's use of onomatopoeia achieves metrical and stylistic effects and results in rhythm that is spirited and forceful.

In the 1,537 word that comprise 'A meri iest', alliteration does not seem to be a conscious literary device. The following verse, however, is one of the few outstanding examples of initial and stressed alliteration:

> He *w*axyng *w*elnygh *w*ood.[139]

The above line trenchantly describes the merchant's wrath upon realizing the malicious designs the friar had for him when he took out his mace and arrested him. In perfect keeping with consistency of character delineation, More, the author omniscient, does not put many words into the mouth of the merchant, who was introduced to us through his own speech and actions as a reticent and suspicious man. As a matter of fact, throughout the entire poem the merchant speaks only three times with three short lines each time. His remarks are insincere, especially when he tells the friar that he is getting along very well; yet, he is most eager to hear the good spiritual tidings he brings.

The alliterative *th's* in the next three lines immediately follow the thrice alliterated *w's*: *w*axyng, *w*elnygh, *w*ood. The angry merchant gives vent to his emotions in a vehement outcry:

> . . . horson *th*efe.
> Wi*th* a mischefe,
> Who ha*th* *t*augh*t* *th*e *th*y good.[140]

The last verse 'Who hath taught the thy good' implies that the sergeant alone could not have contrived this crafty scheme, for his mind is too dull and obtuse for such matters. He is merely called a 'horson thefe',[141] while the adroit scheming is attributed to someone else. It is readily apparent that here alliteration is predicated on emotion and avoids becoming ornate or tedious by reason of its functional relationship to dialogue and characterization in the narrative.

Besides the above-mentioned use of the trope *wood* to describe the enraged officer's emotions, Thomas More employs the same word again effectively when he says the sergeant 'was wood for pain'.[142] After being kicked, jostled, and knocked about by the wife and the maid, and after receiving a painful beating from the merchant, his shame, anger, and pain are so intense that he almost goes mad. In the *Oxford English Dictionary* one finds that in the sixteenth century *wood* was a metaphorical expression having the following connotations: enraged, furious, vehemently excited, going beyond all reasonable bounds, and extremely rash or reckless.[143] It is interesting to note that an obsolete usage of the word associated it with a contemptuous appellation for a stupid person – a blockhead; another such connotation signified a person who was going out of his mind – a lunatic.[144]

58

More's use of the word *freered* is recorded first in the *OED*, and his interpretation of it has been followed by two other writers in the sixteenth and seventeenth centuries. This original and vigorous trope is characteristic of More's love of drollery and his optimistic outlook on life. He humorously describes the sergeant who is so pleased and elated with his disguise as a friar that he 'dopped and dooked'[145] and 'toted and peered'[146] and

> His harte for pryde,
> Lepte in his syde,
> To see how well he *freered*.[147]

More uses *freered* in the sense of acting as a friar or playing the friar. The entire poem could probably be synthesized in this one word, and it seems apparent that it is the idea around which the narrative revolves. Like a conscientious technician, he states this theme in the exposition to the ensuing narrative, when he says:

> Whyle that he would
> See how he could,
> In goddes name *play the frere*.[148]

He uses this phrase again in the envoy when he counsels his listeners with emphatic deliberation:

> *Play not the frere,*
> Now make good chere,
> And welcome every chone.[149]

The narrative is effectively sandwiched in between these two statements: 'See how he could . . .'[150] and 'Play not the frere'.[151] The first one clearly foreshadows the moral, while the second emphatically synthesizes it. Each person ought to stick to his own task and not manifest an unhealthy interest in, or assume unasked-for responsibility for some other task which is definitely outside the pale of his activities. Perhaps More had another intention in writing and narrating this ballad which is not as obvious as this moral. He may have used it as a means of diverting the people's concentration from the foibles of the contemporary friars and thus, instead of facetiously satirizing them, in reality he adroitly defends them. 'Play not the frere', he pleads, 'do not meddle into their affairs, and they, in turn, will keep out of yours'. Nevertheless, whether he had only one obvious moral in the poem or an underlying concomitant one, it was his good will that initiated it, his integrity that devised it, and his love of merriment that brought it to fruition.

More's originality in fabricating novel schemes and tropes is particularly obvious in the solution he devises for the young man's ostensibly safe hoarding of his money. The greedy man encloses his gold, not in a pot or cup, where thieves may find it, but in his own heart, where he alone could reap its benefits. As a consequence, money became the 'root of evil' in more ways than one, for it deteriorates his character, oppresses his mind, and burdens his soul with its specious glamour and weight. The following trope is outstanding for directness of thought and originality of construction:

> And by and by,
> Covetously,
>> He *supped it fayre up,*
> *In his own brest,*
> He thought it best,
>> His money to enclose,
> Then wist he well,
> What euer fell,
>> He could it neuer lose.[152]

More's imagery is admirably suited to the subject matter he expounds. His legal training is readily apparent in the vigorous tropes he employs to describe the merchant who aspires to the practice of law:

> *To fall in sute,*
> Tyll he *dispute,*
>> His *money cleane away.*
> *Pletyng the lawe,*
> For euery *strawe,*
>> Shall proue a thrifty man
> With *bate* and *strife,*
> But by my life,
>> I cannot tell you whan.[153]

A device that More uses with great dexterity is inversion of the natural order of words, a scheme called hyperbaton[154] in Tudor figures of rhetoric. Although the syntax is reversed, it is not awkward and its contribution to the rhythmical emphasis of the verse justifies its use. The examples that follow are a felicitous illustration of this scheme:

> Up *they hym* lift.
> And with yll thrift,
>> Hedlyng a long the stayre,
> Downe *they hym* threwe,
> And sayd adewe,
>> Commaunde us to the mayre.[155]

Among the other salient tropes in this poem are the following six figures which, according to Tudor rhetoric, can be classified as paroemia,[156] since they depict a commonly-quoted proverb, or have some vestiges of a proverb in them:

1. An old trot
   That can God wot,
      Nothyng but kysse the cup.[157]

2. And for your sake,
   Let me be bake,
      But yf I do this cure.[158]

3. His *harte for pryde,*
   Lepte in his syde,
      To see how well he freered.[159]

4. And say an austen fryre,
   Would with him speke,
      And *matters breake.*[160]

5. But drewe himself a side,
   To saint Katherine,
      Streight as a line.[161]

6. And men had sworne,
   Some man is borne,
      To haue a lucky howre.[162]

More's skill in narrative technique is apparent even in his choice of verbs. He uses 'says' eight times in the narration when he, as the author omniscient, speaks in his own voice in a direct, matter-of-fact tone to give advice to the audience or to render indirect statements in a situation devoid of emotion and irony. On the other hand, when the characters experience emotional disturbances of fear and anxiety and when the scene is coloured by ironical innuendoes and duplicity of thinking and acting, 'quod' is used. For example, of the nine times that 'quod' is employed in the narrative, it appears five times in the dialogue between the maid and the sergeant and twice in the ensuing dialogue between the merchant and the officer:

In dede *quod* he,
It hath with me,
   Bene better than it is.
Syr *quod* the frere,
Be of good chere,
   Yet shall it after this.

For Christes sake,
Loke that you take,
No thought within your brest.[163]

Quod was the predominant form used from 1350–1550. It was a variant of *quoth,* which ultimately was derived from *cwap.*[164] More uses this form to link the two interrupted parts of a direct quotation, while he employs the word *sayd* or *say* to introduce an uninterrupted direct quotation as can be seen in the following lines:

The frere than *sayd,*
Ye be dismayd,
With trouble I understande.[165]

Pithiness of form and smoothness of rhythm are achieved by the following three Tudor figures of rhetoric: (1) apocope – omitting the last letter or syllable of a word – as in *fayre may*[166] for *fayre mayd*; (2) prosthesis – adding a letter or syllable at the beginning of a word – as for example in *Adowne*[167] for *down*; and (3) aphaeresis – omitting a letter or syllable at the beginning of a word – as in *minishes*[168] for *diminishes.*

According to Tudor rhetoric, the introduction, which consists of sixty lines, can be classified in the category of *amplification.* Henry Peacham, a sixteenth-century rhetorician, defines this figure as 'a certain affirmation which by large and plentiful speech moves the minds of the hearers and causes them to believe that which is said'.[169] He further adds that by using this rhetorical device the orator 'may prevail much in drawing the mindes of his hearers to his owne will and affection: He may winde them from their former opinions, and quite after the former state of their mindes'.[170] This is exactly what More does in the amplification of his initial and underlying theme; to achieve this objective convincingly, he uses the methods of comparison and accumulation.[171] He states his premise that it is always best for every man to apply himself to one business only, and then proceeds to convince his audience of this tenet by citing nine examples of men whose covetous pursuit of another craft ended in failure. He substantiates his argument with the following comparisons in order to clarify and emphasize the thesis of his narrative: a plea that lay people should 'play not the frere'.[172]

Present craft	*Coveted one*
1. hosiers	making shoes
2. smythe	painting
3. draper	to go to writyng scole
4. olde butler	becum a cutler
5. an olde trot	administer phisick[173]

6.	man of lawe	wenyng to ryse by marchaundise
7.	merchant	pletyng the lawe
8.	hatter	smatter in philosophy
9.	pedlar	waxe a medlar in theology

After thoroughly expounding his introductory assertion and supporting it with the affirmation of 'Wyse men',[174] More narrates the experience of a sergeant who actually played the friar. Thus, the ninth craft of a 'pedlar waxing a medlar in theology'[175] leads into the narration of an analogous incident in which a sergeant uses a religious disguise to achieve his crafty purpose.

In the course of the poem there are abundant examples of litotes, which Puttenham defines as, 'Tempering our sence with wordes of such moderation, as in appearunce it abateth it but not in deede'.[176] The following three examples are conspicuous:

1. When the young man who wished to avoid the ubiquitous presence of the sergeant-of-law went to Saint Katherine's, he certainly did not go:

> For devocion,
> Or promocion . . .[177]

Apropos of the fact that it was a custom in sixteenth-century England to celebrate St. Katherine's day on November 25 with feasting and merry-making,[178] the following lines throw some light on his purpose in going there and the nature of his activities:

> There spent he fast,
> Till all was past,
> And to him came there meny,
> To aske theyr det,
> But none could get,
> The valour of a peny.[179]

On the other hand, however, he may have gone to Saint Katherine's to avoid 'promocion'[180] for, as A. W. Reed points out, 'promoters' were informers. Since the merchant was extremely anxious to escape from them, he may have made his abode in that place.

More employs litotes with such consistency in characterization, action, and dialogue that this trope adds humour and excitement to the narrative. For example, when the young spendthrift endeavours to avoid the courtesies of the sergeant-of-law, who was ready to wait upon him 'as sone as on the mayre',[181] he does so from motives of utility and foresight rather than from the intentions ascribed to his action in the following lines:

> But he doubtlesse,
> Of his mekenesse,
>   Hated such pompe and pride.[182]

In passing, one can note an example of subtle humour. The young man who was so slow and apathetic in applying himself to physical work but so capable and shrewd in sensing danger in any form, must have fully realized that the sergeant-of-law who wished to 'wait' upon him was actually lying 'in wait'[183] for him.

A third example of litotes is found in the dialogue of the disguised sergeant when he assures the vacillating maid that his business with the 'sick' man is comforting in nature and conducive to his spiritual welfare:

> Quod he maystresse,
> No harm doutlesse:
>   It longeth for our order,
> To hurt no man,
> But as we can,
>   Euery wight to forder.[184]

The phrase 'Euery wight to forder' in the last verse contains a subtle understatement in the word *forder*, which means to further one's cause or to give assistance. The feminine rhymes: *order, forder*, are a good clincher to the friar's hypocritical words; for, surely his true order, the sergeants-of-the-law, *forder* i.e., *further*, the administration of just punishment to culprits.

Yet, as he debonairly said these words, he must have adjusted the mace hidden beneath his flowing scapular in comforting reassurance that the arrest will soon take place. As soon as the two men are left alone,

> The frere with euyll grace
> Sayd, I rest the,
> Come on with me,
>   And out he toke his mace.[185]

In this poem litotes appears to be More's figurative and stylistic forte. He uses words adroitly to express meanings directly opposite those intended. He further employs understatements to increase the verbal effect, but derision and mockery are not apparent in these statements. The use of this trope gives the poem dramatic potentialities, provides an outlet for emotional vindication, and adds sparkling zest and humour to it.

Even though the ballad is written in simple language and is geared to the understanding and interests of Tudor craftsmen, More employs words which have symbolic connotations. The line of demarcation between the metaphor and symbol is a delicate one, and the distinction, for the most part, appears to be in the terminology used rather than the idea portrayed. Professor R. M. Eaton defines 'simple symbols as objects taken by a mind to stand for other objects'.[186] He further states that 'the significance of these undefined simple symbols rests on direct experience because they are an integral part of the presentation of the object to which they refer'.[187] René Wellek and Austin Warren give a more exact definition of a symbol, and they show its relationship to the metaphor in their excellent chapter on 'Image, Metaphor, Symbol, Myth'. They make the following succinct distinctions in this fourfold hierarchy of imagery: 'An "image" may be invoked once as a metaphor, but if it persistently recurs, both as presentation and representation, it becomes a symbol, may even become part of a symbol (or mythic) system'.[188]

Since 'symbolism is the representation of reality on one level of reference by a corresponding reality on another',[189] the very essence of 'A meri iest', namely, the act of 'playing the frere',[190] is to be understood on more levels than merely the literary one. Surely, Thomas More did not assume naively that the individuals who comprised his audience would engage in the diverting sport of literally imitating a friar in dress and action. His adamant injunction in the epilogue to 'playe not the frere'[191] takes on metaphoric significance which implies not to make sport of or to jest at another's expense, mock at, to befool, or delude.[192] In the light of this assertion he urges his audience to refrain from the following activities: (1) not to meddle in other crafts; (2) not to pretend to be what one is not; (3) not to undermine the religious prestige of the friars.

On first glance the words, *hedge* and *gown* do not appear as symbols, but when they are seen in the context of the poem, their symbolic significance becomes more readily apparent:

> With visage stout,
> He bare it out,
>   Euen unto the hard *hedge*,
> A month or twaine,
> Till he was faine,
>   To lay his *gown* to pledge.[193]

Hedge is the obsolete form for *edge* and More's use of this word in the second and third verse above is quoted in the *Old English Dictionary*.[194] It is used as a substantive and is formed on the verb phrase *hedge in*, which meant the securing of a debt 'by including it in a larger one for which better security is obtained'.[195] The laying of 'his gown to pledge'[196] further substantiates this meaning of the word, for it implies the making of a bet or investing in some other speculation in order to compensate for one's loss.

The word *gown* similarly means more than its mere literal signification denotes. 'To laye his gowne to pledge' symbolizes one's integrity, one's security, one's hope of retrieval. Deuteronomy, XXIV, 10–13, implies the taking away of such a pledge, but the word *raiment* is used here instead of *gown*. The last of the three verses reads:

> But thou shalt restore it to him presently before the going down of the sun that he may sleep in his own raiment and bless thee . . .[197]

In Morris Palmer Tilley's *A Dictionary of the Proverbs in England in the Sixteenth and Seventeenth Centuries*[198] the symbolic use of this word is found: 'The *gown* is his that wears it and the world his that enjoys it'.

The symbol *golde* signifies the greed and avarice of the young man who hoarded his money best by 'supping it up / In his owne brest'.[199] This money led him to the 'lusty sporte',[200] the 'joly company',[201] and the 'mirth and play',[202] he engaged in so extravagantly. Thus, the gold became a scepter in his hand which he swayed at will and before whose majesty friend and foe bowed obsequiously.

More's use of this symbol can be equated with three sixteenth-century proverbs:
1. Gold goes in at any gate except heaven's.
2. Gold is the fruit that is always ripe.
3. All is not gold that glisters.

Another expression which throws some light on the interpretation of the poem is found in the word *tyde*.[203] It denotes an opportune time, a season, or while; however, it connotes an anniversary or festival of the Church: chiefly in the names of holy seasons or saints' days, St. Andrew's tide, All-Hallow-tide, Easter-Tide, Shrovetide. In the sixteenth century it signified a village feast or fair taking place on the festival of the patron saint of the parish. To ascribe this meaning to the word tyde in the context of the poem seems logical in view of the fact that the young man

> . . . drewe himself a side,
> To saint Katherine,
> Streight as a line,
>   He gate him at a *tyde*,
> For devocion,
> Or promocion,
>   There would he nedes abyde.[204]

The symbolism inherent in the word *howre* dates back to the beginning of the *Old Testament*, for the ancient Hebrews did not divide the day into hours; the day was divided into four parts, the night into three. But afterwards when the Jews came under the Roman rule they followed the Romans in dividing the night into four parts which they called watches because they relieved their sentinels every three hours.[205] In John 12.27, when Jesus suffers excruciating agony in the Garden of Olives, He says: 'My soul is troubled, Father, save me from this *hour*'. Prior to that, when He is arrested in the Garden of Gethsemane, He says to the multitude which came to apprehend Him: 'When I was daily

66

with you in the temple, you did not stretch forth your hands against me. But this is your *hour* and the power of darkness' (Luke 22.53).

Connotations for *hour* were derived from the French, *a la bonne heure* – at a fortunate time, or conversely, 'in an evil hour'.[206] In 'A meri iest', the significance of *howre* is bound up with the idea of fortune, as the following lines exemplify:

> And men had sworne,
> Some man is borne,
>   To have a lucky howre . . .[207]

Ananda K. Coomaraswamy says pertinently in an enlightening article on symbolism: 'Whoever wishes to understand the real meaning of these figures of thought that are not merely figures of speech must have studied the very extensive literature of many countries in which the meanings of symbols are explained, and must have learned himself to think in these terms'.[208] 'In this universal language', he adds, 'the highest truths have been expressed . . . without this kind of knowledge, the historian and critic of literature and literary styles, can only by guesswork distinguish between what, in a given author's work, is individual, and what is inherited and universal'.[209] It seems apparent that a symbol has more gradations of meaning than a metaphor. It has philosophical implications and reflects the thoughts, customs, and convictions of people. It is closely integrated into the fabric of everyday usage and takes on a prosaic appearance. A metaphor, on the other hand, is novel in its representation, arresting in the attention it evokes, and confined to fewer levels of meaning.

The literary values of 'A meri iest' can be epitomized as follows:

1.   It is built on a concrete contemporary incident and is geared to the interests of a heterogenous audience who represent various crafts in sixteenth century England.

2.   In the realm of 'psychological' values, the auditory and kinesthetic images play the strongest role. Their effectiveness depends chiefly on the oral delivery and dramatic ability of the narrator and on the short but emphatic scenes which lead swiftly and forcefully to the climax. The emotional element in the poem is a little weak, but since by its very nature it was meant to be droll and facetious, this is no serious impediment to its literally merit. Its function was primarily to entertain and secondary to teach, and it achieves both objectives in a psychologically satisfying manner.

3.   The poem's greatest literary merit lies in its 'technical' values, especially in the areas of rhythm and diction. Thomas More wrote this ballad at a time when the vernacular was not the ordinary vehicle of literary expression and when Poulter's measure and Skeltonic meter were looked upon as great literary accomplishments. According to Fitzroy Pyle,

> . . . the poetry of St. Thomas More deserves to be held in esteem, if it were only for the interest of its rhythms . . . On the whole, then More has a far greater measure of metrical consistency than the majority of

his contemporaries of the early sixteenth century. And in one respect – in the management of his rhythms in which he repeatedly displays unquestionable artistic feeling – he stands head and shoulders above them all but Skelton.[210]

The imagery in this poem, on the other hand, is not emotive or profound. The ballad contains merely a handful of tropes, and those More uses are so closely intertwined with the common usage of his day that they exhibit no great originality of thought or expression. The symbols used are not unique or provocative, and they add little colour and significance to the sound and meaning structure of the poem. Nevertheless, considering the nature of the occasion, the function of the ballad, and the intellectual level of the audience before him, his directness and the simplicity of his diction may have been a deliberate attempt to establish empathy between himself and his Tudor listeners.

In the area of 'technical' values, Thomas More exhibits skill in creating vigorous and fast-moving scenes which precipitate a forceful and dramatic climax and are followed by a pertinent and brief dénouement. Vividness of characterization and scintillating dialogue give the poem a pronounced narrative appeal and make it effective for public entertainment. In regard to the point of view, More employs the omniscient method successfully, for the most part. A few slight inconsistencies occur, however, when he steps out of his role occasionally to speak to the audience in his own voice rather than in the voice of the impersonator. This personal communication of ideas paradoxically seems to be an integral part of the poem and does not offend or irritate the reader or listener since the author's statements are devoid of ostentation and moralization.

The 'ideational' values are based on the philosophical and ethical standards of the day, which were usually embodied in a moral appended to the literary work or implied in the course of the poem. The moral aspect was an integral part of the literary pattern of sixteenth-century verse and hence, Thomas More, like his contemporaries, makes it obviously auxiliary to his main purpose, that of entertaining his audience with 'a meri iest'. Nevertheless, the author is not clear in his portrayal and enunciation of the ethical values in the ballad. After reading the poem several times, one still wonders if retribution was administered justly, for the merchant who amassed a score of debts without the slightest endeavour to pay the money back was as culpable as the sergeant who set the trap for his arrest. The officer of the law is severely punished for his crafty deed, while the rich young man outwits him and his debtors successfully through cunning and physical strength.

In spite of the apparent lack of justice, one experiences at the end a release of tension because the humour, aided by rhythm, diction, imagery, and symbol, is psychologically satisfying. With the aid of onomatopoetic devices and particularly of the kinesthetic images inherent in them, the entire poem takes on clearness of view and relevancy of theme. 'A meri iest how a sergeant would learne to playe the frere' is more than a simple facetious narration of a humorous incident; it is a serious and pointed satire aimed at purifying and strengthening the sixteenth-century guilds and in building up the self-esteem of the middle-class merchant. From a technical point of view, the poem presents a well-balanced narrative coloured by virile imagery, strengthened by well-chosen diction, and perfected by concrete symbolism.

1. *Works*, I, 15.
2. William Herbert, *Antiquities of the Inns of Court and Chancery* (London, 1804), pp. 369–370.
3. *Ibid.*, p. 358.
4. William Herbert, *History of the Twelve Great Livery Companies of London* (London, 1836), II, 533–535.
5. *Ibid.*, 535
6. Reverend Alfred B. Beaven, *The Alderman of the City of London* (London, 1908), I, 155, 274.
7. Ames, *Citizen Thomas More and His Utopia* (Princeton, New Jersey, 1949), p. 185, citing John Watney's *Thomas of Acon.*
8. Elsie Vaughan Hitchcock, ed., *The Lyfe of Sir Thomas Moore, Knights, written by William Roper* (London, 1935), p. 9.
9. *Works*, I, 'A Mery Iest,' C.ii^v G. 3–14.
10. 'A meri iest,' C.i^r A. 5–8, B. 1–2.
11. Lewis, p. 133.
12. *An old trot*, old woman, usually disparaging.
13. 'A meri iest,' C. i^r E. 1–8. F. 1–4.
14. Ames, p. 43.
15. *Ibid.*, p. 77.
16. *Ibid.*
17. 'A meri iest,' C. i^r F. 6–8.
18. John Lesley, *The History of Scotland* (Edinburgh, 1830), p. 76.
19. 'A meri iest,' C. i^r F. 9–14.
20. *Ibid.*, C. i^r F. 15. 0. 1–2.
21. *The Art of the Short Story* (Chicago, 1913), pp. 21–37.
22. 'A meri iest,' C. i^r B. 9–14.
23. *Ibid.*, C. i^r B. 15–16. C. 1–4.
24. *Ibid.*, C. i^r C. 6–11.
25. *Ibid.*, C. 12–14. D. 1–3.
26. *Ibid.*, D. 8–9.
27. *Ibid.*, D. 10–15.
28. *Ibid.*, C. i^r E. 4–11. F. 1–4.
29. Robert J. Blackham, *The Soul of the City London's Livery Companies* (London, [n.d]), p. 91.
30. *Ibid.*
31. 'A meri iest,' C. i^r B. 4–5.
32. *Ibid.*, B. 6–8.
33. 'A meri icst,' C. i^r G. 2–9.
34. *OED*. IX, 361.
35. 'A meri iest,' C. i^r G. 10–13.
36. *Ibid.*, C. i^r G. 13–14. H. 1–4.
37. *Ibid.*, C. i^v B. 3–4.
38. *Ibid.*, C. i^v H. 10.
39. *Ibid.*, C. i^v A. 9–14.
40. *Ibid.*, C. i^v B. 4–9.
41. *Ibid.*, C. i^v C. 7.
42. *Ibid.*, C. i^v D. 13–16.
43. *Ibid.*, C. i^v B. 13–15. C. 1–6.
44. *Ibid.*, C. i^v E. 2–3.
45. *Ibid.*, C. i^v E. 6–8.
46. John M. Berdan, *Early Tudor Poetry* (New York, 1920), p. 225.

47. *Ibid.*, p. 223.
48. 'A meri iest,' C. i^r E. 8.
49. *Ibid.*, C. i^v E. 12–14.
50. *Ibid.*, C. i^v E. 15–17. F. 1–3.
51. *Ibid.*, C. i^v F. 10–15.
52. *Ibid.*, C. i^r B. 4.
53. *Ibid.*, C. i^v G. 7–12.
54. *Ibid.*, C. i^v H. 2–9.
55. *Dopped and dooked*, ducked and curtsied.
56. 'A meri iest,' C. ii^r. A. 3–8.
57. *Ibid.*, C. ii^r 1–6.
58. *Ibid.*, C. ii^r B. 7–9.
59. *Ibid.*, C. ii^r B. 9–11.
60. Elsie Vaughan Hitchcock, ed., *Harpsfield's Life of More* (London, 1932), p. 17.
61. 'A meriiest,' C. ii^r G. 13–16. H. 1–2.
62. *Lyst*, the lobe of the ear.
63. 'A meri iest,' C. ii^v H. 12. C. 11. A. 1–8.
64. *Ibid.*, C. ii^v F. 1–6.
65. *The*, thrive.
66. 'A meri iest,' C. ii^v F. 12–17.
67. *Ibid.*, C. ii^v G. 1–12.
68. *Ibid.*, C. i^r A. 5.
69. *Ibid.*, C. i^r G. 2–4.
70. *Ibid.*, C. i^v D. 10.
71. *Ibid.*, C. i^v E. 2–3.
72. *Ibid.*, C. i^v F. 12–15.
73. *Ibid.*, C. ii^v B. 7–8. C. 9.
74. *Ibid.*, C. ii^r D. 8–10.
75. *Ibid.*, C. ii^r D. 14. E. 1–5.
76. *Ibid.*, C. i^v H. 3–5. *ure*, used.
77. *Ibid.*, C. ii^r E. 5–8.
78. *Ibid.*, C. ii^r F. 7–15. G. 1–16.
79. *Ibid.*, C. ii^r G. 9–12.
80. Cleanth Brooks, *Understanding Fiction* (New York, 1943), p. 584.
81. 'A meri iest,' C. i^r G. 11–13.
82. *Ibid.*, C. i^r G. 5–6.
83. *Ibid.*, C. i^r H. 5–10.
84. *Ibid.*, C. i^r H. 14. C. i^v A. 1–8.
85. *Ibid.*, C. i^r B. 3. 4.
86. *Ibid.*, C. i^v B. 6.
87. *Ibid.*, C. i^v C. 7.
88. *Ibid.*, C. ii^r H. 8–12. C. ii^v A. 1–7.
89. *Ibid.*, C. ii^v A. 12–13.
90. *Ibid.*, C. ii^v B. 12–15.
91. *Ibid.*, C. i^v G. 1–12.
92. *Ibid.*, C. i^v H. 1–2. 6–8.
93. *Ibid.*, C. ii^r A. 4–8.
94. *Ibid.*, C. ii^v F. 2–5.
95. *Ibid.*, C. ii^r F. 5–15. G. 1.
96. *Ibid.*, C. ii^r B. 13.
97. *Ibid.*, C. ii^r B. 15. C. 1.
98. *Ibid.*, C. ii^r C. 2–7.
99. *Ibid.*, C. ii^r D. 9–10.
100. *Ibid.*, C. ii^v C. 7–12.
101. *Ibid.*, C. ii^v C. 13–14. E. 1–4.
102. *Ibid.*, C. ii^v E. 5–10.
103. Ward and Waller, II, 402.
104. 'A meri iest,' C. ii^r F. 14–15. G. 1.
105. Walter Morris Hart, 'Ballad and Epic: A Study in the Development of the Narrative Art,' *Studies and Notes in Philology and Literature XI* (Boston, 1907), p. 102.

106. Louise Pound, *Poetic Origins of the Ballad* (New York, 1921), p. 166.
107. *Ibid.*, p. 174.
108. *Ibid.*
109. William Carew Hazlitt, *A Hundred Merry Tales* (London, 1887), Preface, pp. iii, vi–vii, ix.
110. W. J. Courthope, *A History of English Poetry* (New York, 1895), I, 434.
111. 'A meri iest,' C. i^r A. 5–8. B. 1–8.
112. *Works*, I, 231.
113. 'A meri iest,' C. i^r F. 6–15. G. 1–2.
114. William Carew Hazlitt, *Early Popular Poetry of England* (London, 1866), pp. 272–273 (Arnold's *Chronicle*, Sig. N. 6).
115. 'A meri iest,' C. ii^r G. 6–15. H. 16–17.
116. Delcourt, p. 10.
117. *Ibid.*, pp. 10–11.
118. *Ibid.*, p. 12.
119. 'A meri iest,' C. ii^r F. 10–16. G. 1–5.
120. *Ibid.*, C. ii^r E. 2–8.
121. *Ibid.*, C. ii^r A. 15. B. 1–5.
122. *Ibid.*, C. ii^r B. 6–16. C. 1.
123. *Ibid.*, C. ii^v C. 1–12.
124. *Ibid.*, C. i^r E. 4–11. F. 1–4.
125. *Ibid.*, C. ii^v E. 11–17. F. 1–5.
126. *Ibid.*, C. i^r E. 4–11. F. 1–4.
127. *Ibid.*, C. i^v G. 1–12.
128. Donald A. Stauffer, Poetic Diction,' in *A Dictionary of World Literature*, ed. Joseph T. Shipley (New York, 1953), p. 99.
129. 'A meri iest,' C. ii^v C. 10–14. E. 1–4.
130. Albert C. Baugh, *History of the English Language* (New York, 1935), p. 282.
131. A. W. Reed's method of indication is here used. See 'Philological Notes,' *Works*, I, 194–195.
132. Warren Taylor, *Tudor Figures of Rhetoric* (Chicago, 1937), p. 41.
133. 'A meri iest,' C. ii^v A. 2. F. 3.
134. *Ibid.*, C. ii^v A. 3–8.
135. *Ibid.*, C. ii^v A. 12–14.
136. *Ibid.*, C. ii^v A. 15–17. B. 1–9.
137. Charles William Kent, *Study of Poetry* (Charlottesville, 1895), p. 72.
138. 'A meri iest,' C. ii^v B. 10–15.
139. *Ibid.*, C. ii^r H. 11.
140. *Ibid.*, C. ii^r H. 12. C. ii^v A. 1–2.
141. *Ibid.*, C. ii^r H. 12.
142. *Ibid.*, C. ii^v E. 13.
143. *OED*, X, 261.
144. *Ibid.*
145. 'A meri iest,' C. ii^r A. 6.
146. *Ibid.*, C. ii^r A. 11.
147. *Ibid.*, C. ii^r A. 12–14.
148. *Ibid.*, C. i^r F. 11–13.
149. *Ibid.*, C. i^r G. 11–13.
150. *Ibid.*, C. i^r F. 12.
151. *Ibid.*, C. i^r G. 11.
152. *Ibid.*, C. i^v B. 1–9.
153. *Ibid.*, C. i^r D. 7–15.
154. Taylor, pp. 32–33.
155. 'A meri iest,' C. ii^v E. 11. F. 1–5.
156. Taylor, p. 45.
157. 'A meri iest,' C. i^r C. 5–7. *Kysse the cup*, to take a sip of liquor.
158. *Ibid.*, C. i^v H. 5–7. *Let me be bake*, to harden by heat.
159. *Ibid.*, C. ii^r A. 12–14. *Harte for pryde, Lepte in his syde*, to be ecstatic with joy.
160. *Ibid.*, C. ii^r D. 4–6. *Matters breake*, to discuss matters.
161. *Ibid.*, C. i^v E. 2–4. *Streight as a line*, to go at once; straightforward.
162. *Ibid.*, C. i^v C. 13–14. D. 1. *To haue a lucky howre*, to have good luck.

163. *Ibid.*, C. ii^r F. 3–11.
164. *OED*, VIII, 79.
165. *Ibid.*, 'A meri iest,' C. ii^r F. 1–3.
166. *Ibid.*, C. ii^r C. 14.
167. *Ibid.*, C. ii^r E. 5. C. ii^v C. 12.
168. *Ibid.*, C. ii^r A. 2.
169. Taylor, p. 3.
170. *Ibid.*
171. *Ibid.*
172. 'A meri iest,' C. ii^v G. 11.
173. *phisick*, a cathartic or purge. *OED*, VII, 806.
174. *Ibid.*, C. i^r A. 5.
175. *Ibid.*, C. i^r E. 4–6.
176. George Puttenham, *The Arte of English Poesie*, ed. Edward Arber (London, 1869), p. 195.
177. 'A meri iest,' C. i^v E. 6–7.
178. *OED*, II, 185.
179. 'A meri iest,' C. i^v E. 9–14.
180. *Ibid.*, C. i^v E. 7.
181. *Ibid.*, C. i^v D. 10.
182. *Ibid.*, C. i^v D. 11–13.
183. *Works*, I, 195.
184. 'A meri iest,' C. ii³ C. 2–7.
185. *Ibid.*, C. ii^r G. 13–15, H. 16.
186. Ralph Monroe Eaton, *Symbolism and Truth* (Cambridge, Mass., 1925), p. 39.
187. *Ibid.*
188. René Wellek and Austin Warren, *Theory of Literature* (New York, 1949), p. 194.
189. Coomaraswamy, 'Symbolism' in Shipley ,p. 405.
190. 'A meri iest,' C. i^r F. 13.
191. *Ibid.*, C. ii^v G. 11.
192. *OED*, VII, 976.
193. 'A meri iest,' C. i^v E. 15–17. F. 1–3.
194. *OED*, V, 188.
195. *Ibid.*
196. 'A meri iest,' C. 1^v E. 17.
197. *The Holy Bible*, Douay Version (Baltimore, 1930), p. 211.
198. (Ann Arbor, Michigan, 1950), p. 272.
199. 'A meri iest,' C. i^v B. 3.
200. *Ibid.*, C. i^v C. 7.
201. *Ibid.*, C. i^v C. 9.
202. *Ibid.*, C. i^v C. 10.
203. *Ibid.*, C. i^v E. 5.
204. *Ibid.*, C. i^v E. 2–8.
205. Alexander Cruden, ed., *A Complete Concordance to the Holy Scriptures of the Old and New Testaments* (Chicago, 1916), p. 293.
206. *OED*, V, 417.
207. 'A meri iest,' C. i^v C. 13–14. D. 1.
208. 'Symbolism,' in Shipley, p. 408.
210. Fitzroy Pyle, p. 76.

CHAPTER III

'NYNE PAGEAUNTES':

REFLECTIONS ON MAN'S LIFE

The introduction to Thomas More's verses on the 'Nyne Pageauntes' is prefaced by the following inscription, which reveals a few pertinent facts regarding the execution of the poem, but throws little light on the circumstances and occasion of its composition:

> Mayster Thomas More in his youth deuysed in hys fathers house in London, a goodly hangyng of fyne paynted clothe, with nyne pageauntes, and verses over of euery of those pageauntes: which verses expressed and declared, what the ymages in those pageauntes represented: and also in those pageauntes were paynted, the thynges that the verses over them dyd (in effecte) declare, which verses here folowe.[1]

The eight rhyme royal stanzas that follow signify the stages in man's life according to Thomas More's interpretation, namely: Childhood, Manhood, Venus and Cupid, Age, Death, Fame, Time, and Eternity. The ninth and the last stanza entitled 'The Poet' consists of twelve verses which cogently synthesize More's views on life. Unlike the other verses which are wirtten in English, this climactic verse is written in Latin.

Already as a youth Thomas More must have thought deeply about the significance of life, the futility of fame and riches, and the salutary remembrance of death. The two happy and profitable years spent in the household of John Cardinal Morton, the Archbishop of Canterbury, sharpened the twelve-year-old boy's intellect and gave him a zest for 'the "New Learning" [which] originally meant the study of the classics, especially of the newly introduced Greek'.[2] The wise and witty prelate, who, 'to prove a man's spirit and wit would engage him in a battle of words and was pleased if he found him a worthy opponent',[3] recognized quickly the boy's inherent capacity for learning and 'for his better furtherance'[4] therein, placed him at Oxford. The aged Chancellor had himself been 'one of the most eminent sons of the University'[5] and had chosen it for his young protégé, being fully cognizant of his interest and enthusiasm for the study of Greek manuscripts, which allured the new humanists and opened for them tantalizing vistas of learning. When the fourteen-year-old and bright-eyed lad entered Oxford, news of Columbus' discovery of a new continent and of Cabot's ambition to cross the ocean and go beyond the lands found by Columbus in order to reach the nearest point of Asia, filled the hearts and minds of the students with new adventure in life, new zest for learning, and an insatiable desire to probe hitherto unknown literary manuscripts. Pertinently

John Edwin Sandys tells us in his *Harvard Lecture on the Revival of Learning* that this revival 'was not only concerned with the "discovery of man"; it was also concerned with the discovery of manuscripts'.[6]

The theme for More's pageants and the verses inscribed under them depicting the various stages in man's life may have been inspired by a Byzantine manuscript of the fourteenth or fifteenth century. This valuable work presumably was written by Dionysius, monk of Fourna d'Agrapha, and contains instructions for the art of painting and directions for the representation of symbolic and moral subjects. The theme that appears to have direct influence on Thomas More's paintings and on the nature of the verses inscribed beneath them is a morality entitled 'The foolish life of the deceitful world', arranged in three concentric circles of which the seven ages of man formed a part.[7]

In his life of Thomas More, Chambers makes the observation that nearly a generation before More's time, a monk of Canterbury, William Selling, who was sent to finish his studies at Canterbury College, had been given leave to make the Italian tour and had brought Greek manuscripts back to England.[8] Sandys further adds a few illuminating facts which give more meaning and emphasis to Chamber's observation. Speaking of the 'Revival of Learning', he says:

> ... the first Englishman, who studied Greek, was a Benedictine monk, William Tilley, of Selling, near Canterbury (d. 1494). 'Night and day' (we are told) 'he was haunted by the vision of Italy, that land, which, next to Greece, was the nursing mother of men of genius'.[9] He paid two visits to Italy, in 1464 and in 1485 ... On his return he became prior of Christ Church, Canterbury, and paid special attention to Greek ... In the school of Christ Church he inspired his nephew, Thomas Linacre, with a love of classical learning.[10]

Dionysius' manuscript may have been among those which attracted the interest of the young humanist, Thomas More, whose eagerness to learn Greek was also heightened by William Grocyn's return to Oxford from Italy.

Another reputable biographer of More, Father Bridgett, assumes that he resided at Canterbury Hall, which, being intended principally for the study of the canon and civil law,[11] was also the residence of the Benedictine monk, William Selling, as well as a 'home of Greek studies'.[12] This manuscript may have come into More's hands and may have served as an incentive and pattern for his reflections on the stages of man's life. In these allegorical verses on 'a goodly hangyng of fyne paynted cloth'[13] Thomas More combined the Renaissance type images of Cupid, Fame, and Death with the medieval Christian treatment and interpretation. Since this interesting and curious Byzantine manuscript appears to have influenced the youthful More directly, it is given in full according to John Winter Jones' 'Observations on the Origin of the Division of Man's Life into Stages':

> On the outside of the third and largest circle, make the seven ages of man in the following manner. At the bottom, on the right hand side,

make a little child ascending; write before it, on the circle, 'child of seven years'. Above this child make one larger, and write 'child of fourteen years'. Higher still, make a young man with moustachios, and write 'youth of twenty-one years'. Above on the top of the wheel, make another man, with a growing beard, seated on a throne, his feet upon a cushion, his hands extended on each side, holding in the right a sceptre, and in the left a bag full of money; he wears royal garments, and a crown upon his head. Under him, on the wheel, write 'young man of twenty-eight years'. Under him on the left side, make another man, with a pointed beard, stretched out, with his head downwards, and looking up: write 'Man of forty-eight years'. Under him make another man with grey hair, stretched on his back and write 'Mature man of fifty-six years'. Under him make a man with a white beard, bald, stretched out, his head downwards, his hands hanging down, and write 'Old man of seventy-five years'. Then under him make a tomb, in which is a large dragon, having a man in his throat, head downwards, and of whom only the half can be seen. Near this in the tomb is Death, with a scythe, which he strikes into the neck of the old man, whom he endeavours to pull down. Without the circle write the following inscriptions near the mouths of the persons: –

Near the little child, 'When, having mounted, shall I arrive at the top?' Near the child, 'O! Time, turn quickly, in order that I may soon arrive at the top'. Near the youth, 'Behold, I have got so far that I shall soon seat myself upon the throne'. Over the young man, 'Who is king as I am? Who is above me?' Near the mature man write 'Wretch that I am, O Time, how thou hast deceived me!' Near the old man, 'Alas! alas! O Death, who can avoid thee?' Near the tomb, these words: 'Hell, all-devouring, and death!' Near him who is swallowed up by the dragon, 'Alas! who will save me from all-devouring Hell!' – Didron, *Iconographic Chretienne*, p. 409.[14]

Not only did the significant ideas in this manuscript possibly fascinate More, but the symbolic figures of the wheel signifying a cycle in man's life must have also conjured in his mind the 'wheel of fortune' concept which was later to have an almost hypnotic influence on his writings. Man's eternal destiny, the reason for his existence, and his insatiable quest for happiness were apparently the young scholar's subject for meditation and study. Thought conditioned him for meditation, meditation led to contemplation and contemplation found expression in allegory. Henry Osborn Taylor says pertinently: 'The devices of the mind have a history as old as humanity . . . The mind seeking to express the transcendentals, avails itself of symbols'.[15] The morality plays with their allegorical interpretations affected, not only the lives of the people, but also the literature of succeeding ages. Homer's *Iliad* and *Odyssey* with their scandalous myths of the gods very likely shocked 'the Greek ethical intellect, which thereupon proceeded to convert them into allegories'.[16] However, already in the first drama of creation in the Garden of Eden, the serpent representing evil, the tree of life, the gate of Paradise, and the forbidden fruit are typical examples of the spontaneous connotations man instinctively gives to his thoughts and emotions. Allegory, then, is rooted in the soil of thought and is nurtured on the seeds of contemplation. The medieval age, which produced so many great thinkers and profound schoolmen, was truly an age of allegory. 'By the time of Augustus', says Henry Osborn Taylor, 'the habit of finding an allegory everywhere had become so universal that learned men deemed that no great writer would write save in allegories'.[17] It is no wonder, then, that the sixteen-year-old amateur in the fine arts drew upon his aesthetic powers of mind and imagination to produce a work of art which would give expression to his strong inner convictions on life and show others how to combine the natural with the supernatural.

Even as a youth Thomas More exhibited a sound and firm independence of mind and a penetrating insight which enabled him to recognize things at their true value. He never imitated slavishly, but expressed his own convictions with candour and originality. He was a man of integrity in his writing as well as in his conduct; consequently, he deviated from the current interpretations of fame, fortune, time, and death and went further than most of his fellow humanists by bringing into play the soul of man and his eternal destiny.

The custom of writing verses for paintings on tapestries was not an unusual one, for in 1516 one finds that Nicholas Ellenbog, a Benedictine monk and a contemporary of More's, 'writes to a friend asking for verses to put under paintings of the Doctors of the Church, which are to adorn the walls [of a new library]'.[18] In tapestry-designing, painting, and verse-making, a humanist could truly exercise his triple skill as designer, artist, and poet. Allegory was an excellent medium for him to display the mental acumen necessary for drawing forth morals and subtle meanings from the fables. A humanist delighted in this type of work, for its beauty fascinated him, its obscurity challenged him, and its possibility of drawing good therefrom inspired him. Although steeped in the spirit of the Middle Ages, Thomas More eagerly imbibed delectable drafts of 'the new learning' and made his own synthesis of the best that was in the Medieval and Renaissance culture. One can picture him at Oxford perusing the Greek manuscripts with curiosity and delight and reading with deliberate pace and careful scrutiny Boccaccio's *Genealogy of the Gods*, 'the chief link between the mythology of the Renaissance and that of the Middle Ages'.[19]

In what way does this young humanist show originality of thought and individuality of treatment? The verses, on the whole, are not profound in symbolism nor strikingly original in imagery. The smooth rhythm in the eight rhyme royal verses and the ninth twelve-lined stanza, however, proves More to be a meticulous literary technician during an age when prosody was still in its experimental stage. The originality of theme and structure is seen perspicuously in the following areas:

1. More depicts eight stages of man's existence and epitomizes them with a

ninth stanza on his evaluation of life. The ancient stanza writers or those contemporary with him depict seven or ten stages and omit, for the most part, the final synthesis.

2.   More's concern is not only with man's temporal existence, but also with his life hereafter, for he does not stop with death but carries his allegorical personification into the realm of eternity.

3.   In addition to the obvious stages in man's life such as childhood, youth, manhood, old age, and death, he personifies the forceful drives and ambitions of man, namely, love, the desire for fame, and his innermost spiritual yearning for immortality of soul and body.

4.   Thomas More's creativeness of mind and dexterity in organization is apparent in his skillful coalescence of all nine stanzas, seen especially in the technique whereby one estate triumphantly conquers the other.

5.   A salient feature of the young scholar's verses on the stages of life is the fact that one verse leads coherently to the other and flows from it with pleasing unity and coherence. Thus, it presents a well-rounded picture of man's life, considering both the now and the hereafter, and recognizes his innate desire for love, fame, and self-preservation.

The verses are not eloquent, but the ideas are powerful and rich in their connotations. Simplicity of diction invigorates the poetic style, perspicuity of thought adorns it, and well-knit organization integrates it into a pleasing pattern of the tapestry of life. Thomas More uses allegory in these nine verses in a human and personal manner and gives it such an air of verisimilitude that the stock figures seem to come from real life and enunciate their message almost audibily to us. The pictures the aspiring humanist paints on 'a goodly hangyng of fyne paynted clothe'[20] are not neatly-penned poetic formulas and isolated units of expression; each is admirably united to the preceding verse in thought and structure as well as to the succeeding one in cumulative design and arrangement. For example, the youth who rides 'a good and lusty stede',[21] scorns the child who plays with 'a cockstele and a ball'[22] and considers himself far superior to him physically and mentally. The lover, on the other hand, pierced by Cupid's 'fyry dart',[23] is destined to become a child again as a thrall in the services of Venus's son, Cupid. Old age, 'with lokkes thynne and hore',[24] is so engrossed with weightier matters that he merely dismisses the childish game of the boy and the idle business of the youth. Death, in turn, commands the 'sage father greatly magnifyed'[25] to descend from his chair of authoritative experience and wisdom and to forego his pride since no one in this world can escape his power. Fame, whose chief living is in the 'voyce of people',[26] and who causes them to live in spite of death in perpetual memory, vigorously defies death's universal power. But, neither is Fame victorious in her tenacious clutch on man's reputation, for Time 'with horyloge in hande'[27] pities her for such naive self-confidence and superciliousness and assures her that it is he who will destroy the world and be the king thereof. Lady Eternity, crowned with an imperial crown, has no need to boast as she reminds Time that her empire 'infinite shall be',[28] whereas his reign will come to nought. With deep insight into the meaning of life, the poet in the ninth stanza synthesizes the alternative praise and scorn in each personified image, and offers his solution to the enigma of man's life. He epitomizes it with the assertion that 'joys, praise and honour, all retire on a speedy foot'[29] and only the love of God remains.

It is indeed a lamentable fact that the University Registers for the year 1463–1505 are deficient,[30] for we do not have any tangible evidence of Thomas More's matriculation there. In his *Athenae Oxonienses* Anthony Wood scrupulously records the names of the famous writers and bishops who had their education at Oxford University,[31] and More's name is not mentioned. He did not stay to take his degree because, as Hutton tells us, 'At Oxford a degree in Law could not be obtained without seven years study after the completion of the Arts',[32] and the shrewd father may have considered this 'a waste of time'.[33]

Although the young scholar was called home by his adamant father in 1494 after less than two years at Oxford and placed at New Inn 'for a study of the laws of the realm',[34] his love and attraction for the fine arts was not diminished by this fact. Mallet tells us in his *History of the University of Oxford* that More's 'friends gathered round him in London', that 'he wrote omnivorously', and 'found time not for law only but for verses, history, epigrams, theology'.[35] It may be that he painted these pageants accompanied by verses on the stages of man's life to prove to his father that classical study as indulged in by the humanists was by no means incompatible with righteous living and even striving after perfection. One could be a humanist and Christian at the same time without jeopardizing one's eternal salvation; one could read and translate Greek manuscripts without defiling one's mind, heart, or character.

The nine 'verses over of euery of those pageauntes: which verses expressed and declared, what the ymages in those pageauntes represented . . .'[36] have no specific title; therefore the writer, following the precedent established by More's biographers, alludes to them as the 'Nyne pageauntes'. A clear understanding of what was meant by *pageaunt* in the sixteenth century will help to elucidate the general framework of the poem, its architectonic arrangement, and the rhetorical pattern it follows. This word had many meanings among which 'dumb show', 'stage', 'tableau', and 'spectacle' point to its versatility of use. The *Oxford English Dictionary* lists Thomas More's 'Nyne pageauntes' under the following specific definition: A scene represented on tapestry.[37] M. Lyle Spencer[38] and E. K. Chambers[39] give scholarly and comprehensive accounts of the origin and nature of the pageants in their discussion of mystery and morality plays.

The word *pageant* was used synonymously in the sixteenth century with the word *triumph*, and Chambers points out that it is 'doubtless a translation of the Italian *trionfo*, a name given to the *edifizio* by the early Renascence, in deliberate reminiscence of classical terminology'.[40] Andrea Mantegna's 'Triumph of Caesar' was depicted on a series of tapestries which adorned the walls of a palace in Mantua in the early fifteenth century. The medieval *chambre de tapisserie* was indeed no figure of speech, for ostentatious pageantry and triumphal processions gave expression to the spirit of the age. As a matter of fact, these 'hangings' were not only ornamental but also functional and utilitarian, for in churches particularly they served both as embellishment for special festive occasions and as a protection from draughts in inclement weather.

The fact that the idea of 'triumph' is inherent in the sixteenth century connotation of the word *pageant* is well borne out by Thomas More. The nine-stanza poem is a series of triumphs beginning with Childhood's triumph over his toys and ending with the Poet's triumph over the futility of fame and the vanity and deceitfulness of this world.

Thomas More probably uses the word *pageant* in the primary sense of a scene represented on a 'goodly hangyng of fyne paynted clothe',[41] while in its cumulative sense his *pageants* represent allegorical personifications in hierarchical order in the stages of man's life. A third meaning can be applied to it, namely, that of a part played by one in a performance or in real life, as for example, 'to play one's pageant'.[42] Similarly, in More's 'Pageauntes' we find the personifications achieving life-like characteristics as they play their parts on the stage of man's intellect, illumined by supernatural faith, strengthened by hope, and perfected by charity. The very fact that he used this medium for the expression of his ideas indicates that he was a link between the medievalists and the humanists of his day. Figuratively speaking, his ideals and convictions were rooted deeply in the soil of the Middle Ages, while the blossoming of his thoughts was stimulated by the brilliancy of the novelty and vigour of the 'New Learning' of the Renaissance.

E. K. Chambers convincingly brings out in his discussion of 'Moralities, Puppet-Plays, and Pageants'[43] that *pageant* has a two-fold meaning of a *scene* or act from a medieval mystery play and a *stage* on which a scene is exhibited or acted. Thus, it shows some influence of the religious drama of Christian England. Since in its etymological source the word *pageant* comes from the Latin *pagina* signifying the leaf of a book or the page of a manuscript, the first meaning – *scene* – is closer to the original denotation of the word. The two meanings, however, are merged in the Dumb Show spectacle in which the *scene* and *stage* are harmoniously combined.

From the deeply religious spirit of the Middle Ages the *pageant* drew its vigour and strength as a vehicle for elevating the people's minds to God and showing them the path of virtue. From the new and stimulating humanism of the Renaissance it received a forceful impetus to re-interpret man's happiness in terms of the 'here and now' and it endeavoured to add splendour, glory, and power to his earthly existence. The debate between virtue and vice, the body and soul, the mind and the senses, gradually led to the triumph spectacles that became such an integral and fascinating part of Renaissance glory and tradition. The triumph of sin in the Garden of Eden was luring men away from the beauties of a virtuous life and the salutary remembrance of a future life of eternal bliss or misery. Describing this phase of the Renaissance in Italy, J. A. Symonds says, 'The saint or angel became an occasion for the display of physical perfection, and to introduce "un bel corpo ignudo" into the composition was of more moment to them than to represent the macerations of Magdalen. Men thus learned to look beyond the relique and the host, and to forget the dogma in the lovely forms which gave it expression'.[44] The genius of Michelangelo, Titian, Boticelli, and Giotto, however, found an outlet in depicting Christian themes from the Old and New Testaments and from the Apocryphal Gospels. With glowing colours and in perfect delineation of forms they portrayed Christ's victory on the cross, His ascension into heaven; on the triumphal arches in their cathedrals and churches they presented Christ enthroned in majesty and in the glory of the Apocalypse.

The treatment that Thomas More gives his poem, 'Nyne pageauntes', admirably fuses the best that is in each school of thought. The form and structure he uses is Renaissance, while his point of view towards his subject matter is medieval. With a firm hold on the teaching of Christianity, he dipped his quill into the rich fluid of Renaissance culture. Like his contemporaries, More was powerfully impressed with the 'Trionfi' of Petrarch, and imitated him in his subjectivity and preoccupation with style and form. Unlike Petrarch, however, he did not pursue 'art for art's sake' but made the truth and beauty of the substance of his poem his chief concern. Petrarch's Laura is described vaguely, and the author deliberately 'left the face blank, as it were, so that each lover might fill the space with the portrait of his own inamorata'.[45] Thomas More's personifications have clearly outlined delineations with specific characteristics and definite functions, and the poet leaves little room for filling in the blank descriptions. Petrarch was a master of style, however, and a lyricist whose melody and grace opened on the continent a new era of poetry. More was an apprentice in the art of versification and a novice in craftsmanship whose interest in poetry was superseded by preoccupation with legal matters. Nevertheless, although more than one hundred and fifty years apart, the two men exhibited a marked predilection for the classics, absorbing interest in the works of St. Augustine, and a strong penchant to write poetry in their vernacular language. Both writers also inveighed against the fickleness of Fortune, were drawn to the 'Peacefulness of Monastic Life',[46] and were deeply concerned with government administration and affairs.[47]

Francesco de Sanctis aptly summarizes Petrarch's role in the formation of a new era of humanism in the following eloquent words:

> Myths, symbols, theological abstractions, are all behind us; we are standing at last in the full light of day in the temple of human consciousness. The sphinx is unveiled: man is found.[48]

Dante's 'Beatrice' was no longer a concept or a symbol but became a sentiment personified in Petrarch's 'Laura'.[49] Thomas More built his poem on the 'Petrarch sentiment' and gave it philosophical dimensions and a religious character. Although pronouncedly below the Tuscan versifier in craftsmanship, he endeavoured to portray the complete man with peculiar propensities and characteristics

80

in each successive stage of his life instead of a series of triumphs which are directly related to the mythical figure of Laura.

Petrarch's 'Triumphs', which A. W. Reed concedes to be More's prototype for the 'Nyne pageauntes', are not considered successful as a whole. The term *triumph* meant to the Tuscan poet, judging by the context of the six poems forming the 'Trionfi', a composition presenting a large number of persons moving processionally under the dominance of a single figure, suggested by the historic triumphal processions of ancient Rome. The term also reminds one of the 'Triumph of Death' in the famous 'Dance of Death' painting by Holbein as Death leads all his victims to the judgment seat of God in a triumphal procession. The first of Petrarch's six triumphs is the conquest of Love, followed, in turn, by the triumphs of Chastity, Death, Fame, Time, and Eternity.

The fact that these six *triumphs* are also called *pageants* links them still more closely with More's 'Nyne pageauntes', and shows some apparent relationship to them. The blind French poet, Bernardus Andreas of Toulouse, who was patronized by Henry VII for his scholarship, was influenced by Petrarch's 'Triumphs' and wrote a series of twelve triumphs in which he compared the labors of Hercules to the King's exploits. Stephen Hawes, More's contemporary and four years his senior, wrote the 'Passetyme of Pleasure', a 5,800-line allegory in rime royal verse in which the concluding pageants of Age, Death, Fame, Time, and Eternity are analogous to More's allegorical sequence. Petrarch's 'Trionfi' adumbrates the poems of Bernardus Andreas and Stephen Hawes, and seems to have had an influence on More's 'Nyne pageauntes'.

The Renaissance aspect of Thomas More's poem mirrors his interest in man, the full realization of his physical, mental, and spiritual consciousness, and shows a penetrating Christian insight into his future destiny. The young poet uses the framework of the medieval morality play for the enunciation of his ideas in the nine verses ascribed to the nine pageants on the hangings of rich cloth. The characters personify abstractions, and as in the fifteenth century morality, 'The Castle of Perseverance', and more particularly in the Chester 'Adoration of the Magi', they speak in the first person. For example, Herod introduces himself to the audience in the following words so analogous to the method of introduction used by More:

> For I am king of all mankinde,
> I byd, I beat, I loose, I bynde,
> I maister the Moone; take this in mynde
> that I am most of mighte. (ll. 169–172)

The next stanza recalls Hamlet's description of Herod's 'ranting manner':

> I am the greatest aboue degree,
> That is or was euer shall be.
> The Sonne it dare not shyne on me
> if I byd hym goe downe. (ll. 173–176)[50]

Similarly, in the folk play of St. George, which Hardin Craig presumes 'may be an infinitely degenerated survival of a medieval miracle play on St. George',[51] the protagonist of the Lutterworth play, Prince George, says:

> I am Prince George, the champion bold,
> And with my sword I won three crowns of gold;
> I slew the fiery dragon and brought him to the
>   slaughter
> And won the King of Egypt's only daughter.[52]

More's verses in the 'Nyne pageauntes' are cast within the framework of the first person and the voice is that of the peaker, who personifies the abstractions that cumulatively make up the pattern of man's existence. Thus, Childhood, representing a carefree youngster at play, says:

> I am called Chyldhood, in play is all my mynde,
> To cast a coyte, a cokstale, and a ball.
> A toppe can I set, and dryue it in his kynde.
> But would to god these hatefull bookes all,
> Were in a fyre brent to pouder small.
> Than myght I lede my lyfe alwayes in play:
> Whiche lyfe god sende me to myne endying day.[53]

The integral worth of the 'Nyne pageauntes' lies in the felicitous combination of sound and meaning structure, which was calculated to evoke the proper emotional responses from the observer or reader. The first three stanzas on 'Childhood', 'Manhood', and 'Venus and Cupid' are conventional representations and do not contain any novel ideas or treatment. The next four rhyme royal stanzas on 'Age', 'Death', 'Fame', and 'Time' personify these ideas according to classical interpretation, but the accompanying description of them and their characteristic function is given original and virile Christian treatment. The eighth stanza on 'Eternity' succinctly closes this cycle of the drama of man's life and shows the 'mobilite'[54] of earthly things. The most original and convincing feature of these pageants, however, is the concluding stanza on 'The Poet', in which Thomas More speaks in his own voice and with unflinching conviction states his philosophy of life. To the conventional number of five or six panels in a series, More added three more depicting Childhood, Youth, and the Poet. An influence of humanism can be seen here, for he places emphasis on man and the development of his mental powers as well as physical maturity.

Since voice and address form one of the salient characteristics of this poem, their meaning and the application of the method used will now be discussed. In his stimulating address on *The Three Voices*,[55] T. S. Eliot discusses the function of each voice in poetry and drama. He maintains that the first voice

82

– that of the poet talking to himself – and the second voice – the poet talking to his audience – are found together in non-dramatic poetry. The third voice is the voice of poetic drama and here he distinguishes between the voice of the dramatic character, for example, Caliban in 'The Tempest', and the voice of the author in a dramatic verse monologue as 'Browning talking aloud through Caliban'[56] in 'Caliban upon Setebos'. As a matter of fact, one voice alone is seldom heard since it is a natural thing for the voices to overlap, and all that really matters is that the principle of harmony should not be violated.

Accepting the plausibility of this explanation and applying it to More's poem on the 'Nyne pageauntes', one finds the third voice, the voice of poetic drama, used predominantly. A close study of this poem discloses its similarity in theme and function to the miracle and morality plays of the fourteenth and fifteenth centuries. Every stanza is a lively personification of an abstract idea presented in a highly dramatic manner, and a little imagination on the observer's or reader's part easily brings the characters to life. Thus, a poetic drama akin to the morality play would be enacted before one's very eyes.

In eight of the verses it is not the author's voice that is heard, but the voice of the dramatic characters who enunciate their own conventional ideas, not necessarily More's. The ninth verse, however, succinctly echoes the young humanist's voice as he clinches the architectonic poem with sincere statements of his view on life embodying his philosophy thereof.

The author's feeling towards his subject, the tone or his attitude towards his listeners, and his intention, which is 'the conscious or unconscious aim of the effect he endeavours to produce',[57] are also necessary factors for explication here. To avoid overlapping, which is likely to occur in a discussion of this nature, the following enumerations will help to make the analysis more pithy and cogent:

1. Feeling – polemical because it appears that Thomas More wishes to prove that classical culture can be interpreted in the light of Christianity.
2. Tone – More's attitude towards his listeners is one of uncertainty and inferiority; being a youth according to chronology of years and a humanist according to inclination and study, he endeavours to produce a work of art effulgent with provocative ideas and allegorical interpretations that will convince his elders and will palliate the antagonism towards the 'New Learning'.
3. Intention – to assert himself as a Christian thinker who can harmoniously fuse classicism with religion, and to give vent to the surging aspirations that are pent up in his mind and heart.

The most salient and pleasing feature of the 'Nyne pageauntes' is its interesting dramatic character. Every component stanza is a sententious morality play in its embryonic stage of development and contains a setting, protagonist, plot, climax, and dénouement. For example, the following seven verses on Fame will illustrate this point:

Main character   Fame, I am called, maruayle you nothing,
Description   Though I with tonges am compassed all rounde

Setting	For in voyce of people is my chiefe liuyng.
Plot	O cruel death, thy power I confounde.
Climax	When thou a noble man hast brought to grounde.
Dénouement	Maugry thy teeth to lyue cause hym shall I,
	Of people in parpetuall memory.[58]

Each of the remaining seven rhyme royal stanzas can be described in the same manner as above since they also contain dramatic elements of setting, characterization, and plot development in an embryonic stage. The foregoing analysis permits the speculation that this poem on the 'Nyne pageauntes' may have been one of the several interludes Thomas More is reputed to have written as a youth.[59] William Holden Hutton, a nineteenth-century biographer of More whose originality of approach is refreshing, makes the subtle observation that in these verses the young humanist was applying 'that sense of form and style'[60] which he had learned at the University. He conjectures that these stanzas inscribed under the nine allegorical representations of the ages of man were written during some Oxford vacation. He attributes to them a 'certain elegance of force'[61] and a superiority over the ballad of the 'Mery Iest'.

To the harmonious fusion of form and style the young aspirant in literary craftsmanship added an architectonic structure by means of which each succeeding stanza is built on the preceding one. This method enables him to achieve pleasing unity of structure, felicitous harmony in subject-matter, and a forceful elegance of emotional impact. The dramatic element inherent in the poem, as a whole, lies primarily in the cyclic sequence of ideas and the circular progression of stanzaic structure. In the first five stanzas a movement of expansion is apparent wherein meaning is explored; in the succeeding four stanzas a movement of identification in terms of symbolic imagery asserts itself. The diction in the poem is not turgid or banal. As a matter of fact, every word is shaped by the author to answer a specific need and to evoke the appropriate emotional response from the reader. The rhythm, More's forte in poetry, is in its experimental stage here, and certain cumbrous lines are forced into the mold of iambic pentameter by an amateur in English verse.

The pattern of Thomas More's punctuation, consisting of a functional use of commas, periods, colons, and parentheses presents an interesting and curious study. The first point for the consideration of this phase of his writing is the following question: Did More deliberately insert these punctuation marks, or were they added by the printer? William Hastell, his nephew who published his works, was a learned man and conscientious printer; William Roper, who assembled his writings for publication, could also have made some notable emendations in this regard.

On the other hand, Thomas More was a grammarian of no mean ability, and his interest and proficiency in grammar and rhetoric has been obscured by his polemical tracts, legal accomplishments, and political success. William Nelson, who makes an illuminating study of this neglected phase of More's career, opens a new and fascinating aspect of Morean scholarship with his observations:

... the period about which the 'English' biographical tradition is least informative is that during which More was most interested in the humanities, since Roper, the primary source of the school of hagiographers, became More's son-in-law only after More had left academic study for the business of the royal court.[62]

He further points out that Thomas More not only loved and imitated the ancient classical writers but also had the 'art of expression'[63] which he acquired from them. In this article Nelson gives proof and evidence that More 'was a student of grammar and rhetoric, and intimate friend of professional grammarians, and himself a teacher of the subject . . .'[64] Augustine's *De Civitate Dei* was a favourite book of the humanists, and St. Augustine himself was a professor of rhetoric before writing it. More's fascination with this utopian book was not merely based on its religious subject matter, but exhibited his interest also in its humanistic features. The historical and philosophical lectures the young More gave on it advanced 'the cause of the "New Learning".'[65]

Thomas More's pattern of punctuation is predicated on rhetorical emphasis and a clear, effective interpretation of the text. The sentences that comprise the stanzas are perspicuous and persuasive, and their significant form and nature necessitate the use of pauses in vocal utterance and of punctuation or pointing, as it was called in the sixteenth century, in its written form. Although the invention of printing forms an important era in the history of punctuation, the art of pointing is already seen in the productions of ancient rhetoricians and grammarians.

More's rhetorical punctuation in terms of prosodic theory and structure can be seen in the light of stylistic rhetoric which was taught in the late fifteenth and early sixteenth centuries. A learned poetic allegory entitled 'The Court of Sapience', used in English classrooms at this time, synthesizes the functions of the seven liberal arts in which 'Dame Rethoryke, Modyr of Eloquence',[66] plays an important part. Since More's 'Nyne pageauntes' can be analyzed in terms of the rhetorical devices then in vogue, the following excerpt throws some light on the method he employed:

> She taught theym all the craft of endyntyng,
> Whyche vyces bene that shuld auoyded be.
> Whyche ben the coloures gay of that konnyng,
> Theyre difference and eke theyre propurte;
> Yche thyng endyted how hit shuld peyntyd be;
> Distinccion she gan clare and discus,
> Whyche ys coma, colon, periodus.[67]

Dame Rhetoric then proceeds to list the vices of style as enumerated by Quintilian, including the following: meanness or extravagance, meagerness, sameness, superfluous elaboration, perverse affectation, and cacemphaton (combining sounds which produce an ill effect); second in this list are the colours, which include the schemes and tropes; third is the topic of painting or word picture, illustration, and vivid description; and lastly, the *comma*, the *colon*, and the *periodus* are discussed, not as arbitrary marks of punctuation, but as a section referring 'to the whole question of rhythm in style'.[68]

In the writings of Cicero as well as in Quintilian, the *comma* or *incisum* is the expression of a thought in a group of words, comparable to a phrase consisting of less than eight syllables; the colon or *membrum* is a thought expressed in a larger group of words, possibly in a clause of eight to seventeen syllables; and the *periodus* or *circuitus* is a thought expressed in a complete sentence which was usually made up of four *cola*. Since Thomas More's sentences in the 'Nyne pageauntes' appear to be built on this theory, a further explanation will help to elucidate the young poet's method. In speaking of the periodic or *compact* style as opposed to the free-running style, Aristotle says:

> By a period I mean a portion of speech that has in itself a beginning and an end, being at the same time not too big to be taken in at a glance. Language of this kind is satisfying and easy to follow.[69]

More applies Aristotle's theory on the periodic style by using the sentence which is complete in itself and the one divided into parts, namely, the simple and antithetical statements, as the following illustration exemplifies:

Complete in itself 1. I whom thou seest with horyloge in hande,
Am named tyme, the lord of euery howre.
2. I shall in space destroy both see and lande.[70]

Simple, antithe- 3. When thou a noble man hast brought to grounde
tical statement Maugry thy teeth to lyue cause hym shall I,
Of people in parpetuall memory.[71]

Antithetical in 4. These thynges become a *very man* in dede,
each of the two Yet thynketh *this boy* his peuishe game swetter,
members But what no force, his reason is no better.[72]

The above excerpts from the 'Nyne pageauntes' prove that More's punctuation depends primarily on the logical interpretation of the statement, the rhetorical effect it produces, and the rhythmical quality which is indigenous to it.

McKerrow points out the fact that punctuation in the sixteenth century was unstable and unreliable. In spite of this limitation More was consistent in his theory and his practice of it, as the following statement by A. W. Reed exemplifies:

> ... If More's Preface [to the First Boke of the Dialogue] be read in the three editions it will be found that the punctuation of the 1529 edition is lighter than that of the second, 'newly oversene by Sir Thomas More'. It is probably nearer to the original MS. of More; for if we assume that More's State Letters show his practice, he relied mainly on the full stop, making very sparing use of the comma or *virgula*.[73]

Reed further assumes that 'More certainly passed and possibly inspired the punctuation of the revised edition of 1531, the pointing of which is followed in the 1557 edition'.[74]

Nevertheless, even in Rastell's carefully edited poems in the 1531 edition, one finds places where a lack of precision and consistency is obvious. One example of inconsistency at this time is the fact that the early printers used a period, colon, or a virgule (/) at the end of a sentence. The question mark was formed by reversing the semicolon. In 1509 Wynkyn de Worde, who printed More's *Life of John Picus*, made use of the following five points: the period, the semicolon, the comma, the interrogative, and the parenthesis.[75] Caxton, on the other hand, used only three points: a virgule marking off a word group or phrase, a colon marking a distinct syntactical break or pause, and a full stop marking either the end of the sentence or a brief pause.[76] George Henry Vallins' statement on the instability of punctuation reflects its inconsistency even in the eighteenth century:

> In the work of eighteenth century writers, colons, semicolons, and commas seem to jostle one another unceremoniously, with little regard for their relative values; and the grammarians themselves find some difficulty in distinguishing one from the other.[77]

One cannot be definitely certain that the punctuation marks embodied in the English poems were made by More. As a matter of fact, the heavy use of the comma at the end of the lines and the ambiguous use of the period where a comma would be more meaningful, seem to be the work of the printer, Rastell. On the other hand, the medial commas, the rhetorical use of the colon, and the dramatic use of the parenthesis appear to be, as A. W. Reed asserts, 'newly oversene by Sir Thomas More'.[78] The following sentences may serve to illustrate this point more clearly:

Medial comma	Me nedeth not to bost, I am Eternitee,
	The very name signifyeth well,
	That myne empyre infinite shal be.[79]
Colon	Old Age am I, with lokkes, thynne and hore,
	Of our short lyfe, the last and best part.
	Wyse and discrete: the publike wele therefore
	I help to rule to my labour and smart.[80]
Parenthesis	Therefore sage father greatly magnifyed,
	Discende from your chayre, set a part your pryde,
	Witsafe to lende (though it be to your payne)
	To me a fole, some of your wise brayne.[81]

Thomas More's use of the parenthesis is very interesting. It gives the poem a certain dramatic effect and supports the hypothesis that it may have been rendered orally in the form of a short allegorical presentation reminiscent in part of the medieval morality plays. Here the parenthesis is used as effectively as the Shakespearean 'asides' and does not detract from the statement, but instead adds strength and colour to the ironical implications contained in the verses.

Perhaps More's use of punctuation in his poetry does not justify such a lengthy discourse on it; nevertheless, these observations lead one to a close study of the rhetorical pattern of More's sentences comprising the verses on the 'Nyne pageauntes'. Consequently, one sees in this poem, not only a versifier shaping his words carefully and confining them within a rhythmical framework, but an erudite grammarian and rhetorician. In the fourteenth and fifteenth centuries rhetoric denoted style generally, whether in prose or in verse, and *rhetor* or *rhetorien* meant master of style and was a term freely applied to poets.[82] As a matter of fact, Mallet tells us in his *History of the University of Oxford* that 'the word "Poeta" was often used for a classical scholar'.[83]

These nine allegorical poems are truly studies in stylistic rhetoric and as such can be analysed according to the following divisions:
1.   Arrangement or organization
2.   Amplification and abbreviation
3.   Style and rhetorical devices.

Pertinent parts of Jean de Garland's *Poetria*, in which he adapts the rhetorical style to poetics, will serve our purpose for the analysis of the nine pageants. The arrangement or organization is also called *Dispositio*, and the following five questions help to establish its identity and function:
1.   *Ubi* – Where? The theme may be taken from persons, from examples and proverbs, and from etymologies.
2.   *Quid* – What? What is one able to find? In the qualities or faults of perons; in the examples and the proverbs, in the etymologies, an abundant harvest of traits may be a means to praise or to disparage.
3.   *Quale* – What sort of ideas? The ones which express reality directly or those which are understood only by manner of their insinuation.
4.   *Ad quid* – In view of what end? In order to foresee the true and the useful.
5.   *Qualiter* – In what way? By the application of the seven *colours* the effect of which is to adorn and to amplify the idea, that is to say:
     a. The bringing together of two words different in meaning but similar in sound
     b. A transferring, metonymy
     c. A repetition of the same word at the beginning of several sentences
     d. Gradation or climax
     e. Explanation of one expression by another
     f. A marking out, limiting, defining or explaining a definition
     g. A conversation, disputation, discussion.[84]

Garland's initial analysis of poetry is suited admirably to the explication of More's 'Nyne pageauntes', and the five underlying questions help to exemplify his inherent technique and method of approach:
1.   *Ubi?* His theme is taken from the proverb that 'All is vanity and vexation

of spirit', and from Augustine's famous aphorism that 'Restless is the heart of man until it rests in God'.

2. *Quid?* One finds that these statements quoted above are meaningful and convincing, for they have been proven perennially in the examples of men from all stages of life.

3. *Quale?* These ideas are expressed directly in the course of the nine stanzas by the use of the rhetorical devices of *apostrophe* and *antithesis*, and at the end they are clearly enunciated by the poet.

4. *Ad quid?* In the age of the 'New Learning', when humanism hypnotized man with the realization of the power of the human intellect, Thomas More wished to prove man's dependence upon God for happiness and security.

5. *Qualiter?* He does this satisfactorily by depicting the stages of man's life beginning with Childhood through Manhood, Age, and Death. The allegorical personifications of Fame and Time continue the method of gradation, and thus bring the climax, Eternity, into focus. He employs disputation to prove that life does not end with the grave, but that an eternity of endless bliss or misery awaits man.

The 'Nyne pageauntes' adheres closely to the norms for medieval rhetoric, and presents a fine study in *amplification* and *abbreviation*. Professor J. M. Manly, who made a detailed study of Chaucer and his debt to the rhetoricians,[85] names six principal means of amplification: Description, Digression, Apostrophe, Prosopopeia or Effectio, Periphrasis or Circumlocutio, and Expolitio.

Amplification by means of description is a prominent feature of Thomas More's poetical method in this poem. This figure of amplification is called *Energia* in Tudor rhetoric and includes *Mimesis*, *Characterismus*, *Dialogismus*, and other terms too numerous and overlapping to mention. The generic term which Puttenham refers to in *The Arte of English Poesie* as *Energia* is derived from the Greek word *argos* 'because it geueth a glorious lustre and light'.[86] He further explains that they call the latter term *Energia* from *ergon* 'because it wrought with a strong and vertuous operation; and figure breedeth them both, some seruing to giue glosse onely to a language, some to giue it efficacie by sense . . .'[87]

According to classical theory, definite rules were followed by the poets and rhetoricians for the description of persons: (1) these descriptions were conventional in nature, and as Faral tells us, 'un portrait complet comprend deux parties et traite successivement du physique et du moral';[88] (2) they stressed the qualities and traits of a person in addition to his physiognomy; (3) praise or blame was the object of every description.

More's descriptions of Age, Death, Fame, and Time follow the conventional style but do not bore the reader with a drawn-out enumeration of physical and moral qualities. They are described laconically but sufficiently well for a knowledge and appraisal of the part they play on life's stage. The above four abstractions are described in the opening lines which serve the twofold function of introduction and description:

> Old Age am I, with lokkes, thynne and hore,
> Of our short lyfe, the last and best part.[89]
>
> . . . .
>
> Though I be foule ugly lene and mysshape,
> Yet there is none in all this worlde wyde,
> That may my power withstande or escape.[90]
>
> Fame I am called, maruayle you nothing,
> Though I with tonges am compassed all rounde
> Far in voyce of people is my chiefe liuyng.[91]

Thomas More does not become guilty of excessive dilation in the amplification of his subject matter, but keeps the description tightly bound within the framework of a rhyme royal verse. For this purpose he employs not only verbal delineations of physical traits, but also describes the characters by their representative actions or by the effect these actions produce. For example, youth delights in his attainment of manhood which means that now he can engage in the following activities:

> Manhood I am therefore I me delyght,
> To hunt and hawke, to nourishe up and fede,
> The grayhounde to the course, the hawke to the flyght,
> And to bestryde a good and lusty stede.[92]

The young man delights in the realization of his manhood, which is characterized by strength and vitality, just as the Renaissance humanist exulted in the consciousness of his potentialities and in the power of his mental acumen. Venus and Cupid are classical personifications signifying the love that conquers a man's heart; and More apparently assumes that their description, personality, and function are well-known facts. He enumerates three of their attributes which seem to overlap one another, but in Tudor rhetoric and poetics this apparent repetition adds vigour and eloquence to the passage:

> Who so ne knoweth the *strength*, *power* and *myght*,
> Of Venus and me her lytle sonne Cupyde . . .[93]

One of the important functions of description, besides that of dilation of subject matter for the sake of clarifying the idea, is the arousing of praise or censure, which results from the peculiar nature of the person or object described. In the eighth verse on 'Eternitee', More's praise of this estate is not blatant or reprehensible, but is brought into the context of the lines with force and perspicuity:

Me needeth not to bost, I am Eternitee,
The very name sygnifyeth well,
That myne empyre infinite shal be.[94]

From the above examples it is obvious that Thomas More abandoned the long
and digressing features of medieval dilation and adapted his method of amplification sententiously to the matter and form of the 'Nyne pageauntes'. Instead
of several lines of description, he uses one or a few epithets which aptly describe
the person or object. The Latin grammarians had two classes for the adjective.
In the first class were nouns substantive, for example: kind, cold, appropriate.
The words in the second class never stood alone, but were always added or
'adjected' to a noun. They could be used *attributively* as in a 'wise ruler',
appositively as in 'a ruler, wise and good', and *predicatively* as in the 'ruler is
wise'. Stephen Hawes refers to the 'nowne substantyve' in the 'Pastyme of
Pleasure': 'A nowne substantyve Might stand wythout helpe of an adjective'.[95]
The following analysis may be helpful in showing the grammatical, rhetorical,
and poetic usages More employs in his technique of amplifying his verses by
using the technique of descriptive epithets:

GRAMMATICAL — TO INSTRUCT

Nouns Adjective		*Nouns Substantive*
chargeable matters		strength, power and myght
childish game		mobilite
ydle bysinesse		pride and bostyng
simple fame		liuyng
noble man		pryde

Attributive	*Appositive*	*Predicative*
short lyfe	lokkes, thynne and hore	his reason is no better.
endlesse flowre	lyfe, the last and best part	Though I be foule, ugly,
		lene and mysshape . . .
mortal Tyme	tyme, the lord of euery	Manhod I am.
great pryde	howre	
tender syde	name, an endlesse flowre	myne empyre infinite
		shal be.
wise brayne	me her lytle sonne Cupyde	I am Eternitee.
cruel death	To me, a fole . . .	
	Thou, mortall Tyme . . .	

RHETORICAL — TO PLEASE

Hyperbaton —   Inverting the natural order of words in a sentence to emphasize the idea.

these hatefull bookes all   a name eternall
pouder small   myne empyre infinite shal be.
in a fyre brent   to lyve cause hym shall I
his peuishe game swetter   Of people in parpetuall memory.

Voice —   The concrete references to the first, second, and third person
                 give the poem an oratorical and dramatic effect.

First Person :   myne endyng day   my fyry dart
                   our short lyfe   my chiefe liuyng
Second Person : thy great pryde   thy tender syde
                   your wise brayne   be to your payne
Third Person :   her lytle sonne   these hatefull bookes all
                   children small   his peuishe game swetter.

POETIC — TO MOVE

Adjectives which by nature of their description evoke an emotional response:
great pryde – emotion of hatred   fyry dart – emotion of love
tender syde – sympathy   wise brayne – pride and esteem
last and best part – contentment   wyse and discrete – satisfaction
cruel death – anger   simple fame – contempt
hatefull bookes all – disgust   chargeable matters – responsibility
maugry thy teeth – vengeance   pride and bostyng – disdain.

Physical Description   *Description of Abstract Ideas*
Lytle sonne   name eternall
children small   empyre infinite
a good and lusty stede   mortall Tyme
lokkes, thynne and hore   ydle bysinesse
foule ugly lene and mysshape   wyse brayne
fyry dart   great pryde
worlde wyde   cruel death
pouder small   perpetuall memory
childish game   simple fame
endyng day   endlesse flowre

Digression, as a means of amplification, includes anticipatory passages and
comparisons. If it is placed skillfully in the structural pattern of the work, it
does not detract from the unity and coherence of the poem or work of art, but
may even strengthen or embellish it effectively. In the 'Nyne pageauntes' Thomas
More does not digress by anticipating some new scene or event that will come
later, nor does he use *sententia* or *exempla* to illustrate the subject at hand. The
matter and form of the nine pageants is set up against the tapestry of pictorial

delineation, and the verses are so compact that digression in this case would indeed be a *tour de force* not worth striving for. There is only one instance where the young poet employs a subtle and extended use of this figure, namely, in the aside he uses when Death says to Age:

> Therefore sage father greatly magnifyed,
> Discende from your chayre, set a part your pryde,
> Witsafe to lende (though it be to your payne)
> To me a fole, some of your wise brayne.[96]

Here the digressing passage which is enclosed in parentheses is a deviation that is dramatic and auricular rather than figurative and rhetorical. Furthermore, it strongly suggests a pantomime or stage representation and gives one the impression that it was meant to be delivered orally.

More's paucity in the use of digression as an effective medieval means of amplifying one's subject matter is complemented by Goerge Puttenhan's distrust of it in Book III, 'Of Ornament', in *The Arte of English Poesie*:

> This manner of speech is termed the figure of digression by the Latines, following the Greeke originall, we also call him the straggler by allusion to the souldier that marches out of his array, or by those that keep no order in their marche, as the battailes well ranged do: of this figure there need be geuen no example.[97]

Exhibiting the initiative of a humanist and the audacity of an innovator, the young More, steeped in classical studies and medieval conventions, departed from the accepted traditions and molded his ideas to fit a new literary form rather than let the old form mold his ideas. Instead of using rhetorical devices and poetic conventions in a monotonouts and stereotyped fashion, he places the nine verses on the stages of man's life within the framework of one unifying and pervasive amplifying figure, namely, apostrophe, which becomes the form and the spirit of the poem. Each of the nine consecutive stanzas devotes the last three, four, or five lines to the function of apostrophe, which in its Greek etymological meaning denotes a 'turning' to some object or person. A speaker interrupts his discourse and addresses the object, person, or personified abstraction, but does so under the strain of some emotion or in the joy of its exhilarating effects.

In the first verse on 'Chyldhood' the child interrupts his enumeration of playful activities and speaks with disgust of 'hatefull bookes' that interrupt his pursuance of pleasurable pastimes. Here, however, he does not address this inanimate object directly in the role of the first person, but speaks in the third person as he gives vent to his pent-up emotions:

> But would to god these hatefull bookes all,
> Were in a fyre brent to pouder small,
> Then myght I lede my lyfe alwayes in play:
> Whiche lyfe god sende me to myne endyng day.[98]

If More had used the figure apostrophe in the generally accepted sense, then the child's address to the books directly would indeed be naive and fatuous. Reason guided the young humanist at all times, even at the expense of departing from literary conventions and accepted forms.

The third verse on 'Venus and Cupyde' has a five-line illustration of apostrophe in which Cupid tauntingly and prophetically addresses the complacent youth:

> Thou Manod shalt a myrrour bene a ryght,
> By us subdued for all thy great pryde,
> My fyry dart perceth thy tender syde,
> Now thou whiche erst despysedst children small,
> Shall waxe a chylde agayne and be my thrall.[99]

Following this pattern, Old Age, 'Wyse and discrete', turns aggressively to Cupid, the god of love, in the fifth line of his verse, and fully aware of his specious approach, says:

> Therefore Cupyde withdrawe thy fyry dart,
> Chargeable matters shall of loue oppresse,
> The childish game and ydle bysinesse.[100]

Proud and disdainful Fame enters upon the scene and 'confounds' the power of Death; in her vengeance she promises that a man's name and reputation shall live in spite of Death's annihilation:

> O cruel death, thy power I confounde,
> When thou a noble man hast brought to grounde,
> Maugry thy teeth to lyue cause hym shall I,
> Of people in perpetuall memory.[101]

Time, 'the lord of every howre', looks upon Lady Fame with supercilious sympathy and, in conquering her, he preserves his equanimity of mind and haughty self-assurance:

> O simple fame, how darest thou man honowre,
> Promising of his name, an endlesse flowre,
> Who may in the world have a name eternall,
> When I shall in proces distroy the world and all.[102]

Lady Eternity triumphs over Time, and to denote her conquest she is 'crowned with an imperial crown'.[103] However, instead of having a glorious crescendo effect on these series of conquests, More portrays her in a drab and prosaic manner. She speaks to Lord Time not as a regal sovereign evoking respect and admiration for her wisdom and discretion, but as a typical Renaissance humanist discoursing on the astronomical phenomena of the sun and moon:

94

Thou mortall Tyme euery man can tell,
Art nothyng els but the mobilite,
Of sonne and mone chaungyng in euery degre,
When they shall leue theyr course thou shalt be brought,
For all thy pride and bostyng into nought.[104]

Apparently, Thomas More did not intend Eternity to synthesize the poem and win the final laurel of victory, for he reserves this special function for the Poet. Here one sees More's humanistic approach, for he makes the individual the triumphant victor in the poem. Man with intelligence and free will can conquer the frivolity of childhood, the complacency of manhood, the power of love, the self-assurance of old age, the enigma of death, the speciousness of fame, the amplitude of time, and thus assure for himself, with the grace of God, an eternity of bliss. More's poet in the last stanza is a representative humanist who speaks in Latin, unlike the personified abstractions who utter their thoughts and sentiments in the vernacular. That the technique of adding the poet's enunciation of a philosophy of life was not a common one, is evidenced by the fact that Stephen Hawes in his famous *Pastyme of Pleasure* (1509) has Fame write the epitaph of Graund Amoure, while Time and Eternity pronounce the final exhortation of the poem.[105] Petrarch also ended his 'Trionfi' with the final conquest of Eternity, thus keeping this succession of victories within the medieval framework, which was supported, emphasized, and crowned by allegory.

The Poet mirrors Thomas More's own philosophy of life and depicts him as a true Christian humanist, who considered not only man's mind but also his soul. It is indeed admirable that at so early an age, possibly at the age of sixteen, More recognized the false allurements of this world's pleasures, and following the exhortation of St. Augustine, was convinced that the human heart is restless 'until it rests in God'. As a matter of fact, his interest in Augustine can be traced not only to the *City of God* and his *Confessions*, but also to the fact that this renowned doctor of the Church was at one time a professor of rhetoric and the author of a treatise on aesthetics. As a contemporary Renaissance scholar, Donald Lemen Clark, puts it 'in fact, Augustine never quite got over being a professor of rhetoric'.[106] More profited by Augustine's mistakes, and early in life recognized values at their true worth and led a life that was virtuous and edifying.

In order to fully understand the comprehensive design of the poem as a whole and to realize the unity of its structure, it is necessary to give an English translation of the Latin stanza. A prose translation of it by Bradner and Lynch follows:

If anyone finds pleasure in looking at these pictures because he feels that, although they are products of the imagination, still they represent man truly and with remarkable skill, then he can delight his soul with the actual truth just as he feasts his eyes on its painted image. For he will see that the elusive goods of this perishable world do not come so readily as they pass away. Pleasures, praise, homage, all things quickly disappear – except the love of God, which endures forever. Therefore, mortals, put no confidence hereafter in trivialities, no hope in transitory advantage; offer your prayers to the everlasting God, who will grant us the gift of eternal life.[107]

Viewed as a whole, Thomas More's 'Nyne Pageauntes' are not only designed to please but also to instruct. In his final exhortation, he is perspicuous, eloquent, and forceful. Perspicuity is seen in the clear explanation he gives of the allegorical significance of the verses, eloquence is achieved by his rhetorical exclamations, and strong feeling testifies to the presence of deeply-rooted convictions. The Tudor humanist does not consider allegory as an end in itself and a means of embellishing a poetic pattern, but as a powerful force for the inculcation of new ideas or the strengthening of old ones. Thus, he encourages the reader or listener to contemplate the good, true and beautiful while 'he delights the eyes with false images'.[108] Apropos of the 'deceiving' function of allegory, Sir John Harington makes this scintillating remark while giving *A Brief Apology for Poetry*:

> This is then that honest fraud in which (as *Plutarch* saith) he that is deceived is wiser than he that is not deceived, and he that doth deceive is honester than he that doth not deceive.[109]

Closely allied with apostrophe in function but at the other polarity of it in meaning, is the figure of *prosopopeia*, which Puttenham describes as 'the Counterfait in personation'. 'No prettier examples can be given to you thereof, than in the Romant of the rose translated out of French by Chaucer, describing the persons of auarice, ennuie, old age, and many others, whereby much moralitie is taught', he says.[110] By means of this figure the absent are introduced as present and inanimate objects and abstract ideas are represented as living. *Prosopopeia* or *Effictio* was used extensively for purposes of amplification and often formed the framework for the whole literary composition. It sometimes takes the form of a *débat*, as in Froissart's charming piece which represents his dog and horse discussing their master and the journeys he compels them to make with him.[111] Geoffrot cites numerous examples of this figure in his *Poetria*, among which are the following: a lamentation of the Holy Cross, Rome weeping upon the death of Caesar, and a farewell of an old tablecloth to the table.[112] In apostrophe the speaker addresses the inanimate object, personified abstraction, dead or absent person, while in *prosopopeia* the object, abstraction, dead or absent person, addresses an audience or some particular person or object. The address, however, is not a necessary feature of prosopopeia, for the dead or absent person or the inanimate object may be merely represented as living by attributing lifelike characteristics to them. In this sense the figure is known today as personification. Furthermore, the essence of apostrophe signifies a digression in thought and an interruption in speech, and its highly emotional strain causes an exclamatio[113] of sorrow, pity, joy, and exultation.

96

The 'Nyne Pageauntes' taken as a whole are developed around this figure of prosopopeia, which serves as the framework for the poetic pattern More devised. The stages of man's life: Childhood, Manhood, Old Age, and Death, are invested with life-like qualities by means of graphic descriptions. The classical allusion to Venus and Cupid, the personified abstractions of Fame, Time, Eternity, and the synthesizing voice of the Poet are likewise given human attributes. They introduce themselves and then hurl an abusive invective on their predecessor in order to assure themselves of the palm of victory. Seen in this light, each of the eight verses contains both prosopopeia and apostrophe, as the following verses exemplify:

Prosopopeia	Old Age am I, with lokkes, thynne and hore,
	Of our short lyfe, the last and best part.
	Wyse and discrete: the publike wele therefore,
	I help to rule to my labor and smart . . .
Apostrophe	Therefore Cupyde withdrawe thy fyry dart,
	Chargeable matters shall of loue oppresse,
	The childish game and ydle bysinesse.[114]

The poem is cast within the mold of prosopopeia, while apostrophe gives it a characteristic feature which recalls to mind the medieval *débat*. Chambers' definition of *débat* shows some definite analogy with the composition of More's 'Triumphs' insofar as it contains not only the dialogue but also the assertion of superiority. It is 'a kind of poetical controversy put into the mouths of two types or two personified abstractions, each of which pleads the cause of its own superiority, while in the end, the decision is not infrequently referred to an umpire in the fashion familiar in the eclogues of Theocritus'.[115] In the framework of More's poem, then, the Poet takes on added significance as he performs this function of ascertaining who receives the palm of victory in the final triumph. Seen in this light, the 'Nyne pageauntes' can be linked with such allegorical poems as Henri d'Andelli's 'Bataille des Vins' or 'Le Mariage des Sept Arts et des Sept Vertus'.[116] Instead of merely two people engaging in dialogue, More presents nine personified characters forming a cyclic sequence. A dialogue between two abstractions invested with human qualities does take place, nevertheless, and in all there are five dialogues spoken in the first person and addressed to the third person. The abstraction 'Childhood' addresses the books not directly but in a third person reference, while 'Manhood' scorns the frivolity of Childhood also in the third person. The poet voices his address to the audience or the readers of these 'Nyne Pageauntes', and they are strongly made aware of the fact that it is in reality the voice of More himself cogently expressing his views on life, its purpose and significance.

Because the amplification in the poem is achieved largely through the figures of prosopopeia and apostrophe, the framework of voice and address is particularly interesting and effective here. Aristotle makes three divisions which determine the form of the poem and illustrate its meaning. Thus, (1) the speaker may speak at one moment in narrative and at another in an assumed character, as Homer does; or (2) he may remain the same throughout, without any such change; or (3) the imitators may represent the whole story dramatically, as though they were actually doing the things described.[117] In the 'Nyne Page-auntes' More employs the first voice reference, while the addressee is the conventional second person reference:

		Voice	Addressee
1.	Chyldhood	First Person	Assumed audience – Second Person Plural
2.	Manhood	„ „	Assumed audience – Second Person Plural
3.	Venus and Cupyde	„ „	Manhod – Second Person Singular
4.	Age	„ „	Cupyde – Second Person Singular
5.	Death	„ „	Age – Second Person Singular
6.	Fame	„ „	Deth – Second Person Singular
7.	Time	„ „	Fame – Second Person Singular
8.	Eternitee	„ „	Time – Second Person Singular
9.	The Poet	Third Person – Voice of narrator	Second Person Plural – Readers or Listeners

In his illuminating article on 'Voice and Address',[118] Dr. LaDriére combines Plato's and Aristotle's voice distinctions and makes the following classification in which the poet speaks in his own voice or in an assumed one:
(1) Speaks in his own person. – *Diegesis* or *Apangellia* – Pure Exposition, Pure Narration.
(2) Assumes the voice of another person or set of persons and speaks in a voice throughout, not his own. –
Mimesis or 'Imitation' – Dialogue or Dramatic Monologue.
(3) Produces a mixed speech in which the basic voice is the speaker's, but other personalities are at times assumed and their voices introduced. –
Drama and Narrative with direct quotations by other voices.
The entire poem is an appealing study in the structure of 'Voice and Address' relationships. Dr. LaDriére aptly describes this structure when he says: '... the various types of voice-structure and address are in literature what the basic colours of the palette are in painting, or keys in music; the whole tone and

character of a composition is set by the writer's choice among them, and changed by any variation form one to another within the work'.[119]

All of the eight consecutive characters which are really personified abstractions in the 'Nyne pageauntes' speak in an assumed voice which is not the author's, and, since they address one another directly, they engage in the dialogue form of expression. The Poet, on the other hand, is the disguise the author assumes in order to voice his own opinions on life and its various stages. The manipulation of voices in this manner gives the poem flexibility of structure and felicity of expression. Relegating the disguised moral to the very end of the poem is an effective means of avoiding moralization and keeping it within the framework of light and fanciful allegory.

The fifth means of amplification, *periphrasis* or *circumlocutio*, besides expanding the idea, raises the low and commonplace idea to a high stylistic level. George Puttenham in his *Arte of English Poesie* calls this figure a 'dissembler, by reason of a secret intent not appearing by the works, as when we go about the bush, and will not in one or a few words expresse that thing which we desire to have knowen, bu do chose to do it by many words . . .'[120] For example, when we say, 'When they had a while hearkened to the persuasion of sleep' for 'When they had slept a while',[121] we are not expanding the idea, but embellishing it and raising it to a higher stylistic level. More does not use periphrasis in the 'Nyne Pageauntes' because there is no reason to 'dissemble' the idea since the personified abstractions, which made up the 'dramatis personae', introduce themselves clearly and forcefully in their opening lines. Secondly, the verses are short, and the seven-lined rhyme royal stanza emphasizes the particular features of the character with a definite stress on activities rather than mere verbalizations.

Closely related to the above stylistic device is *expolitio*, which Professor J. M. Manly has described as follows: '[It] includes the repetition of the same idea in different words (one form of *interpretatio*) and also the elaboration of an idea by adding the reasons or authorities, pronouncing a generalization with or without reasons, discussing the contrary, introducing a similitude or an *exemplum*, and drawing a conclusion'.[122] Manly adds: 'Although these two figures *periphrasis* and *expolitio* are of minor importance, they nevertheless play a considerable part in the writings of Chaucer, as of most medieval authors'.[123] Upon close examination of Thomas More's poem one finds the literary device of *expolitio* used in the following verses:

Childhod	in play is all my mynde . . . Than myght I lede my lyfe alwayes in play.	Repeating the idea of play
Manhod	Manhod I am therefore I me delyght . . . . . But what no force, his reason is no better.	Expressing Satisfaction

Venus and *Cupyde*	Who so ne knoweth the strength, power and myght,	
	Of Venus and me her lytle sonne Cupyde . . .	Pronouncing a generalization
	Now thou whiche erst despysedst children small,	
	Shall waxe a chylde agayne and be my thrall.	Discussing the contrary
Age	Of our short lyfe, the last and best part.	Drawing a conclusion
Deth	To me a fole, some of your wise brayne.	Implying the contrary
Fame	Fame I am called, maruayle you nothing,	Elaborating by giving reasons
	Though I with tonges am compas- sed all rounde	
	For in voyce of people is my chiefe liuying.	
Time	I shall in space destroy both sea and land	Repeating the same idea in different words
	When I shall in proces distroy the world and all.	
Eternitee	Me nedeth not to bost, I am Eternitee,	Drawing a conclusion
	The very name signifyeth well,	
	That myne empyre infinite shall be.	

The seventh device used to amplify the subject matter of poetry is the figure *comparison*, which has for its function pointing out similarities between like or unlike persons or things. It is also called *syncrisis*, which compares unlike things or persons in one sentence, as for example: 'A wise son maketh a glad father; but a foolish son is the heaviness of his mother' (Prov. 14, 1–2).

John Hoskins (1566–1638) in his *Directions for Speech and Style* states: 'Comparison is either of things contrary, equal, or things different'.[124] The comparing of equal things is not as forceful as the comparison of things unequal or different. The third comparison overlaps with the figure *contrarietas* or antithesis of negation and affirmation; therefore, the two will be treated together in the same discussion. Cornificius, a friend of Cicero, well-versed in literature, while discussing *similitudo* defines it thus: 'Similitudo est oratio traducens ad rem quampiam aliquid ex re dispari simile'. In other words, the similarity or comparison is a development which applies to an idea certain borrowed elements

100

from a different idea.[125] In twentieth-century poetics these tropes are called simile and metaphor, the latter being an implied comparison in its most general meaning, and the former, an explicit comparison characterized by the use of *like* or *as*. *Comparison* preserves its literalness, and it is essentially in this feature that the difference between the present day simile or metaphor and comparison is found. The few examples of this trope can be tabulated as follows:

1. *Venus* and *Cupyde* Thou Manhod shalt a myrrour bene a ryght.
                    Comparison of things different.

2. *Age* Olde *Age* am I, with lokkes, thynne and hore,
            Of our short lyfe, *the last and best part*.
            Comparison of things equal.

3. *Deth* To me a *fole*, some of your *wise brayne*.
             Comparison of contraries or contrarietas (antithesis of affirmation).

4. *Time* Promising of his *name*, an *endlesse flowre*.
             Comparison of things different.

5. *Eternity* Thou *mortall Tyme* every man can tell,
             Art nothyng els but the *mobilite*,
             Of sonne and mone chaungyng in euery degre.
             Comparison of things equal.

John Hoskins' thesis in support of amplification will serve as a fitting synthesis to the discussion thereof in the analysis of More's 'Nyne Pageauntes':

> To amplify and illustrate are two the chiefest ornaments of eloquence, and gain of men's minds two the chiefest advantages, admiration and belief. For how can you commend a thing more acceptably to our attention than by telling us it is extraordinary and by showing us that it is evident? There is no looking at a comet if it be little or obscure, and we love and look on the sun above all stars for these two excellencies, his greatness, his clearness: such in speech is amplification and illustration.[126]

Hoyt H. Hudson makes the observation that amplification employed in this sense means magnification and emphasis rather than dilation. Consequently, it refers more to the subject than the language of discourse.[127] Subject matter can be magnified or minimized by means of language in the following ways: (1) by choice of word; (2) by successive contrasts of terms; (3) by incrementum: building up several degrees of emphasis; (4) by comparison with something less or more striking which will make the thing compared seem greater (or less) inferior by contrast; (5) by ratiocination: enlarging an incidental matter so as to imply the point itself; (6) by accumulation achieved through a repetition of synonyms.[128]

Amplification thus gives rise to two structures: the paratactic and the hypotactic. Parataxis is the placing of prepositions or clauses one after another without indicating by connecting words the relation of subordination between them. For example, 'He laughed; she cried'. Here the co-ordinatives are placed side by side as opposed to syntactic structure, which shows the connection and relation in a sentence, since it is a harmonious adjustment of parts. Hypotaxis is dependent and subordinate in construction and, to make a hypotactic element paratactic, the joining connective which shows this relationship is merely omitted.

Thomas More's poem on the 'Nyne pageauntes' makes use of both the paratactic and the hypotactic structure in the amplification of his subject. This dilation in each stanza consists of the description of the actions of the first three personified abstractions, 'Chyldhod', 'Manhod', and 'Venus and Cupyde', in the first three stages of man's life. The poet then emphasizes the physical descriptions of 'Age' and 'Deth', while 'Fame' and 'Time' are delineated in terms of one outstanding symbol. The description of 'Eternitee' is, in the writer's estimation, the most colorless of all, and the young humanist's interest in the 'New' science outweighs his poetical ability in these verses.

Thomas More uses amplification in the sense of emphasis rather then mere dilation for two reasons: (1) the nature and form of the treatment he gives the 'Nyne pageauntes' requires brevity; (2) the individualized descriptions of the personified abstractions necessitate emphasis rather than dilation in a seven-line verse. The following will show the paratactic and hypotactic structure More employs on a small scale in these verses:

Parataxis	*Hypotaxis*

I am called Chyldhod,
   in play is all my mynde,
To cast a coyte, a coks-
   tele, and a ball . . .
	A toppe can I set, *and* dryve it
	   in his kynde.
	But would to god these hatefull
	   bookes all,
	Were in a fyre brent to pouder
	   small

The grayhounde to the course,
   the hawke to the flyght . . .
	Manhod I am *therefore* I me delyght,
	Yet thynketh this boy his peuishe
	   game swetter,
	But what no force, his reason
	   is no better.

Fame I am called, maruayle you nothing . . .	

Thou Manhod shalt a myrrour bene
   a ryght,
By us subdued for all thy great
   pryde,
My fyry dart perceth thy tender syde.
	Now thou whiche erst despysedst
	   children small,
	Shall waxe a chylde agayne and
	   be my thrall.

Me nedeth not to bost,
I am Eternitee,
The very name signifyeth well.

Discende from your chayre, set a
  part your pryde,
Witsafe to lende (though it be to
  your payne)
To me a fole, some of your wise brayne.

Therefore Cupyde withdrawe thy
  fyry dart.

Therefore sage father greatly
  magnifyed . . .

When they shall leve theyr course
  thou shalt be brought,
For all thy pride and bostying
  into nought.

Abbreviation, which is the antithesis of amplification, is a poetical device, and if properly used, it adds elegance and force to the poem. Chaucer employed the two principal means of the use of absolute construction, and especially the figure called *occupatio*, that is, the refusal to describe or narrate extensively, in *The Squire's Tale* with striking poetic effect. Likewise, Sidney used abbreviation effectively in his *Arcadia* by his two obvious methods of diminishing single terms: (1) by denying the contrary, as for example, *not misliked*; (2) by denying the right use of the word and attributing this usage to the error of others, as for example: 'Those fantastical-minded people which children and musicians call lovers'.[129]

Thomas More uses the rhetorical scheme asyndeton as his principal means of abbreviation to achieve the desired rhetorical and poetic effect he wanted his allegory to attain. By means of this figure two or more words or clauses follow one another without interlinking conjunctions. The following four examples are conspicuous ones in More's poem:

I am called Chyldhod, in play is all my mynde,   C. iii^r A. 4.
The grayhounde to the course, the hawke to the flyght, C. iii^r B. 8.
Discende from your chayre, set a part your pryde . . . . C. iii^v B. 2.

Thomas More's verses are such coherent periods[130] of rhetorical thought and structure that a short discussion of style will not be amiss in the analysis of this poem. Furthermore, in the Renaissance as well as in the medieval period, figures of words which were divided into tropes and schemes and figures of thought were enumerated under style. These figures added perspicuity, elegance, and force to poetry in general.

George Puttenham devotes Chapter V of the third book of *The Arte of English Poesie* to a discussion of style, which he defines as follows:

Stile is a constant & continuall phrase or tenour of speaking and writing, extending to the whole tale or processe of the poeme or historie, and not properly to any peece or member of a tale: but is of words speeches and sentences together, a certaine contriued forme and qualitie, many times naturall to the writer, many times his peculier by election and arte, and such as either he keepeth by skill, or holdeth on by ignorance, and will not or peraduenture cannot easily alter into any other.[131]

103

'Style is the man' applies also to Thomas More's case, for in his style of writing poetry one can detect the careful rhetorician and the precise logician. His use of parallel structure, the piling up of nouns and adjectives to achieve a cumulative effect, the subordinating and coordinating functions of well-chosen connectives, and his vigorous use of infinitives – all point to his efficiency and skill in the art of rhetoric. On the other hand, each stanza can be loosely compared to a syllogism with a major premise, a minor premise, and a conclusion. For Example, the one on Chyldhod may be analysed thus:

Major premise	I am called Chyldhod, in play is all my mynde,
Minor premise (specific examples)	To cast a coyte, a cokstele, and a ball. A toppe can I set, and dryue it in his kynde.
Conclusion or *Application* (in reference to the nature of Chyldhod)	But would to god these hatefull bookes all, Were in a fyre brent to pouder small. Than myght I lede my lyfe alwayes in play: Whiche lyfe god sende me to myne endyng day.[132]

'Therefore' does not appear to be a poetical word; yet More uses it four times in three different ways: (1) as a medial connecting link, 'Manhod I am *therefore* I me delyght . . .'; (2) the final connecting link, as for example in 'Wyse and discrete: the publike wele *therefore*'; (3) the initial word used to enforce the speaker's address as in the following two examples: '*Therefore* Cupyde withdrawe thy fyry dart', and '*Therefore* sage father greatly magnifyed . . .' The use of the word 'therefore' implies logical reasoning and the proof or the refutation of an established premise, and consequently, savors of judiciary proceedings and of the sanctions of the law courts.

More's adroit use of parallelisms adds felicity to his expression and gives the verses a poetical touch. This parallel structure is composed mostly of infinitive forms, and these give vigour to the first person nouns and pronouns and add strength to the active voice verbs. Childhood and Manhood introduce themselves in the opening lines of the verse and then inform us that their pleasure is to participate in the following action peculiar to their state in life:

Chyldhod	I am called Chyldhod, in play is all my mynde,
	. . . .
	To cast a coyte, a cokstele, and a ball. C. iii^r A. 5.
Manhod	Manhod I am therefore I me delyght
	To hunt and *hawke, to nourishe* up and *fede.* C. iii^r B. 7.

The remaining four uses of infinitive forms give emphasis to the meaning of the verse and accentuate its rhythm:

Manhod	And *to bestryde* a good and lusty stede.	C. iii[r] B. 9.
Age	I help *to rule* to my labour and smart.	C. iii[v] A. 2.
Deth	Witsafe *to lende* (though it be to your payne).	C. iii[v] B. 3.
Fame	Maugry thy teeth *to lyue* cause hym shall I.	C. iii[v] C. 4.

A means of amplification which Thomas More uses very dexterously for purposes of rhetorical emphasis and poetical embellishment is the figure accumulation, which in Tudor figures of rhetoric is termed synathroismos.[133] It is the heaping together of words which signify things of like nature. John Hoskins in his *Directions for Speech and Style* reminds us that Cicero used it often in his orations but seldom exceeded three such cumulative enumerations. Others, among whom Thomas More can be numbered, 'follow it to four clauses',[134] as can readily be seen in the examples from his verses that follow:

Deth	Though I be foule ugly lene and mysshape (4)	C. iii[v] A. 10.
Venus and Cupyde	Who so ne knoweth the strength, power and myght	(3) C. iii[r] C. 8.
Chyldhod	To cast a coyte, a cokstele, and a ball.	(3) C. iii[r] A. 5.

Puttenham praises this figure in *The Arte of English Poesie* (1589) and attributes earnestness and force to it when he says:

> Arte and good pollicie moues us many times to be earnest in our speach, and then we lay on such load and so go to it by heapes as if we would winne the game by multitude of words & speaches, not all of one but of diuers matter and sence, for which cause the Latines called it *Congeries* and we the *heaping* figure . . .[135]

This figure obviously is very appropriate for the triumph scheme in More's 'Nyne pageauntes' whereby one personified abstraction endeavours to conquer the preceding one in order to establish and ascertain its superiority over it.

Perhaps more than any other rhetorical device, More's well-integrated use of coordinating and subordinating connectives makes each stanza a unified and comprehensive structural pattern. In the first stanza, on 'Chyldhod', the introductory connective *But* in line four connects the first part of the stanza, which is the exposition of the child's frame of mind, with the succeeding two lines which take the form of a desire in the subjunctive mood. The sixth line begins with *Than* and is followed by the application of the child's dream to what would constitute real happiness for him. Although a multiple use of connectives in one short verse ordinarily makes it prosaic and dull, in More's case his connectives, predicated on coordination and subordination, give the verses a narrative flavor and a cyclic movement, which is comparable to the reaching of a climax. In the hands of an unskilled rhetorician the result may have been less felicitous, and the poem may have been marred instead of strengthened by these inclusions.

In the second stanza, on 'Manhod', the connectives *Yet* and *But* in the last two verses provide the antithesis which gives it a forceful conclusion:

> *Yet* thynketh this boy his peuishe game swetter,
> *But* what no force, his reason is no better.[136]

In the third stanza, on 'Venus and Cupyde', the connective *Now* in the sixth verse has the flavor of dialogue and consequently gives it a dramatic quality:

> *Now* thou whiche erst despysedst children small.
> Shall waxe a chylde agayne and be my thrall.[137]

The stanza on 'Deth' contains five connectives, two of which are coordinating ones while three are used subordinately:

Subordination	*Though* I be foule ugly lene and mysshape,
Coordination	*Yet* there is none in all this worlde wyde,
Subordination	*That* may my power withstande or escape,
Coordination	*Therefore* sage father greatly magnifyed,
Subordination	*Witsafe* to lende (*though* it be to your payne) . . .[138]

In the next stanza, on 'Fame', the subordinating conjunction *Though* links the first line cogently with the second, while the coordinating conjunction *For* in the third line intrepidly resolves the suspicion the specious description of Fame may have conjured in the minds of simple people:

> Fame I am called, maruayle you nothing,
> *Though* I with tonges am compassed all rounde
> *For* in voyce of people is my chiefe liuyng.[139]

The relative pronouns *Who* and *Whom* and the introductory adverb *When* give unity, cohesion, and force to the complex sentences without making the verses unduly prosaic and verbose:

> I *whom* thou seest with horyloge in hande,
> Am named tyme, the lord of euery howre,
> I shall in space destroy both see and lande.
> O simple fame, how darest thou man honowre,
> Promising of his name, an endlesse flowre,
> *Who* may in the world have a name eternall,
> *When* I shall in proces distroy the world and all.[140]

In his discussion of the influence of medieval rhetoric on Chaucer's poetry, Professor Manly peremptorily dispenses with the treatment of 'Style and its

Ornaments' calling it a 'vast and tangled jungle'.[141] 'The tangle', he says, 'is suggested by the fact that there are recognized, defined, and discussed thirty-five colours, or figures of words, twenty figures of thought, and ten varieties of tropes, with nine more sub-varieties. These figures fall into two very distinct classes: first, those in which human emotion and aesthetic feeling have always found utterance – metaphor, simile, exclamation, rhetorical question, and the like; and second, a vast mass of highly artificial and ingenious patterns of word and thought, such as using the same word at the end of a line as at the beginning, heaped-up rhymes, and alliteration'.[142]

Style, or *elocutio*, the third part of medieval rhetoric, deals primarily with the choice and arrangements of words in a sentence. Such words should be chosen which are clear, elegant, and appropriate. It presupposes further that the sentences be grammatically correct, artistically arranged, and adorned with figurative language. As a matter of fact, to the rhetorician, the glory and acme of style lay in the use of figures of thought, sound, and language. The classification of these figures can, however, become such an exasperating and confused process that the following brief and simplified outline will serve our purpose adequately:

I.   Figures are divided into figures of words, thought, and sound.

    A. Figures of words may be divided into tropes and schemes.

    B. A trope (from the Greek *to turn*) is a word turned from its original or literal signification to another, on account of some resemblance. Examples: metaphor, metonymy, synecdoche, etc.

    C. A scheme is a figure of arrangement in which words are used in their literal sense but are arranged or repeated in an unusual or artificial way as in alliteration or in balanced phrases (parison).

II. Figures of thought are forms of language in which the words are used in their proper and literal signification, but in which the figure consists in a turn of thought. Examples: apostrophe, comparison, climax, etc.

III. Figures of sound or what Puttenham in *The Arte of English Poesie* calls *Auricular Figures*.[143]

IV. Overlapping among these figures is inevitable, for one may be at the same time a figure of word as well as a figure of thought.

Thomas More does not pad his nine stanzas making up the 'Nyne pageauntes' with excessive ornamentation or with an involved framework of rhetorical devices, but employs these devices functionally rather than ornamentally. In this regard his practice approximates Erasmus' treatment of figures and his method of amplifying examples, comparisons, and contrasts in the *De Copia*.[144]

Likewise, John Hoskins in the sixteenth century dispensed with the lengthy and technical classification of figures and listed them according to their functional purposes of (1) variation; (2) amplification, and (3) illustration. Since there is little difference between the last two categories, that of amplifying and that of illustrating the subject matter, they will be merged into one heading in the following analysis of More's figurative devices:

Figures Used to Vary the Subject Matter

Figures of words : Tropes

1. *Metaphor –* translates a word from its literal signification to another which it commonly does not denote at all.

Venus and Cupyde	Thou *Manhod* shalt a *myrrour* bene a ryght.	C. iii^r C. 9.
Time	Am named *tyme*, the *lord* of euery howrc.	C. iii^v D. 2.
Time	Promising of his *name*, an endlesse *flowre*.	C. iii^v D. 5.

2. *Metonymy –* substitutes for the name of a thing the name of an attribute or an adjunct.

Fame	For in *voyce* of people is my chiefe *liuyng*.	C. iii^v C. 1.
Fame	Maugry thy *teeth* to lyue cause hym shall I.	C. iii^v C. 4.
Fame	Though I with *tonges* am compassed all rounde.	C. iii^v B. 10.

3. *Synecdoche –* indicates a part by naming the whole or the whole by a part.

Chyldhod	I am called *Chyldhod*, in *play* is all my *mynde*.	C. iii^r A. 4.
Deth	Witsafe to lende (though it be to your payne) To me a fole, *some* of your wise *brayne*.	C. iii^v B. 3–4.

Figures of words : Schemes

4. *Epanodos –* repeats the first word of a passage in the middle or the middle word at the end.

Chyldhod	Than myght I lede my *lyfe* alwayes in play: Whiche *lyfe* god sende me to myne *endyng* day.	C. iii^r A. 9–10.
Time	Promising of his *name*, an *endlesse* flowre . . .	C. iii^v D. 5–6.

5. *Climax* – leads by degrees to make the final word or statement the synthesis of its meaning.

Time	I shall in space destroy both see and lande.	
	. . . .	
	When I shall in proces distroy the world and all.	C. iii^v D. 3–7.

6. *Apodioxis* – rejects the argument of an opponent as absurd, impertinent, or false.

Manhod	Yet thinketh this boy his peuishe game swetter, But what no force, his reason is no better.	C. iii^r B. 11. C. 1.
Age	Chargeable matters shall of loue oppresse, The childish game and ydle businesse.	C. iii^v A. 4–5.

7. *Hyperbaton* – inverts the natural order of words or phrases in a sentence to emphasize the idea.

Manhod	Manhod I am therefore *I me delyght.*	C. iii^r B. 6.
Age	Chargeable matters shall *of love oppresse.*	C. iii^v A. 4.
Deth	Yet there is none in all *this worlde wyde.*	C. iii^v A. 11.
Fame	*Maugry thy teeth* to lyue *cause hym shall I, Of people* in parpetuall memory.	C. iii^v C. 4–5.
Time	Promising *of his name*, an endlesse flowre . . .	C. iii^v D. 5.

8. *Asyndeton* – forms a series of words or clauses without interlinking conjunctions.

Manhod	To hunt and *hawke, to nourishe* up and fede,	C. iii^r B. 7.
	The grayhounde to the *course, the hawke* to the flyght.	C. iii^r B. 8
Deth	Discende from your *chayre, set a* part your pryde	
	Witsafe to lende (though it be to your payne) . . .	C. iii^v B. 2–3.

9. *Ecphonesis* – exclaims vehemently some emotion or passion, as wonder and admiration, despair, wishing, indignation, derision, etc.

| Manhod | Yet thynketh this boy his peuishe game swetter, | |
| | But what no force, his reason is no better. | C. iii^r B. 11. C. 1. |

10. *Optatio* – declaring a wish to either God or men.

| Chyldhod | But would to god these hatefull bookes all, | |
| | Were in a fyre brent to pouder small. | C. iii^r A. 7–8. |

11. *Erotesis* – affirms or denies a point strongly in the form of a question to which no answer is expected.

| Venus and Cupyde | Who so ne knoweth the strength, power and myght, | |
| | Of Venus and me her lytle sonne Cupyde . . . | C. iii^r C. 7–8. |

12. *Isocolon* – Constructing sentences of equal members of successive phrases or clauses.

Manhod	To hunt and hawke, to nourishe up and fede,	
	The grayhounde to the course, the hawke to the flyght,	
	And to bestryde a good and lusty stede.	C. iii^r B. 7–9.

13. *Metathesis* – changing the natural order of letters within a word, for example, *brids* for birds.

Chyldhod	Were in a fyre *brent* to pouder small	
	. . . . .	C. iii^r B. 8.

14. *Apophthegm* – expressing a truth in a short, pointed way.

Fame	Maugry thy teeth to lyue cause hym shall I	
	Of people in parpetuall memory.	C. iii^v C. 4–5.

15. *Anastrophe* – an unusual arrangement of words or clauses within a sentence.

Time	Who may in the world have a *name*	
	eternall . . .	C. iii^v D. 6.

Figures Used to Amplify and Illustrate the Subject Matter

Figures of Thought –

1. *Hyperbole* – exaggerates ideas or emotions in order to emphasize their importance.

Venus and Cupyde	Who so ne knoweth the strength, power and myght . . .	C. iii^r C. 8.
Deth	Though I be foule ugly lene and mysshape . . .	C. iii^v A. 10.
Time	Therefore sage father greatly magnifyed . . .	C. iii^v B. 1.

2. *Irony* – expresses in words a meaning directly opposite that intended.

Time	O *simple fame*, how darest thou man honowre.	C. iii^v D. 4.

3. *Prosopopoeia* – attributes to a beast, to an inanimate object or to an idea the characteristics of a living person.

Age	Chargeable matters shall of *loue oppresse*,	
	The childish game and *ydle bysinesse*.	C. iii^v A. 4–5.
Fame	For in *voyce* of people is my chiefe liuyng.	C. iii^v C. 1.

Fame	Maugry thy teeth to *lyue* cause him shall I,	
	Of people in parpetuall *memory*.	C. iii^v C. 4–5.
Manhod	Yet thinketh this boy his *peuishe game swetter*.	C. iii^r B. 11.

4. *Epitheton* – qualifies the subject with an appropriate adjective.

Chyldhod	Whiche lyfe god sende me to myne *endyng day*.	C. iii^r A. 10.
Manhod	And to bestryde a *good* and *lusty stede*.	C. iii^r B. 9.
Venus and Cupyde	By us subdued for all thy *great pryde* . . . My *fyry dart* perceth thy *tender syde* Now thou whiche erst despysedst *children small* . . .	C. iii^r C. 11. D. 1–2.
Age	Therefore Cupyde withdrawe thy *fyry dart*, *Chargeable matters* shall of loue oppresse, The *childish game* and *ydle bysinesse*.	C. iii^v A. 3–5.
Eternitee	Thou *mortall Tyme* euery man can tell . . .	C. iii^r A. 8.

5. *Antithesis* – Expresses contrasted ideas in adjoining phrases or clauses.

Age	*Chargeable matters* shall of loue oppresse, The *childish game* and *ydle bysinesse*.	C. iii^v A. 4–5.
Deth	To me a *fole*, some of your *wise brayne*.	C. iii^v B. 4.
Fame	When thou a *noble man* hast brought to *grounde* . . .	C. iii^v C. 3.
Eternitee	When they shall leue theyr course thou shalt be brought, For all thy *pride* nad *bostyng* into *nought*.	C. iii^r A. 11. B. 1.

6. *Peristasis* – amplifies the subject by giving circumstances of persons or circumstances of places, time, occasion.

112

Fame	Fame I am called, maruayle you nothing, Though I with *tonges am compassed all rounde* For in voyce of people is my chiefe liuyng.	C. iii^v B. 9–10. C. 1.

7. *Paralepsis* – emphasizes a point by pretending to pass it unnoticed.

| Eternitee | *Me nedeth not to bost*, I am Eternitee
The very name signifyeth well. | C. iii^r A. 5–6. |

8. *Epergesis* – places two substantives together without a verb, the second defining the first as in an appositive.

| Age | Olde Age am I, with lokkes, thynne and hore,
Of our short *lyfe*, the last and best part. | C. iii^r D. 9–10. |

9. *Apostrophe* – Addresses directly some person or thing, animate or inanimate, present or absent.

| Fame | *O cruel death*, thy power I confounde. | C. iii^v C. 2. |
| Time | *O simple fame*, how darest thou man honowre. | C. iii^v D. 4. |

10. *Paraphrasis* – states the same idea in other ways.

| Time | O simple fame, how darest thou man *honowre*,
Promising of his name, an endlesse *flowre*,
Who may in the world have a *name eternall*. | C. iii^v D. 4–6. |

11. *Parenthesis* – inserts as an aside a word, phrase, or sentence within a sentence which is complete in itself.

| Deth | Witsafe to lende (though it be to your payne) . . . | C. iii^v B. 3. |

113

12. *Accumulation* – heaps together words which signify things of a like nature.

Venus and Cupyde	Who so ne knoweth the strength, power and myght . . .	C. iii^r C. 8.
Deth	Though I be foule ugly lene and mysshape . . .	C. iii^v A. 10.

13. *Metabasis* – moves from one point to another by use of a linking summary.

Deth	*Therefore* sage father greatly magnifyed Discende from your chayre, set a part your pryde.	C. iii^v B. 1–2.
Age	Wyse and discrete: the publike wele *therefore*, I help to rule to my labour and smart.	C. iii^v A. 1–2.

14. *Characterismus* – description of the body or the mind of a person.

Age	Olde Age am I, with lokkes, thynne and hore, Of our short lyfe, the last and best part,	C. iii^r D. 9–10.
	Wyse and discrete.	C. iii^v A. 1.

The figures which Puttenham calls 'auricular' are characterized by sound, accent, and time; they are found in single words, clauses of speech, and complete sentences.[145] However, it is drawing the line of demarcation too sharply to say that these figures appeal to the ear only without having any impact on the mind. To this class belong the following figures: hyperbaton, parenthesis, asyndeton, metathesis, isocolon, epanodos, epergesis, and anastrophe. These schemes and tropes have been included in the above lists under the Figures of Words and Figures of Thought.

The figures Thomas More uses in 'The Nyne Pageauntes' are so adroitly interwoven into the texture of the thought and the framework of his poetical pattern that they do not stand out as patches of ostentatious display. Hoskins' injunction in this regard, 'But let discrecion bee the greatest and generall figure of figures',[146] can well apply to More's style, which has for its aim the saying of a thing plainly rather than ornately. With this purpose in mind, he employs clear diction which the nuances of rhetorical art do not pervert or distort. A. W. Reed lists only seven words and phrases which may be unintelligible to the modern reader in his 'Philological Notes' to More's poem, which consists of fifty-seven lines. Of these seven, three refer to a child's game popular in the sixteenth century, one is a scheme used for rhetorical emphasis, while one is a colloquial expression which, because of its eloquence and pithiness, aptly fits the domain of poetry. Apropos of the last expression, 'Maugry thy teeth',[147] in addition to Reed's note interpreting it as 'however unwilling (thou) Death mayest be',[148] the word 'maugre' which means 'in spite of, notwithstanding all one can do', was often used with beard, cheeks, eyes, face, heart, mind, mouth, nose, visage, and will following it. He does not include the expression 'But what no force'[149] which may puzzle modern readers; perhaps he assumes that this expression can readily be understood from its context. The literal meaning of these words, however, is 'it maketh no force, it does not matter, or simply, no matter'.[150]

The strength of Thomas More's diction in these verses consists in a virile use of fifty-six verbs, including the infinitives which strike the keynote of engrossing activity; of eighty-seven nouns, fifty-one of which are abstract and thirty-six concrete; and of forty adjectives which add luster and colour to the words they describe and modify. According to twentieth-century standards, the poem may appear prosaic and bereft of imagery, but on the other hand, its simplicity and cogency adumbrate the style of Jonson, Dryden, and Addison.

Since the poem has already been considered as a whole in the treatment of it thus far, only a few pertinent remarks remain to be made about each stanza individually.

The first stanza, 'Chyldhod', is simple in its connotation and apparently devoid of complex figurative devices. Its chief merit, however, lies in its smooth and felicitous rhythm which harmonizes effectively with the theme of the poem as well as the painting on the tapestry.

> I am / callèd Chyld / hod in play / is all / my mynde /
> To cast / a coyte / a cok / stele and / a ball /
> A toppe / can I set / and dryue / it in / his kynde /
> But would / to god / these hate / full book / es all /
> Were in / a fyre / brent / to pou / der small /
> Than, myght / I lede / my lyfe / al wayes / in play /
> Whiche lyfe / god sende / me to / myne en / dyng day /

Lines one, two, three, and six, contain three inversions, which give the verses sufficient flexibility to prevent monotony of sound structure. The substitutions in the first and third lines give them pleasing versatility, while the spondee and the pyrrhic add emphasis and dramatic quality to the entire stanza.

The mood of these verses is light-hearted and gay and is supported by the tone quality, which is patterned and accentuated by the skillful use of the vowel sounds connotating joy and frivolity. Professor Tolman gives an interesting account of the emotional suggestiveness of vowel sounds in his essay on 'The symbolic Value of English Sounds'. He uses the following table for his interpretation:

i as in little	i as in I	oo as in wood
e „ „ met	u „ „ due	ow „ „ cow
a „ „ mat	a „ „ what	o „ „ gold
e „ „ mete	a „ „ father	oo „ „ gloom
ai „ „ fair	oi „ „ boil	aw „ „ awe
a „ „ mate	u „ „ but	

'The sounds at the beginning of this scale', he says, 'are especially fitted to express uncontrollable joy and delight, gayety, triviality, rapid movement, brightness, delicacy, and physical littleness; the sounds at the end are peculiarly adapted to express horror, solemnity, awe, grief, slowness of motion, darkness, and extreme or oppressive greatness of size . . .'[151]

Thomas More uses the vowels placed at the beginning of the scale, namely, the i, a, and e to set the tempo for the poem and to determine its tone quality. Thus, in the first line of verse the following vowels are used:

$$I a / a y / o i a / i a / y y /$$

The y in 'my mynde' and 'Chyldhod' has the sound of a long i which is in keeping with the spirit of the rest of the verse. In the second line, continuity and progression of action are effectively shown through the repeated usage of the vowels of o and a which are used eight times in a line of verse which consists of ten syllables:

$$o a / a o i / a o / e a / a a /$$

The anapest in the third line preceded and followed by iambuses gives it a rapid, twirling movement while the vowel sounds of e and i attach to it a spirit of conviction and determination:

$$a o / a i e / a y / i i / i y /$$

True to Tolman's scale of 'Symbolic Value of English Sounds' the vowel u and the digraph ou change the tone pattern in the fourth line and presage fear, anxiety, and disappointment:

$$u o u / o o / e a / u o o / e a /$$

The fifth verse resumes the child's carefree attitude, and in hopeful anticipation of complete freedom from the drudgery of books, the light vowels of e, i, o, and a, are again used to form the pattern of tone quality in this line:

$$e i / a y / e / o o u / e a /$$

With what joy and eagerness the child envisions a bright and carefree future is evident in the next line, which is composed of e's, i's (or y's having the same sound), and a's:

ey / ie / yy / aa / ia /

The last verse ends with an emphatic and hopeful plea for a life free from care, anxiety, and mental strain:

iy / oe / eo / ye / ya /

The emotional impact of the sound pattern and tone quality is further emphasized by the skillful use of the caesura. It sets the tone for the poem and adjusts itself functionally to the idea denoted by the words and suggested by the vowel pattern as illustrated above. The regular medial caesura was used widely in the early Elizabethan period, and More employs it with felicity and grace whenever the sense and the theme of the poem necessitate it. He further employs the caesura to facilitate the reading of the verses and to lend life and vigour to the painting depicted in the tapestry by giving it dramatic and lifelike qualities of dialogue:

I am called Chyldhod // in play is all my mynde /

In like manner More uses a medial caesura in the third line:

A toppe can I set // and dryue it in his kynde /

The two caesuras which follow are placed after a stressed syllable for the sake of rhetorical emphasis, while the third one after an unstressed syllable precipitates a sigh of hoped-for relief:

But would / tŏ gód // thĕse háte / fŭll boók / ĕs all /
Weře in / aˣfyré / brént / tŏ póu / deř smáll /
Thán myˣght / I léde / m̆y lýfe // al waˣyes / in pláy /
Whiˇche lyfe / god sénde / mĕ // tŏ / m̆yne end / yˇng dáy /

The rhyme scheme pattern in this rhyme royal stanza is made up of the following rhymes: a b a b b c c

mynde	a
ball	b
kynde	a
all	b
small	b
play	c
day	c

The first three verses bring out the essence of childhood, i.e., 'in play is all my mynde', and the favourite pastimes of a carefree youngster are enumerated with refreshing vitality. The fourth verse is coloured with emotional intensity and overshadows the brightness of his happy life with a presentiment of discouragement and resentment, 'But would to god these hateful books all . . .'. In the fifth line a definite and hopeful decision is made, but in theory only, as the child gives vent to his pent-up emotions by saying that he desires that the books should be 'in a fyre brent to pouder small'. After releasing his anger on the source of this oppression of his childhood happiness, he again becomes joyous and hopeful and says ecstatically:

Than myght / I lede / my lyfe / alwayes / in play.[152]

He ends his expository declamation with a prayer saying:

Whiche lyfe / god sende / me to / myne end / yng day.[153]

The imagery in this stanza is not strikingly original, but neither is the subject matter it alludes to. Apropos of this fact, there is consistency of theme and structure and a levelling down of the style to the idea represented in the first line, 'I am called Chyldhod, in play is all my mynde'. One can presume that the painting on the hanging of rich cloth was emblazoned with colourful and scenic representations of the stages of man's life; therefore, the same richness of imagery and an overemphasis on rhetorical art would make the tapestry surfeited with excessive ornamentation. The simplicity and vigour of the nine verses against the colourful pictorial designs prevent them from becoming unduly pompous and give them a balance that is pleasing and a tone that is wholesome and refreshing.

In the second pageaunt was paynted a goodly, freshe, younge man, rydyng upon a goodly horse, havynge an hawke on his fyste, and a brase of grayhoundes folowyng hym. And under the horse was paynted the same boy, that in the first pageaunte was playing at the tope and squyrge. And over this second pageant the wordyng was thus.

Manhod I am therefore I me delyght,
To hunte and hawke, to nourishe up and fede,
The grayhounde to the course, the hawke to the flyght,
And to bestryde a good and lusty stede.
These thynges become a very man in dede,
Yet thynketh this boy his peuishe game swetter,
But what no force his reason is no better.[154]

In the second pageant we see a colourful picture of a healthy and handsome young man exulting in the glory of his newly-achieved manhood and finding

118

delight in typical manly sports. The image is truly Renaissance in character, and the last two lines with their reference to the 'mind', are indicative of More's interest in humanism and its influence upon him.

> Yet thynketh this boy his peuishe game swetter,
> But what no force, his reason is no better.[155]

As the lad grows older he acquires more reason and learning, and not only his activities change but also his convictions and outlook on life. As childhood is characterized by play and irresponsibility, so too the distinctive features of manhood are self-complacency and pride.

> Manhod I am therefore I me delyght.[156]

It is a delight in the exercise of one's strength and vitality and an exuberant joy in the participation in outdoor sports. With scorn and disdain the supercilious youth looks back upon days gone by in his childhood and is confirmed in his belief that

> These thynges become a very man in dede.[157]

What the top and squyrge (whip) are to the young lad, the hawk and steed are to the sophisticated youth. Falconry, long lost to us, has always been considered a noble art and one closely associated with royalty. Stephen, King of England, is represented as bearing the hawk on his hand as a proof of royal blood.[158] The emperor, king, prince, duke, earl, baron, knight, esquire, lady, and young man had each a different type of hawk designated for his or her sport and enjoyment. These birds were held in such esteem that the laws against injuring them or destroying their eggs stipulated a year's imprisonment.[159]

Horse-racing likewise was confined almost entirely to persons of rank among our early ancestors. It was contrasted advantageously with card-playing, dicing, and stage plays by an old Puritanical writer of Elizabeth's time. This sport was practised for sheer amusement in the sixteenth century, and unlike the practice of it today, the race took place generally to find out the qualities of the animal. The youth in this stanza is interested primarily in riding 'a good and lusty stede' rather than engaging the animal in a race. On the other hand, he finds manly sport and delight in nourishing and feeding the 'grayhounde to the course' and 'the hawke to the flyght'. These are the things that become a man, and so he pities the lad engaged in childish play with tops and balls, for 'his reason is no better'.

The rhythm, tone quality, and diction harmonize effectively with the theme and structure of these seven verses. They lack imaginative appeal, but apparently this objective is not the poet's aim. Rather than to incite the emotions, More directs his appeal to the mind of the speaker in each stanza. The rhythm, composed for the most part of iambic pentameter, is made flexible and pleasing by the inclusion of four inversions and four substitutions in verses one, three, five, six, and seven:

> Mán hŏd / I am / ther fŏre / I me / dĕ lyght /
> Tŏ hunte / ånd hawke / tŏ nour / rishe up / and fede /
> The gray / hounde tŏ / thĕ course / thĕ hawke / tŏ thĕ flyght /
> And tŏ / be stryde / å good / ånd lus / tў stede /
> These thynges / be come / a vé / rў man / iň dede /
> Yet thyn / keth this boy / his pe / uishe game / swet tĕr /
> But what / nŏ force / his rea / soň iš nŏ / bet tĕr /

The inversion in the first verse, namely, / Mán hŏd / emphasizes the initial word, which is the key word in this stanza, and the inversion / therfore / shows the relationship of the ideas that follow. The two compound infinitives give the line strength and vigour, and the regularity of the meter sets the pace for anapestic substitution in the next verse. The second foot in the seventh line is a good example of a hovering accent whereby it may be either an iamb or a spondee according to the mood of the verse and the interpretation of the reader. The first foot in the fifth line may likewise be an iamb if regularity of rhythm is aimed at, or a spondee if emphasis and variation are the objectives:

> Thĕ gray / hounde tŏ / thĕ course / the hawke / to thĕ flyght /
> . . . .
> But what / ňo force / his rea / soň is nŏ / bet tĕr /
> . . . .
> Thesĕ thynges / bĕ come / å vé / rў man / iň dede /[160]

The assonance consisting of the *th* pattern seen in lines one, three, five, and six slows down the tempo of this verse and seems to give it a deliberate horse-trotting pace as, for example, can be seen in line three:

> *Th*e grayhounde to *th*e course, *th*e hawke to *th*e flyght.[161]

Line five strengthened by the initial *th* blend gives it a reflective tone:

> *Th*ese *th*ynges become a very man in dede . . .[162]

The emotional element in this verse can be summed up in two words: self-complacency and scorn. These characteristic features of the sophisticated young

120

man at first sight appear to be paradoxical, but since they emanate from one source, pride, they flow from one channel, i.e., love of self.

The diction is as clear as the hunter's horn calling the greyhounds to the hunt and as direct as the hawk's flight into the sky. Few words savour of an archaic usage and the syntax, in most cases, is such as one would accept today. The glaring example, however, of strained syntax in the first line ending with 'therefore I me delyght', enables the thought to be expressed forcefully. It also gives one the impression that the 'me' the young man discovered is a separate entity from the child he used to be, and this discovery of his new personality is the cause of untold joy and ecstasy. The word 'peuishe' in the sense of 'foolish, trifling, or silly' is an appropriate epithet for game. This use of it is much more closely related to its original meaning of arousing the emotions because of some foolish act than the circumscribed meaning one finds for it today.

Thomas More exhibits an admirable unity of design in this poem by his technique of linking the preceding stanza to the succeeding one. Thus, youthful desires and the consciousness of one's maturity are superseded by the tenacious hold of the power of Venus and Cupid over the heart and mind of man. The idea in this stanza resembles an early sixteenth century tapestry which belongs to the Flemish school of art. It consists of five subjects, the fourth one which concerns us, being called the 'Triumph of Cupid'. The central figure, Cupid, winged and blindfolded, sits high upon a pedestal that rises from an altar, red with curling flames. He is in the act of loosing an arrow from his bow. In the foreground is seen a procession of famous men and women whom the god of love (Cupido) attacks with his darts.[163]

In Jean de Meun's *Roman de la Rose*, Venus is delineated as a symbol of leisure which opens the way to the amorous life as opposed to the active and contemplative life.[164] This goddess of love is portrayed by the Latin poet Manilius with a mirror in her hand, the three Graces as her attendants and her little son, Amor, either at her side or painted on her girdle.[165] The last representation is of more concern to us since Thomas More alludes to the mirror in the third verse:

Thou Manhod shalt a myrrour bene a ryght.[166]

Cupid, on the other hand, is also delineated in several different ways, the predominant ones being the following:

1. One image shows him riding in a chariot drawn by lions which he has tamed, proof that the power of love is irresistible.

2. In another image he holds a fish in one hand and flowers in the other hand showing thereby that both land and sea are subject to the laws of love.

3. In this picture lightning is seen expending itself in vain against his wings and his weapons without affecting him in the least – he is made stronger as a result of this encounter.[167]

Cupid's arrows, wings, and blindfolded eyes have been favourite topics of discussion for scholars throughout the ages. His arrows signify the poignancy and directness with which love wounds the heart of man and maid; the wings portray the speed and swiftness which bear thoughts of the loved one to the lover's mind; the blindfolded eyes depict the abruptness and finality of love at first sight. Thomas More's Cupid apparently complied with this Renaissance description, for in line five one reads:

My fyry dart perceth thy tender syde.[168]

Exultingly Venus' son announces his triumph over the heart and mind of the sophisticated young man as he assures him in verses six and seven that the intoxicating power of love will make him his thrall:

Now thou whiche erst despysedst children small
Shall waxe a chylde agayne and be my thrall.[169]

The diction in this verse presents an interesting study of word accumulation and epithet building. In the first line of the poem one observes a crescendo effect of strong nouns which intensify and magnify the weight and prestige of Cupid's sway over men's hearts. But he alone is not able to achieve this desired effect; Venus, his mother, is ever at his side and stimulates him to complete victory. The 'great pryde of Manhod' is finally subdued as Cupid's 'fyry dart' perceth man's 'tender syde'. The two together with their 'strength, power and myght', overthrow the strength of man's convictions, the power of his reasoning, and the force of his resolutions.

The rhymes are not forced and affected but flow naturally from the thought content and carry the reader forward to a climactic conclusion. The third verse presents a strikingly appropriate metaphor wherein manhood is compared to a mirror not only in the sense of being a faithful reflection of the conquest of love over his proud and scornful heart, but especially in the now obsolete sense of serving as a warning to others and reflecting something to be avoided.[170] The phrase 'a ryght' following the verb 'shalt . . . bene' is used as an adverb meaning 'indeed', 'assuredly', or 'in a proper or fitting manner'.[171] Thus, it emphasizes the idea of punishment and retaliation which Cupid administers to the youth for resisting the power and attractions of love. In the end the god of love conquers and the young man, waxing 'a chylde agayne', becomes Cupid's 'thrall'.

After delineating childhood with its irresponsibility, manhood with its sophisticated pride, and Venus and Cupid with the magnetic attractions of love, there is a rather long interval of time before the next stage in man's life is presented. The fourth pageant exhibits a personification of Age with 'lokkes, thynne, and hore'. This picture is indeed a generally accepted and even stereotyped presentation, but it is the next line that startles the reader's passivity and challenges his acceptance of the general estimate of this stage of man's life:

Of our short lyfe, the last and best part.[172]

How few people consider old age the last and best part of life, and how surprising it is that Thomas More in the prime and vigour of his youth should have made this inference! Obviously, then, this conviction was born of deep reflection on life and serious contemplation of the passing joys of this world's goods. In these verses especially, More's humanism shows up brilliantly, for he takes a weather-beaten symbol and with a few meaningful words gives it new interpretation. This inference and conviction of the last stage of man's earthly life being the 'best part' of his existence is so contrary to the Epicurean motto, 'Eat, drink and be merry, for tomorrow you die', that it could be enunciated only by one whose eyes were set upon eternity's shores.

An interest in astronomy was rife in the sixteenth century, and it formed one of the four Arts of the Quadrivium at the University of Oxford.[173] In all probability, the young More studied this science with diligence and enthusiasm. The ages of life could be determined from the signs of the zodiac and corresponded to the four seasons of the year and the four temperaments of man as against the background of the four major colours of the solar spectrum.[174] Since the youthful More designed and possibly painted these pageants himself, the colours mentioned here have special bearing and significance, for they, then, add a new insight to his poem:

Seasons	Ages of life	Temperaments	Colours
Spring	Childhood	Sanguine	Red
Summer	Youth	Choleric	Yellow
Autumn	Maturity	Melancholic	Black
Winter	Old Age	Phlegmatic	White

Unlike the conventional portrayals of Old Age depicting a decrepit person whose presence one willingly avoids, whose voice no longer commands, and whose wise counsels are no longer heeded, Thomas More's representation of Old Age is virile, respectful, and elevating. At this stage of man's life he pictures him as:

Wyse and discrete: the publike wele therefore,
I help to rule to my labour and smart.[175]

More probably had his own father whom he loved, feared, and revered, in mind when he added wisdom and discretion to the above portrayal. His father, Judge John More, lived to a ripe old age and enjoyed the prestige, comfort, and security that respect and wisdom are heirs to. More's thoughts of him are kind and loving, sincere and grateful, and the words these thoughts evoked are in direct harmony with Holbein's famous crayon sketch of his father, who was then in his seventy-sixth year. Harpsfield, who based his account of the old judge on More's filial words, describes him thus:

> A man very virtuous, and of a very upright and sincere conscience, both in giving of counsel and judgment; a very merciful and pitiful man; and among other his good qualities and properties, a companionable, a merry, and pleasantly conceited man.[176]

The fact that John More became Judge of the King's Bench when he was in his seventy-second year testifies to his vigour of mind and alacrity of spirit. He lived to see his son's elevation to the Chancellorship, but was fortunately spared the sight of the sufferings and trials which took place within the next five years of More's life. Roper gives us a short but penetrating glimpse into the character of the wise father and dutiful son and portrays the affectionate relationship of understanding that existed between them:

> When Sir John lay on his death bed, Sir Thomas according to his duty, oftentimes with comfortable words most kindly came to visit him, and at his departure out of this world with tears, taking him about the neck, most lovingly kissed and embraced him, commending him into the hands of Almighty God.[177]

The sage father delineated on the tapestry sits in a chair which symbolized his authority and his control over the concupiscence of the eyes and the flesh, while Venus and Cupid are portrayed vanquished under his feet. This grave man has no inclination or time for the affairs of Cupid, which are so trivial and frivolous in comparison with the weighty matters of the public commonwealth. Reason controls his passions and subjugates the vagaries of youth as the following lines testify:

> Chargeable matters shall of loue oppresse,
> The childish game and ydle bysinesse.[178]

But even this wary and sagacious man did not fully escape the magnetism of Cupid's arrow of love, for in line five he indirectly implies that he too had been wounded by it:

> Therefore Cupyde withdrawe thy fyry dart.[179]

In view of the perspicuity of reason Old Age after a virtuous life is rewarded with, it is indeed remarkable that the young More, in whom the flame of passion was not subdued by age, should have such a penetrating insight into the fickleness of the allurements of youthful love.

The caesuras in this verse emphasize the sense and fit in with the serious and retrospective mood of the poem. The commas are timed to keep pace with the slow tempo as the following verses illustrate:

> Old Age am I, // with lokkes, thynne and hore,
> Of our short lyfe, // the last and best part.[180]

124

The colon in line three adds emphasis and necessitates a longer pause. It ends with a note of finality:

> Wyse and discrete: /// the publike wele therefore,
> I help to rule // to my labour and smart.[181]

The diction is clear and, for the most part, composed of monosyllables, particularly in the description of Old Age in the opening lines which consist of nineteen such short words before a disyllable is reached in verse three. The use of the word 'therefore' twice – at the end of the third line and the beginning of the fifth – points to the logical trend of thinking the verse follows. The verses appear to be bereft of emotion, but then in old age, man's passions are subdued, and his craving for excitement and pleasure is under control. The word 'smart' in line four may be used in the obsolete sense of 'severe or hard upon one' or it may employ the connotation of 'mental pain or suffering, grief, sorrow, or affliction'.[182] These two connotations fit in with the meaning of the line:

> I help to rule to my labour and smart,[183]

for ruling the commonwealth not only gives honour, wealth, and prestige, but it also offers a good share of mental anguish, grief, and disappointment.

The representation of Death as 'foule ugly lene and mysshape' in the following fifth verse is sharply reminiscent of the delineation of the famous 'Dance of Death' painted on the walls of a cloister situated on the north side of St. Paul's Cathedral. Hollar describes it for us in the following words:

> This was a single piece, a long train of all orders of men, from the Pope to the lowest of human beings; each figure has as his partner, Death; the first shaking his remembering hour-glass.[184]

Almost every church of eminence was decorated with this memorable frieze, and even the bridges in Germany and Switzerland were ornamented with its figures. John Lydgate, a monk of Bury in the Benedictine Abbey in Suffolk, translated a poem on this subject from the French verses which were inscribed under a painting of the same kind in St. Innocent's cloister in Paris. Lydgate's verses became an important adjunct to the 'Dance of Death' frieze in St. Paul's cloister. Allusions to its striking and powerful influence are seen in the work of William Langland in 'The Vision of Piers the Plowman' and in More's unfinished 'Treatise upon These Words of Holy Scripture, Remember the Last Things, and Thou Shalt Never Sin'. In the fifth stanza of the 'Nyne pageauntes' More graphically alludes to the following portrayal of death, which made a deep and lasting impression upon him as a youth:

> But if we not only hear this word 'deth', but also let sink into our hearts the very fantasy and deep imagination thereof, we shall perceive thereby that we were never so greatly moved by the beholding of the Dance of Death pictured in Paul's, as we shall feel ourselves stirred and altered by the feeling of that imagination in our hearts.[185]

The second and third verses forcefully synthesize the powerful meaning the 'Dance of Death' conjures, particularly in his tenacious and fatal grasp on the life of each human being:

> Yet there is none in all this worlde wyde,
> That may my power withstande or escape.[186]

In a book written in the fifteenth century, a conversation between Death and a widower contains this provocative passage:

> As soon as man is born, so soon has he received the pledge that he must die.[187]

The Black Death in the middle of the fourteenth century turned the people's thoughts to the wholesome remembrance of death. Some individuals raised their minds and hearts to God and repented their past sinful life, while others indulged passionately in the drowning pleasures of the senses and this world's goods in order to escape the dreadful thought of their misery. To avert the latter attitude, in many places a canvas stretched on a frame was suspended from a rope in the churches, containing on one side a beautiful youth and a maiden looking at themselves in a mirror, and on the other, a picture of Death with scythe or shovel and with his body entwined with worms and snakes. Every breath of wind turned the picture round, and thus, the rapid change from life to death was exhibited.[188]

In More's verses, Death jeeringly addresses the sage old father sitting complacently in his chair, and he says to him:

> Therefore sage father greatly magnifyed,
> Discende from your chayre, set a part your pryde.[189]

Then, with contempt ringing in his voice and a hypocritical smile hovering about his lips, one can almost see him in his mind's eye bow obsequiously before this respectable and domineering old man, as he says:

> Witsafe to lende (though it be to your payne)
> To me a fole, some of your wise brayne.[190]

The petition Death enunciates in the last two lines does not seem to be sincere at all but, conversely, implies a pungent tone of sarcasm and an envious attitude of wishing to maintain his superiority. This remark is irony in the sense that it expresses a meaning directly opposite the one intended. Death calls himself a 'fole' but by the same token he manages dexterously to subjugate even the Pope, the Emperor, the Bishop, the Bailif, the Astronomer, the Sergeant-at-Law, and all classes of people under his domination when, commanded by a higher authority, God Himself, he cuts the thread of their life for them. His own description of himself as a 'fole' is in keeping with his loathsome external

126

appearance. Thomas More makes a fitting comparison of the appearance of death and the effects of envy on man's heart and mind in his unfinished treatise on 'The Four Last Things', Speaking in glaring language of the hideous effects of sin, he says:

> And it so drinketh up the moisture of the body and consumeth the good blood, so discoloureth the face, so defaceth the beauty, so disfigureth the visage, leaving it all bony, lean, pale, and wan, that a person well set awork with enuy needeth none other image of death than his own face in a glass.[191]

In the sixth pageant More alludes to Lady Fame, who is encompassed all around with tongues and whose chief living is in the voice of the people. This powerful and supercilious lady conquers not only age, but death also lies vanquished at her feet. With convincing tones and a sneer on her face, she says belligerently:

> O cruel death, thy power I confounde.
> When thou a noble man hast brought to grounde
> Maugry thy teeth to lyue cause hym shall I,
> Of people in perpetuall memory.[192]

The ending couplet to these verses, besides adapting itself to frequent quotation, contains literary merit and technical excellence. One finds not only music and pleasing rhythm in these lines, but also an admirably devised metaphor in the phrase, 'Maugry thy teeth', which is reminiscent of death's gruesome skull. In spite of death's apparent victory, Lady Fame has such confidence in her own power and exhibits such superciliousness that she loudly proclaims her ability to make man live after death in the perpetual memory of people. Another apt metaphor is found in verse three of this stanza:

> For in voyce of people is my chiefe living.[193]

As Lady Fame thrives on her own caprices, her nourishment comes from the voice of the people which re-echoes throughout time's labyrinthine corridors long after man has left his earthly abode. She is not so sure, nevertheless, of the people's reaction to her specious power of immortality nor of their sincere attitude regarding her own person. Therefore, to gain their confidence and win their affection, she bids them disregard their questioning scrutiny of her integrity when she states boldly in lines two and three:

> Fame I am called, maruayle you nothing,
> Though I with tonges am compassed all rounde.[194]

Then, with a sweeping gesture savouring of pride and belligerency, she denounces death and asserts her power over her cadaverous kingdom:

> O cruel death, thy power I confounde.[195]

Thomas More's youthful but penetrating spirit pierces beyond the thin and glamorous veil of fame, and his Christian interpretation transcends the barrier of human glory and reaches out into the timeless stretches of Eternity. For him spirit is more important than matter, and a truly virtuous life more fruitful than wisdom which natural knowledge gives. He was a humanist with his foot on two continents – earth and heaven. With his eyes focused on spiritual values, he viewed this short life primarily as a preparation for the next.

The tropes he uses are taken from human physiognomy and are consistent with the nature of the personifications in the poem. As a matter of fact, they may be summed up in three connotative words: tongue, voice, and teeth. To Lady Fame, the tongue and voice are ascribed consistently, for through them man's fame is spread abroad. Death, on the other hand, is described in terms of the teeth, which immediately correlates this picture with the loathsome portrayal of death in St. Paul's cloister, which evidently made a deep and lasting impression on this young humanist.

More's personification of Lady Fame encompassed all around with tongues is an interesting and significant one. Hawe's famous 5,770-lined rhyme-royal allegory, 'The Pastime of Pleasure', also depicts Lady Fame riding on a palfrey 'encircled with tongues of fire'.[196] This work was printed in 1509. Since Stephen Hawes was the groom of King Henry the Seventh's chamber and since More was a member of Parliament, both men may have shared a mutual interest in poetry. Furthermore, Hawe's personified abstractions of Time and Eternity at the end of his poem seem to be closely patterned after More's interpretation and description of them.[197] The 'Nyne pageauntes' may have been written and the tapestries exposed to interested onlookers before 1509, since Thomas More supposedly wrote these pageants in his youth and thus assuredly before his thirty-first year. If the arduous dilettante in the art of poetry coined this symbolic figure which Shakespeare later used for the personification of Fame for his Rumour in the Chorus to *Henry the Fifth*,[198] then indeed Thomas More is to be credited with striking originality, which testifies to his poetic ability and initiative in the area of imagery. Perhaps, his characteristic interpretation of fame may help to support this presumed claim to the originality of this provocative image. For him Lady Fame is the proud and capricious sister of Lady Fortune against whom More waged a constant battle and whose speciousness he made it his lifelong ambition to expose. Almost every poem he writes or treatise he pens has a direct or an indirect allusion to Fame or Fortune, and the two states are so closely allied together that one seems to be predicated on the other. The connotation of 'tonges' as Thomas More uses the term is prefixed by the introductiory adverb 'Though', which significantly changes its meaning from something complimentary to something derogatory. At one time the interpretation of 'tonge' taken in a metaphorical sense was 'eulogy or fame'.[199] It could also be interpreted, however, as 'the stinging organ'[200] or as 'speech distinguished from or contrasted with thought and action'.[201] In this sense, then, it is closer to the 'tonges' referred to in the confusion of Babel than to the 'tonges of fire' on Pentecost Day. That the derogatory interpretation was used extensively during the sixteenth century is partially borne out by the fact that John Heywood's *Proverbs and Epigrams* (1562) contains the following epigram among many others with which More was undoubtedly familiar: 'Thy tounge runth before thy wit'.[202]

The meter in this sixth verse is vigourous and in parts a little rough, but this irregularity is in total agreement with the boasting of Lady Fame. In the first line of verse, the strong stresses approximate what Hopkins later called sprung rhythm and which have for their prototype heightened and current speech coloured by emotion. An example is evident in the irregularity the following verse exhibits:

$$\text{Fáme Î / am̂ cál / lêd már / uayle yóu / nó thing } /^{203}$$

The inversion in the first foot, / Fáme Î / strikes an emphatic note and this vigorous trochee movement is followed by three smooth iambuses. The fifth foot, / nó thing / is also a trochee.

The second verse has a more regular cadence:

$$\text{Thoûgh Î / with toñges / âm cóm / pâs sêd / all roúnd } /^{204}$$

Verse three affords a pleasing variation from the regularly-stressed iambic pentameter by reason of the initial substitution and final inversion:

$$\text{Fôr iñ voýce / of péo / ple iš / mŷ chiefe / li uŷng } /^{205}$$

The rhythm in verse four is composed of uninterrupted iambic pentameter. This line is characterized by a unity of impression and an integrated progression of words evoked by powerful emotion and a desire to give vent to belligerent feelings of antipathy and revenge:

$$\text{O cŕu / el death / thy pó / wêr Î / côn fouñde } /^{206}$$

Line five is regular and contains five consecutive iambuses which mirror the spirit of defeat this verse portrays:

$$\text{Wheñ thóu / a}^{x}\text{nó / blê mán / hâst broúght / tô groúnde } /^{207}$$

The two inversions in the first and fourth foot of line six add vehemence and force to Lady Fame's announcement of vengeance:

$$\text{Máu grŷ / thy teéth / tô lyúe / caúse hŷm / shall Î } /^{208}$$

Besides an iamb in the first and third foot and an anapest in the fourth, the meter contains two pyrrhics; these unaccented syllables mitigate the harshness of her overbearing tone and add a touch of feminine pride to her vaunting:

Of péo / ple iň / pǎr pé / tǔ all mé / mǒ rỳ /[209]

The seventh stanza is one of the best of the nine pageants because of its imagery and sententiousness. It has great emotional intensity and skillfully reveals the author's own convictions, which are brought to a firm conclusion in the verses depicting the conquest of Time over Fame:

> I whom thou seest with horyloge in hande,
> Am named tyme, the lord of euery howre.[210]

Lord Time gives Lady Fame a poignant insult in the most innocuous way when he calls her Ladyship 'simple'. Thus, he deprives her of glory, pomp, and ostentation and strips her of power and prestige. With a condescending attitude that chagrins her and a scoffing demeanor that outrages her, he says:

> O simple fame, how darest thou man honowre,
> Promising of his name, an endlesse flowre,
> Who may in the world haue a name eternall.[211]

Then, asserting his own power, he says forcefully and convincingly:

> When I shall in process distroy the world and all.[212]

The tone and attitude of the assumed voice keep pace with the accompanying changes in rhythm, assonance, and tone colour. As Time has the fluctuating and world-pivoting hourglass under his control, so too, Thomas More exhibits discipline and mastery in the manipulation of the rhythm in this verse, which is opposed to Lady Fame's loud and blatant boasting. Time is sure that he will conquer his jealous foe; therefore, there is equanimity in his thoughts which are reflected in the equanimity of the smooth-flowing meter. Lady Fame, on the other hand, boasts so flagrantly of her power precisely because she is afraid of losing it. She holds on to it tenaciously and is completely crushed when she, and not the 'noble man hast [been] brought to grounde'[213] by Death. Lord Time is so blinded with self-confidence and pride that he does not even give a thought to the possibility of an eternal life after he destroys the entire universe. The rhythm in Lady Fame's verses begins with strongly accented beats denoting the striding tone of her assertions, but end on a gentle and conciliatory note. The verses on Time, however, begin vigorously and end defiantly:

Í whom̆ / thŏu sèest / with hŏ / r̆y lŏg̀e / ĭn hánde /

. . . .
Whĕn Í / shăll ĭn prò / cĕs dĭs tróy / the wórld / ănd áll /[214]

The substitutions in the form of two consecutive anapests in the second and third foot of the last verse place an emphasis on the disyllabic words 'proces' and 'distroy'. The rhythm employed in this line reflects a steadiness of purpose and manifests a cool, malicious penchant for revenge.

The epithet used to describe 'name' as an 'endlesse flowre'[215] is a good and appropriate trope. It implies a subtle use of irony, for by its very nature a flower is destined to wither and die. Yet, this idea of assumed immortality should have conjured up in the mind of personified Time the existence of a future eternal life. There are no other striking images in this verse, but bitter and derisive satire breathes through it. At first glance Time seems to portray equanimity and self-control, but then reveals his true intent when, blinded with fury, he speaks of destroying the world and all things in it.

It is Eternity, however, that gives us genuine peace and comforting joy, for she conquers not only Death and Fame, but Time as well; yet, she remains simple and humble in spite of all her conquests. Her empire is infinite, indeed, and with appropriate decorum she defies Lord Time as she says to him:

> Thou mortall Tyme euery man can tell,
> Art nothyng els but the mobilite,
> Of sonne and mone chaungyng in euery degre,
> When they shall leue theyr course thou shalt be brought,
> For all thy pride and bostyng into nought.[216]

The epithet 'mortal' attributed to Time is a death blow to him and, truly, no one but a supernatural and immortal being would have the boldness and courage to administer it.

As in the preceding stanzas, More's voice again pierces the veil of the disguised speaker in the verses that follow, for here he enunciates his own belief about astronomy:

> Art nothyng els but the mobilite,
> Of sonne and mone chaungyng in euery degre.[217]

These verses indicate real interest in science and not a slavish belief in the powers of astrology to mold men's humours, which belief still clouded the minds of Englishmen in the sixteenth century. The line, 'Of sonne and mone chaungyng in euery degre', indirectly implies a belief in Ptolemy's geocentric universe, or conversely, it simply alludes to the rising and the setting of the sun.

Thomas More's speculations concerning astronomy reveal a curiosity of mind and an attitude divorced from superstititious belief. Henry VIII also manifested a keen interest and an open mind in regard to astronomy. Of all his counsellors he chose More to discuss with him 'the diversities, courses, motions, and operations of the stars and planets'.[218] He must have listened to More's ex- postulations with secret admiration, for he esteemed him for his convictions which were strongly opposed to those of his fellow-men.

Unlike the other stanzas which have seven lines, this one has eight, which signifies that More was not bound by prosodic convention but placed more emphasis on thought content rather than on structure and form. The rhyme scheme, in view of this fact, differs from the other rhyme royal stanzas and is a b a b c c d d.

This stanza does not have profound imagery, but then, its allusion to science precludes thought-provoking epithets and figurative discourse. It is significant that in the realm of transcendental and spiritual values, More becomes scientific and practical in this poem; whereas in the delineations of Youth, Fame, Death, and Time, he is imaginative and metaphorical. Consequently, it is apparent that for him belief in eternity and faith in the immortality of the soul was as real as the physical development of man and as positive as the fact that every man must die. In each of the seven stanzas the voice expresses a desire to gain some good and to excel its competitor; Eternity alone is satisfied and content with her state. She possesses all things now and hopes for no new and startling victory. She enjoys the 'endyng day' of Childhood's play, the maturity and 'reason' of Manhood, the 'strength, power and myght' of Cupid's darts, the 'wisdom and discretion' of Old Age, the power and equality of Death, the brilliancy and prestige of Fame, the domination and potency of Time, and the eternal bliss of God's endless day.

The verses in this stanza are, for the most part, run-on lines which approximate the pattern of ordinary speech. Verses four, five, and six are a good example of this technique:

> Thou mortall Tyme euery man can tell,
> Art nothyng els but the mobilite,
> Of sonne and mone chaungyng in euery degre.[219]

The thought unit and line structure do not end here but continue in circular progression until a climactic end is reached:

> When they shall leve theyr course thou shalt be brought,
> For all thy pride and bostyng into nought.[220]

The diction consists of strong and clear nouns adorned by three adjectives, powerful in their connotative and spatial qualities. The following diagram may be helpful in seeing the unity and design of the diction More employs in this verse:

Nouns   Eternitee, name, empyre, Tyme, man, course, mobilite, sonne, mone, degre, pride, and bostyng.

132

Adjectives	Infinite, mortal, and chaungyng.

Infinite describes: Eternitee, name, and empyre.

Mortal describes: Tyme, mobilite.

Chaungyng describes: Man, sonne, mone, degre, course, pride, bostyng.

In the last stanza, which is written in Latin, the youthful More takes off his mask and speaks to us in his own voice. To add prestige to his message and to communicate his ideas more effectively, he sits in the poet's chair and enunciates his convictions on the value of life. He employs the medium of the Latin tongue, which may imply that these verses were addressed to an educated audience who spoke this language fluently. Then, too, having written one hundred and sixty-seven epigrams in Latin, he was adept in using this medium for the expression of his innermost thoughts and convictions. Following a spiral pattern, this last stanza has twelve lines, while the one preceding it has eight, and all the other stanzas have seven lines each. Since the writer of this dissertation is analysing More's English poems, only the ideas contained in this concluding Latin stanza will be discussed, for they clinch the poem's meaning and give unity and emphasis to its allegorical dichotomy.

The tenets of these convictions fall into the following framework of spiritual and philosophical values:

1. The soul feeds on truth.

2. The goods of this world are fragile.

3. Joys, honour, and praise are fleeting.

4. The love of God is a permanent thing.

5. The good are rewarded with eternal life.

6. God's grace is needed in order to persevere.

This culminating twelve-lined stanza has a threefold approach and appeal: (1) the first four lines make an appeal to man's intellect, and the approach is made through the senses; (2) the next four lines stir man's emotions and, hence, the rhetorical question here is very apropos: 'Joys, praise and honour, all retire on a speedy foot; whatever remains ecxept the love of God?'[221] In the last four lines the will is moved to action; and a resolution, 'Yield up your faith in inconsiderable things and offer your vows to God',[222] is strongly advocated.

This last verse, characterized by philosophical speculation and rich in spiritual thought, efficaciously clinches the nine pageants and gives the reader or the onlooker a sense of climactic unity in the subject matter presented and the structural form used. Looking at the succession of scenes in one's life which begin with Childhood and end with Eternity, one is urged to consider and to look forward to an eternity of everlasting happiness or perpetual misery.

Algernon Cecil, who wrote an interesting description of Thomas More as a scholar, a statesman, and a saint, gives an excellent summary of the 'Nyne pageauntes', which More devised as a youth in his father's house in Cripplegate Ward in London. He asserts that the subject of these verses is not merely the pageant of life, but 'perhaps more truly the dance of death'.[223] With penetrating insight into the meaning structure of this poem, he says:

> As we look back over these crude verses, we see that the kaleidoscope which they cause to revolve is nicely calculated to show that the pains of dissolution, even to old age, even at death, issue continually in nobler being. Still in his teens, More had in fact worked out a scheme of life permitting no man to grow really old. Life, if its phases are not the series of steppingstones to higher things of the later Poet, resolves itself, into the ludicrous decline of Jacques's seven stages or the strutting player and idiot's tale of Macbeth's conclusion. It was in More's bones, so to say, to see it as a progress, revealing more than it removes, rendering back a fuller joy of youth than that which it takes away. There was nothing new in this; for it is a leading motif in the liturgy of the Mass to which he daily listened.[224]

1. *Works*, I, 332, C. ii^v. H. 2–8.
2. Chambers, p. 84.
3. James A. Williamson, *The Tudor Age* (New York, 1953), p. 37.
4. Chambers, p. 64.
5. H. C. Maxweel Lyte, *History of the University of Oxford* (London, 1886), p. 333.
6. (Cambridge, Eng., 1905), p. 30.
7. John Winter Jones, 'Observations on the Origin of the Division of Man's Life into Stages,' *Archaeologia*, XXXV (London 1853), 167–189.
8. Chambers, p. 65.
9. Leland, *Scriptores Britannici*, p. 482. Cited in Sandys, p. 197.
10. Sandys, pp. 197–198.
11. Rev. Thomas Edward Bridgett, *Life and Writings of Blessed Thomas More* (London, 1924), p. 9.
12. Chambers, p. 65.
13. *Works*, I, 'Nyne pageauntes,' C. ii^v. H. 3.
14. Jones, pp. 167–168.
15. Henry Osborn Taylor, *The Medieval Mind: A History of the Development of Thought and Emotion in the Middle Ages* (New York, 1919), II, 68.
16. *Ibid.*
17. Henry Osborn Taylor, *The Classical Heritage of the Middle Ages* (New York, 1901), p. 98.
18. Percy Stafford Allen, *The Age of Erasmus* (Oxford, 1914), p. 91.
19. Jean Seznac, *The Survival of the Pagan Gods* (New York, 1953), p. 220.
20. *Works*, I, 'Nyne pageauntes,' C. ii^v H. 3.
21. *Ibid.*, C. iii^r B. 9.
22. *Ibid.*, C. iii^r A. 5.
23. *Ibid.*, C. iii^r D. 1.
24. *Ibid.*, C. iii^r D. 9.
25. *Ibid.*, C. iii^v B. 1.
26. *Ibid.*, C. iii^v C. 1.
27. *Ibid.*, C. iii^v D. 1.
28. *Ibid.*, C. iiii^r A. 7.
29. *Ibid.*, C. iiii^r C. 1.

30. Charles Edward Mallet, *A History of the University of Oxford* (London, 1924), I, 425, n. 1.
31. *Athenae Oxonienses: An Exact History of All the Writers and Bishops Who Have Had Their Education in the Most Antient & Famous University of Oxford*, Volume I, (London, 1721).
32. Hutton, p. 17.
33. *Ibid.*
34. R. W. Chambers, p. 66.
35. Mallet, I, 425.
36. *Works*, I, C. ii^v H. 2–8.
37. *OED*, VII, 374.
38. M. Lyle Spencer, *Corpus Christi Pageants in England* (New York, 1911).
39. E. K. Chambers, *The Medieval Stage*, 2 vols. (Oxford, 1931).
40. *Ibid.*, II, 176.
41. 'Nyne pageauntes,' C. ii^v H. 3.
42. *OED*, VII, 374.
43. E. K. Chambers, II, 149–176.
44. John Addington Symonds, *Renaissance in Italy* (New York, 1888), I, 18–19.
45. Berdan, p. 458.
46. Ernest Hatch Wilkins, *A History of Italian Literature* (London, 1954), p. 90.
47. Petrarch wrote a treatise 'Concerning the Best Administration of Government' which may have had some influence on More's *Utopia*.
48. Francesco de Sanctis, *History of Italian Literature*, trans. John Redfern (New York, 1931), p. 289.
49. *Ibid.*
50. Spencer, p. 237.
51. Hardin Craig, *English Religious Drama of the Middle Ages* (London, 1955), p. 330.
52. *Ibid.*, p. 331.
53. 'Nyne pageauntes, C. iii^r A. 4–10.
54. 'Nyne pageauntes, C. iiii^r A. 9.
55. Thomas Stearnes Eliot, *The Three Voices* (New York, 1954), pp. 5–39.
56. *Ibid.*, p. 13.
57. Ivor Armstrong Richards, *Practical Criticism: A Study of Literary Judgment* (New York, 1950), p. 182.
58. 'Nyne pageauntes', C. iii^v B. 9–10. C. 1–5.
59. Thomas Warton, *History of English Poetry* (London, 1840), III, p. 98.
60. Hutton, p. 12.
61. *Ibid.*
62. Nelson, p. 337.
63. *Ibid.*, p. 338.
64. *Ibid.*
65. Hutton, p. 21.
66. Wilbur Samuel Howell, *Logic and Rhetoric in England, 1500–1700* (Princeton, 1956), p. 120.
67. *Ibid.*, p. 21. See *Institutio Oratoria*, 8. 3. 44–60.
68. *Ibid.*
69. *Aristotle's Rhetoric*, trans. W. Rhys Roberts (New York, 1955), p. 182.
70. 'Nyne pageauntes', C. iii^r D. 1–3.
71. *Ibid.*, C. iii^r C. 3–5.
72. *Ibid.*, C. iii^r B. 10–12.
73. Works, II, [46].
74. *Ibid.*
75. Frederick W. Hamilton, *Punctuation* (Chicago, 1920), p. 4.
76. George Henry Vallins, *The Pattern of English* (London, 1956), p. 149.
77. *Ibid.*, p. 152.
78. *Works*, II, 46.
79. 'Nyne pageauntes,' C. iiii^r A. 5–7.
80. *Ibid.*, C. iii^r D. 9–10, C. iii^v A. 1–2.
81. *Ibid.*, C. iii^v B. 1–4.
82. Charles Sears Baldwin, *Medieval Rhetoric and Poetic* (New York, 1928), p. 292.
83. Mallet, I, 180, n. 6.

84. Edmond Faral, *Les Arts Poétiques Du XII Et Du XIII Siècle* (Paris, 1924), pp. 378–380.
85. John Matthews Manly, *Chaucer and the Rhetoricians* (London, 1926), Warlon Lecture on English Poetry, XVII, 10-13.
86. George Puttenham, *The Arte of English Poesie*, ed. Gladys Doidge Willcock and Alice Walker (Cambridge, Eng., 1936), p. 143.
87. *Ibid.*
88. Faral, p. 80.
89. 'Nyne pegeauntes,' C. iii^r D. 9–10.
90. *Ibid.*, iii^v A. 10–12.
91. *Ibid.*, iii^v B. 9–10, C. 1.
92. *Ibid.*, C. iii^r B. 6–9.
93. *Ibid.*, C. iii^r C. 8–9.
94. *Ibid.*, C. iiii^r A. 5–7.
95. *OED*, I, 112.
96. 'Nyne pageauntes,' C. iii^v B. 1–4.
97. Puttenham, ed. Arber, pp. 240–241.
98. 'Nyne pageauntes,' C. iii^r A. 7–10.
99. *Ibid.*, C. iii^r C. 10–11. D. 12–14.
100. *Ibid.*, C. iii^v A. 3–5.
101. *Ibid.*, C. iii^v C. 2–5.
102. *Ibid.*, C. iii^v D. 4–7.
103. *Ibid.*, C. iii^v D. 9. iiii^r A. 1.
104. *Ibid.*, C. iiii^r A. 8–12.
105. Berdan, p. 80.
106. Clark, p. 122.
107. Bradner and Lynch, p. 238.
108. 'Nyne pageauntes,' C. iiii^r B. 7.
109. Gregory Smith, ed., *Elizabethan Critical Essays* (Oxford, 1904), II, 199.
110. Puttenham, ed. Willcock and Walker, p. 139.
111. Manly, p. 13.
112. Faral, p. 73.
113. Manly, p. 12.
114. 'Nyne pageauntes,' C. iii^r D. 9–10. C. iii^v A. 1–5.
115. E. K. Chambers, I, 79.
116. *Ibid.*, I, 79–80, n. 5.
117. Aristotle's *Poetics*, trans. Ingram Bywarer (New York, 1954), p. 226, 1148a20.
118. Shipley, p. 442.
119. Shipley, p. 443.
120. Puttenham, ed. Willcock and Walker, p. 193.
121. Hoskins, pp. 46–47.
122. Manly, p. 13.
123. *Ibid.*,
124. Hoskins, p. 17.
125. Faral, p. 68.
126. Hoskins, p. 17.
127. Hudson, ed., p. 73, n. 54^b.
128. Shipley, p. 22.
129. Hoskins, p. 35.
130. Aristotle's *Treatise on Rhetoric*, trans, Theodore Buckley (London, 1872), p. 230. A period is a form of words which has independently in itself a beginning and ending, and a length easily taken in at a glance.
131. Puttenham, ed. Willcock and Walker, p. 148.
132. 'Nyne pageauntes,' C. iii^r A. 4–10.
133. Taylor, p. 55.
134. Hudson, ed., p. 25.
135. Puttenham, ed. Arber, p. 243.
136. 'Nyne pageauntes,' C. iii^r B. 11. C. 1.
137. *Ibid.*, C. iii^r D. 2–3.
138. *Ibid.*, C. iii^v A. 10–12. B. 1. B. 3.
139. *Ibid.*, C. iii^v B. 9–10. C. 1.

140. *Ibid.*, C. iii^v D. 1–7.
141. Manly, p. 14.
142. *Ibid.*, pp. 14–15.
143. Puttenham, ed. Willcock and Walker, p. 160.
144. Hudson, ed., Introduction, p. xx, n. 19.
145. Puttenham, ed. Willcock and Walker, pp. 160–161.
146. Hudson, ed., Introduction, p. xx.
147. 'Nyne pageauntes,' C. iii^v C. 4.
148. *Works*, I, 196. Fifth page, C. 4.
149. 'Nyne pageauntes,' C. iii^r C. 1.
150. *OED*, IV, 420.
151. A. H. Tolman, 'The Symbolic Value of English Sounds,' in Raymond Macdonald Alden's *An Introduction to Poetry* (New York, 1909), pp. 218–219.
152. 'Nyne pageauntes,' C. iii^r A. 9.
153. *Ibid.*, C. iii^r A. 10.
154. *Ibid.*, C. iii^r A. 11. B. 1–11. C. 1
155. *Ibid.*, C. iii^r B. 11. C. 1.
156. *Ibid.*, C. iii^r B. 6.
157. *Ibid.*, C. iii^r B. 10.
158. Frederick Hodgetts, *The English in the Middle Ages* (London, 1885), p. 190.
159. *Ibid.*, pp. 193–194.
160. 'Nyne pageauntes,' C. iii^r B. 8. 12. 10.
161. *Ibid.*, C. iii^r B. 8.
162. *Ibid.*, C. iii^r B. 10.
163. George Leland Hunter, *Tapestries, Their Origin, History and Renaissance* (New York, 1912), p. 398.
164. *Ibid.*, p. 107.
165. *Ibid.*, pp. 2–4–205.
166. 'Nyne pageauntes,' C. iii^r C. 10.
167. Hunter, p. 102.
168. 'Nyne pageauntes,' C. iii^r D. 1.
169. *Ibid.*, C. iii^r D. 2–3.
170. *OED*, VI, 489.
171. *Ibid.*, VIII, 675.
172. 'Nyne pageauntes,' C. iii^r D. 10.
173. Mallet, p. 182. The other three Arts of the Quadrivium were Music, Arithmetic, and Geometry.
174. Seznec, p. 47.
175. 'Nyne pageauntes,' C. iii^v A. 1–2.
176. Harpsfield, quoted in Chambers' *Thomas More*, pp. 53–54.
177. Roper, quoted in Bridgett's *Life and Writings of Blessed Thomas More* p. 241.
178. 'Nyne pageauntes,' C. iii^v A. 4.
179. *Ibid.*, C. iii^v A. 3.
180. *Ibid.*, C. iii^r D. 9. E. 1.
181. *Ibid.*, C. iii^v A. 1–2.
182. *OED*, IX, 262.
183. 'Nyne pageauntes,' C. iii^v A. 2.
184. Wenceslaus Hollar, *The Dance of Death; from the Original Designs of Hans Holbein* (London, 1816), pp. 16–17.
185. *Works*, 'The Four Last Things,' I, 467–468.
186. 'Nyne pageauntes,' C. iii^v A. 11–12.
187. Woltmann, p. 248.
188. *Ibid.*, p. 249.
189. 'Nyne pageauntes,' C. iii^v B. 1–2.
190. *Ibid.*, C. iii^v B. 3–4.
191. *Works*, I, 481.
192. 'Nyne pageauntes,' C. iii^v C. 2–5.
193. *Ibid.*, C. iii^v C. 1.
194. *Ibid.*, C. iii^v B. 9–10.
195. *Ibid.*, C. iii^v C. 2.

196. Stephen Hawes, *The Pastime of Pleasure*, Early English Texts, Original Series 173, ed. William Edward Mead (London, 1927), P. 11, 11. 176–177.
197. Warton, II, p. 405.
198. *Ibid.*, p. 417.
199. *OED*, X, 129.
200. *Ibid.*, p. 128.
201. *Ibid.*, p. 129.
202. *Ibid.*, p. 128.
203. 'Nyne pageauntes,' C. iii^v B. 9.
204. *Ibid.*, C. iii^v B. 10.
205. *Ibid.*, C. iii^r C. 1.
206. *Ibid.*, C. iii^v C. 2.
207. *Ibid.*, C. iii^v C. 3.
208. *Ibid.*, C. iii^v C. 4.
209. *Ibid.*, C. iii^v C. 5.
210. *Ibid.*, C. iii^v D. 1–2.
211. *Ibid.*, C. iii^v D. 4–6.
212. *Ibid.*, C. iii^v D. 7.
213. *Ibid.*, C. iii^v C. 3.
214. *Ibid.*, C. iii^v D. 1. D. 7.
215. *Ibid.*, C. iii^v D. 5.
216. *Ibid.*, C. iiii^r A. 8–11. B. 1.
217. *Ibid.*, C. iiii^r A. 9–10.
218. Roper quoted in Ernest Edwin Reynolds' *Saint Thomas More* (London, 1953), p. 137.
219. 'Nyne pageauntes,' C. iiii^r A. 8–10.
220. *Ibid.*, C. iiii^r A. 11. B. 1.
221. *Ibid.*, C. iiii^r C. 1–2.
222. *Ibid.*, C. iiii^r C. 7–8.
223. Algernon Cecil, *A Portrait of Thomas More, Scholar, Statesman, Saint* (London, 1937), p. 16.
224. *Ibid.*, p. 17.

CHAPTER IV

'A RUFUL LAMENTACION':

EXPERIMENTATION WITH FORM

In *The Arte of English Poesie* (1589), George Puttenham describes the form and purpose of poetical lamentations and, endeavouring to add dignity to this kind of writing, says:

> Lamenting is altogether contrary to reioicing, euery man saith so, and yet it is a peece of ioy to be able to lament with ease, and freely to poure forth a mans inward sorrowes and the greefs wherewith his minde is surcharged . . . Such funerall songs were called *Epicedia* if they were song by many, and *Monodia* if they were uttered by one alone, and this was used at the enterment of Princes and others of great accompt, and it was reckoned a great ciuilitie to use such ceremonies . . .[1]

When Queen Elizabeth of York, the wife of Henry VII and the mother of Henry VIII, died in childbed on February 11, 1503, Thomas More paid national tribute to her memory by expressing his sentiments in 'A ruful lamentacion on the deth of quene Elizabeth . . .' A. W. Reed attributes movement and inspiration to this verse and says that 'as an English versifier he [More] is here at his best'.[2] Reverend Thomas E. Bridgett considers this poem to be of such great promise that, 'had he [More] given himself to this species of composition, [he may] have anticipated something of the beauties of the Elizabethan poets'.[3] That this elegy is a poem of unusual historical significance and true literary merit is further substantiated by the interesting comment made by Thomas Warton in his *History of English Poetry*. He speaks perfunctorily of More's English poems, which he includes only on the basis that they are the 'productions of the restorer of literature in England',[4] and hence, deserve to be noticed. However, after quoting four stanzas from 'A ruful lamentacion', he adds, 'I am of opinion that some of the stanzas have strokes of nature and pathos, and deserve to be rescued from total oblivion'.[5]

It was customary for scholars to make an offering of verse at court,[6] and this elegy, patterned after Italian models, reflects the young humanist's interest and preoccupation with Italian verse forms. Warton tells us that this poem 'is evidently formed on the tragical soliloquies which compose Lydgate's paraphrase of Boccace's book *De Casibus Virorum Illustrium*, and which gave birth to the *Mirror for Magistrates*, the origin of our historic dramas'.[7]

Thomas More's elegy is cast in the form of a soliloquy and contains twelve stanzas in rhyme royal verse, each one closing with the haunting refrain, 'lo now here I lie'. The poem follows a definite conventional pattern, and the

139

pervasive use of *apostrophe* enables the voice of the deceased speaker to become the focal point of the poem. The dead Queen, 'the eldest daughter of Edward IV, who by her marriage to Henry VII, had joined the White Rose to the Red'.[8] poignantly takes leave of her husband, her five children,[9] her four sisters, and all her subjects who loved and esteemed her so much that they appendixed to her the title of 'Good'.[10] She exhorts them solicitously to think of death and eternity, and to profit from her example since wealth, power, and pleasure are of no avail when that dread hour approaches. With the same tenderness and charity that characterized her during life, she addresses her family, friends, and servants in the first person, thus creating a bond of love and familiarity between herself and them. The elegy is predicated on Thomas More's favourite theme – the transiency and insatiability of earthly happiness and the salutary effects of a remembrance of death and eternity.

The first stanza gives us the pattern that More used for his effective voice and address structure. On it the entire poem is built. Inconsistency of form does not mar it, neither does digression in point of view jeopardize its literary merit:

> O ye that put your trust and confidence,
> In wordly ioy and frayle prosperite,
> That so live here as ye should neuer hence,
> Remember death and loke here uppon me.
> Ensaumple I thynke there may no better be.
> Your selfe wotte well that in this realme was I,
> Your quene but late, and lo now here I lye.[11]

In this speech construct, one single voice is heard throughout the poem – that of a personality assumed by the author in imagination – and the reference to 'I' and 'me' prove this point with unmistakable clarity. The last line of the stanza 'Your quene but late, and lo now here I lye', indicates the present status of the speaker: she has recently died, and, pointing to her bed which will soon be exchanged for a coffin, she sets herself as an example for others to profit therefrom. The theme of the poem, as well as the elaboration of its twelve stanzas, centers around the profound 'Dance of Death' motif and concentrates on one of its significant triumphs, namely, the death of a queen who must, however unwillingly, leave all her precious possessions and join the procession of death's victims who follow in his cadaverous train.

The voice reference is simple, direct, and forceful, while the attitude of the speaker is one of deep concern, maternal solicitude, and profound sympathy for those who are so engrossed in wordly pleasure that they are totally oblivious to the proximity of death and the vast timelessness of eternity. Nevertheless, in the speaker's voice one does not detect a tone of chiding or supercilious vaunting, but only poignant wistfulness at the speed and certainty with which ancestry, riches, honour, and wealth desert one at the hour of approaching death. It is indeed admirable that the twenty-five-year old More could so

140

vicariously experience the feelings of the deceased Queen and enunciate her longings with such sensitivity and compassion. There is delicacy in the diction he uses, charm in the tropes and schemes he employs, and a tenderness in the ideas enunciated to the accompaniment of such soothing and lilting rhythm.

The first person referend is used consistently throughout the poem, with most of the description taking place in the past tense, while the lithe and pleasing refrain is in the present tense. The stanzas are composed of a variety of sentence patterns; the supplicating imperative sentences which achieve periodic abruptness in a cyclic manner; the pensive interrogative statements which attain an exquisite cumulative effect by means of the initial alliteration used; the poignantly-expressed exclamatory sentences which state a truism dramatically; and the emphatic declarative sentences that carry the action of the poem to its climactic conclusion. An example of this rhetorical and varied sentence pattern follows:

Imperative   O ye that put your trust and confidence,
       In worldly ioy and frayle prosperite,
       That so liue here as ye should neuer hence,
       Remember death and loke here uppon me.
               Seventh Page. A. 2–5.

Interrogative   Was I not born of olde worthy linage?
       Was not my mother queene my father kyng?
       Was I not a kinges fere[12] in marriage?
       Had I not plenty of euery pleasaunt thyng?
               Eighth Page. A. 1–4.

Exclamatory   O bryttil welth, ay full of bitternesse,
       Thy single pleasure doubled is with payne.
               Eighth Page. C. 1–2.

Declarative   Yet was I late promised otherwyse,
       This yere to live in welth and delice.
               Eighth Page. B. 3–4.

In eighty-four lines of iambic pentameter verse interspersed with a few final hexameter lines, the reference to the personal pronoun 'I' occurs thirty times, while the objective reference to 'me' is found in seven places. The first person reference to 'my' or 'myne' is used eighteen times, and this use of the possessive pronoun begins significantly in the sixth stanza, when a definite and pronounced change in the addressee takes place. In the concluding seven stanzas the good Queen, spouse, and mother addresses her husband, her children, and her four blood sisters; and last of all, she commends her soul to the mercy of God.

In view of this fact, the poem may be said to be divided into two structural parts which are predicated on the different types of addressees and the Queen's immediate relationship to him or her in life. The mechanism of the address in this poem presents an interesting study and accounts for its felicitous sound structure and emphatic meaning structure. This technique gives rise to an adroit use of rhetorical elements of style such as syntax, sentence structure, figurative language composed of colours and conceits, paratactic and hypo-tactic arrangement, and a consistent pattern of meaning references.

In the *apostrophe* used in the first line of the first stanza, 'O ye that put your trust and confidence', the addressee is the designated universal 'you' who put their trust 'in worldly ioy and frayle prosperite'. More specifically, the deceased Queen is addressing the people of her realm, her devoted subjects, for she implies this distinction when she says:

> Your selfe wotte well that in this realme was I,
> Your quene but late, and lo now here I lye.[13]

Her poignant references to her royal ancestry, her regal parents, the dowager Queen Elizabeth Woodville, and her father, Edward IV, uttered in emphatic rhetorical statements, connote the people's awareness of her heredity and prestige. As if to re-affirm the conviction she has arrived at too late and to forewarn others of a similar disillusionment, she asks them in a voice betraying self-reproach and compunction:

> Was I not borne of olde worthy linage?
> Was not my mother queene my father kynge?[14]

The third stanza is particularly interesting on account of the transitions of voice and address that take place. In the first three lines the Queen appears to be in a reminiscing mood and muses to herself as she says audibly:

> If worship myght haue kept me, I had not gone.
> If wyt myght haue me saued, I nede not fere.
> If money myght haue holpe, I lacked none.[15]

The use of the subjunctive mood correlated with references to 'worship', 'wyt', and 'money' heightens the wistful tone of the poem as the futility of striving for these transient goods is made clearly manifest. The three concluding clauses, 'had not gone', 'nede not fere', and 'lacked none', are diversified in diction and paratactic in structure; they form a balance to the pensive speculation of the subjunctive mood in the first clause. The speaker then addresses God in an exclamatory tone which implies rumination on the past rather than a prayerful cry of the soul to its Creator:

> But O good God what vayleth all this geare.[16]

The three lines that follow are strongly reminiscent of the morality play 'Every-man', and the words 'deth', 'messangere', 'obey', 'remedy', 'sommoned', show this influence:

> When deth is come thy mighty messangere,
> Obey we must there is no remedy,
> Me hath he sommoned, and lo now here I ly.[17]

In both the morality play and this poem, Death is the messenger of God, who summons man irrevocably to appear before His judgment seat to give an account of his deeds. The idea of the 'Dance of Death' is inextricably bound with the underlying idea in 'Everyman', and obvious or implied references are made to both works in 'A ruful lamentacion'. Hardin Craig in his recent book, *English Religious Drama of the Middle Ages*, makes the interesting supposition that the origin of the English morality play is a dramatic development of the 'Dance of Death' theme.[18]

Structurally the above reference constitutes a slight inconsistency in voice and address, for the personal pronoun 'I' shifts to the universal plural 'we' in line six, then reverts again to the personal, objective 'me' in the following line. The addition of the refrain 'and lo now here I ly' to the three lines, so analogous to 'Everyman' in diction and theme, gives them a note of originality as they alter the meaning structure by delimiting it to a specific person, Queen Elizabeth, the mother of Henry VIII.

In stanza four the good Queen continues to address her immediate circle of family and friends and the wider range of her faithful subjects as she muses painfully on the false promises of astrology:

> Yet was I late promised otherwyse,
> This yere to liue in welth and delice.[19]

A break in the voice and address pattern suddenly occurs and the thread of verisimilitude is broken when Elizabeth, forgetful of her listeners, poignantly upbraids the augury of the stars and says with acrid disappointment:

> Lo where to commeth thy blandishyng promyse,
> O false astrology and deuynatrice,
> Of goddes secretes makyng thy selfe so wyse?[20]

In the face of immediate death such mental meanderings and retrospective verbalizations are plausible, which would not otherwise be so; therefore, this structural inconsistency is no serious blemish on the poet's art. The author skillfully brings his readers back to the definite scene of the situation, and they hear the dying Queen again addressing the group surrounding her bedside:

> How true is for this yere thy prophecy?
> That yere yet lasteth, and lo nowe here I ly.[21]

143

Thomas Warton quotes this stanza together with three others in the *History of English Poetry*, and his comment on More's dissentient attitude towards astrology is so significant that it deserves to be quoted here:

> In the fourth stanza she [the Queen] reproaches the astrologers for their falsity in having predicted that this should be the happiest and most fortunate year of her whole life. This, while it is a natural reflection in the speaker, is a proof of More's contempt of a futile and frivolous science, then so much in esteem.[22]

In the ensuing analyses of the separate stanzas, the subject of astrology and the early Renaissance attitude towards it will receive greater treatment. This excerpt on More's abhorrence of a popular science strengthens his status as a humanist and shows how he could depart from traditional thinking and form his own judgment on a widely-accepted and popular belief.

The fifth stanza begins with a scintillating apostrophe to wealth, and the inclusion of it in the first line makes the sound structure diversified and pleasing. As a matter of fact, the elements that make up the sound pattern in the first six stanzas resemble a variegated tapestry with synchronized pastel shades blending into a harmonious chiaroscuro. Although the diction is felicitous and the rhythm is good, the structural element of the addressee in this stanza is ambiguous. The reader does not know definitely whether the languishing Queen is addressing all seven verses to the personified concept of 'welth' or whether she is making a public self-accusation before those individuals surrounding her bedside who had been the obvious receptors of her reminiscing speech thus far. As if speaking to a person she is vehemently reproaching, she says:

> O bryttil welth, ay full of bitternesse,
> Thy single pleasure doubled is with payne.
> Account my sorrow first and my distresse,
> In sondry wyse, and recken there agayne,
> The ioy that I haue had, and I dare sayne,
> For all my honour, endured yet haue I,
> More wo then welth, and lo now here I ly.[23]

One has only to compare the above excerpt with Chaucer's 'Envoy to Fortune' to realize the close similarity between the two:

> Prynses. I prey yow of yowre gentilesses
> Lat nat this man on me thus crye and pleyne
> And. I. shal quyte yow yowre bysynesse
> at my requeste as thre of yow or tweyne
> that but yow lest releue hym of hys peyne
> preyeth hys best frend of his noblesse
> That to som betere estat he may attayne.[24]

144

Beginning with the sixth stanza until the end, i.e., the twelfth, the queen becomes more realistic and conscious of her surroundings, as seen in the verbalizations she addresses to the immediate members of her family. She speculates first on the castles and towers that were once part of her glorious possession:

Where are our Castels, now where are our Towers?[25]

Professor A. W. Reed, who praises this poem for its 'inspiration' and 'movement', comments favorably on its historical significance:

> The poem has a wealth of allusion which alone must save if from neglect.
> It refers to Henry's new buildings at Richmond; to the Henry VII Chapel
> 'that costly work of yours', then a-building; it refers to the recent death
> of Arthur, Prince of Wales, and to his childwidow, Katharine of Aragon;
> it speaks of the approaching marriage of Elizabeth's daughter Margaret
> to James of Scotland; Prince Henry is mentioned, and his sister Mary,
> 'bright of hue', and the Queen's sisters are all addressed, Cicely, Ann,
> Katharine, and Bridget, of whom More was to write again at greater
> length in the opening paragraph of his *Richard III*.[26]

With an affection comparable to that which is lavished on an only child, Elizabeth of York addresses Richmond Castle, where she spent so many soothing and tranquil moments and where she and her children found relaxation and joy:

Goodly Rychmonde sone art thou gone from me.[27]

In a third reflex action, which is a little too swift and incongruous for a sustained unity of effect in the voice and address pattern, she turns to her husband, Henry VII, and laments the fact that she will never see his 'costly worke' at Westminster:

At westminster that costly worke of yours,
Myne owne dere lorde now shall I neuer see.[28]

Even at a moment which would justify dejection of spirit and self-pity, she thinks of her loved ones rather than of herself as she adds with sincerity in a subdued tone of voice:

Almighty god vouchesafe to graunt that ye,
For you and your children well may edefy.
My palyce bylded is, and lo now here I ly.[29]

Turning to her spouse, Henry Tudor, the Earl of Richmond, with whom she, Elizabeth of York, daughter of Edward IV, lived harmoniously for seventeen years, she bids him farewell in these words:

> Adew myne owne dere spouse my worthy lorde,
> The faithfull love, that dyd us both combyne,
> In marriage and peasable concorde,
> Into your handes here I cleane resyne,
> To be bestowed uppon your children and myne.[30]

Little has been said about the marital relationship of Henry VII with Edward IV's eldest daughter, but James A. Williamson in a recent book entitled *The Tudor Age* throws some light on it in the following paragraph:

> In January 1486 Henry, already completely recognized as king, married the heiress of the Yorkish claim, having thus taken care that none could say that he owed his position in any part to her. Their mutual relations continued tranquil and presumably happy, with no recorded infidelities. The queen was the king's faithful and sensible wife, but hardly a great public figure. She bore him children and exercised little practical influence.[31]

Mindful of the fact that it is the disguised voice of Thomas More enunciating the dying Queen's addresses and poignant farewells, one is impressed with the masculine tenderness that parallels a woman's devotion and affection for her children. The following wistful lines have great empathetic value, since More himself was in an analogous position when Jane Colt's death left him with four little motherless children. It was up to him to 'supply the mother's part also', for the 'neither young nor handsome widow'[32] he married a few months after the death of his beloved wife, was more adept in being a scrupulous house-keeper than a tender mother. The lines that follow are, consequently, a sincere echo of his own anxiety in this matter:

> Erst wer you father, & now must ye supply,
> The mother's part also, for lo now here I ly.[33]

One wonders how Henry VII fulfilled this trust; for, avariciousness being the weak point of his character, his vulnerable 'Achilles' heel', he was more solicitous about the accumulation of wealth and the diplomatic marriage alliances of his children with a view to his own welfare, than the sympathetic love and understanding of his offspring. Surviving his wife for six years, he died at the age of fifty-two and was laid to rest beside her in the magnificent Chapel in Westminster Abbey, to which the speaker alludes in the poem.

The good Queen's next address is directed to her eldest daughter, Margaret, who was born at Westminster in 1489. Unlike her gentle mother and sedulous father, she later became a bane rather than a blessing. A few days before the death of her mother she was married by proxy at the age of fourteen years in a marriage alliance arranged by her father, to James IV of Scotland, a man of thirty and one of the most gallant princes of his day.[34] The solicitous mother refers in these verses to the sorrow that her daughter's approaching separation was destined to bring when the Scottish King would claim her for his bride:

Farewell my doughter lady Margarete.
God wotte full oft it greued hath my mynde,
That ye should go where we should seldome mete.[35]

She sadly reviews the abrupt turn of events her death has precipitated as she says in line five:

Now am I gone, and haue left you behynde.[36]

Didacticism, which is as incongruous as an anachronism in Twentieth-century drama, is softened here by the haunting mood which envelopes the poem. The speaker changes the first person 'I' to the plural we" as she looks into space and addresses humanity at large:

O mortall folke that we be very blinde,
That we least feare, full oft it is most nye.[37]

Then, alluding to her present state and approaching death, she reverts to the singular pronoun and brings the speech construct into direct focus as she says in the ending line of this verse:

From you depart I fyrst, and lo now here I lye.[38]

The following stanza contains three terse and integrated farewells to the mother of Henry VII, the Lady Margaret, Countess of Richmond, to Elizabeth's daughter-in-law, Katherine of Aragon, and lastly to her own dear child, Prince Arthur, who died in his nineteenth year. She solicits Lady Margaret Beaufort to be of good cheer and to comfort her son and exhibits edifying self-forget-fulness in these last moments of her life. At this trying and crucial moment, her concern for the welfare of others is indeed praiseworthy. Then, displaying true Christian spirit and sentiment, she beseeches them to pray for her soul:

It booteth not for me to wepe or cry,
Pray for my soule, for lo now here I ly.[39]

The 'Farewell' of the two preceding stanzas is changed to an 'Adew' in the following one. The meaning remains the same, but the pattern of the sound structure is altered with gratifying results. This 'adew' is addressed to Henry VIII, her dashing and jovial young son, who was twelve-years-old at the time of his mother's death. In the same stanza she bids 'adew' to her daughter Mary, who was not more than five years of age when she lost her mother. The greatest tenderness, however, is the farewell she gives to her new-born daughter Kate as she laments the fact that the dear child will never know her mother:

Adew swete hart my little doughter Kate,
Thou shalt swete babe suche is thy desteny,
Thy mother neuer know, for lo now here I ly.[40]

It is significant that Thomas More's wife, Jane Colt, after six years of presumably happy married life, died also in childbirth; and this fact is borne out by
Erasmus, who 'hints at a dead child'.[41] Another slight but impressive factor
which shows More's personal interest in the death of the good Queen consists
in the names he gave his own children: Elizabeth, Margaret, and Cicely, names
suggesting the Queen's immediate family.

The eleventh stanza contains an address to the Queen's four sisters: Cicely,
Anne, Katherine, and Bridget. The first three sisters are spoken to in one group,
and, after having addressed them by name individually, she tenderly calls them
'my welbeloved sisters three'. She devotes a separate stanza to her youngest
sister, Lady Bridget, who became a Dominican nun at Dartford. The recollec-
tion of Bidget's renunciation of worldly honor and riches serves as a point of
comparison with her own life. Absorbed in this reverie, she says meditatively,
more to herself than to those surrounding her bedside:

Lo here the ende of worldly vanitee.[42]

Again there is an ostensible disruption in the voice and address framework when,
in the fifth and sixth verses, Elizabeth of York speaks to a designated 'you',
addressing in this speech construct all those who have dedicated themselves to
a virtuous life, whether in the cloister or in the world, for she does not specify
any distinction here:

Now well are ye that earthly folly flee,
And heuenly thynges loue and magnify.[43]

Having indulged in this pious reverie, she immediately comes back to her surroundings, orientates herself to her dolorous situation, and solicits alms for her
soul in the form of prayer:

Farewell and pray for me, for lo now here I ly.[44]

The hour of death is approaching fast, and the tempo of the last stanza is
accelerated as Queen Elizabeth bids adieu to her lords, ladies, servants, and
commons, and commends herself to God's mercy, all in one final stanza:

Adew my lordes, adew my ladies all,
Adew my faithfull seruauntes euery chone,
Adew my commons who I neuer shall,
See in this world wherfore to the alone,
Immortall god verely three and one,
I me commende thy infinite mercy,
Shew to thy servant, for lo now here I ly.[45]

She humbly calls herself God's 'servant' in the last line, makes a beautiful act of faith in the Holy Trinity, and manifests confidence in the infinite mercy of the Redeemer. Although her musing is pensive and her reverie is melancholy, there is an apparent absence of the frustration of soul that sin and concomitant despair bring at the hour of death. When Elizabeth, the White Rose of the House of Plantagenet, died from consumption in her thirty-seventh year, her death was deeply lamented by her subjects, who, because of her unselfishness, modesty, and meekness called her 'the good Queen Elizabeth'.[46]

'A ruful lamentacion of the deth of quene Elisabeth' is a beautiful example of an extended pattern of voice and address in spite of a few minor inconsistencies inherent therein. One can summarize the functions of the voice as follows: the first three stanzas are enunciated by the Queen; the fourth and fifth stanzas are indirect enunciations of Thomas More's reflections on astrology and wealth; the sixth and seventh stanzas clearly belong to the voice of the Queen; in the eighth, More pierces the veil of the disguised voice, and for a brief moment asserts his own voice as he assumes a didactic tone, which is again repeated in stanza eleven with the same slightly irritating effect; while stanzas nine, ten, and twelve are the consistent and unmistakable articulations of Queen Elizabeth.

In the context of the addressee one notices more discrepancies and inconsistencies, but the general framework is as follows: the voice address is made sixteen times to a specific 'you', i.e., to the Queen's husband, mother-in-law, children, and sisters; three times to a personified abstraction, i.e., to astrology, wealth, and Richmond Castle, and four times to a designated 'you' which implies a circle of family members and friends surrounding her bedside. The voice becomes crystallized in the form of a soliloquy four times, and performs the function of an *apostrophe* three times as the Queen directs her address to God in stanzas three, ten, and twelve.

Sound and meaning structure are inextricably woven into an analysis of the above voice and address pattern, but an endeavour will be made to throw more light on each of these two phases which constitute such an integral part of this lilting and haunting elegy.

The efficacy of the sound structure in this poem depends on the principle of sameness and difference which gives it beauty, melody, and versatility. A skillful poet and meticulous craftsman, Thomas More takes the refrain, 'Lo now here I ly', and builds twelve rhyme royal stanzas around it. The structure he uses is architectonic in the sense that the central idea remains the same from the beginning till the end, but it is dilated and embellished by the accumulating data in each succeeding stanza. Consequently, the pattern follows a temporal unity which enables the reader to perceive the time gradation in the various events of the Queen's life. The emphasis is dramatic, and a strong, sensory appeal is made to the emotions, which makes the poem tender without becoming sentimental and tragic without descending into melodrama. The progression in this elegy appears to be circular, for the speaker always returns to the same starting point repeated in the haunting refrain, 'Lo now here I ly'.

E. E. Reynolds in his recent book, *Saint Thomas More*, reiterates Maynard's and Chambers' conclusions regarding More's metrical skill in this particular poem when he says: 'The third thing, the lament on the death of Queen Elizabeth (1503) deserves more consideration, for here Thomas More showed a metrical skill that makes one regret he did not develop this vein of poetry'.[47] More than fifty years ago Sidney Lee made a provocative comment regarding More's neglected poems when he said that 'More at times achieves metrical effects which adumbrate the art of Edmund Spenser'.[48]

The principle of sameness and difference in the sound structure gives rise to paratactic structure, which makes the dilation of the theme pleasing and sonorous. Melody in the poem is achieved by the underlying cadence, the regularity of which is strengthened by the ending refrain, while versatility results from the relation of the movement of stresses.

Parataxis in the sentence structure knits the component elements of the stanza, and thus forms a more coherent and felicitous sound pattern. This effect is increased when it is adorned with *anaphora*, or initial repetition, which gives it a pensive, rhythmical quality:

> *Was I not* borne of olde worthy linage?
> *Was not* my mother queene, my father kyng?
> *Was I not* a kinges fere in marriage?[49]

The variety of sentences used, such as declarative, interrogative, imperative, and exclamatory, diversify the paratactic structure and prevent it from becoming pompous and saccharine. More's use of the interrogative sentence is of particular interest in this elegy because it implies a soliloquy and is cast in the form of a dramatic monologue. Thus, it gives the lines a lilting rhythm and a haunting melody. These poignant interrogations are full of pathos, and they are uttered, not with pretentious vaunting but with a humble realization that 'rychesse, honour, welth, and auncestry', forsake even a royal personage at the inexorable hour of death. The four question marks Thomas More uses in the above stanza not only increase the musical quality of the cadence, but they also tend to stress the final accent of the last syllable in the line, which is determined by the raising of the voice at the end of the interrogative statement.

Thomas More's knowledge of rhetoric, oratorical ability, and love of poetry are instrumental in helping him to produce a work of art. The influence of the rhetoric is evident in the syntax, inversions, and variety of sentence structure; the oratorical ability is manifested in the elegance and force which characterize the style of this elegy; and the predilection for poetry is obvious in the knowledge of the metrics displayed and in the effective use of schemes and tropes. More proves himself to be an adept grammarian as well as a skillful versifier, for the punctuation marks he uses in this poem have a direct bearing on its rhythmical quality and tone color pattern. He uses these marks functionally and correlates them admirably with the pronounced mood of the poem. The period, for example, allows for further meditation on the statement uttered by the dying Queen, as is evident in these lines:

> If worship myght haue kept me, I had not gone.
> If wyt myght haue me saued, I nede not fere.
> If money myght haue holpe, I lacked none.[50]

The seven interrogation marks that are used in the course of the poem strike a personal note which is sustained appropriately by the pronoun 'I'. Sympathy and tender compassion are thus evoked as the reader or listener hears the dying Queen recount her noble ancestry and extol her royal lineage. She does not do this through the medium of declarative statements, for they would then color her autobiographical remarks with obnoxious egotism. In order to confirm her realization of the transiency of earthly goods and to convince others of the incompletion and futility of striving for honour and riches, she uses rhetorical questions with grandiloquent effect. Two typical statements illustrating this point follow:

> Was I not a kinges fere in marriage?
> Had I not plenty of euery pleasaunt thyng?[51]

Since the commas, which are often replaced by periods in the course of printing, do not portray accurately More's rhetorical style, they need not concern us here. This omission or misplacement may be ascribed to the negligence of the printer, and in More's day this inaccuracy was a prevalent problem, since punctuation was by no means standardized. The use of the colon, on the other hand, can be ascertained from the context of the statement which includes it:

> Mercifull god this is a strange reckenyng:
> Rychesse, honour, welth, and auncestry
> Hath me forsaken and lo now here I ly.[52]

One may argue the point that the punctuation marks may have been inserted by the printer in a loose and haphazard fashion; hence, they do not reflect More's conscious efforts in this regard. The nature of the sentences, however, is such that they require a certain kind of punctuation mark and, consequently, the variety of sentence structure on More's part implies the concomitant variety of punctuation marks with which these statements end either in oral speech or in writing. Even if the printer were careless in supplying these marks, the meaning and syntax of the sentences would require them.

From a rhetorical point of view also, the poem is a very interesting study in paratactic and hypotactic structure, with the latter indicating the syntactical pattern of the sentences. The present tense verbs create a direct, conversational tone, the preterite tense adds wistfulness and pathos to the lines, while the

151

future tense displays fear and trepidation. The following lines illustrate this technique:

Present Tense Verbs (underlined once)	O ye that *put* your trust and confidence . . . That so *liue* here as ye SHOULD neuer hence . . . *Remember* death and *loke* here uppon me.
Preterite Tense (underlined twice)	Me hath he SOMMONED, and lo now here I *ly*. Thy single pleasure DOUBLED is with payne. *Account* my sorrow first and my distresse.
Future Tense (underlined thrice)	At westminster that costly worke of yours, Myne owne dere lorde now SHALL I neuer SEE. Thou SHALT swete babe suche *is* thy desteny, Thy mother neuer KNOW, for lo now here I *ly*.

The use of the subjunctive mood in the third rhyme royal stanza together with the initial *anaphora* in the first three lines designated by 'If', determines the wistful mood of the elegy and concomitantly affects its rhythm:

$$\text{If w\H{o}r / ship m\H{y}ght / ha\u{u}e k\'ept / m\v{e} I h\'ad / n\H{o}t go\'ne /}$$
$$\text{If w\H{y}t / myg\H{h}t h\u{a}ue / m\'e sa\H{u}ed / I n\'ede / n\H{o}t fe\'re /}$$
$$\text{If m\'o / n\v{e}y myght / ha\u{u}e holp\'e / I lac\H{k} / ed no\'ne /}$$

The accent is placed not on the potentially powerful 'if' determinant, but on the seductive words, 'worship', 'wyt', and 'money', which are closely linked with the verbal phrase 'myght haue'. This functional subjunctive combination of 'if' and 'myght' seems to point to the false glamour of worldy enticements and to reveal a certain lack of security which the indicative mood might have conveyed. The dynamic verbs which complete the static auxiliaries 'myght haue' are chosen appropriately to correlate with the nouns and to complement their meaning. The three pithy sentences in the indicative mood which complete the subjunctive clauses possess strength of diction and virility of connotation. Their predication on the negative gives these lines a note of finality and assurance.

The twelve units of speech construct comprising 'A ruful lamentacion' are coherent units of sound pattern tied together by rhyme, alliteration, consonance, and assonance. The verses, however, are not overcharged with alliteration, for *anaphora* is used to achieve an analogous rhetorical effect. Nevertheless, wherever More does use alliteration, the vowel and consonant sound texture is strengthened thereby, and the poetical beauty of the verses is enhanced. The five alliterated *f*'s in the ending couplet of the eighth stanza form a consistent extension of the initial *f* in the first word, 'Farewell' and the medial word 'folke' in the fifth line. Repetition of the same letter is not overdone, and a salubrious balance is achieved when set against the three strong medial verbs which begin with the hard sound of *g*. In order to recognize the alliterative pattern at a glance, one has only to read the whole stanza as here quoted:

152

> *F*arewell my doughter Lady Margarete.
> God wotte *f*ull o*f*t it *g*reued hath my mynde,
> That ye should *g*o where we should seldome mete.
> Now am I *g*one, and haue le*f*t you behynde,
> O mortall *f*olke that we be very blynde.
> That we least *f*eare, *f*ull o*f*t it is most nye,
> *F*rom you depart I *f*yrst, and lo now here I lye.[53]

The six alliterated *s*'*s* in the following two lines of stanza ten give them a tone of softness and evoke sympathy on the part of the reader:

> Adew *s*wete hart my little doughter Kate
> Thou *s*halt *s*wete babe *s*uche i*s* thy de*s*teny . . .[54]

A wholesome sense of balance is shown in the next line as the pliable and tender quality of the *s* sound is contrasted against the firm *th* sound:

> *Th*y mo*th*er neuer know, for lo now here I ly.[55]

This same line contains a good illustration of the vowel assonance in the words 'know' and 'lo'. The assonance and consonance pattern adds most to the euphonic melody of the poem. The following stanza contains five accented *e*'s in the first five end-rhymes and twenty altogether in these five lines of verse:

> O y*e* that put your trust and confid*e*nce,
> In worldly ioy and frayle prosp*e*rit*e*,
> That so liue h*e*re as y*e* should n*e*uer h*e*nce,
> R*e*member d*e*ath and lok*e* h*e*re uppon m*e*.
> *E*nsaumple I thynke there may no better b*e*.[56]

The recurrence of the same consonantal sounds, namely, *rd* and *n*, forms the consonance in the end-rhymes of the seventh stanza:

> Adew myne owne dere spouse my worthy lo*rd*e,
> The faithful loue, that dyd us both comby*n*e,
> In marriage and peasable conco*rd*e,
> Into your handes here I cleane resy*n*e,
> To be bestowed uppon your children and my*n*e.[57]

Like a skillful artificer in words who wishes to deepen the gamut of tonal effects, Thomas More uses incomplete and imperfect rhyme to achieve the quality of dissonance which does not mar the rhythmical effect, but embellishes it. Examples of incomplete rhyme are interspersed throughout the entire poem, the most outstanding ones of which are the following: (1) in stanza one, 'confi-

153

dence and hence'; 'prosperite and be'; (2) in stanza two, 'auncestry and ly'; and (3) in stanza eleven, 'vanitee and flee'. A striking example of imperfect rhyme is found in the opening lines of stanza six in the first and third end-rhyme: *'Towers'* and *'yours'*. This rhyme, also called false rhyme, suspended rhyme, or tangential rhyme, retains the identity of the consonantal arrangement, and when used dexterously, produces pleasing and sonorous effects.

The most salient characteristic of Thomas More's rhyme scheme in this elegy is his successful use of feminine rhymes, which vary from the two-syllable rhyme to the four-syllable ones. To avoid over-femininity in the end-rhymes, he adroitly links them with a vigorous masculine rhyme in a chiasmatic pattern, as the following four lines of stanza one illustrate:

O ye that put your trust and confidence,	a
In worldly ioy and frayle prosperite,	b
That so live here as ye should never hence,	a
Remember death and loke here uppon me.	b

To further elucidate this point, 'confidence' is a feminine rhyme while 'hence' is masculine; in like manner, 'prosperite' is feminine while 'me' is a masculine rhyme. The fourth and sixth stanzas present an analogous technique in rhyme structure, for 'devynatrice' a four-syllable rhyme is followed by the masculine rhyme 'wyse', and 'edefy' rhymes vigorously with 'ly'.

Perhaps, the following diagram will give a better overall picture of this quantitative aspect of the poem's sound structure which gives it acoustic value and underlies diversity in the underlying pattern of unity:

Stanza	*Feminine rhymes*	*Masculine rhymes*
One	2	5
Two	4	3
Three	2	5
Four	5	2
Five	3	4
Six	2	5
Seven	4	3
Eight	2	5
Nine	2	5
Ten	4	3
Eleven	3	4
Twelve	3	4

On the whole, then, the feminine rhymes which form such a great part of Italian poetry are indigenous to this elegy, which, being the lament of a dying Queen, is overshadowed by a languishing mood and a haunting refrain.

It is an interesting feature in prosodic experimentation on More's part to realize how successfully he could use various rhyme scheme patterns to produce harmonious rhythm and euphonic effect. Theodore Maynard, who reiterates platitudinous remarks about More's English poetry, sees in this particular metrical effect some originality and value. Pertinently he says:

> It is perhaps the earliest of the adumbrations of the Spenserian stanza, in that More concludes the Chaucerian seven-line stanza, at that time called 'balade or ballet', with a hexameter line.[58]

Because of the important relation these hexameter lines, 'adumbrating the art of Spenser',[59] bear to the Spenserian stanza, the five couplets containing the refrain are quoted in full:

Stanza Six	For you and your children well may edefy. My palyce bylded is, and lo now here I ly.
Stanza Seven	Erst were you father, & now must ye supply, The mothers part also, for lo now here I ly.
Stanza Eight	That we least feare, full oft it is most nye, From you depart I fyrst, and lo now here I lye.
Stanza Ten	Thou shalt swete babe suche is thy desteny, Thy mother neuer know, for lo now here I ly.
Stanza Eleven	And heuenly thynges loue and magnify, Farewell and pray for me, for lo now here I ly.

The effect of the six-syllable line is achieved, to a great extent, through the medium of the terse monosyllables which form the six words of the refrain, 'for lo now here I ly'. The accents on the second, fourth, and sixth phonograms strengthen the principle of sameness on which this felicitous metrical effect is predicated. This same principle can be paralleled harmoniously with the principle of difference which, crystallized in the area of sentence structure patterns and rhyme forms, combines the eighty-four verses comprising the twelve stanzas into a veritable work of art.

According to Maynard, the function of the alexandrine has never been described better than by Saintsbury:

> Despite its great bulk and the consequent facilities which it offers for the vignetting of definite pictures and incidents within a single stanza, the long Alexandrine at the close seems to launch it towards its successor *ripae ulterioris amore*, or rather with the desire of fresh striking out in the unbroken though wave-swept sea of poetry.[60]

In tracing 'The Formation of the Spenserian Stanza' Maynard quotes the tenth stanza from Thomas More's lamentation on the death of Queen Elizabeth and sees in the hexameter line 'a perhaps unconscious incipience of the Spenserian stanza'.[61]

The principle of sameness in the sound structure of the poem is further seen in the rhyme scheme pattern which determines its identity as rhyme royal verse: a b a b b c c. The accent in the rhymes is also regular, for the most part, as the following diagram shows:

Regular accented rhyme		*Unaccented, 'misplaced' or 'strained' accent rhyme*	
gone	– none	thyng	– reckenyng
delice	– deuynatrice	lorde	– concorde
payne	– agayne – sayne	Towers	– yours
linage	– marriage	supply	– I ly
combyne	– resyne	estate	– fortunate – Kate
chere	– fere – dere	vanitee	– flee
mynde	– behynde – blinde	every chone	– alone – one
mother	– nother	Margarete	– mete
adew	– hew	Katheryne	– myne

In an age when 'the force, compass, and capacity of harmony were untried',[62] More's efforts in achieving felicitous rhythms are indeed praiseworthy. He uses iambic pentameter as his basic meter and varies it with wellplaced and felicitous substitutions. The first stanza has pleasing regularity which avoids becoming monotonous or trite:

> O ye / that put / your trust / and con / fidence /
> In world / ly ioy / and frayle / pros pe / ri te /
> That so / lyue here / that ye / should ne / uer hence /
> Re mem / ber death / and loke / here up / pon me /
> En saum / ple I thynke / there may / no bet / ter be /
> Your selfe / wotte well / that in / this realme / was I /
> Your quene / but late / and lo / now here / I lye /

The fourth verse ends with a trochee and spondee which give color and force to the Queen's injunction as she points to herself and urges those around her to profit from her tragic example. The anapestic foot in the fifth verse is the occasion for a medial caesura and enables the stress to be placed on the key word, 'thynke'.

Vigorous trochees make the second stanza resound with poignant lamentation and acrid self-accusation. Verses five and six, in particular, exemplify these inversions:

> Mer ci / full God / this is a / straunge re / ckenyng /
> Ry chesse / ho nour / welth // and aun / ces try /

156

The medial caesura after the third foot is a characteristic technique of More, which he uses often with gratifying results. He further varies the rhythm by adding an extra short syllable at the beginning of the second or third foot in the verse. As a consequence, the regularity of the iambic pentameter is prevented from becoming boring, and this relaxation and flexibility of the underlying meter produces wholesome effects. Note, verses three and four of this same stanza:

> Wăs I nŏt / ă king / ĕs fere / in măr / ri ăge /
> Hăd I / not plĕn / tў of eŭe / rў / pleă / săunt thўng /

On the other hand, to sustain the regularity of the meter he uses *hyperbaton* effectively without ostentation or artificiality. Verse two of stanza three illustrates this technique:

> If wўt / mўght *haŭe* / *me saŭĕd* / I nedĕ / nŏt fere /

Hyperbaton adds vigor and force to the sixth verse and alters the mood of the poem which hitherto was gentle and languishing:

> *O^xbeў* / *we^xmust* / therĕ i̸s / nŏ rĕ / mĕ dў /

The syntax inversion in the last verse gives trenchant emphasis to the words of the Queen as she dejectedly points to herself and says:

> *Mĕ hăth* / *hĕ som* / *mŏ nĕd* / ănd lŏ / nŏw here / I lў /

The first verse of the fourth stanza evokes a meditative mood with the introductory monosyllable 'yet'. This pensive atmosphere is sustained by the three medial anapests which, in More's characteristic fashion, give the fivestress line buoyancy and flexibility. The poignant question inherent in lines three to five is written in an inverted rhetorical style which accentuates and facilitates the smoothness of the rhythm:

> Lŏ where / tŏ come / mĕth thў bland / ĭsh ĭng / prŏ mўse /
> O false / as^xtrŏ / lă gў / ănd dĕ vў / ăna trice /
> Of god / dĕs sec / retes mak / kyng thy self / sŏ wўse /

One cannot read these lines from More's lamentation without recalling to mind Chaucer's rhyme royal verses on 'The Complaint of Mars':

> O wŏ / fŭl Mars / ă las / whăt maist / thŏu seўn /
> Thăt in / the păl / eўs ŏf / thy dis / tŭr baunce /
> Art thŏu left / bў-hynde / in pĕ / ril tŏ / bĕ sleўn[63]

157

The iambic pentameter which makes up the following lines of the fifth stanza, with the exception of two pyrrhic substitutions, is divested of monotony and banality by the richness of its onomatopoetic imagery:

O brýt / til welth / aý full / óf bit / tér nesse /
Thy sin / gle pléa / sure dóu / bled is / with paýne /

The freshness and originality of the *prosopopoeia* or what in twentieth-century parole is termed personification, is evident in the words, 'bryttil', 'bitternesse', and 'payne'. These words attribute human characteristics to wealth and its ensuing pain, with the exception that 'bryttil' is applied to things rather than to human beings. This word, nevertheless, is so pregnant with sound appeal and kinesthetic experience that More's use of it in this context is a felicitous addition to his poetry. It is a word that he uses often to connote the transiency of this life and the speciousness of wealth, honor, and fortune. The author of the *Mirror for Magistrates* employs this word in the same context as Thomas More fifty years later. He says with keen insight and subtle appreciation of the true value of an elusive quality or state of being: 'To shew by patarne of a prince, how brittle honour is'.[64]

The first verse of the sixth stanza contains the following brilliant substitutions, which are accentuated by the interrogation point at the end of the rhetorical question:

Whére are / our Cás / tels nów / where are / our Tów / ers?

There is enough rhythmical diversification in this verse with two trochees, to warrant the regularity of iambic meter in the next six lines which, without this pleasing and refreshing irregularity, would descend into jingling and common-place meter.

The run-on lines in the next stanza give coherence and strength to the basic rhythmical pattern into which mold, all seven lines are set. To show their functional use in rounding out the rhythm and in accentuating the thought rather than striving merely for metrical effects, the following symbols will be used: (0) run-on lines; (//) normal pause; (///) heavy pause.

A déw / mýne owne / deré spóuse // mý wór / thy lorde ///
The fáith / full loúe / that dýd / us bóth / com býne / (0)
In már / ri age // and péa / sa ble / con córde /
In tó / your hándes / here /// I cleáne / re syne /
To bé / be stowed / up pon / your child / ren and myne /
Erst wére / you fa / ther & nów // must yé / sup ply / (0)
The mó / thers part / al so /// for ló // now here // I lý /

158

The 'Adew' in the seventh stanza is changed to a 'Farewell' in the eighth one. The alliterated *f*'s add beauty to the lines and make up for the lack of substitutions which give variety to the other stanzas.

The light and heavy stresses in the ninth stanza follow a consistent pattern in lines one, two, three, five, and seven; in lines four and six the trochee and the two spondees give the verses vigor and dramatic intensity.

> Fare well / my dough / ter La / dy Mar / ga rete /
> God wotte / full oft / it gre / ued hath / my mynde /
> That ye / should go / where we / should sel / dome mete /
>
> Now am / I gone / and haue / left you / be hynde /
> O mor / tall folke / that we / be ve / ry blinde /
> That we / least feare / full oft / it is / most nye /
> From you / de part / I fyrst / and lo / now here / I lye /

The tenth stanza has all end-stopped lines, and only the concluding couplet is here quoted from it:

> Thou shalt / swete babe / such is / thy des / te ny /
> Thy mo / ther ne / uer know / for lo / now here / I ly /

In the eleventh stanza the words that are heavily stressed are those that articulate the transitoriness of worldly possessions and pleasures and extol the wisdom of turning one's mind heavenward and of longing for heavenly things. In the context of this rhyme royal stanza the heavily-stressed syllables are the following:

Verse one   – all lightly stressed syllables
Verse two   – Fare-well, wel be-lo-ued
Verse three – all lightly stressed syllables
Verse four   – Lo, end, world-ly va-ni-tee
Verse five   – ye, fol-ly, flee
Verse six   – he-uen-ly, loue, mag-ni-fy
Verse seven – Fare-well, pray, me, lo, ly.

The twelfth and last stanza of this wistful elegy begins with three lines characterized by *anaphora*, which enhances its euphonic effect. The farewells addressed to the lord, ladies, and 'faithfull seruauntes euery chone' serve as a fitting finale to this 'ruful lamentacion on the deth of Quene Elisabeth mother to king Henry the eight and wife to king Henry the seuenth'. Commensurate with the philosophy and ideals of a Christian humanist, the poem ends on a Christian note as the good Queen commends herself to the infinite mercy of God. She has exhibited poignant sorrow but manifested no despair; she has rued her attachment to worldly honor and riches, but trusted until the end in the mercy and goodness of Christ, the Redeemer of mankind.

The epitaph which Thomas More appended to this lamentation in Latin and in English is a fitting tribute to the good and noble Queen. The Latin epitaph is composed of ten lines, while the English one has eighteen lines of pentameter couplets. Both epitaphs are printed in Richard Hill's *Commonplace Book*, compiled from the Balliol MS. 354, which ranges from A.D. 1508 to 1536.[65] Since for some reason these epitaphs were not included in Thomas More's *English Works*, edited by William Rastell in 1557, the English epitaph is quoted in full here:

> Here lith the fresshe flowr of Plantagenet;
> Here lith the white rose in the rede sete;
> Here lith the nobull quen Elyzabeth;
> Here lith the princes departid by deth;
> Here lith blode of owr contray royall;
> Here lith fame of Ynglond immortall;
> Here lith of Edward the IIIIth a picture;
> Here lith his dowghter & perle pure;
> Here lith the wyff of Harry, owr trew kyng;
> Here lith the hart, the joy & the gold rynge;
> Here lith the lady so lyberall & gracius;
> Here lith the pleasure of thy hows;
> Here lith very loue of man & child;
> Here lith insampull, owr myndez to bild;
> Here lith all bewte, of lyung a myrrour;
> Here lith all vertu, good maner & honour;
> God grant her now heuyn to encrese,
> & owr kyn Harry long lyff & pease![66]

Although Henry VII married Elizabeth Plantagenet at the advice of his mother, the Countess of Richmond, for purely political reasons, she, the eldest daughter of Edward IV and the rightful heir to the English throne, probably did more to heal England's wounds than her avaricious husband. With Elizabeth's consent to the marriage after the decisive Battle at Bosworth, the union of the Houses of York and Lancaster was consolidated. The day she was summoned to meet her illustrious and victorious husband at Westminster, she took as her motto, 'Humble and Reverent'.[67] It was no easy thing for her, a Yorkist, to submit herself to a Lancastrian who delayed her coronation for two years and fulfilled his promise first after she had presented him with a male heir to the throne.[68] Nevertheless, in spite of a life of disillusionment and suffering, she was happy and content in the thought that she made a gift to her country by uniting the Red and White Rose into one Tudor Rose.

Henry VIII was only twelve years old when his mother, Queen Elizabeth, died; but he kept her memory alive in his heart throughout the thirty-eight years of his reign. The greatest tribute he paid to his mother, to whom he was always very devoted, was to name the daughter of his second marriage 'Elizabeth'[69] after her. The young prince Harry, who already in his eighth year manifested an interest in poetical accomplishments, must have been impressed favourably with Thomas More's eulogy of his beloved mother. The eighteen-line epitaph penned by Thomas More in honour of Queen Elizabeth, not only extols her virtues but also tactfully brings in her husband, Henry VII, and renders him tribute as 'owr trew kyng'.[70] This phrase must have been veritable music to Henry VII's ears, for during most of the twenty-four years of his reign he struggled aggressively to support his claim to the English throne. More's elegy on the death of Elizabeth of York may have been instrumental in obtaining for him a representation in the new Parliament of 1504, although he was only twenty-five years old at the time.

The praises Thomas More lavishes on the Queen are not mere verbal enunciations of obsequious devotion; they constitute a sincere encomium to one who merited the title 'Good' by those who were her subjects. The following outline briefly enumerates and summarizes the nature of these praises:

1.	fresshe flowr of Plantagenet	9.	princes departid by deth
2.	white rose in the rede sete	10.	blode of owr contray royall
3.	nobull quen Elyzabeth	11.	fame of Ynglond immortall
4.	of Edward the IIIIth a picture	12.	the pleasure of thy hows
5.	his dowghter & perle pure	13.	very loue of man & child
6.	wyff of Harry, our trew kyng	14.	insampull, owr myndez to bild
7.	the hart, the joy & the gold rynge	15.	all bewte, of lyvyng a myrrour
8.	the lady so lyberall & gracius	16.	all vertu, good maner & honour

The last couplet is refreshingly original, as the poet, through the medium of *hyperbaton*, inverts the order of words to achieve good end rhyme; he does this, however, without sacrificing the sense by making it artificial or fatuous, and achieves instead a strikingly creative effect:

> God grant her now heuyn to encrese,
> & owr kyn Harry long lyff & pease!

'A ruful lamentacion of the deth of quene Elisabeth' has overtones of Petrarch's rhetorical questions in the third of his six 'Triumphs', namely, 'The Triumph of Death'. One has merely to compare the two interrogatory statements which achieve such a genuine poetic effect and are so contiguous to the elegiac form:

'The Triumph of Death'	'A ruful lamentacion'
Where is that wealth? where are those honors gone?	Where are our Castels, now where are our Towers?

Scepters, and crownes, and roabes
    and purple dye?
And costlie myters, sett with
    pearle and stone?
O wrethc who doest in mortall
    things affye.[71]

Fortune som bitter with your
    sweetes compound.[72]

Goodly Rychmonde sone art thou
    gone from me . . .
Rychesse, honour, welth, and
    auncestry
Hath me forsaken and lo now here
    I ly.[73]

O bryttil welth, ay full of
    bitternesse,
Thy single pleasure, doubled is
    with payne.[74]

Likewise, Lydgate's 'An Envoy on Rome', which completes Book II of the
Fall of Princes, is replete with rhetorical interrogations which constitute such a
pleasing and sonorous sound pattern in poems characterized by the lamentation
of a person, object, or thing:

> Wher be thyn Emperours, most souereyn off renoun?
> Kynges exiled for outraious lyuyng? (ll. 4467–4468).

> Where is the palace or royall mancion,
> With a statue clere of golde shining
> By Romulus wrought & set on that dongeon? (ll. 4481–4483).

> Wher is become thi dominacioun?
> The grete tributis [enrichyng] thi tresours? (ll. 4509–4510).

The historical allusions this poem contains make it a memorable one indeed.
These references are amalgamated into the thought content of the twelve
rhyme royal stanzas; therefore, they form a large part of the analysis of the
meaning structure of the poem and are considered concomitantly with it.

    One of the most curious allusions in this elegy is the reference to the tenacious
belief in the powers of astrology in the sixteenth century. Unlike his predecessors and many of his colleagues, Thomas More boldly asserts his denial of the
efficacy of this superstitious astronomical power. In the dying words of Queen
Elizabeth one hears this Christian humanist enunciating his ideas and convictions about the powers alleged to science which belong indubitably to God
alone. Elizabeth of York says with sardonic bitterness in her tone of voice:

> Yet was I late promised otherwyse,
> This yere to liue in welth and delice.
> Lo where to commeth thy blandishing promyse,
> O false astrolagy and deuynatrice,
> Of goddes secretes makyng thy selfe so wyse?
> How true is for this yere thy prophecy?
> That yere yet lasteth, and lo now here I ly.[75]

It was believed that planets possessed special attributes and exerted a powerful influence over men's lives. The planet's position in the heavens, especially at the moment of one's birth, determined one's destiny and was alluded to as 'casting the horoscope'.[76] To cast a horoscope the astrologer divided the circle of the universe into four segments. These he subdivided into twelve equal parts and numbered them from one to twelve. Knowing the hour and day of birth and, whenever possible, the precise moment the person was born, the astrologer looked into Ephemerides, and by the conjunctions of the planets he determined the infant's prospects and even his occupation in life. For example, spinning was attributed to Aries, music to Gemini, hunting to Leo, and language and scholarship to Virgo.[77] It is no wonder that the Church became alarmed over the popularity of this belief, and while admitting the importance of astronomical studies, she was very conscious of its dangers. Among the humanists in the fifteenth century, Pico della Myrandola was an honourable exception to this avid credence in astrology. He would often say: 'Nothing can more foster evil than the belief that the heavens and not man are the cause of it'.[78]

Henry VIII shared More's curiosity and interest from a purely scientific point of view in the heavenly phenomena, and he would often discuss with him matters of astronomy and geometry. Oftentimes at night, Roper tells us, they would watch the stars and planets and consider their courses, motions, and operations.[79] More condemned belief in the stellar horoscope as pure superstition, and whenever the occasion presented itself, he staunchly expressed his conviction. From the Queen's censure on the deception of astronomical predictions, one gets the impression that she consulted the horoscope for an answer to the question of what this particular year would have in store for her. She says reproachfully in the opening lines of the fourth stanza:

> Yet was I late promised otherwyse,
> This yere to liue in welth and delice.

Belief in the supernatural powers of astrological predictions was so common that every court had its practising astrologer, and all the universities had their professors of this science.[80] C. E. Mallet tells us that 'practically all the great medieval mathematicians were astronomers and that all medical science was supposed to be governed by the stars.'[81]

Thomas More's convictions regarding the futility and perniciousness of this popular belief paralleled those of John Lydgate, who, in his *Court of Sapience*, a learned poetic allegory of 330 stanzas, devotes 115 lines to Astronomy, which mirrors the current beliefs of the fifteenth century. In the poem, Astronomy is personified as a heavenly dame while Astrology, her maid, is described thus:

> Whiche somtyme is kyndely and precyous,
> And otherwhyle ouer-moche superstysous.[82]

163

Not to leave any dubious connotation in the reader's mind, Lydgate goes on to explain what he means by the above equivocation:

> She is kyndely, whan that she sheweth clere
> The sonnes cours, the mone, the sterres eke,
> And doth nothyng but as kynd doth her lere;
> But whan she lust in sterres for to seke
> The byrthe of man, whyche hole, [whiche] shal be seke,
> And wyl dyuine, and preche thyng for to be,
> Unkyndely than and unleful is she.[83]

In the following rhyme royal stanza the same poet gives credit to Isidore for the logical refutation of this rife belief:

> For yf man were in his natyuyte
> Constreyned to his sondry actes al,
> Theym for to doo ryght by necessyte,
> Why shold good men haue lawde in specyal,
> Or myslyuers to punysshement be thral?
> Good Isidorus maketh this reson
> In dampnynge of this fals oppynyon.[84]

In view of the fact that Thomas More was only twenty-five years old at the writing of this poem, one can admire his integrity of character and fortitude in enunciating his convictions so intrepidly. History gives no insight as to whether or not Elizabeth of York had really consulted the horoscope; nevertheless, the poem gives tangible indication that she was aware of the predictions for the year 1503; but, on the other hand, it does not imply that she believed in them.

The White Rose of the Plantagenet garden was surrounded by thorns, and the trials and vexations of mind and heart that she endured as wife and consort of King Henry VII outweighed the joys and honours of regal reign. Perhaps, the following lines are intermingled with an exaggeration of the actual facts to make the poem more romantic in its audience appeal; nevertheless, historical data agrees with it in its general scope:

> O bryttil welth, ay full of bitternesse,
> The single pleasure doubled is with payne.
> Account my sorrow first and my distresse,
> In sondry wyse, and recken there agayne,
> The joy that I haue had, and I dare sayne,
> For all my honour endured yet haue I,
> More wo then welth, and lo now here I ly.[85]

There is an obvious sense of unity in these verses which begin with 'welth' and end with it. Elizabeth of York is referring here not only to financial security but also to emotional adjustment, peace of mind, and interior joy. Luckily, she

164

possessed a sense of equilibrium and knew how to direct her interests and affections into other channels, which became a redeeming feature of her marital life. In her royal consort, Henry VII, she did not find the love and comradeship her affectionate nature needed; therefore, she poured out all her love on her children and lived for them alone. When the first child, a son, Arthur, and the heir to the royal throne, was born at Winchester in September, 1486, his birth was hailed with as much gladness and triumph as had attended his father's and mother's marriage. The union of the rival houses of York and Lancaster was celebrated with bonfires, banquets, and pageants, and white and red roses figured prominently.[86] It is an interesting historical fact that the first male heir was named after King Arthur, since Henry VII and his mother, the Countess of Richmond, prided themselves on their regal ancestry which went as far back as the great British King Cadwallader.

Since the Londoners strongly resented the King's heir having been born at Winchester, Elizabeth's second child was born at Westminster to appease them. It was a girl, and she was called Margaret after the King's mother, Lady Margaret Beaufort. In the eighth stanza the dying Queen laments the fact that it is not Margaret who will go on a long journey, but she who never dreamed that her death would come before her eldest daughter's departure:

> Farewell my doughter Lady Margarete.
> God wotte full oft it greued hath my mynde,
> That ye should go where we should seldome mete.
> Now am I gone, and haue left you behynde,
> O mortall folke that we be very blinde,
> That we least feare, full oft it is most nye,
> From you depart I fyrst, and lo now here I lye.[87]

Perhaps it was good that the good Queen did not probably know that her daughter's future husband easily and quickly passed from his mourning for Margaret Drummond, the fair, unhappy woman whom he had secretly married in his youth and who, together with her two sisters, had been killed by an unknown murderer to prevent the King's open acknowledgment of her as his wife.[88] Unlike her saintly mother, 'the good Queen Bess', Lady Margaret, who became the Queen of Scotland in her youth, was a great thorn not only in the side of Scotland, but England as well. She had spent her life in persistent determination to gratify her own mean and low inclinations in utter disregard of the claims of others. After her husband's death she became regent of the country during her son, James V's minority. For marrying the Earl of Angus, however, she was deposed from this regency. She sued for a divorce from her second husband, Angus, but her efforts to free herself from him were violently opposed by her brother, Henry VIII of England, who sent a Roman Catholic priest down to Scotland to remonstrate with the insubordinate wife in vain.

It was fortunate that Queen Elizabeth was spared the heartaches and disappointments her daughter's selfishness and levity would have caused her. Truly, she was most unlike her good, gentle mother and her silent, cautious father; if, like him, on the other hand, she had a great desire for money, she had an equal propensity for spending it extravagantly.

In June, 1491, a second son was born at Greenwich. Elizabeth loved him with a delight that made the disappointments of her marriage life bearable. The unforeseen future heir at this time to the throne of England was named Harry, and he lived up to his jolly, dashing name. In the tenth stanza of this mournful elegy the Queen-Mother bids adieu to him in these pithy but solicitous words:

> Adew lord Henry my louyng sonne adew.
> Our Lorde encrease your honour and estate.[89]

She had a strong, tender love for her twelve-year-old son, Henry, and often while observing him in his vigorous and robust sport, she had a secret premonition that he, and not the pale and sickly-looking Arthur, would be the next successor to the English throne. There is a note of finality in her farewell to Henry, and it may be careful design on the poet's part or merely an undeliberate euphonic device that the Queen employs the term 'adew' for both father and son, while for her daughters and sisters she uses the term 'farewell'. With a mother's prophetic look she seems to pierce the veil of the future as she prays that God increase his honour and estate.

Queen Elizabeth next addresses her four-year-old daughter, Mary, and bequeaths to her the legacy of virtue, wisdom, and good fortune. She was the fifth child and exceedingly dear to Elizabeth, since her fourth child, named after her own mother, Elizabeth Woodville, had died young. Hence, there is no mention of her in the lamentation. Princess Mary was such a lovely child that tradition states that the probability of her growing up the most beautiful princess in Europe was taken into account at the disposal of her hand – personal considerations rarely thought of in state alliances.[90] Fittingly, then, More puts the phrase describing Mary's beauty already as a child, 'Adew my doughter Mary bright of hew',[91] into the context of the dying Queen's lamentation verse. Little Mary inherited the docility and sweetness of her good and virtuous mother, and not only her rare beauty, but also her modesty and gravity enchanted all she came in contact with. At the age of sixteen her marriage to King Louis XII of France, who was then infirm and sixty years of age, made her the Queen Consort of France. Her reign, however, was of very brief duration, beginning in October of 1515 and ending on the last day of that same year. She married Charles Brandon, the Duke of Suffolk, and like her mother, she was a good and devoted wife. Like her mother, too, she died at the age of thirty-seven, after previously receiving a severe blow in the death of her only son, a boy of eleven years of age.[92]

Elizabeth's most poignant and tender words are addressed to her youngest daughter, Kate, who was destined never to know her mother:

> Adew swete hart my litle doughter Kate,
> Thou shalt swete babe suche is thy desteny,
> Thy mother neuer know, for lo now here I ly.[93]

Although the voice of history is articulate about the lives of her other children, very little or almost nothing is narrated of the youngest child, who also probably died while young. Of her seven children, four died young, namely, Edmund, Arthur, Katherine, and Elizabeth, leaving Margaret, Henry, and Mary to grow up

The birth of the last child, which precipitated Elizabeth's death, was designated on account of some occult reason of Henry's to take place in the royal appartments adjacent to the Tower. The rooms were damp, the time of delivery was in winter, and Henry VII was aware of the fact that his wife suffered acutely with the ague. But Elizabeth's retorts to the remonstrations of her sisters, who were embittered and displeased with such treatment, was: 'When a Tudor commands, one must obey. Henry never does anything without a reason'.[94] In the course of a week oppressed by anxiety and worry and tormented with the ague, which passed into consumption, Queen Elizabeth died on her thirty-seventh birthday, February 11, 1503.[95] Warton gives us an interesting detail concerning the Queen's death when he says: 'The queen died within a few days after she was delivered of this infant, the princess Catherine, who did not long survive her mother's death'.[96]

Thomas More knew the royal family, and he maintained an enthusiastic and lively interest in the children of the royal Tudor household. This fact gives the poem verisimilitude and interest. More had taken his friend, Erasmus of Rotterdam, in the year 1499 to meet the children of Henry VII. Thomas More was at that time twenty-one years old and full of the merry wit, which was so characteristic of him all through his life, and it was this fun-loving mischief that prompted him to play a joke on his friend. Apparently, More and the young nine-year old Prince Henry VIII must have been on quite friendly terms, for it appears that they together concocted a drollery which caused the Dutch scholar chagrin but evoked a belated poem from his pen.

In spite of pronounced differences of nature and temperament, Elizabeth testifies to the faithfulness of her spouse in stanza seven:

> Adew myne owne dere spouse my worthy lorde,
> The faithfull loue, that dyd us both combyne,
> In marriage and peasable concorde,
> Into your handes here I cleane resyne,
> To be bestowed uppon your children and myne.[97]

Henry VII did not marry after his Queen died, but this was not because of love or loyalty to her memory, but simply because prospects for three other subsequent political marriage alliances failed him. He was forty-nine when his wife died, and he contemplated obtaining a papal dispensation which would enable him to marry the nominal widow of his lately-deceased son, Arthur, the Prince of Wales. When Katherine of Aragon and all others who were consulted protested vehemently against this unnatural marriage, he transferred his proposals to her widowed sister, Joanna. The last proposal was directed to a third widow, the Austrian Princess Margaret of Savoy; but this offer also was not accepted, and Henry died on April 21, 1509, in his fifty-fourth year having survived the Queen by five years.[98]

In stanza nine Queen Elizabeth bids farewell to her husband's mother, Lady Margaret, the Countess of Richmond, the 'venerable Margaret'[99] of Gray's verse and the mother of a race of kings. A loving, mutual relationship existed between Queen Elizabeth and her mother-in-law, to whom she went for advice and guidance, especially after her own mother had been sent away to the Convent of Bermondsey. Margaret of Richmond outlived her daughter-in-law by six years and her son by a few months. He was a dutiful and affectionate son towards her and always manifested great outward respect for her; yet, as Bacon adds significantly, 'not listening to her'.[100] The first three lines of this ninth stanza are addressed to Elizabeth's mother-in-law, whom the dying Queen exhorts to submit wholly to God's will in this instance:

> Farewell Madame my lordes worthy mother,
> Comfort your sonne, and be of good chere,
> Take all a worth for it wil be no nother.[101]

According to the *OED*, 'nother' is a variant for 'other' or 'an other'; hence, the verse simply means: 'take all things as they come, for the will of God has ordained that it should be so'. Nevertheless, 'nother' is a poor, watered-down rhyme which gives one the impression it was chosen for lack of a better and more meaningful one. This line may also allude to Henry's possible marriage after the Queen's death. Thus, she may have wished to placate her mother-in-law's anxiety concerning the rumours to which Henry's attitude towards his wife gave rise.

> Farewell my doughter Katherine late the fere
> To prince Arthur myne owne chyld so dere,
> It booteth not for me to wepe or cry,
> Pray for my soule, for lo now here I ly.[102]

Katherine's mother, Isabella of Castile, was a friend of Columbus, and her father, Ferdinand of Aragon, was the conqueror of the Moors. At the age of three the little girl Katherine was promised in marriage to Arthur, the Prince of Wales, who was then only a babe of twenty months. From her fourth year the future bride was called the Princess of Wales, and she corresponded in Latin with her future husband. Henry VII was not only gratified with the success of this political alliance which strengthened his kingdom, but he was also pleased with his daughter-in-law's physical appearance, decorum, and dignity. Only six months after their marriage Arthur died, either from a development of a consumptive malady or from a sudden outbreak of the plague. Being called back to London after her husband's early death, Katherine remained at the English court for nine years, the poor victim of the avaricious King Henry and the covetous King Ferdinand, her father, who wished to maintain at any cost the Anglo-Spanish alliance.[103]

Even Elizabeth of York must have been aware of the suspicion when she was sent to the Tower for the delivery of her seventh child that Henry was anxious to wed Katherine himself rather than imperil this alliance. Nevertheless, two years after the death of Arthur, Katherine, in spite of her reluctance, was betrothed to his brother Henry Tudor, who was only a boy of twelve while she was a young widow of eighteen. Six years later in June of the year 1609 and six weeks after the death of King Henry VII, Katherine and Henry were married. In the middle of the festivities, tidings arrived of the death of the King's grandmother, the highly respected and loved Margaret of Richmond. The exhortation addressed to Katherine by Elizabeth in the last verse of the ninth stanza, 'Pray for my soule', was faithfully carried out by her daughter-in-law, who was often found kneeling on the hard, cold floor of the church praying for her loved ones.

After bidding adieu to her husband, mother-in-law, daughter-in-law, and children, the Queen turns to her loving sisters, who lived with her in the royal castle and whose presence gave her the sympathy and companionship her forever-busy husband denied her. She addresses them affectionately by name and in a separate line commends her fourth sister, Bridget, for embracing the religious life:

> Lady Cicyly, Anne, and Katheryne,
> Farewell my welbeloued sisters three,
> O lady Briget other sister myne,
> Lo here the ende of worldly vanitee.
> Now well are ye that earthly folly flee,
> And heuenly thynges loue and magnify,
> Pray for my soule, for lo now here I ly.[104]

Thomas More's unfinished *History of King Richard the Third* begins with a brief description of the children of Edward IV: Edward, Richard, Elizabeth, Cicely, Bridget, Anne, and Katherine. Their names appear in the first line of the above stanza according to their seniority, while Bridget, who became a contemplative nun in Dartford, is given distinction by having her name set apart from the others. There is reverence in these lines, and they mirror the young humanist's predilection for things of the spirit.

The Queen's three lovely sisters became the brides of English noblemen: Anne was honorably married to Lord Howard, who afterwards became the Earl of Surrey. Thomas More alludes to Cicely, the eldest of the three as 'not so fortunate as fair'.[105] When her rich, old husband died, she no longer made a secret of her love for Sir Robert Kime, a gentlemen of Lincolnshire. Of Kathe-rine's lot More tells us that for a long time she fluctuated between wealth and adversity, and at last through the kindness and generosity of her nephew, King Henry VIII, she was given prosperous estate befitting her birth and virtue. Bridget, the youngest of Edward IV's five daughters, was happy and content in the convent, which fact gave her mother untold joy and her sisters, an edifying example of worldly renunciation.

The last stanza is a synthesis of sorrow and hope in which the Queen bids farewell to the lords and ladies who served her and commends herself to the mercy of God. With her last words she explicitly proclaims her belief in the Blessed Trinity when she says:

Immortall god verely three and one.[106]

Then humbly calling herself the servant of God, she places her hope in Christ's merits as she implores Him to have pity upon her soul.

William Rastell, More's nephew, who collected and printed his *English Works*, dedicated his praiseworthy task to the Queen of England, Mary Tudor. She was the third but only surviving child of Henry VIII and Catherine of Aragon. As a young woman she knew four foreign languages, was skilled in music and embroidery, and manifested piety and courage to a remarkable degree. In the year 1535 when Thomas More courageously and devoutly gave his life as a pledge of his belief in the universal authority of Peter's successor, the Supreme Pontiff, Princess Mary was nineteen years of age. More's beautiful example of steadfast faith and intrepid loyalty at the hour of his death, his zeal for truth, and the integrity of his character must have impressed her deeply. When she was crowned Queen in 1553, his example shone brilliantly in her actions, for, like him, she made her conscience her guide in all matters.

Just a year before her death in 1557, which was precipitated by an incurable disease,[107] but worn out, perhaps still more by many misunderstood and futile attempts to reconcile England with Rome, Queen Mary graciously accepted Rastell's petition to become the patron of Thomas More's *English Works*.

In the dedication to the 1557 edition, William Rastell gives eloquent testimony to the esteem Thomas More had for her in these words:

> . . . and for that also that Syr Thomas More (the author of these workes) whyle he lyved, dyd beare towardes your highnesse a speciall zeale, an entier affection, and reverent devocion: and on thother syde lykewyse your grace (as it is well knowen) had towardes him in his life time, a benevolent mynde and synguler favoure, not onelye for his great learn-ynge, but also for his moch more vertue.[108]

On the whole, 'A ruful lamentacion' is a moving and eloquent poem. The rhythm is pleasing to the ear and particularly vibrant with lyric qualities. The aural effect is strengthened by the vowel and consonant pattern which gives rise to assonance and alliteration, and hence makes it adaptable to singing or oral delivery. The rhymes, for the most part, are dependent upon the thought developed by the artistic treatment of the theme and aid the poet in avoiding the censure of stressing the sound pattern to the exclusion of the meaning structure. A. W. Reed sees in this poem 'unusual historical interest'[109] and an elegy with 'a wealth of allusion which alone must save it from neglect'.[110]

1. Puttenham, ed. Willcock and Walker, pp. 47–49.
2. *Works*, I, 16.
3. Bridgett, p. 15.
4. Warton, III, 94.
5. *Ibid.*, III, 97.
6. Bridgett, p. 15.
7. Warton, III, 96.
8. R. W. Chambers, p. 91.
9. Her daughter-in-law, Katheryne, is referred to as the fifth child. Of Elizabeth's seven children, four died young.
10. Henrietta Keddie, *Tudor Queens and Princesses* (London, 1896), p. 157.
11. 'A ruful lamentacion,' Seventh Page. D. 2–8.
12. *Fere*, wife.
13. 'A ruful lamentacion,' Seventh Page. D. 7–8.
14. *Ibid.*, Eighth Page. A. 1–2.
15. *Ibid.*, A. 8–10.
16. *Ibid.*, A. 11.
17. *Ibid.*, A. 12. B. 1–2.
18. Craig, p. 348.
19. 'A ruful lamentacion,' Eighth Page. B. 3–4.
20. *Ibid.*, B. 5–7.
21. *Ibid.*, B. 8–9.
22. Warton, III, 97.
23. 'A ruful lamentacion,' Eighth Page. C. 1–7.
24. Frederick J. Furnivall, ed., *Chaucer's Minor Poems*, Chaucer Society, 1st series (London, 1880), 318.
25. 'A ruful lamentacion,' Eighth Page. C. 8.
26. *Works*, I, 16.
27. 'A ruful lamentacion,' Eighth Page. C. 9.
28. *Ibid.*, C. 10. D. 1.
29. *Ibid.*, D. 2–4.
30. 'A ruful lamentacion,' Eighth Page. D. 5–9.
31. Williamson, p. 20.
32. Bridgett, p. 113.
33. 'A ruful lamentacion,' Eighth Page. D. 10. Ninth Page. A. 1.
34. Keddie, p. 159.
35. 'A ruful lamentacion,' Ninth Page. A. 2–4.
36. *Ibid.*, A. 5.
37. *Ibid.*, A. 6–7.
38. *Ibid.*, A. 8.
39. *Ibid.*, B 4–5.
40. *Ibid.*, B. 10. C. 1–2.
41. Bridgett, p. 55.
42. 'A ruful lamentacion,' Ninth Page. C. 6.
43. *Ibid.*, C. 7–8.
44. *Ibid.*, C. 9.
45. *Ibid.*, C. 10. D. 1–6.
46. Keddie, p. 157.
47. Reynolds, p. 49.
48. Lee, p. 60.
49. 'A ruful lamentacion,' Eighth Page. A. 1–3

50. *Ibid.*, A. 8–10.
51. *Ibid.*, A. 3–4.
52. *Ibid.*, A. 5–7.
53. *Ibid.*, Ninth Page. A. 2–8.
54. *Ibid.*, B. 10. C. 1.
55. *Ibid.*, C. 2.
56. *Ibid.*, Seventh Page. D. 2-6.
57. *Ibid.*, Eighth Page. D. 5–9.
58. Theodore Maynard, *Humanist as Hero, The Life of Sir Thomas More* (New York, 1947), p. 24.
59. Lee, p. 60.
60. George Saintsbury, *History of English Prosody* ,I, 366–367, quoted in Theodore Maynard, *Ballade, Rime Royal, and Spenserian Stanza* (Catholic University of America, Washington, D.C., 1934), p. 111, no. 15.
61. Maynard, p. 120.
62. Mackintosh, p. 16.
63. Lines 106–108. Furnivall, p. 76.
64. *OED*, I, 1114.
65. Roman Dyboski, ed., *Songs, Carols and Other Miscellaneous Poems* (London, 1907), pp. 97–100. The Latin epitaph and its English version are not in the edition of 1557. The Latin verses are given in Weever's 'Ancient Funerall Monuments,' ed. 1631, p. 476, as 'transcribed out of a Manuscript in Sir Robert Cotton's Library . . . ' *Ibid.*, n. 84, p. 185.
66. Dyboski, pp. 99–100. [The letters *th* are here used instead of the character p. 84, which joined to the *e* forms the word *the*].
67. Margaret Campbell Barnes, *The Tudor Rose* (Philadelphia, 1953), p. 311.
68. *Ibid.*, p. 196.
69. Harrison, I, 39.
70. Dyboski, ed., p. 100, line 9.
71. Frances Berkeley Young, 'The Triumphe of Death,' transl. Countess of Pembroke, *PMLA*, XXVII (March 1912), 57.
72. *Ibid.*, p. 55.
73. 'A ruful lamentacion,' Eighth Page. C. 8–9. A. 6–7.
74. *Ibid.*, C. 1–2.
75. *Ibid.*, B. 2–8.
76. Sir Thomas D. Barlow, *The Medieval World Picture and Albert Durer's Melancholia* (Cambridge, Eng.,), p. 3.
77. *Ibid.*, p. 3.
78. *Ibid.*, p. 8.
79. William Roper, *Lyfe of Sir Thomas More, Knighte*, ed. James Mason Cline (New York, 1950), p. 19.
80. Florence M. Grimm, 'Astronomical Lore in Chaucer, '*Studies in Language, Literature and Criticism*, No. 2 (Lincoln, 1919), 54.
81. Mallet, I, 190.
82. Robert Spindler, ed., *The Court of Sapience* (Leipzing, 1927), p. 207, 11. 2099–2100.
83. *Ibid.*, 11. 2101–2107.
84. *Ibid.*, 11. 2185–2191.
85. 'A ruful lamentacion,' Eighth Page. C. 1–7.
86. Keddie, p. 154.
87. 'A ruful lamentacion,' Ninth page. A. 2–8.
88. Keddie, p. 162.
89. 'A ruful lamentacion,' Ninth Page. B. 6–7.
90. Keddie, p. 177.
91. 'A ruful lamentacion,' Ninth Page. B. 8.
92. Keddie, p. 191.
93. 'A ruful lamentacion,' Ninth Page. B. 10. C. 1–2.
94. Barnes, p. 307.
95. Keddie, pp. 156–157.
96. Warton, III, 97, n°.
97. 'A ruful lamentacion,' Eighth Page. D. 5–9.
98. Keddie, p. 157–158.

99. *Ibid.*, p. 143.
100. *Ibid.*, p. 149.
101. 'A ruful lamentacion,' Ninth Page, A. 9–10. B. 1.
102. *Ibid.*, B. 2–5.
103. Keddie, pp. 200–202.
104. 'A ruful lamentacion,' Ninth Page. C. 3–9.
105. *Works*, I, 399.
106. 'A ruful lamentacion,' Ninth Page. D. 5.
107. Harrison, I, 148.
108. *Works*, I, 324.
109. *Ibid.*, I, 16.
110. *Ibid.*

CHAPTER V

'CERTAIN METERS':

MORE'S DENOUNCEMENT OF FORTUNE

William Rastell's definite statement that Sir Thomas More 'caused'[1] his verses on 'Certain meters' to be printed at the beginning of the *Boke of Fortune* helps to explain the reason More had for writing forty-six rhyme royal stanzas on 'Fortune'. The nine stanzas comprising the prologue and epilogue are not in Rastell's 1557 edition, but Robert Wyer had printed the complete series of poems separately – 'most probably before Rastell had them printed'.[2]

If the poem on the 'Nyne pageauntes' is an amateur exercise in the art of writing poetry, if the ballad of 'a meri iest' is an elaboration of a contemporary incident according to medieval treatment, if 'A ruful lamentacion' is a successful and promising experimentation with the use of a poignant refrain, if the verses inspired by Pico's life are a skillful adaptation of a religious theme to the art of poetry, the poems on 'Fortune' represent the acme of Thomas More's perfection in this art. Sidney Lee was probably thinking of the verses comprising the last poem when he said:

> Critics have usually ignored or scorned his [More's] English poetry. Its theme is mainly the fickleness of fortune and the voracity of time. But freshness and sincerity characterize his treatment of these well-worn topics . . .[3]

Clive S. Lewis highly praises these verses for the *Boke of Fortune* and, while attributing 'real value'[4] to the lamentation on the death of Queen Elizabeth, concedes greater merit to this poem. Like Mr. Lee, he sees in these verses a foreshadowing of Spenser, and in addition, notices a resemblance to Sackville:

> Here, on a characteristically medieval theme, and in firmer metre, we have something like an anticipation of Spenser's court of Philotime in the underworld, and allegorical figures which are not much below Sackville's.[5]

A detailed study of these verses is revealing, for, the works that influenced Thomas More, his attitude towards fortune, and the outlet that these verses provided for his pent-up feelings on this subject are clearly manifested therein.

Shortly after the death of the good Queen Elizabeth, a political incident occurred which imperiled More's life, but at the same time may have been an indirect and remote occasion for the writing of these elaborate verses on fortune. In 1504, the nineteenth year of the reign of Henry VII, when More was twenty-six years old, he received the great privilege of being elected a member of the new Parliament in the spring of that year. After a long and barren interim of seven years' inactivity of Parliament, Henry VII called a meeting but not for the purpose of mending grievances as all England anxiously looked forward to and hoped for. In reality he demanded from Parliament the grant of a large sum of money as a dowry for his eldest daughter Margaret, who was entering a marriage alliance with James IV of Scotland. As a result, the people, already heavily laden with taxes, would again be taxed severely. The barons and nobles, who fully realized the aggression and the injustice of the king's demands, cowered in fear and obsequiousness before him. The youthful More received his first but lasting impression of court hypocrisy and intrigue in this Parliament. Perplexed and bewildered, he listened how first one speaker and then another upheld the king's egotistic and unjust demands and how old, wise, and experienced men betrayed the cause of truth and integrity rather than incur the King's anger. After two readings of the bill had been passed and acquiescence had been made to the King's unjust request, Thomas More, a 'beardless boy',[6] rose for the last debate and eloquently and vehemently opposed the bill to the silent admiration and surprise of everyone present. He listened to the promptings of his own conscience in this crucial case and concomitantly awakened the conscience of those around him – but he paid dearly for this frank avowal of truth and sincere exhortation to righteousness. As a consequence, his father, who was to have been one of the collectors of the new tax, was committed to the Tower, and Thomas More was obliged to go into hiding for peril of his life. He had even resolved to go over seas, but the death of Henry VII in the year 1509 altered his decision.[7]

Warner, who published the *Memoirs of the Life of Sir Thomas More* in the year 1758, informs us that during these four years More 'diverted himself with Music, Arithmetic, Geometry, Astronomy, and studying French; and in this retirement he made himself a perfect master of History'.[8] For four years More lived in confinement, during which time he married in the year 1505, studied the life of the great Italian humanist, Pico della Mirandola, and, choosing him as a model for emulation, translated his works from the Latin into the vulgar tongue. His four children were born during these intervening years. In 1508 occurred a fact to which Chambers gives credence, namely, that in this year Thomas More 'was visiting the Universities of Paris and Louvain, and this may have been preparatory to an intended sojourn abroad'.[9]

These years of More's retirement were ostensibly a loss to his public life, but what a precious boon they were for his literary achievements! It is highly probable that most of his English poems were written during this period. Russell Ames, in his book *Citizen Thomas More and His Utopia*, believes that this incident of More's earliest political experience is grossly exaggerated and, regarding his clandestine activities at this time he says:

> A tradition among Roman Catholic and Anglo-Catholic scholars suggests that he was in serious danger of losing his life because of the displeasure of the king over his conduct in parliament, and that he would have fled abroad had the king not died. He did visit the universities of Louvain

and Paris in 1508, perhaps looking for a safer berth; but if so, he did not let his intention interfere with his raising a family or gaining employment. At Lincoln's Inn in 1507 he became Pensioner, then Butler, and loaned money for a building; and long before Henry VII died in April 1509, More had established his important connection with the Mercers of London.[10]

The very fact that he 'caused' the 'certain meters for the *Boke of Fortune*' to be prefaced to this particular book testifies to his knowledge of French and to the realization of the pernicious influence the contents of this work exerted on the minds of the readers. The first Italian copy of the *Boke of Fortune* was translated into French and edited in the year 1500 and shortly after translated into English by Caxton. Its complete French title was *Le Livre de Passetemps de la Fortune des Dez*, and to the four stanzas in French, More added forty-two stanzas in the English Language. In the Prologue he alludes in the third stanza to the 'french Cronycles'[11] which, in addition to the English and Latin chronicles he had read, give him some justification for expressing himself in poetry despite the fact that he is only an amateur in the 'contryuyng of these matiers'.[12] Chaucer, likewise, had written a poem on the subject of Fortune. It is interesting to see how closely More's organization of subject matter and treatment resembles Chaucer's in this respect. Both poems are divided into six parts, contain the plaintiff's arguments and Fortune's responses, and end with an envoy. Chaucer's epithet for describing the world as 'wretched'[13] and his felicitous refrain, 'For fynaly fortune, I the deffye'[14] clearly recall Thomas More's attitude towards this fickle Queen.

The contents of More's 'certain meters' consist of the following parts: (1) the Prologue made up of three rhyme royal stanzas in English; (2) two French stanzas with English versions (3) 'the wordes of Fortune to the people', comprised of six rhyme royal stanzas; (4) 'Thomas More to them that trust in Fortune', consisting of twenty-four stanzas; (5) 'Thomas More to them that seke Fortune', comprised of seven stanzas; (6) two French stanzas entitled 'Fortune speketh'. A separate edition of these poems exists bound up with six other curious political tracts in the interesting and curious *Boke of the Fayr Gentylwoman . . . Lady Fortune* printed by Robert Wyer around 1538. The title page is decorated with a woodcut of Lady Fortune and the following descriptive and lengthy title is indicative of its nature and design: *The Boke of the fayre Gentylwoman, that no man shulde put his truste, or confydence in: that is to say, Lady Fortune: flaterynge euery man that coueyteth to haue all, and specyally, them that truste in her, she deceyueth them at laste.* The title is a perfect synthesis of the contents of the poem and illustrates the fact that it was a powerful factor in altering people's ideas and in convincing them of the variability and ultimate deceitfulness of fortune.

Another curious and interesting woodcut was composed of numbers which were arranged in the following order:

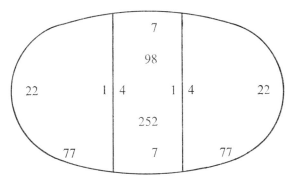

In the *Boke of Fortune* one's future was determined by an involved and integrated process of numbers resulting from the throw of dice and corresponding to the planet's negative and positive vibrations,[15] and predicated on the day and hour of a person's birth.

It may be interesting, in conjunction with More's vituperative remarks about the throwing of dice and the ensuing astronomical and numerical divinations, to see by way of a very brief summary, what the Hebraic system of planetary numbers consisted of:

0 Space, 1 the Sun, 2 the Moon, 3 Mars, 4 Mercury,
5 Jupiter, 6 Venus, 7 Saturn, 8 Uranus, 9 Neptune.

The corresponding days were: 1 Sunday, 2 Monday, 3 Tuesday, 4 Wednesday, 5 Thursday, 6 Friday, 7 Saturday, 8 Uranus was the first of the new octave, the point of disruption; and 9 Neptune was the state of chaos, the nebula of the new order of existence.

Likewise, there were seven colors – tones in a musical gamut – and seven spirits or Archangels whose names were:

Michael   – the Sun   Raphael – Mercury
Gabriel   – the Moon   Zadkiel – Jupiter
Madimial – Mars   Uriel   – Venus
                             Samiel   – Saturn

A great number of people in More's time believed that from these correspondences it followed that there were seven types of human beings, each born under the dominant influence of a planetary ray, color, and tone.[16]

The *Boke of Fortune* was an amusing game or an engrossing pastime revolving around a set of twenty questions analogous to those found in fortunetelling books: Shall my life be happy and fortunate or not? Does my sovereign lady love me? Is my wife good or bad? The title page contained a woodcut of Fortune's wheel which symbolized Lady Fortune's immediate connection with the answers to these highly personal and poignant inquiries. The answers ultimately depended on a combination of numbers obtained by a throw of dice, and fifty-six answers were given to each question since there were fifty-six possible combinations of a single throw of three dice. In the English version, which differs very slightly from the Italian and French ones, the inquirer is sent to kings, philosophers, and lastly astronomers, for his respective answer which appears in verse quatrains. Consequently, Thomas More's references in the course of the poem to Julius, Darius, and Alexander, to Socrates, Pythagoras, and Democritus, have pertinent significance, as well as his allusions to 'the rolling dice'[17] and to the predictions of astronomy which he adamantly disapproves of and castigates with conviction and sincerity.

In medieval literature Fortune was delineated as having two faces, one beautiful, the other ugly. Boccaccio depicts her in *De Casibus Virorum Illustrium*, a work which profoundly influenced More, as a strange figure having great stature, a threatening look in her eyes, a cruel and horrible face, and long, thick hair hanging over her mouth.[18] Her capricious change in mood is symbolized by her specious smile or foreboding frown. She is often blind as, for example, in Boethius' *Consolation of Philosophy*, to show that she has no regard for merit or integrity of thought or conduct. Likewise, she is depicted with many hands, the right and left signifying good and evil fortune respectively. Her multiple postures, too, have significance: (1) she stands with one foot on a globe and the other on an upright wheel – positions symbolic of her unsteadiness; (2) she is sometimes asleep but wakes up when she pleases; (3) she lives on an island which has both fruitful and barren trees; and (4) her abode has incessant variations of scenery where both Zephyr and Boreas blow. Her wheel turns incessantly; it cannot stop, for if it should, she would then cease to be Fortuna, which is synonymous with changeableness. This capricious Lady is often compared to the moon, for as it varies from day to day and controls the shifting tides, so too, she continuously changes her face, motives, and actions and thus, turns the tide of mankind.[19]

The 'Certain meters' for the *Boke of Fortune*, as well as the 'Lamentation of Queen Elizabeth', were also published in the *Commonplace Book of Richard Hill*,[20] Citizen and Grocer of London, who was a contemporary of Thomas More. Since the latest date in this book is 1536, the poems may have been published during More's own life time and probably appeared before the separate Wyer edition.

Thomas More's scintillating treatment of the concept of Fortune in these forty-two stanzas (including the five English stanzas in the prologue) is in perfect keeping with the idea of a game or pastime. In Boethius' *Consolation of Philosophy* – a work which obviously influenced More – Lady Fortune enjoys playing games with human beings in which she exalts them or debases them in turn. Of these the most common are chess and dice and the game of the shuttlecock to which Jean de Meun refers in the *Roman de la Rose*.[21] Howard Patch describes Fortune in the following words: '. . . she is just the envious, vindictive creature to throw dice with mankind and shout her laugh of triumph when she wins, to set traps for the sufferer, to snare the unwary, to wage petty warfare on the defiant'.[22]

Thomas More portrays this pagan goddess as a supercilious queen whose powers are relegated to temporal and mundane affairs, for the most part, but whose favour can also be courted for health and the bestowal of children – two instances where she infringes on God's rights. The pagan interpretation is especially seen in the last of the four sections in which '. . . she kepeth euer in store / From euery manne some parcell of his wyll, / That he may pray therefore and serue her styll'.[23] The court, where she is very much at home, is a suitable environment for the exercise of her capricious and fickle reign as she bestows kingships, empires, and crowns gratuitously and then captiously takes them away again. Her highness' jeering and over-confident attitude may be summed up in the words: 'Regno, Regnavi, Sum sine Regno, Regnabo'.[24] Medieval art has personified these powers for us and inscribed them on the famous wheel, which is such an indispensable accoutrement of the fickle Queen. On the top of the wheel is a crowned youth sitting on a throne and holding a sceptre; at the right is a figure falling, his crown dropping from his head; at the bottom is a figure prostrate; on the left is a man climbing, extending his hands towards the youth at the top.[25] Thomas More's tenth stanza in the section wherein he gives advice to those who trust in Fortune faithfully parallels the pictorial delineation of the 'formula of four'[26] – *regnabo, regno, regnavi, sum sine regno*, with a verbal description cast in the seven-line mold of a rhyme royal stanza. It reads:

Alas the folysh people can not cease,	
Ne voyd her trayne, tyll they the harme do fele.	
About her alway, *besely they preace*.	*Regnabo*
But lord how he doth thynk hym self full wele.	
That may set once *his hande uppon her whele*.	*Regno*
He holdeth fast: but *upward as he flieth*,	Regnavi
She whipeth her whele about, and *there he lyeth*.	*Sum sine regno*.

By citing examples of internal evidence from the lines of the poem itself, one can obtain a comprehensive and accurate picture of Thomas More's delineation of Fortune which will indicate the origin and cult of his particular treatment of her. The following lines describe the cult and functions of this puissant Queen, while the traditions that this description belongs to are briefly appended to it:

Royal powers	Mine high estate power and auctoritie.	
	line A. 3. Tenth page	*The pagan tradition*
Temporal goods	That richesse, worship, welth, and dignitie,	
	Joy, rest, and peace, and all thyng fynally,	
	That any pleasure or profit may come by,	
	To mannes comfort, ayde, and sustinaunce,	
	Is all at my deuyse and ordinaunce.	

	ll. A. 5–9. Tenth page	*Quasi-pagan* Power over spiritual goods is denied her.
Arbitrary *despotism*	Without my favour there is nothyng wonne. line A. 10. Tenth page	*Fortuna Panthea* Exalted position in the Roman Empire is hers.
Respect for man's *free will*	Eche man hath of him self the gouernaunce, Let euery wight than folowe his owne way. ll. D. 9. Tenth page, A. 1. Eleventh page	*The Renaissance tradition* Man is master of his fate.

Thomas More, who was thoroughly acquainted with the development of the Fortuna cult, gives a classical presentation of this pagan goddess when he describes her in the following epithets, phrases, or lines:

Sometyme she loketh as louely fayre and bright, As goodly Venus mother of Cupyde.	Eleventh page B. 5–6.
But this chere fayned, may not long abide.	Eleventh page B. 8.
Then as a bayte she bryngeth forth her ware, Siluer, gold, riche perle, and precious stone.	Eleventh page C. 9. D. 1.
Fortune at them laugheth, and in her trone Amyd her treasure and waueryng rychesse, Prowdly she houeth as lady and empresse.	Eleventh page D. 4–6.
Above her commeth all the world to begge.	Twelfth page A. 5.
And yet her brotell giftes long may not last.	Twelfth page B. 8.

Thomas More uses the classical interpretation of Fortune turning the wheel on which the estate of mankind depends, and not the concept of Fortune in Roman art in which she stands on the wheel and is turned with it, or that of the wheel, independently of her controlling the vicissitudes of man's life. Like Boethius, who portrays the goddess turning the wheel herself, More's Lady is in charge of human affairs, and instead of being a participant in its reversals, she is a haughty and jeering spectator of them. This interpretation is seen in the following lines pertaining to the rotation of the wheel and the goddess' turning of it according to her caprices:

180

She whirlith about and pluckith away as fast,
And geueth them to an other by and by.[27]

He holdeth fast: but upwarde as he flieth,
She whippeth her whele about, and there he lyeth.[28]

Having described her as 'mighty, varyable, inconstaunce, slypper, frayle, and
full of treason',[29] More, her avowed enemy, gives convincing and substantial
arguments for her overthrow. Man can resist Fortune's alluring sway and avoid
succumbing to her specious power with the threefold weapons of poverty,
virtue, and stoicism. Showing a marked acquaintance with the poverty convention employed by Boccaccio in *De Casibus Virorum Illustrium* and following the
advice of Boethius, who recommended virtue and stoicism as efficacious defenses
against the power of this capricious Queen, Thomas More synthesizes his wise
advice in the following rhyme royal stanza:

Wherefore yf thou in suretye lyst to stande,
Take pouertes parte and let prowde fortune go.
Receyue nothyng that commeth from her hande:
Loue maner and vertue: they be onely tho.
Whiche double fortune may not take the fro.
Then mayst thou boldly defye her turnyng chaunce:
She can the neyther hynder nor auaunce.[30]

As opposed to the inconstancy of Fortune's goods, More offers the 'Summum
Bonum' in the form of poverty which gives freedom through detachment; virtue,
which ennobles man's mind and soul; and stoicism, as is expressed in Thomas
More's advice 'to them that seke fortune':

And though in one chaunce Fortune you offend,
Grudge not there at, but beare a mery face.[31]

The second line of the stanza quoted above, 'Take pouertes parte and let prowde
fortune go', shows the influence of Boccaccio's delineation of the medieval type
Fortune in his *De Casibus Virorum Illustrium*, in which he vividly describes the
struggle for supremacy between proud Fortuna and aggressive Poverty. The
aspect of free will, which contravenes the pagan concept of the goddess, is skillfully tied up with the description of Fortuna; therefore, the excerpt from
Boccaccio quoted below will further manifest Thomas More's acquaintance
with his work and the concomitant influence it exerted on this poem:

The fable is told by Andalus, who relates how Poverty was sitting at
the crossroads, dressed in a coat with a hundred holes [as opposed to
Fortune's hundred hands] and deep in melancholy, when Fortune
smiling proudly passed by. Rising with a harsh and bitter countenance,

Poverty demanded, 'Foolish one, why smilest thou?' Fortune replied, 'I am looking with wonder at thee and thy dearth, thy pallor, fleeing thy friends, and arousing dogs'. Poverty, angered by the words and hardly withholding her fists, answered: 'Lo, Fortuna, foolish judge, part-goddess, why dost thou slander me? I deny that my estate is caused by thee; for I am here by my own free-will'.[32]

In the struggle that ensues, Poverty is victorious, but she is not boastful and arrogant in victory; she exercises pity and graciousness towards her opponent by not breaking her wheel, but imposes a law upon her and releases her. More's phrase 'take pouertes parte' elicits an association with this incident from Boccaccio's book as it recalls the struggle for prestige between the two contestants.

It is curious and interesting that Boccaccio refers to Fortuna as 'part-goddess', which indicates that her role in the Roman Empire as 'Fortuna Panthea' and the homage and worship that was rendered to her gradually diminished. Likewise, Thomas More presents her not as a goddess, but as a puissant and liberal queen who bestows her gifts capriciously upon whom she pleases and then wantonly takes them back again whenever she has a fancy to do so. In More's poem she has no control over man's will, which she respects and stands in awe of, but in the following two instances, she infringes on the Creator's functions: (1) 'To some she sendeth children',[33] and 'Some manne hath good, but chyldren hath he none; (2) Some man hath both, but he can get none health'.[34] The bestowing of children and health is God's prerogative; therefore, it appears that More takes Boccaccio's view in portraying her, in a small part only, as a 'part-goddess'. The woodcut on the title page of *The Book of the Fair Gentlewoman, Lady Fortune*[35] depicts her as the 'Fortune of Abundance', an ancient Roman cult that survived in the idea of the 'Giver', the 'Bestower of Riches'. She appears in this woodcut with a part only of her symbol, the cornucopia; with a light heart and smiling face, she lavishes her gifts upon her devotees freely and haphazardly. In another cut describing the same personification, she wears an ugly scowl on her face and has a threatening look in her eyes – indication of her vindictiveness and inconstancy.

Boethius gives a clear description of the pagan goddess in his *Consolation of Philosophy* and, while attributing power and prestige to her, he worships the Christian God without showing how the two can be reconciled. His character delineation of Fortuna is in accord with classical literature, and he suggests a partial solution to this paradoxical problem by making the pagan goddess subject to Divine Providence. It is in Dante, however, that the reconciliation is realized for, in the seventh canto of the *Inferno*[36] the capricious goddess becomes a ministering angel entirely subject to God and His Divine Will.[37]

When numerous temples were being dedicated to the honour of 'Fortuna Panthea' and she was absorbing the functions of the other gods,[38] the Romans escaped her wanton rule by limiting her powers. Thus, reason was chosen as an antidote gainst her unreason; wisdom, as a substitute for her folly, and a life of virtue, as opposed to a life of wantonness and erratic vagaries. In medieval literature, particularly in Boethius, Boccaccio, and Dante, the remedy was not to prize her transient gifts, but to honour and serve God and live a life of virtue. Thomas More also shows an acquaintance with the remedies some outstanding French writers of the early fifteenth century advocated against Fortune's power. Jean Froissart's advice, to reject Fortune's gifts, parallels More's suggestion to take on a stoic attitude towards Fortune's bestowal of favours, while Eustace Deschamps' counsel to practise fortitude and prudence finds its acme in Christian stoicism.[39]

More's urgent and sagacious advice to 'Love maner and vertue: they be onely tho / Whiche double fortune may not take the fro',[40] stresses the permanency and stability of these spiritual goods as opposed to the mutable gifts of Lady Fortune. By 'maner' he implies a good moral character, integrity of mind, and rectitude of character which is the foundation for a virtuous life. Barclay uses this word in the same context in his 'Shyp of Folys' when he quotes an old proverb which 'Sayth that good lyfe and maners makyth man'.[41]

In the two concluding French stanzas, which are not in the 1557 Rastell edition, the writer[42] employs the 'ubi sunt formula' which Boethius has made famous in his *Consolation of Philosophy* with the line rendered in the French: 'mais où sont les neiges d'antan!'[43] After suggesting remedies against the hypnotic power of Lady Fortune, he gives thirty-three tragic examples of kings, emperors, philosophers, and gods and goddesses who had succumbed to her wily embrace, climbed her treacherous wheel, and then were cast from it with shame and degradation.

More's English rendition of the French verses shows the influence of the *Roman de la Rose* in which Reason discusses her work and accepts her existence as obvious.[44] This 'fair gentlewoman' is called 'Fortune perverse et contraire / Que la mole et la debonnaire'.[45] Jean de Meun candidly exposes her characteristic perniciousness in his work *Roman de la Rose* which Petrarch's *De Remediis* parallels very closely.

Howard Rollin Patch pithily shows the relationship between the two works in the following précis:

> Good Fortune deceives and fools.[46] She seems to be loyal; she gives her promises of worldly felicity. Mounted on her wheel, men think they shall never fall. They think they have many friends, but when they lose their wealth, they learn their true friends. When she dwells with men, she troubles their minds; she nourishes them in ignorance. When they fall, she gives them vinegar. Only our true friends remain with us under those circumstances. She has power over nothing really good. All good things are enclosed in one's self. Fortune has control over the rest of the gifts of this world, and takes and gives them at her caprice, whereby she makes fools smile and grieve . . .[47]

Jean de Meun brings in the example of Socrates 'who was never glad in prosperity nor sad in adversity'.[48] Both writers, Petrarch and the author of the second part of the *Roman de la Rose*, stress the fact that man should strive with Fortune and that he would eventually subdue her.[49]

The Prologue to 'Certain meters' consists of three rhyme royal stanzas which serve as a vindication for Thomas More, who wrote despite the fact that he considered himself a dilettante in this art. The first stanza gives proof of his wide reading in the fields of poetry, oratory, and philosophy. Duly impressed with the classical elegance of scholars and the erudite eloquence of their utterance as well as their profundity of thinking, he becomes almost petrified with fear at the sight of his own inadequacy. He uses the figure of a dead tree in a fresh and original context and acknowledges his deficiency in emulating their noteworthy endeavours. This humble poet says with sincerity and humility:

> Halfe amased I am and as a deed tre
> Stonde styl, ouer rude for to brynge forth
> Any fruyte or sentence, that is ought worth.[50]

The run-on line, '. . . as a deed tre / Stonde styl', characterized by the *s* alliteration and followed by *hyperbaton* '. . . ouer rude *for to brynge* forth / Any fruyte or sentence, that is *ought worth*' is emphatic from the standpoint of both poetry and oratory.

The second stanza has historical value and throws significant light on the literary achievements of the Tudor period. Thomas More deprecates the fact that 'unlerned men nowe a days, wyll not spare / To wryte, to bable, theyr myndes to declare',[51] and so, taking advantage of this established precedent, he, too, will 'declare' his mind on a topic which impressed itself indelibly on his intellect and engaged him in practical repudiation of its theories. More, who later was to pursue heretics relentlessly but tactfully, is seen here castigating the vagaries of the capricious goddess with sincerity and zeal. Although young in years, he manifested intellectual curiosity and a love of reading. He gives indication of keen perception to criticize and evaluate what he reads judiciously, for he describes the cunning and the writing skill of these quacks as 'not worth a strawe'.[52]

More enumerates these pseudo literary writers and philosophers. He significantly begins with the French chronicle writers and then adds the English and Latin authors. This stanza has depth, style, and force; therefore, it merits quotation in full:

> Some in french Cronycles, gladly doth presume
> Some in Englysshe, blyndly wade and wander
> Another in laten bloweth forth a darke fume
> As wyse as a great hedded Asse of Alexandre
> Some in Phylosophye, lyke a gagelynge gandre
> Begynneth lustely the browes to set up
> And at the last concludeth in the good ale cup.[53]

This Christian humanist's verses, which were prefixed to the popular *Boke of Fortune*, were designed to add literary merit to it. More's prologue and introductory poems give evidence of genuine learning in spite of the fact that he considers himself to be a mere dilettante in writing.

The two rhyme royal English stanzas that follow the French stanzas and that belong to the section not included in Rastell's 1557 edition, describe Fortune as 'mighty & varyable',[54] but 'slypper, frayle, and full of treason'.[55] She gives her gifts to those who are unworthy of them; she spoils the just man and enriches the unjust. She kills young men and lets the old live, but neither does she forever cherish the one who falls in her favour nor forever forsake him whom she takes joy in oppressing. Thus, More points out in this poem that Dame Fortune's salient vices are variability, which does not take man's integrity of character into consideration, and cruelty, which finds satisfaction and joy in oppressing people and making them miserable.

The ending poem entitled 'Fortune speketh' is in French and it consists of two stanzas, eight lines apiece. They are not meritorious from a literary point of view. Their main interest, however, lies in the 'ubi sunt' formula, which provides a setting for the enumeration of Biblical personages, kings, philosophers, and pagan deities. In the first line of the first stanza, the addressee asks Fortune: 'Where is David and Solomon, Methuselah, Joshua, Maccabees, Holofernes, Alexander, and Sampson?'[56] He inquires next about Julius Caesar, Hector, Pompey, Ulysses and his great fame, King Arthur, Godfrey, Charlemagne, Darius the Great, Hercules, and Ptolemy.

The 'ubi sunt' continues in the second stanza with the inquiry, 'What has become of Pharaoh, the felon king?' The writer curiously alludes to Job as 'le courtais', and then enumerates the philosophers: Aristotle, Hippocrates and Plato; Judith, Esther, Boethius, and Penelope; and these, in turn, are followed by Dido, Pallas, Juno, and Medea. Guinevere and the noble Helen, Palamides, and Tristan conclude this enumeration. The refrain, 'They are all dead, and this world is a vain thing',[57] appropriately concludes both stanzas. The catalogue of kings, philosophers, and Biblical personages is pertinent since in the *Boke of Fortune* the inquirer, having chosen a question from Fortune's wheel, is directed to a wood-cut representation of a king, then is sent to one of twenty philosophers, each of whom has a page to himself, and finally to an astronomer who gives him the answer to his interrogation. This catalogue concludes the three poems with a total of nine stanzas which are not in the Rastall or Campbell edition.

The first section of the poem entitled 'The wordes of Fortune to the people' is composed of six rhyme royal stanzas which rhyme ababbcc. The speaker in this poem is the personified abstraction, Fortune, who introduces herself to the readers in terms of her deeds, namely, the bestowal of her gifts, and not in terms of physical description. In the hierarchy of values which give her fame and prestige, she counts 'high estate, power and auctoritie' as the outstanding prerogatives. It is significant, however, that this puissant Lady herself reminds man that 'he hath of him self the governaunce',[58] and it is ultimately up to him to succumb to her glamour and solicit her favour or to reject her solicitations. She concludes dishearteningly: 'And he that wyll be a beggar, let hym be'[59].

Thomas More uses the rhetorical scheme of accumulation or synathroismos and achieves thereby an effect of emphasis and perspicuity .The goddess boasts that 'richesse, worship, welth, and dignitie',[60] are at her willful disposal and that 'any pleasure or profit'[61] that is conducive to man's comfort, sustenance, or aid is within her power to bestow upon him. She not only lures him with the promise of wealth, dignity, and honour, but she also promises him gifts of mind and soul, namely, 'ioy, rest, and peace'.[62] The last line of the stanza definitely states that her power to bestow these favours and gifts upon man is her own prerogative, and thus she is totally independent of divine aid:

> Is all at my deuyse and ordinaunce.[63]

The second stanza begins with an egocentric statement, which serves as the proposition she wishes to defend:

> Without my favour there is nothyng wonne.[64]

Then, in three pithy run-on sentences she substantiates her thesis with proof for her assertion, and ends with an inference that 'Better [it] is to be fortunate than wyse'.[65] She arrives at this conclusion, for she firmly believes that 'Without good happe there may no wit suffice'.[66]

The medial caesura is forceful and vigorous:

> And therefore hath there some men bene or this,
> My deadly foes and written many a boke,
> To my disprayse. //[67]

Thomas More cleverly incorporates Aesop's fable of the fox and the grapes into this stanza. The capricious Queen compares these writers, who speak so derogatorily of her and her ubiquitous power, to the fox who was not successful in his attempt to reach the grapes. Consequently, since the wily animal tried desperately and failed, he began to 'defy' the grapes, for it was not in his power to possess them. Pleasing rhythm and economy of verbiage make these lines good poetry:

> Thus lyke the fox they fare that once forsoke,
> The pleasaunt grapes, and gan for to defy them,
> Because he lept and yet could not come by them.[68]

Angry and chagrined, Lady Fortune takes on a disconcerted attitude: 'But let them write',[69] she says in a defeated tone, and defiantly adds 'theyr labour is in vayne'.[70] She tries forcefully to convince her addressee or reader that one who is bereft of her protection and favour lives in penury and pain – a burden to himself and others. She cannot force their will; she can merely appeal to their senses, and thus she glamorously balances a life in wealth, honour, and mirth against distress, hunger, and pain.

More brings out Dame Fortune's specious advice effectively with the use of accumulation or synathroismos in verse two of the following fourth stanza, alliteration in verse three, and epitheton in verses four, five, and six:

> For well ye wote, *myrth, honour,* and *richesse,*
> Much better is than *p*enury and *pa*yne.
> The *nedy* wretch that lingereth in distresse,
> Without myne helpe is ever *comfortlesse,*
> A very burden *odious* and *loth,*
> To all the world, and else to him selfe both.

The voice of Lady Fortune in the fifth stanza urges the addressee to consider duly the benefits and privileges of her royal favour, particularly in raising her devoted protégé to power and prestige and promising him 'A common wele to gouerne and defende'.[71] The use of *epitheton* to make her appeal more alluring is a good rhetorical device for enhancing her solicitation: '*mighty* power, *excellent* degree, *blist* condicion'.[72] The first line, 'But he that by my fauour may ascende'.[73] implies a reference to the wheel, Fortune's famous symbol, on which man turns from the cradle to the grave. The delicate use of 'may' indicates his free will in ascending this ominous and perilous wheel, for when he once deliberately ascends it, he places himself in Fortune's power. To lure him to this precarious ascent, she holds out to him the fragrant flower of 'ioyfull rest and peace'.[74] It is significant that in More's poem, this inconstant Lady often entices her dubious admirers with the Renaissance penchant for joy, rest, and peace of mind. She tactfully balances wealth, power, and prestige with tranquility of spirit and serenity of mind; but here her power ends, for she can not penetrate into the spiritual life of man's soul which is strictly God's domain. Prophesying worldly honour and success, joined irrevocably to a life of peace and rest, she exclaims exultantly:

> O in how blist condicion standeth he.[75]

But that is not all – she assures her addressee – for not only will he himself enjoy the fruit of this prosperity, but also those he governs will likewise be secure and happy:

> Him self in honour and felicite,
> And over that, may forther and encrease,
> A region hole in ioyfull rest and peace.[76]

'Forther' in line two is used in the archaic sense of 'helping, assisting, or promoting',[77] and the association of it with 'region' implies a Utopian concept of an ideal commonwealth.

Lady Fortune's rule comes to an end here; she is no longer the pagan goddess in More's poem, in whose honour temples were erected and who was worshipped as a deity by men who obsequiously solicited her favour. She says in the opening lines of stanza six, with finality and abruptness:

> Now in this poynt there is no more to say,
> Eche man hath of him self the gouernaunce.

The next five lines in this stanza reflect the attitude of Thomas More, the Christian humanist, rather than the consistent pagan attitude of Fortuna. Consequently, one notices a slight shift in voice as More's convictions are articulated and these, in turn, seem incongruously placed in the mouth of the fickle Queen, who respects no one's feelings but her own. Reechoing Augustine, Aquinas, Boethius, and Aristotle on the matter of man's free will, More puts the following words into Fortuna's mouth:

> Let every wight than folowe his owne way,
> And he that out of pouertee and mischaunce,
> List for to live, and wyll hym selfe enhaunce,
> In wealth & richesse, come forth and wayte on me.

One can almost see the scorn on the proud Lady's face and hear the haugthy tone of her jeering voice as she utters the last line with a toss of her head:

> And he that wyll be a beggar, let hym be.

The second section of the Fortune poems, according to the Rastell edition, is entitled 'Thomas More to them that trust in fortune'. Here More no longer employs the voice of the goddess Fortuna in which she described herself so alluringly, but speaks to his audience in his own voice. He addresses his message to a specific addressee in the person of 'thou', but in the clause that follows he includes all individuals who are merely interested in heaping up this world's goods. Thus, he directs his sincere advice to the following types of people:

1. Thou that art prowde of honour shape or kynne,

2. [Thou] That hepest up this wretched worldes treasure,

3. [Thou whose] fingers are shrined with gold,

4. [Thou who art] With fresh apparayle garnished out of measure,

5. [Thou who] wenest to haue fortune at thy pleasure.

It is to this particular group of individuals whose vulnerability lies in pride, avariciousness, vanity, covetousness, sloth, and concupiscence that Thomas

More speaks with a desire to change their attitude and convince them of Fortune's speciousness. He realizes that mere theorizing will not perform this abrupt change in them; therefore, he urges them to look at Dame Fortune and see for themselves how changeable, pernicious, and capricious she is. 'Cast up thyne eye', he says, 'and loke how slipper chaunce, / Illudeth her men with chaunge and varyaunce'.[78] The goddess Fortuna is inconsistently identified in this line with the concept 'chaunce', which ultimately goes back to the Anglo-Saxon use of the Germanic term 'Wyrd' or to the Latin idea of 'Fate'. The injunction to 'cast up thyne eye' is slightly analogous to the dream technique which enables a person to see strange sights with the eyes of his imagination and to experience unearthly joy in exotic surroundings. Thus, assuring himself of his addressee's interest and attention, the poet presents to his reader Lady Fortune's sycophants, who solicit her diverse gifts, and then are, in turn, mercilessly flung from her wheel. From the panorama of the historical personages, More verbally conjures before the spectator's eyes the defeat of mighty Julius, Darius, the worthy king of Persia, and the fall of Alexander, the great conqueror. The Poet's procession of illustrious figures also includes those noble individuals who defied Fortuna's allurement, such as the renowned Greek philosophers, the wise Socrates, Aristippus, Pythagoras, Heraclitus, and Democritus – all of whom were devoted followers of Lady Poverty, who gave them freedom of mind and detachment from worldly goods in order to aid them in seeking the highest wisdom.

While stressing the subject matter of the poem by making it clear and forceful, Thomas More does not neglect the metrical aspect of its verses. He artistically molds his ideas into the conventional five-stress line as the second stanza in this section illustrates:

> Some tyme / she lo / keth as loue / ly fayre / and bright /
> As good / ly Ve / nus mo / ther of / Cu pyde /
> She beck / eth and / she smil / eth on eu / ery wight /
> But this / chere fay / ned may / not long / a bide /
> There com / meth a cloude / and fare / well all / our pryde /
> Like a / ny ser / pent she / be gin / neth to swell /
> And look / eth as fierce / as an / y fu / ry of hell /

The first line begins with a spondee which sets the tone for the ensuing slow, deliberate movement. The anapests carry this movement forward and thus prevent the verses from becoming monotonous. The alliteration of the letter *s* as in line three, 'She becketh and she smileth', and of the letter *c* as in the fifth line, 'There cometh a cloude', adds immensely to the musical quality of the stanza. The two similes in the ending couplet are effective from the standpoint of rhythm, imagery, and alliteration:

Like any *s*erpent *s*he beginneth to *s*well,
And looketh as *f*ierce as any *f*ury of hell.

The antithesis used in comparing Lady Fortune to 'goodly Venus, mother of Cupyde' and signifying her appearance 'as louely fayre and bright' is made effective by describing her as a swelling 'serpent' and a 'fierce . . . fury of hell'. The third and fourth lines: 'She becketh and she smileth on euery wight / But this chere fayned may not long abide', / have kinesthetic appeal, for one can almost see this supercilious Lady smiling graciously and beckoning erring mankind to place its confidence in her power and to set its hands upon her treacherous wheel of destiny. The next powerful line, 'There commeth a cloude and farewell all our pryde', is indicative of the wily Lady's divergent moods as she, without reason, becomes changed in appearance and attitude. Her dress and accoutrements remain the same, but the smile she previously wore now becomes a scowling frown, while her attitude is mirrored in her malicious deeds and unreasonable caprices.

The third stanza contains two of More's favourite and frequently used epithets, namely, 'brotle' in verse one and 'wretched' in the following verse. What a refreshing and original trope he builds around the words, 'we brotle men'. Spelled 'brittle' in our day and age, the word connotes the frailty and vacillation of man in overcoming false allurements and snarling temptations. Here the speaker merges himself with the group of individuals who comprise the listening attitude of the addressee for he says, 'we brotle men' and not 'you brotle men'. In a humble manner so characteristic of the great humanistic scholar, Thomas More descends in spirit from the speaker's platform and, acknowledging the frailty of human nature, he says apologetically:

(So wretched is our nature and so blynde).[79]

He deplores the fact that men look at appearances only; for 'As soone as Fortune list to laugh agayne',[80] they surround her throne like sycophants and, cringing before her, give her honour by requesting favours from her perfidious hands. In his book *The Goddess Fortuna in Medieval Literature*, Howard R. Patch compares her frailty, which is 'frail and brittle in termperament',[81] to glass. 'Her fickleness, too', he says, 'includes her treachery. Her face may smile, but she stings just the same, and thus she resembles a serpent or (even better) a scorpion'.[82] She is furthermore so envious and vindictive that she is jealous of man's prosperity and having given it to him merely as a bait to have him enter her service, she withdraws all her favours from him. Thus, the higher she raises her devotee in wealth and prosperity, the lower he falls when she perceives his opulence and prestige.

To achieve poetical and rhetorical emphasis More again skillfully employs epitheton in line four:

With *fayre* countenaunce and *disceitfull* mynde.

Although composed of six words only, this line contains a graphic example of antithesis and is characterized by sententiousness and directness of appeal. The last three lines are cast in the form of hyperbaton, and they make extremely effective poetry. They are embellished with striking personification and a piquant simile:

> To crouche and knele and *gape after the wynde*,
> Not one or twayne but thousandes in a rout,
> *Lyke swarmyng bees* come flickeryng her aboute.[83]

More here touches the vulnerable spot of the devoted followers of Lady Fortune, for as in a mirror he shows them just how they look and act when they lower their dignity and self-esteem to crouch obsequiously before this fickle goddess in order to solicit her transient favours. Like bees they flicker about her throne but, instead of gathering honey from the flowers of her bountiful gifts, they find that they have gathered gall and wormwood instead. How great their disillusionment must be when this proud, fickle Lady casts them from her wheel of glorious destiny, but then, it is too late for them to realize their folly.

The next stanza is indeed an eloquent one, rich in imagery and felicitous in rhythm and hence, deserving to be quoted in full:

> Then as a bayte she bryngeth forth her ware,
> Silver, gold, riche perle, and precious stone:
> In which the mased people gase and stare,
> And gape therefore, as dogges doe for the bone.
> Fortune at them laugheth, and in her trone
> Amyd her treasure and waureryng rychesse,
> Prowdly she houeth as lady and empresse.[84]

Lady Fortune is delineated here so graphically that in one's imagination she can easily be seen proudly hovering over mankind as a royal Empress of the people whose obeisance is extremely dear to her. She not only alluringly smiles now that she sees them at her feet, but laughs gleefully 'amyd her treasure and waveryng rychesse'. In the epitheton 'waveryng' as applied to 'rychesse' More strikes a delightfully fresh and apt trope. This image describes not only the state of mutability of the riches, but of Lady Fortune's character in general – the instability of her throne, the oscillation of her wheel, and the vacillation of her decisions.

The first verse of this famous stanza presents the proud Empress displaying her wares with a charlatan's skill before the quick-moving eyes of her greedy spectators: 'Silver, gold, riche perle, and precious stone'. The on-lookers, who perceive only the superficial value of these items, open wide their eyes in amazement as 'the mased people gase and stare'. To describe their foolish scuffle, More uses an appropriate simile, which four centuries ago was much more original than it is today, namely, 'as dogges doe for the bone'. Fortuna's

191

favour truly becomes the bone of contention between all parties, for it is the deceitful Lady's aim to beguile her sycophants. The recipients of her royal gifts, on the other hand, desire passionately to remain in her graces forever. Enthroned in glory, she laughs at their ignorance and folly. One sees in her delineation, stamped with egotism and frivolity, another picture of a boastful, but puissant Lady who later was to come to life in Erasmus' *Encomium of Folly*. Professor Allen says of her:

> ... Folly rose up to play, smiling, dancing Folly, singing her own praise. Harmless, almost charming, she seems as she comes on, with no sign of danger; then in a trice her rapier has found out the joints of the harness. The smarting victim stamped with indignation ... It was to Folly's insidious attack that the sufferers traced the beginning of their misfortunes.[85]

Could it be that Erasmus's delightful delineation of Lady Folly was influenced by More's characterization of Fortuna? Erasmus published the *Encomium of Folly* in 1511, while More's verses on Fortune were probably written shortly after 1500 when the *Book of Fortune* was translated from the French into English.

With the aid of classical imagery that surpasses by far the imagery used in the 'Nyne pageauntes', Thomas More, Fortune's avowed enemy, pierces the veil of duplicity that envelopes her. The love of truth that motivated him later in his castigation of heretics now leads him to expose her depravity. The true nature of the fickle Queen is thus revealed as he introduces her attendants to us:

> Fast by her syde doth wery Labour stand,
> Pale Fere also, and Sorow all bewept,
> Disdayn and Hatred on that other hand,
> Eke restless watche fro slepe with trauayle kept,
> His eyes drowsy and lokyng as he slept,
> Before her standeth Daunger and Enuy,
> Flattery, Dysceyt, Mischiefe and Tiranny.[86]

T. E. Bridgett considers this stanza 'striking and harmonious, and [one which] might have been written by Spenser or by Gray'.[87] William Holden Hutton praises these verses and, commending them highly, says:

> It is impossible to read the lines attentively without being reminded of some picture of Botticelli's. There is the same quaint beauty and far-away suggestiveness of an underlying pathos. More was learning to understand the complexity of life and struggling to embrace, maybe, all its many and divergent interests. His 'Fortune' is like Botticelli's calumny. It appeals as strangely, and as widely, at the parting of two ways of life.[88]

Scarcely eighty years later, the 'prince of the English poets'[89] of the sixteenth century, Edmund Spenser, vividly and artistically described the personification of these vices in Book I, Canot IV, in which Duessa guides the faithful knight

192

to the 'sinful hous of Pryde'.[90] In twenty-one lines of description for each vice, Spenser so admirably delineates these despicable abstractions that one can almost see them executed with glowing colours on a tapestry before one's very eyes. To show a slightly analogous comparison with More's stanza, the first lines of some of Spenser's examples of prosopopoeia follow:

> And by his side *rode* loathsome *Gluttony*,
> Deformed creature, on a filthie swyne.[91]

> And next to him *rode* lustful *Lechery*.[92]

> And greedy *Avarice* by him *did ride*,
> Upon a camell loaden all with gold.[93]

> And next to him malicious *Envy rode*.[94]

> Full many mischiefes follow cruell *Wrath*;
> Abhorred *Bloodshed*, and tumultuous *Strife*,
> Unmanly *Murder*, and *unthrifty Scath*,
> Bitter *Despight*, with *Rancours* rusty knife;
> And fretting *Griefe*, the enemy of life.[95]

Thomas More associates his Lady Fortune with 'Labour', 'Fere', and 'Sorow' on one side, while 'Disdain' and 'Hatred' stand on the other side. He uses descriptive epithets such as 'Wery Labour', 'Pale Fere', and 'Sorow all bewept'. Disdain and Hatred are restless as they 'watche fro slepe with travayle kept', but the six attendants who stand before her throne 'Daunger and Enuy / Flattery, Dysceyt, Mischiefe, and Tiranny' need no epithets to describe them, for their close association with the capricious Queen is self-explanatory.

Likewise, Erasmus's Folly has a similar retinue of attendants, to which fact this boasting Lady testifies:

> And there is no reason I should envy Jove for having a she-goat for his nurse, since I was more creditably suckled by two jolly nymphs; the name of the first Drunkenness, one of Bacchus's offspring, the other Ignorance, the daughter of Pan; both which you may here behold of several others of my train and attendants . . . This, who goes with mincing gait, and holds up her head so high, is Self-Love. She that looks so spruce, and makes such a noise and bustle, is Flattery. That other which sits humdrum, as if she were half sleep, is called Forgetfulness. She that leans on her elbow, and sometimes yawningly stretches out her arms, is Laziness.[96]

Fortunes' devotees see only her glamorous beauty and her powerful sway over external things; their eyes are closed to the parasites that surround her throne; and, hence, they implore her for passing gifts and favours:

About her commeth all the world to begge.
He asketh lande, and he to pas would bryng,
This toye and that, and all not worth an egge.[97]

The anaphora in the following verses adds felicity to the rhythm and elegance to the sound structure, and at the same time helps to show that rhythm in poetry was one of Thomas More's fortes:

He would / in loue / pros / per / à boue / all thyng /
He kne / leth downe / and would / bè made / à kyng /
He for / ceth not / so he / may mo / ney haue /
Though all / the world / ac compt / hym for / à knàve /[98]

The first verse in the next rhyme royal stanza emphasizes the addressee in the second person plural of 'ye':

Lo thus ye see diuers heddes, diuers wittes.

Then follows a trenchant innuendo on Lady Fortune, and the repetition of the 'divers' in this line adds emphasis and force to it:

Fortune alone as diuers as they all
Unstable here and there among them flittes.

Like a vain, capricious child, she suddenly showers her gifts on her adorers, and in doing so her aim is to be admired rather than to be of service to them. She does not look around to see who is in need of her gifts or to whom she can give special aid, but she wantonly upsets the cornucopia of bounty and lo! her favours tumble out and their downpour amuses her. She laughs with glee and looks with delight as her sycophants run, push, and tumble over one another in order to catch at least one of the desired gifts. A few of the more aggressive and agile persons reach out before the others and take all they can hold. She nods her head in temporary approval, for they have spared neither their neighbour's feelings nor exhibited any proper decorum in rapaciously appropriating for themselves everything they can possibly grab at this opportune moment. Many walk away discouraged and are disillusioned, while only a few are the recipients of her royal favour. These 'fortunate' individuals pledge themselves instantaneously to Fortune's untiring service.

Thomas More uses a strong, beautiful simile in this passage, which reminds one of the goodness and forbearance of the Creator, who lets the sun shine on the good and the evil – but this proud Dame is perverse and showers her gifts upon a few individuals only:

Catch who so may she throweth great and small
Not to all men, as commeth sonne or dewe,
But for the most part, all among a fewe.[99]

Again More's famous and pertinent epithet 'brotell' – meaning brittle – is used to describe 'gifts', and the prosopopoeia here is excellent for conveying the idea of change and withdrawal. Lady Fortune amuses herself at the expense of her subjects' heart-breaking chagrin and disappointment, and she tosses the gifts from one admirer to another as if she were engaged in sprightly amusement. This proud Lady is not at all interested in the feelings of her clamouring subjects, and she giddily tosses their hearts around – insensible to their groanings and disillusionments. In convincing language and fluent rhythm More embodies these actions in stanza eight of this section. The Tudor poet takes this opportunity to talk to the people in his own voice:

And yet her brotell giftes long may not last,
He that she gaue them, loketh prowde and hye.
She whirlth about and pluckth away as fast,
And geueth them to an other by and by.
She useth to geue and take, and slily tosse,
One man to wynnyng of an others losse.

The caesura, the pyrrhic, and the spondee in the first line of the ninth stanza are assets to this verse:

And when / she rob / beth one // down goth / his pryde /

The alliteration and the assonance in the next verse augment the excellence of its rhythmical value:

He we / peth and way / leth and cur / seth her / full sore /

The following line proves that meaning is more important to the poet than sound:

But in a whyle when *she loueth hym no more,*
She glideth from hym, and her giftes to.
And *he her curseth* as other fooles do.

The eloquent tenth stanza finds More soliloquizing on the foolishness of the people rather than consistently talking to them on the futility of trusting in Fortune as he had set out to do. Throughout his youth and manhood, he continually strove to reveal to others the despicable results of courting Fortune's favours. In these verses so full of poetical merit, he alludes to the famous symbol of the 'wheel', which certainly had no place later in his ideal commonwealth, *Utopia*:

195

Alas the folysh people can not cease,
Ne voyd her trayne, tyll they the harme do fele.
About her always, besely they preace.
But lord how he doth thynk hym self full wele,
That may set once his hande uppon her whele.

These lines exhibit his pity and sorrow for the people who are so fatuous as
to be deceived by Lady Fortune, only to become a prey to bitter disillusionment
at the end. The last two verses of this stanza give a vigorous and graphic
description of the turning of the wheel by this capricious Lady. Caring little
for their life, prestige, or position, she whips her wheel around as a carefree boy
whips his top for the mere pleasure of seeing it spin:

He holdeth fast: but upwarde as he flieth,
She whippeth her whele about, and there he lyeth.

Having given vent to his arduous feelings in the above soliloquy, Thomas More
again becomes conscious of his plural addressee. The sight of the wheel has
conjured in his mind the fates of illustrious historical figures and Biblical
personages and, surely, if his words cannot move his hearers to abandon the
service of the pagan deity, these tragic examples may persuade them to do so.
   He begins with Julius, who fell 'from his mighty power'; then he presents
before the spectators' eyes the tragedies of Darius and Alexander. The fivefold
anaphora and the tropes used, make this stanza an eloquent beginning for the
ensuing tragedies:

Thus fell Julius from his mighty power.
Thus fell Darius, the worthy kyng of Perse.
Thus fell Alexander the great conqueror.
Thus many mo then I may well reherse.
Thus double fortune, when she lyst reuerse
Her slipper fauour fro them that in her trust,
She fleeth her wey and leyeth them in the dust.

The five epithets employed in the appositive, the nominative, and objective
cases enhance the description of the nouns and add rhetorical force and
intensity to the stanza:

mighty power – object of preposition from
worthy kyng of Perse – in apposition with Darius
great conqueror – in apposition with Alexander
double fortune – nominative case
slipper fauour – objective case

More uses the apocope as in the words *mo* for *more* and *fro* instead of *from* in order to strengthen and beautify the sound structure. The allusions to the historical personages, however, form the essence of the meaning structure of this rhyme royal stanza; therefore, a short commentary on them is in order.

The Mirror for Magistrates, 1559, contains fifty-one stanzas of eight lines apiece describing the rise and fall of Julius Caesar. The verses which refer directly to his ascendancy to power through the goddess Fortuna's graces and to his ignominious downfall will be quoted for the purpose of elucidating the content and showing Thomas More's reason for its incorporation here:

> But glory won the way to holde and keepe the same,
> To holde good Fortune fast a worke of skill,
> Who so with prudent arte can stay that stately dame,
> Which sets up so high upon her hauty hill
> And constant aye can keepe her loue and fauour still,
> He winnes immortall fame and high renowne:
> [But thrise unhappy he that weres the stately crowne].
> If once misfortune kicke and cast his scepter downe.[100]

The once-renowned Emperor urges the princes and nobles to beware of pride. He sets his own tragic example before them and says with self-accusing compunction:

> But sith my whole pretence was glory vayne,
> To haue renowne and rule aboue the rest,
> Without remorce of many thousands slayne,
> Which, for their owne defence, their warres addrest:
> I deme therefore my stony harte and brest
> Receiu'd so many wounds for iust reuenge, they stood
> [By iustice right of Ioue, the sacred sentence good],
> That who so slayes hee payes, the price is bloud for bloud.[101]

The next historical allusion to Darius is a historical and a Biblical one, for it is taken from the *First Book of Esdras* and, as such, was very popular in the sixteenth century. In his *History of English Poetry*, Thomas Warton names 'A playe of the story of kyng Darius from Esdras', in 1565, as one of the surviving religious interludes during Queen Elizabeth's reign.[102] Thomas More calls Darius 'the worthy kyng of Perse' because he brought to pass the completion of the temple of God in Jerusalem and issued a decree to that end:

> And may the God, that hath caused his name to dwell there, destroy all kingdoms, and the people that shall put out their hand to resist, and to destroy the house of God, that is in Jerusalem. I Darius have made the decree, which I will have diligently complied with.[103]

Like his predecessor, King Cyrus of Persia, Darius helped to release the Jews from captivity and even solicited their prayers for God's blessings on him and his children:

> And let them offer oblations to the God of heaven, and pray for the life of the king, and of his children.[104]

The fall of Alexander, 'the great conqueror', was precipitated by sensuality and love of fame. The following rhyme royal stanza from Lydgate's *Fall of Princes* vividly illustrates the vulnerability of one of the world's greatest leaders:

> Thouh Alisaundre was myhti of puissaunce,
> And al the worlde hadde in his demeyne,
> Yit was his resoun under thobeisaunce
> Off flesshli lustis fetrid in a cheyne;
> For in his persone will was souereyne,
> His resoun bridled be sensualite,
> Troublyng the fredam off riht & equite.[105]

Alexander the Great, who 'frequently lamented that his father [Philip] conquered everything, and left him nothing to do',[106] bribed the priests to salute him as the son of their god, Jupiter Ammon, and commanded his army to pay him divine respect and homage. After the defeat of Darius in Asia and the slaying of 2,000 inhabitants in cold blood, he made himself supreme master of Egypt, Media, Syria, and Persia. He died in the thirty-second year of his life, presumably from the effects of poison or excessive drinking, after a brilliant and glorious reign of eight years and twelve months of continued success.[107] Thus, Fortune's favourite son was also whirled from the top of her wheel as a tragic example of her short-lived affection and moodiness of spirit.

Having presented Lady Fortune's prosperous sons before the eyes of his spectators, the poet enlarges upon her maliciousness and capriciousness in the following stanza, which deserves to be quoted in full because of its excellent sound and meaning structure:

> She sodeinly enhaunceth them a loft.
> And sodeynly mischeueth all the flocke.
> The head that late lay easily and full soft,
> Instede of pylows lyeth after on the blocke.
> And yet alas the most cruell proude mocke:
> The deynty mowth that ladyes kissed haue,
> She bryngeth in the case to kysse a knaue.[108]

The first two lines are vigorous in rhythm and cogent in meaning, while the repetition of the word 'sodeynly' gives the verses a dynamic force of abruptness and change. The assonance crystallized in the digraph *ea*, in the long sound of *a*, and in the short sound of *o* in the third and fourth lines adds glamour and effectiveness to the meaning structure, which is both autobiographical and provocative.

The word 'mischeueth' in line two is used as a forcible verb, and its function is analogous to that of a scythe which cuts a large area of grain with one vigorous sweep. 'And sodeynly mischeueth all the flocke' implies that Lady Fortune causes her multitudinous protégés to suffer injury as they meet with misfortune to which she is apathetic.

> The head that late lay easily and full soft,
> Instede of pylows lyeth after on the blocke.

After the 1504 incident in Parliament when 'More was elected a burgess'[109] and had spoken intrepidly in negation of Henry VII's proposed request for a monetary gift for the marriage of his eldest daughter Margaret to the King of Scots, he incurred for himself and his family the anger and enmity of the King. During the years 1504–1509 he lived in constant trepidation for his life, and it is at this time that he planned a sojourn abroad.[110] The 'Certain meters' for the *Boke of Fortune* may have been written during these intervening years, and the above two lines may have been the crystallization of the young fugitive's frequent meditations on this phase of his political career. At the same time, these two verses are prophetic in spirit, for the intrepid Chancellor whose love for truth and justice was not altered or mitigated by his youthful experience at court, deliberately laid his head on the block on Tuesday, July 6, 1535. With his characteristic humour he fondly stroked his auburn beard, put it over the scaffold gently, and with a merry twinkle in his blue-gray eyes asked his executioner not to cut it off for it 'hath not committed treason'.[111]

The fifth verse of this rhyme royal stanza contains the irony and hyperbole which characterizes much of his writing:

> And yet alas the most cruell proude mocke.

It is not the loss of honour, wealth, or life that disconcerts the courtier as much as being chagrined while courting a lady's favour and being exposed as stupid before the public eye. Promising every fair lady he meets his love and giving her his troth, the courtier is horrified when he finds out that the rosy lips he met in osculation are not hers, but some roguish fool's:

> The deynty mowth that ladyes kissed haue,
> She bryngeth in the case to kysse a knaue.

Stanza thirteen is provocative and merits quotation in full:

> In chaungyng of her course, the chaunge shewth this,
> Up startth a knaue, and downe there falth a knyght,
> The beggar ryche, and the ryche man pore is.
> Hatred is turned to loue, loue to despyght.

199

This is her sport, thus proueth she her myght.
Great boste she maketh yf one be by her power,
Welthy and wretched both within an howre.

A scintillating use of antithesis and epigrammatic antimetabole or *commutatio*, i.e., a sentence or statement inversed or turned back, makes this seven-line stanza one of literary merit and deep meaning. The three examples of a combination of this rhetorical trope and scheme follow:

Up startth a knaue	downe there falth a knyght
The beggar ryche	the ryche man pore is
Hatred is turned to loue	loue to despyght

The smoothness of the rhythm is exemplified by the following decasyllabic line:

This is / her sport / thus pro / ueth she / her myght /

The stanza ends with an alliterative verse that engraves itself amost indelibly on the reader's mind:

*Wel*th*y* and wretched bo*th with*in an howre.

Stanza fourteen reflects the influence of Lydgate's *Fall of Princes*, in which the author devotes twenty-nine rhyme royal stanzas to the praise of Poverty. Thomas More describes Poverty also as rejecting the gifts of Lady Fortune 'Wyth mery chere'[112] and looking on how 'fortunes houshold goeth to wrake'.[113] Lydgate delineates Poverty as scorning conquest and vain glory and setting little store by wealth. He quotes Seneca, who says that Poverty is the richest of all things, content in both joy and adversity.

Moral Senec recordeth be writyng,
Richest off thynges is Glad Pouerte,
Euer off o cheer[e], void off all gruchchyng.
Bothe in ioie and in aduersite:
Thoruh al the world[e] last hir liberte,
And hir fraunchise stant in so gret ese,
That off hir fredam no man will hir displese.[114]

In Poverty's train of attendants one finds 'the wyse Socrates', Aristippus, Pythagoras, and many other old and sagacious philosophers. Socrates deliberately espoused Poverty during life so that, freed from the trammels of Fortune's unstable gifts, he could devote his life to meditation and study.
    In Chaucer's poem on 'Fortune', Socrates, likewise, is depicted as a champion of Fortune:

O Socrates thou stidfast chaumpyoun
she neuer myht be thi tormentowr.[115]

Aristippus, a disciple of Socrates, practised Poverty also, but not for the same
noble motives as did his master. A story is told that when he was travelling
through the deserts of Africa, he ordered his servants to throw away the money
they carried, as too burdensome. On another occasion, discovering that the
ship in which he sailed belonged to pirates, he threw all his property into the
sea, saying that he chose rather to lose it than his life.[116]

Pythagoras, the third of the celebrated philosophers that More mentions in
this stanza, wished to be called, not a 'sophist' or 'wise man', but a 'philosopher'
or 'the friend of wisdom'. At the Olympic games, when explaining the new
appellation he wished to assume, he said among other things:

> ... thus, on the more extensive theatre of the world, while many struggle
> for the glory of a name, and many pant for the advantages of fortune,
> a few, and indeed but a few, who are neither desirous of money nor
> ambitious of fame, are sufficiently gratified to be spectators of the
> wonder, the hurry, and the magnificence of the scene.[117]

He urged his pupils to be virtuous, exhorted the females to be modest in their
dress, reasoned with youth to abandon the licentious pursuit of pleasure, and
directed the old to stop amassing money and to spend the rest of their days
seeking the peace and comfort of mind that frugality and benevolence give.[118]

Thomas More's reference to the philosopher Diogenes 'in his tonne'[119]
closely parallels Lydgate's description of the same incident with a similar
stress on the blessings of poverty. This poor but wise philosopher who defied
all riches, lived in a tun[120] which he turned toward the south in cold weather
and toward the north in the summer time. Lydgate devotes three stanzas to his
conversation with King Alexander, who came to visit him and offered him wealth
and great treasures. 'You have no lordship over the sun', said the philosopher
to him, 'and your shadow keeps his rays from me'.[121]

In the next stanza More exemplifies good narrative technique, for he tells a
laconic story within the scope of a seven-line stanza. Bias, one of the seven
wise men of Greece, is in the circle of attendants who surround Lady Poverty.
He saved his native city, Priene, from ruin and in time of great danger engraved
upon the minds of the people the fact that wisdom is to be valued more than
material possessions. Thomas More telescopes the story thus:

> With her is Byas, whose countrye lackt defence,
> And whylom of their foes stode so in dout,
> That eche man hastely gan to cary thence,
> And asked hym why he nought caryed out.
> I bere quod he all myne with me about:
> Wisedom he ment, not fortunes brotle fees.
> For nought he counted his that he might leese.[122]

'Leese' in the last line is used in the sense of 'lose', and the epithet 'brotle' perfectly connotes the frailty and fickleness of Fortune's gifts.

Heraclitus, a renowned Greek philosopher of Ephesus who lived five hundred years before the Christian era, was by nature of such a melancholy disposition that he received the appellation 'mourner'.[123] He spent much of his time weeping at the follies and vicissitudes of human beings and lamenting the frailty of human nature. More summed up this feature of his character admirably in the following three lines:

> Of which the fyrst can neuer cease but wepe,
> To see how thick the blynded people go,
> With labour great to purchase care and wo.[124]

Democritus, who travelled in quest of knowledge throughout Europe, Asia, and Africa, returned home in the greatest poverty, retired to a garden near the city, and devoted himself to study and solitude. According to some authorities,[125] he put out his eyes in order to avoid distraction and, consequently, to apply himself more fervently to philosophical speculation and religious contemplation. He laughed at the follies and vanities of mankind who, distracting themselves with care, become prey to anxiety and hope of material gain which ends in frustration and despair. More says of him:

> That other laugheth to see the foolysh apes,
> How earnestly they walke about theyr japes.[126]

The obsolete meaning for 'japes', according to the *Old English Dictionary*, is a means of deception, fraud, or a trick or device to cheat.

As models of wisdom and virtue, Thomas More holds up 'this poore sect,[127] composed of the philosophers: Socrates, Aristippus, Pythagoras, Diogenes, Bias, Heraclitus, and Democritus before the eyes of his spectators. Thomas More himself was deeply impressed with the profundity of their thinking, which transcended the glamorous allurements of wealth, prestige, and power. Like them he was satisfied 'Onely to take that nature may systayne',[128] and banished 'cleane all other surplusage'.[129] In good, rhythmical five-stress lines he further says of these philosophers:

> They be content, and of nothyng complayne.
> No nygarde eke is of his good so fayne,
> But they more pleasure haue a thousande folde,
> The secrete draughtes of nature to beholde.[130]

While penning the last decasyllabic line More probably had Democritus especially in mind, for he said with sincerity and conviction that 'he would prefer the discovery of one of the causes of the works of nature to the diadem of Persia'.[131]

The eighteenth stanza of this section, 'Thomas More to them that trust in fortune', has a three-fold excellence in the following categories: (1) in the provocative antithesis of its meaning structure, (2) in the felicitous rhythm and sound structure pattern, (3) in the rhetorical balance of its sentence structure. The harmonious combination of these three factors makes it a stanza worth repeating often and memorizing for its sound and meaning structure. It is also a perfect synthesis of the Renaissance concept of a free and happy mind, which is a greater treasure than all the wealth one could obtain in a life-time. Allegiance to the demands of Fortune makes one a slave to passion, a servant to anxiety, and a victim of misery. On the other hand, those happy individuals who freely serve Poverty are masters of their passions, heirs to peace of mind, and victors in the strife between body and soul. How well Thomas More has implied this realization is seen in the stanza in which he alludes to the servants of Fortune:

> Set fortunes servauntes by them and ye wull,
> That one is free, that other euer thrall,
> That one content, that other neuer full,
> That one is suretye, that other lyke to fall.
> Who lyst to aduise them bothe, parceyue he shall,
> As great difference betwene them as we see,
> Betwixte wretchedness and felicite.

Six lines of verse, adorned with anaphora and beautified by pleasing assonance of sound structure, lead coherently and emphatically to the climax in the seventh verse. The delineation is so clairvoyant that one can almost see it engraved on the mosaic of one's mind: Fortune is described as 'wretchedness' while Poverty is delineated as 'felicite'. It seems as if More, who was also an enterprising man of law, put the two estates on a scale, scrupulously weighed the merits of each, and permitted the onlookers to form their own judgments concerning the superiority of the latter. Appropriately, then, he says to them in stanza fourteen:

> Nowe haue I shewed you bothe: chese whiche ye lyst,
> Stately fortune, or humble pouertee.

Thomas More, who was also well-read in theology and had often contemplated one of man's greatest attributes, his free will, invites his audience to choose freely, for this privilege is their God-given prerogative:

> That is to say, nowe lyeth it in your lyst,
> To take here bondage, or free libertee.

Unlike Lady Fortune, who engages in prevarication and deliberately deceives her admirers, More does not equivocate but sincerely shows his public 'both sides of the medal' by presenting the assets and liabilities of each estate. Then they may choose – but first he urges them to weigh and ponder, to evaluate and convince themselves of the wisdom of their choice.

Following a weak fifth line, 'But in thys poynte and ye do after me', the next two lines contain an ironical suggestion:

> Draw you to fortune, and labour her to please,
> If that ye thynke your selfe to well at ease.[132]

Continuing his exhortation in a vein of irony, this master of insight into the nature of the capricious goddess says debonairly to his addressee, whom he feels he still did not persuade to abandon Fortune's service:

> And fyrst, uppon the louely shall she smile,
> And frendly on the cast her wandering eyes,
> Embrace the in her armes, and for a whyle,
> Put the and kepe the in a fooles paradise.[133]

How well the young author of these excellent lines knows the sophistic charms of this deceiving lady, and how thoroughly convinced he is of her true colors and despicable worth! Before even attempting to mount her wheel of destiny, he realizes full well what the detrimental outcomes are and burns with a desire to impart his soul-stirring feelings to others. 'You may join her train of attendants, if you wish', says Thomas More out of respect for the people's free-will, 'But for all that beware of after clappes'.[134]

In what is considered one of the best stanzas in this section, Thomas More expresses his philosophical ideas in hyperbolic and antithetical equations. He now makes a direct appeal to the mind of his addressee since appealing to the emotions alone without gaining the conviction of his reason proves futile and unsuccessful. However, his erudite speculation is far from being dry and boring. Hyperbole gives it colour and animation; antithesis makes it provocative and alluring; prosopopoeia clothes it with vitality and ingenuity. These verses figuratively expose the true nature of Fortune, and their references to clouds, land, and fire make these lines highly artistic:

> Recken you neuer of her fauoure sure:
> Ye may in clowds as easily trace an hare,
> Or in drye lande cause fishes to endure,
> And make the burnyng fyre his heate to spare,
> And all thys worlde in compace to forfare,
> As her to make by craft or engine stable,
> That of her nature is euer variable.

In his 'Philological *Notes*'[135] A. W. Reed does not give the meaning of the word 'Compace', which is certainly unintelligible to the modern reader. Its current meaning in the sixteenth century denoted an 'artifice, a skillful or crafty device, or contrivance'.[136] From 'skillful devising or designing' it passed into the derogatory sense of 'subtilty, cunning, or craft' which later became associated with the modern sense of 'compassing or contriving'. Reed includes the word 'forfare' in his 'Philological Notes' and gives as its definition the synonym 'to perish'.[137] This fifth line, then, takes on intelligible meaning to the twentieth-century reader, for its signifies that the entire world will sooner perish through deceit than that Fortune should become stable who 'of her nature is euer variable'.[138] The epigrammatic quality of these verses appeals to the imagination, impresses itself on one's memory, and adds sparkle, humour, and wit to one's conversation. These memorable sayings are in lines two, three, and four of the twenty-first stanza:

> Ye may in clowds as easily trace an hare,
> Or in drye lande cause fishes to endure,
> And make the burnyng fyre his heate to spare.

Thomas More takes his tropes from the sky, the land, and fire which gives off heat and light; and lastly, he shows his addressee a picture of the world bereft of virtuous men, 'And all thys worlde in compace to forfare'.[139]

Obviously, More's audience still appears sceptical, for he continues his spirited persuasion:

> Serue her day and nyght as reuerently,
> Uppon thy knees as any servaunt may,
> And in conclusion, that thou shalt winne thereby
> Shall not be worth thy seruyce I dare say.[140]

While bent on convincing his addressee and winning his voluntary disavowal of Fortune's power, More does not neglect the rhythmical aspect of his verses. The fluency of the following decasyllabic lines testifies to this fact. The three trochees, moreover, in the second and third verses add dramatic emphasis to the meaning structure of this stanza:

> And look / yet what / she ge / ueth the / to day /
> With la / bour wonne / she shall / hap ply / to mor / row /
> Pluck it / a gayne / out of / thyne hand / with sor / row /[141]

In the twenty-second stanza the poet assumes that he has gained sufficient goodwill on the part of his addressee to consider the argument proposed to him; he now ventures to give him sound, practical advice on how to abandon Fortune's service. Nevertheless, More is still dubious about his audience's attitude, for he says in the first line of the twenty-third stanza:

> Wherefore yf you in suretye lyst to stande.

There is no vacillation in the remedy Thomas More gives 'to them that trust in fortune';[142] and if one wants to lead a useful and happy life, he urges the practice of the following four things:

1. Take pouertes parte
2. Let prowde fortune go
3. Receyve nothyng that commeth from her hande
4. Loue maner and vertue

Plutarch and Aristotle gave Fortune 'a reasonable basis of existence and explained her as the "cause by accident" which is proper only to man, and which is the necessary cause to allow for human free-will'.[143] Juvenal advocated 'prudentia'[144] as a remedy against her powerful sway over man's emotions, and Seneca wrote: 'Unum Bonum esse, Quod Honestum est'.[145] Since her power was thus mitigated and she could no longer be supreme, man's allegiance to her as a puissant goddess was weakened. Petrarch, who referred to the goddess many times, particularly in his work, *De Remediis Ultriusque Fortunae*, advocated wisdom and spiritual devotion against her wiles and hypocritical deceit. The typically Italian Renaissance conception of *Virtù* against Fortune implies that she yields, not to goodness or wisdom, but only to power.[146] In keeping with this concept Machiavelli said that the goddess, being a lady, must be taken by storm.[147] Howard Patch makes a pertinent and scholarly inference concerning the philosophy of Fortune and the remedies against her power when he points to her as the symbol of the restless and confused age:

> And thus the Renaissance welcomes the pagan figure, and gives her an appropriate place in its elaborate theology. Like the time of Augustus in Rome, it is a restless period, with much traffic and discovery, much hazarding of all that one had, much toying with strange gods for the very delight of their strangeness, much questioning (with little passion for an answer). The goddess of chance admirably represented both its weakness and its strength. She is just the deity for the romantically-minded, for those who find life only in flux and change. She represents that conveniently adjustable religion for which certain temperaments long.[148]

Not only does Thomas More advocate the fourfold remedy of poverty, renunciation, mortification, and virtue, but he also recommends aggressiveness in these lines:

> Then mayst thou boldly defye her turning chaunce:
> She can the neyther hynder nor avaunce.[149]

More looks at this vexing problem from all possible angles, and then adds cautiously:

> But and thou wylt nedes medle with her treasure,
> Trust not therein, and spende it liberally.
> Beare the not proude, nor take not out of measure.[150]

Metaphor, aphorism, and alliteration combine to make the next verse emphatic:

> Bylde not thyne house on heyth up in the skye.[151]

He who has little does not live in constant fear of having his possessions taken from him, just as he who is content with his lowly position in life is bereft of the fear and anxiety that power and prestige are heir to. The following fifth line of the last stanza admirably sums up this philosophy in terse diction:

> None falleth farre, but he that climbeth hye.

The two clinching verses, which are coloured by tactful didacticism, go back to pristine nature and have for their setting the 'Garden of Paradise'. 'Remember', says More admonishingly, 'nature sent the hyther bare',[152] and he adds convincingly, 'The gyftes of fortune count them borowed ware'.[153]

The third section, 'Thomas More to them that seke fortune', consists of seven rhyme royal stanzas which stress man's free will in choosing to serve or to reject Lady Fortune. More appears to be a little hesitant in displaying an adamant attitude towards his addressee, for the reference he makes to himself in the first person, objective case, savours of deliberate vindication in this regard. Apologetically he says in line four of the opening stanza:

> Blame ye not me: for I commaunde you not,
> Fortune to trust . . .

In the last two lines which are the best in this stanza, he compares this proud Queen to a lively and irresponsible mare over whom he has no control:

> I have of her no brydle in my fist,
> She renneth loose, and turneth where she lyst.

The next seven lines imply that the speaker and the addressee know one another, for More alludes to 'the rollyng dysc in whome your lucke doth stande', and which, he says almost aggressively, 'Ye knowe your selfe came neuer in myne hande'.[154] Reference here to 'the rollyng dyse' points to its association with the *Boke of Fortune*: one received the answer to one's inquiry into future events or states of the mind of other persons through a complicated process which was initiated with a single throw of three dice. Thomas More openly states his disapproval of diceplaying and considers it unchristian, unmanly, and unethical. He is undoubtedly influenced by Chaucer, who gives his opinion of dice play in the following verses:

> Dycing is very mother of leesings,
> And of deceyte, and cursed forswearings,
> Blasphemie of God, manslaughter, and waste also,
> Of battayle, oughtinessc, and other mo,
> It is reprofe, and contrarie to honour,
> For to beholde a common dicesour.[155]

Nicholas Lyra's little book entitled *Praeceptorium*, in which he gives nine reasons against playing dice, was one of the occasions for the making of laws forbidding this pernicious pastime. In the *Summa Angelica* this art is considered the 'mother of lies, of periuries, theft, of debate, of iniuries, of manslaughter, the very inuention of the deuills of hell: and arte altogether infamous, and forbidden by the lawes of all nations'.[156] Dice-playing was prohibited during the reigns of Richard II and Edward IV; and in the time of Henry VII dice-players were sentenced to the stocks for one whole day. During Henry VIII's reign every housekeeper that kept dice-players within her house forfeited forty shillings.[157]

With a delightful turn of humour which takes the sting out of More's didacticism, he compares Lady Fortune's bounty to a pond in which fishes and frogs swim. He uses a colourful and vigorous trope, to convey his idea: 'Cast in your nette',[158] but then, he immediately adds, 'Holde you content as fortune lyst assyne:'[159] and, again holding his opponent at an arm's length, he asserts, 'For it is your owne fishyng and not myne'.[160]

On the other hand, 'if you offend Fortune', he tells his addressee, 'do not grudge thereat, but beare a mery face'.[161] In the four final lines of this stanza he illustrates Fortune's fickle domination, for at one end of the hierarchy of her gifts is the man who is 'out of her grace / But he sometyme hath comfort and solace',[162] while at the other end is the individual who, not possessing the full bounty of her gifts, is never 'full satisfyed with her behauiour'.[163]

Thomas More brilliantly describes the external features of this imperious Queen as 'stately, solemne, prowde, and hye',[164] and puts his finger on the most vulnerable point of her deceitful character when he exposes the harm she does to human nature itself:

> But for all that she kepeth euer in store,
> From euery manne some parcell of his wyll,
> That he may pray therfore and serue her styll.[165]

The fifth stanza of this third section has rhetorical skill and poetical merit. Anaphora enhances its rhythmical quality, parallelism gives it a sense of proportion and beauty, and accumulation dramatically leads to a crescendo effect. Allusions to these lines are often made by More's biographers, particularly the pungent but not necessarily autobiographical reference to the 'shrewde wyfe'.[166] Because of its technical and felicitous melody the stanza is here fully quoted:

> Some manne hath good, but chyldren hath he none,
> Some man hath both, but he can get none health.
> Some hath al thre, but up to honours trone,
> Can he not crepe, by no maner of stelth,
> To some she sendeth, children, ryches, welthe,
> Honour, woorshyp, and reuerence all hys lyfe.
> But yet she pincheth hym with a shrewde wyfe.[167]

The run-on line in verse three, which carries the meaning over to the next line, proves More to be a poet of no mean caliber and emphasizes the fact the he strives for sense rather than sound. Oftentimes, as in the above stanza, he combines both with very good results.

Having exhausted his subject and shown his addressee both sides of Lady Fortune's glamorous and specious character, Thomas More gives the final counsel to those who followed him in his exposition of her true nature:

> I counsayle you eche one trusse up your packes,
> And take no thyng at all, or be content,
> With suche rewarde as fortune hath you sent.[168]

'Trusse' is an obsolete word which, as the context of the phrase implies, means exactly what it signifies, namely 'to tie in a bundle or to pack'.[169] Above all, More exhorts those who are sympathetic towards his point of view not to solicit Fortune's favours, but to be content with what they have. Thus, stability of temperament, peace of mind, and strengthening of will power will insure for them a well-ordered and happy life.

The seventh and last rhyme royal stanza, with which the entire poem concludes, clearly points to the addressee to whom More's entreaties and exhortations were directed, namely, to the numerous readers of the *Boke of Fortune* who presumably were avid believers in its predictions. The first two verses of this stanza reveal the poet's tact in dealing with this delicate subject:

> All thynges in this boke that ye shall rede,
> Doe as ye lyst, there shall no manne you bynde.

Following the example of Augustine and Thomas Aquinas, Thomas More manifests great respect for man's free will and does not coerce him, but merely presents to him a true picture of the fickle goddess. He has the much-read *Boke of Fortune* in mind when he says adamantly that the things contained therein should not be believed in 'as surely as your crede'.[170] In Thomas More's mind, however, there is no vacillation, no ambiguity, nor any desire to succumb to Fortune's wiles or to pry into the future's unpredictable affairs. With a positiveness that is refreshing and a sanguinity that is relaxing, he ends this poem with his testimony to the prevarication of this art, which is as false 'As are the iudgementes of Astronomye'.[171]

Approximately thirty years after the writing of these verses for the *Boke of Fortune*, Thomas More at the age of fifty-seven was confined to imprisonment in the Tower. As he looked back on his life, he rejoiced that he had never solicited Lady Fortune's gifts nor entered her service. The innocent victim of Henry VIII's displeasure must have smiled as he recapitulated his own sudden rise to power and then his abrupt downfall to misfortune and degradation. Thomas More had, figuratively speaking, been at the top of Fortune's wheel when fame, wealth, and prestige courted him, and then he had been hurled mercilessly to the ground in disgrace and debasement. For this staunch Christian humanist, however, it was not the goddess Fortune who manipulated these pivotal events in his life, but it was God and His Divine Providence who had ordained these events to happen. Hence, More smiles and jeeringly says to this capricious Queen:

> Ay flattering fortune look you never so fair,
> Nor never so pleasantly begin to smile,
> As though thou wouldst my ruins all repair
> During my life thou shalt not me beguile.[172]

Then, full of confidence in God's love and infinite mercy, he adds in a spirit of Christian wisdom and understanding:

> Trust I shall, God, to enter in a while
> Thy haven of heaven sure and uniform,
> Ever after thy calm look I for no storm.[173]

Already as a young man of twenty-five Thomas More realized the absurdity of paying homage to this fickle goddess, and six years before his death he publicly gave testimony to her 'slippery' power. On October 26, 1529, Thomas More took the oath as Chancellor, having accepted the Great Seal from King Henry VIII the day before. The Duke of Norfolk in the King's special commission openly declared 'how worthy he was of the highest preferment in the Kingdom, and how dearly his Majesty loved and confided in him'.[174] Then, attributing to young More the virtues of wisdom, equity, sincerity, and integrity, the Duke added that the exaltation of such a virtuous man to this high office would insure the people of peace and justice and the kingdom of prosperity, honour, and fame.[175] The humble and prudent Chancellor was ruffled by these words of praise, and after 'many expressions of his own unworthiness, of his unwillingness to be a courtier, of his gratitude and dutifulness to the King, and above all of his aversion to this high office which was a weight unsuitable to his weakness, a burden and not a glory, a care and not a dignity',[176] he cast his inward eye on 'flattering Fortune', as he said:

> ... I have cause enough by my predecessor's example, to think honour but slippery, and this dignity not so grateful to me as it may seem to others. For it is a hard matter to follow with like paces or praises a man of such admirable wit, prudence, splendour, and authority; to whom I may seem but as the lighting of a candle when the sun is down. Then the sudden and unexpected fall of so great a man as he was, doth terribly put me in mind, that this honour ought not to please me too much, nor the lustre of this glittering seat dazzle my eyes.[177]

In most of the biographies of Thomas More the ballad to Fortune is included without its title, 'Lewys the lost louer', and with a presumably erroneous first line. Rastell's 'Ey flatering fortune'[178] has become for most authors 'Eye-flattering fortune';[179] Warner and Cline use 'Ay' or 'Aye flattering fortune' and employed in this sense, the word is closer to More's original meaning.

For purposes of clarification and the correction of erroneous lines, Rastell's edition of this ballette[180] follows:

Lewys the lost louer

> Ey flatering fortune, loke thou neuer so fayre,
> Or neuer so pleasantly begin to smile,
> As though thou wouldst my ruine all repayre,
> During my life thou shalt me not begile.
> Trust shall I God, to entre in a while,
> Hys haven heaven sure and uniforme.
> Euer after thy calme, loke I for a storme.[181]

The doomed victim of Henry VIII's revenge and concupiscence wrote this poem with charcoal (all writing materials being taken away from him) for his own pastime in the recapitulation of his vicissitudes in life. He speaks vindictively to Lady Fortune and exults in the fact that she had never beguiled him during life. Now in the face of approaching death More takes on the attitude not of a stoic, but of a Christian who asserts his belief in God's providence and repudiates Fortune's power and authority.

The occasion for this poem was the visit of Thomas Cromwell, the Master Secretary who was sent to More by the King to beguile him with kind words and specious intentions. Thomas More saw through this dissembling incident, which was designed to make him swerve from his decision, and expressed his thoughts and sentiments in the above verse.

'Dauy the dicer' was written in prison also, not in the spirit of foresight which enabled the innocent prisoner to see the trap set for him, but in a facetious mood and with a carefree mind. More does not speak here in his own person but assumes the disguise of 'Dauy the dicer', who has played against Fortune in the game of life but has lost. In this personified guise he amuses himself with writing the following seven lines:

Dauy the dicer

> Long was I lady Lucke your seruing man,
> and now haue lost agayne all that I gat,
> wherfore whan I thinke on you nowe and than,
> and in my mynde remember this and that,
> ye may not blame me though I beshrew your cat,
> but in fayth I blesse you agayne a thousand times,
> for lending me now some laysure to make rymes.[182]

Apparently, this ballette was written without any pretence at real poetry, for it appears to be in its first draft only. Unlike Thomas More's other poems, every line begins with a small letter and some of the endings are trite, as for example, in line three 'nowe and than' and in line four, 'this and that'. Appropriately More does not call the ubiquitous Queen by her usual appellation 'Fortune' but in keeping with the colloquial atmosphere of the poem and the vulgarity of dice-playing, he calls her 'Lady Lucke'.

The most salient feature of this little poem, however, lies in the autobiographical detail concerning More's love for the writing of poetry. When he blesses this Queen of dice-players 'for lending me now some laysure to make rymes', he reverts to a pastime he loves and enjoys. At the same time he pierces the bubble of her pride and hurls at her an innuendo, which is as poignant and keen as it is subtle and suave. Thus, all throughout his life Thomas More waged a relentless war against Fortune; and now, just before going to his execution on Tower Hill, he scoffs at her pretentiousness and derides her power.

1. *Works*, I, 16.
2. *Ibid.*, I, 18.
3. Lee, pp. 59–60.
4. Lewis, p. 133.
5. *Ibid.*
6. R. W. Chambers, p. 87.
7. Hitchcock, p. 17.
8. Ferd[inand] Warner, *Memoirs of the Life of Sir Thomas More* (London, 1758), p. 9.
9. R. W. Chambers, p. 98..
10. (Princeton, New Jersey, 1949), p. 41.
11. *Works*, I, 225, line 15.
12. *Ibid.*, 11. 8–9.
13. Furnival, line 1, p. 316.
14. *Ibid.*
15. Walter Gorn Old (Sepharial), *Fortune Telling By Numbers* (Philadelphia, 1943), p. 29.
16. *Ibid.*, pp. 20–21.
17. *Works*, Thomas More to them that seke fortune.' Fifteenth Page. D. 1.
18. Howard Rollin Patch, *The Goddess Fortuna in Medieval Literature* (Cambridge, Mass., 1927), pp. 42–43.
19. *Ibid.*, pp. 49, 50, 137.
20. Dyboski, pp. 97–100.
21. See *Roman de la Rose*, 11. 6580–6583.
22. Patch, p. 85.
23. 'Thomas More to them seke fortune,' Sixteenth Page, B. 1–2.
24. Patch, p. 164.
25. *Ibid.*
26. *Ibid.*, p. 60.
27. Twelth page, B. 10. C. 1.
28. *Ibid.*, D. 8–9.
29. *Works*, I, 226, 'Certain Meters,' lines 7 and 18.
30. 'Thomas More to them that trust in fortune,' Fifteenth Page, A. 8–11. B. 1–3.
31. *Ibid.*, Fifteenth Page, D. 8. Sixteenth Page, A. 1.
32. Patch, p. 73.
33. 'Thomas More to them that seke fortune,' Sixteenth Page, B. 7. 3–4.
34. *Ibid.*, B. 3–4.
35. Henry Huth, *Fugitive Poetical Tracts*, First Series (Chancery Lane, 1875), Printed for Private Circulation, p. xiii.

36. Lines 76–96, Patch, p. 19.
37. *Ibid.*, p. 19.
38. *Ibid.*, p. 12.
39. Howard Rollin Patch, 'Fortuna in Old French Literature,' *Smith College Studies in Modern Languages*, IV (July 1923), 1–32.
40. 'Thomas More to them that trust in Fortune,' Fifteenth Page, A. 11. B. 1.
41. *OED*, VI, 129.
42. Sufficient proof to certify that More wrote the French verses is lacking.
43. Patch, p. 72. n. 2.
44. Patch, IV (July 1923), 6.
45. *Ibid.*, citing Jean de Meun's *Roman de la Rose*, 11. 4858–61.
46. *Ibid.* Cf. Petrarch, *De Remediis* (*Smith College Studies in Modern Languages*, III, 207), cited in Patch, 'Fortuna in Old French Literature,' IV, 7.
47. *Roman de la Rose*, 11. 4852 ff., cited in Patch, p. 7.
48. *Ibid.*, 11. 5868ff.
49. *Ibid.*, 11. 5900 ff.
50. *Works*, I, 225, 'The Prologue,' 11. 5–7.
51. *Ibid.*, lines 11–12.
52. *Ibid.*, line 14.
53. *Ibid.*, 11. 15–21.
54. *Ibid.*, I, 226, line 7.
55. *Ibid.*, line 18.
56. 'Fortune Speketh,' p. 226, lines 1–8.
57. *Ibid.*, 226–227, lines 7. 14.
58. 'The wordes of Fortune to the people,' Tenth page, D. 9.
59. *Ibid.*, Eleventh page, A. 5.
60. *Ibid.*, Tenth page, A. 1. 5.
61. *Ibid.*, A. 7.
62. *Ibid.*, A. 6.
63. *Ibid.*, A. 9.
64. *Ibid.*, A. 10.
65. *Ibid.*, B. 5.
66. *Ibid.*, B. 4.
67. *Ibid.*, B. 6–8.
68. *Ibid.*, B. 10. C. 1–2.
69. *Ibid.*, C. 3.
70. *Ibid.*
71. *Ibid.*, D. 3.
72. *Ibid.*, D. 2. 4.
73. *Ibid.*, D. 1.
74. *Ibid.*, D. 7.
75. *Ibid.*, D. 4.
76. *Ibid.*, D. 5–7.
77. *OED*, IV, 80.
78. 'Thomas More to them that trust in fortune,' Eleventh Page, B. 3–4.
79. 'Thomas More to them that trust in fortune,' Eleventh Page, C. 3.
80. *Ibid.*, C. 4.
81. Patch, p. 51.
82. *Ibid.*, pp. 51–52.
83. 'Thomas More to them that trust in fortune,' Eleventh Page, C. 6–8.
84. *Ibid.*, C. 9. D. 1–6.
85. Percy Stafford Allen, *Erasmus* (Oxford, 1934), pp. 75–76.
86. 'Thomas More to them that trust in fortune,' Eleventh Page, D. 6–8, Twelfth Page, A. 1–4.
87. Bridgett, p. 15.
88. Hutton, p. 29.
89. A. A. Tunstall, ed., *The Faerie Queene*, 'Memoir of Edmund Spenser' (New York, 1859), p. viii.
90. *Ibid.*, p. 31.
91. *Ibid.*, Canto IV, Stanza 21, p. 35.

92. *Ibid.*, p. 36, stanza 24.
93. *Ibid.*, p. 36, stanza 27.
94. *Ibid.*, p. 37, stanza 30.
95. *Ibid.*, p. 38, Stanza 35.
96. Desiderius Erasmus, *In Praise of Folly*, Sesame Library (London, 1930), p. 11.
97. 'Thomas More to them that trust in fortune,' Twelfth Page, A. 5–7.
98. *Ibid.*, A. 8–11.
99. *Ibid.*, B. 5–7.
100. Joseph Haslewood, ed., *The Mirror for Magistrates* (London, 1815), I, 271–272, Stanza 40.
101. *Ibid.*, I, 275, stanza 51.
102. Warton, III, 270.
103. *The First Book of Esdras*, VI, 12.
104. *Ibid.*, VI, 10.
105. Lines 6252–58, John Lydgate, *Fall of Princes*, Part I, Books I–II (Washington, 1923), p. 177.
106. John Lemprière, *A Classical Dictionary* (London, 1930,) p. 32.
107. *Ibid.*, p. 31.
108. 'Certain meters,' Thirteenth Page, A. 1–4. B. 1–3.
109. Chambers, p. 87.
110. *Ibid.*, Chambers quoting Roper, p. 98, no. 1.
111. Mackintosh, p. 195.
112. 'Thomas More to them that trust in fortune,' Thirteenth Page, C. 2.
113. *Ibid.*
114. Lines 6175–81, Lydgate, I, 174.
115. Lines 17–18, Furnivall, p. 316.
116. Lemprière, p. 77.
117. *Ibid.*, p. 522.
118. *Ibid.*
119. 'Thomas More to them that trust in fortune,' Thirteenth Page, C. 7.
120. *OED*, X, Part I, 464. *Tun*, barrel or a large cask usually for liquids or for various provisions.
121. Line 6245, Lydgate, I, 176, gloss.
122. 'Thomas More to them that trust in fortune,' Thirteenth Page, C. 8–10. D. 1–4.
123. Lemprière, p. 266.
124. 'Thomas More to them that trust in fortune,' Thirteenth Page, D. 7–8. Fourteenth Page, A. 1.
125. Lemprière, p. 198.
126. 'Thomas More to them that trust in fortune,' Fourteenth Page, A. 2–3.
127. *Ibid.*, A. 4.
128. *Ibid.*, A. 5.
129. *Ibid.*, A. 6.
130. *Ibid.*, A. 7–10.
131. Lemprière, p. 198.
132. 'Thomas More to them that trust in fortune,' Fourteenth Page, C. 2–3.
133. *Ibid.*, C. 4–7.
134. *Ibid.*, D. 1.
135. *Works*, I, 194–218.
136. *OED*, II, 704, 711.
137. *Works*, 'Philological Notes,' by A. W. Reed, I, 197. D. 6.
138. 'Thomas More to them that trust in fortune,' Fourteenth Page, D. 8.
139. *Ibid.*, D. 6.
140. *Ibid.*, Fifteenth Page, A. 1–4.
141. *Ibid.*, A. 5–7.
142. 'Thomas More to them that trust in fortune,' Eleventh Page, A. 6–7.
143. Patch, p. 12.
144. *Ibid.*, p. 13.
145. *Ibid.*
146. *Ibid.*, p. 25.
147. *Ibid.*
148. *Ibid.*, pp. 25–26.
149. 'To them that trust in fortune,' Fifteenth Page, B. 2–3.

150. *Ibid.*, B. 4–6.
151. *Ibid.*, B. 7.
152. *Ibid.*, B. 9.
153. *Ibid.*, B. 10.
154. 'Thomas More to them that seke fortune,' Fifteenth Page, D. 1. 3.
155. John Northbrooke, *A Treatise Against Dicing, Dancing, Plays and Interludes* (London, 1843), p. 132.
156. *Ibid.*, p. 133.
157. *Ibid.*, p. 136.
158. 'Thomas More to them that seke fortune,' Fifteenth Page, D. 5.
159. *Ibid.*, D. 6.
160. *Ibid.*, D. 7.
161. *Ibid.*, Sixteenth Page, A. 1.
162. *Ibid.*, A. 3–4.
163. *Ibid.*, A. 6.
164. *Ibid.*, A. 7.
165. *Ibid.*, A. 11. B. 1–2.
166. *Ibid.*, B. 9.
167. *Ibid.*, B. 3–9.
168. *Ibid.*, C. 5–7.
169. *OED*, X, Part I, 430.
170. 'Thomas More to them that seke fortune,' Sixteenth Page, C. 10.
171. *Ibid.*, D. 4.
172. Maurice Adams, ed., *More's Utopia, with Roper's Life* (London, 1890), pp. 48–49.
173. *Ibid.*
174. Warner, p. 53.
175. *Ibid.*, pp. 53–54.
176. *Ibid.*, p. 54.
177. *Ibid.*, p. 55.
178. William Rastell, ed., *The Workes of Sir Thomas More Knyght* (London, 1557), p. 1432.
179. See Chambers, p. 326, Reynolds, p. 319.
180. Rastell refers to these poems as *ballettes*. See *Workes*, p. 1432.
181. *Ibid.*
182. *Ibid.*, p. 1433.

CHAPTER VI

RELIGIOUS THEME WITH
ARTISTIC TREATMENT

From the years 1499–1503 Thomas More lived with the Carthusians in the Charterhouse without taking any vows in order to determine what his vocation in life should be. In the quiet atmosphere of this religious guest house he read the teachings of the Fathers, made a translation with Lily from the Greek Anthology, and prepared his manuscript for a series of lectures on St. Augustine's *De Civitate Dei*. He participated in the spiritual exercises of the monks with devotion and sincerely contemplated choosing a state of life that would be most pleasing to God and most commensurate with His holy will. Stapleton records the fact that it was William Lily who was More's confidant in this speculation concerning his vocation: 'Meditabatur adolescens sacerdotium cum suo Lilio'.[1] At this time also, he probably read the *Life of John Picus, the Erle of Myrandula*, which had been published by the Earl's nephew, Giovanni Francesco Pico, and which Linacre or Colet may have brought from Italy, together with other manuscripts.[2] More than the pressing persuasions of Dean Colet to embrace a married state of life, the beautiful example of the young but renowned Italian humanist seemed to point to Thomas More his own way of life. He sincerely endeavoured to emulate the zeal, detachment, and love of God this great fifteenth-century scholar manifested in the last years of his life. Like his ideal who remained in the world and yet was not of it, More felt he could still be a Carthusian in spirit while serving God in the world and striving zealously after perfection.

Stapleton substantiates this theory when he says that, after Thomas More decided to leave the cloister, he chose Picus as his model:

> [He] determined, therefore, to put before his eyes the example of some prominent layman, on which he might model his life. He called to mind all who at that period, either at home or abroad, enjoyed the reputation of learning and piety, and finally fixed upon John Pico, Earl of Mirandola, who was renowned in the highest degree throughout the whole of Europe for his encyclopedic knowledge, and no less esteemed for his sanctity of life. More translated into English a Latin Life of Pico by his nephew, as well as his letters, and a set of twelve counsels for leading a good life, which he had composed. His purpose was not so much to bring these to the knowledge of others, though that too, he had in view, as throughly to familiarize himself with them.[3]

Thomas More's subsequent life faithfully mirrors the virtues and edifying

216

practices the young Earl performed, and a close examination of these rules of conduct displays a marked affinity between the two men. Only fifteen years More's senior, Pico della Mirandola died from a fever at the early age of thirty-one, while More was a martyr for the faith at the age of fifty-seven. In delineating the character of the Italian humanist whom he chose as his model for life, Thomas More almost unwittingly paints his own portrait:

> He was of cheer always merry and of so benign nature that he was never troubled with anger . . . O very happy mind, which none adversity might oppress, which no prosperity might enhance . . . Not his great substance, not his noble blood could blow up his heart; not the beauty of his body, not the great occasion of sin, were able to pull him back into the voluptuous broad way that leadeth to hell. What thing was there of so marvellous strength that might overturn the mind of him which now (as Seneca saith) was got above fortune? . . . When another man offered him great worldly promotion if he would go to the king's court, he gave him such an answer that he should well know that he neither desired worship nor worldly riches, but rather set them at naught that he might the more quietly give himself to study and the service of God . . . All praise of people, all earthly glory he reputed utterly for nothing: but in the renaying (i.e. denying) of this shadow of glory he laboured for very glory, which evermore followeth virtue as an inseparable servant . . .[4]

This English humanist admired the Italian scholar particularly for the following five things: (1) an incredible wit, (2) a marvellously fast memory, (3) Latin and Greek books and volumes of all manner of literature, (4) indefatigable study, and (5) the contempt of earthly things.[5]

Thomas More begins and ends the *Life of John Picus* in his own words, but follows the Latin text in the rest of the work. He omits cumbersome details of kinship, family history, and earlier studies in 'obscure philosophy'.[6] One notices a preoccupation with style and a concentration on elegance, perspicuity, and forcefulness of expression with a consequent appeal to the mind, emotions, and will of the reader. A. W. Reed makes the interesting observation that 'the presence in More's *Life of Pico* of a considerable body of verse not found in the original reflects in an interesting way the spirit in which More approached his experiment'.[7]

Pico's 'Twelve rules of John Picus Earle of Mirandula . . .' which are short prose apothegms, were translated into English prose by Sir Thomas Elyot and rendered by More into twenty-three stanzas of rhyme royal English verse. It has been assumed that More's interest in Pico della Mirandola is traceable to the poet Skelton, for whom the Italian humanist wrote some laudatory verses which can be found in Dyce's edition of Skelton's *Poetical Works*.[8]

John Skelton was tutor to Prince Henry VIII at the time Thomas More took Erasmus to visit the royal nursery at Eltham. The nine-year-old Prince's interest in poetry is evident from the fact that he jovially challenged Erasmus to offer him a specimen of his poetical powers. The Dutch scholar, who was visiting

England for the first time, tells us this fact honestly and bluntly:

> I went home; and, in despite of the muses, from whom I had long before
> divorced myself, composed, in three days, a poem in alternate hexa-
> meters and iambics, in which I celebrated the praises of Henry VII and
> his children, and the whole nation, and thus soothed my shame and
> sorrow.[9]

Rev. Alexander Dyce, who edited *The Poetical Works of John Skelton*, alludes
to a manuscript in the collection of Mr. B. H. Bright, which consists of *Hymni
Heroici* by Picus Mirandula, in which priase is given to John Skelton.[10] In a
recent book on *Skelton* by H. R. L. Edwards, this current mistake is attributed
to the fact that Pico's *Hymni Heroici* was addressed to various saints, and
Erasmus's manuscript also begins with poems to the Archangels: Michael,
Gabriel, and Raphael.[11] Consequently, the assumption that 'More's interest
in Pico della Mirandola is traceable to the poet Skelton' is untenable in the light
of the above facts. One is more likely to concede to the inferences of Dr. Reed
that John Colet, who was in Italy at the time of Pico's death in 1494, made
Giovanni Francesco Pico's life of his uncle available to him. On the other hand,
Thomas More's intimate relationship with the Italian banker, Antonio Bonvise
of Lucca, of whom More himself said, 'of all frendes most trustye, and to me
most derelye beloued, and as I was wont to call you the apple of myne eye',[12]
may have been the occasion for this vicarious acquaintance which so profoundly
influenced his life.

Another intriguing feature of More's translation of the *Life of John Picus*
is the fact that he dedicated this noble work to Joyeuce Leigh, who had taken
the veil in the convent of Poor Clares outside the walls of London. She was the
daughter of Ralph Leigh of the manor of Stockwell in Lambeth, undersheriff of
London, and his wife, Joyeuce, daughter and co-heir of Sir Richard Culpeper
of Hollingborne. Her brother, Edward Leigh, was four years More's junior and
like him was educated at Oxford, taking a B.A. there in the year 1500. He was
learned in Latin, Greek, Hebrew, and theology, and is reputed to have been a
holy man. In the year 1531, four years before the martyrdom of More, his friend
was made Archbishop of York. Could not More have dedicated the translation
of Pico's *Life* to him rather than to his sister, Joyeuce? One wonders what
motives prompted Thomas More to offer the life of the Italian humanist as a
new year's gift to this young girl whom he calls 'myne hertly beloued syster'[13]
unless it was a mutual interest in striving after perfection that asserted itself
in both of them. Since the Leigh's were old friends of More's and his fellow
parishioners in Walbrook,[14] he and Joyeuce or Jocosa as she was called, must
have known each other for a long time. Could she possibly have been the sweet,
fourteen-year-old girl who stole his heart in his youth and for whom he wrote
his exquisite poem, 'To Eliza whom he had loved in his youth'? Upon reading
the poem carefully, however, one is inclined to dismiss this thought and to
accept the assumption that it was primarily a spiritual attraction that manifested
itself in the love of God, which welded their friendship into such a beautiful

218

mould of self-sacrifice and affinity of interest. In the opening words of the letter addressed to her, he writes:

> Hit is, and of longe tyme hath bene, my well beloued syster, a custome in the begynnynge of the newe yere, frendes to sende betwene, presentes or gyftes, as the wytnesses of theyr loue and frendeshyp and also sygny-fyenge that they desyre eche to other that yere a good contynuance and prosperous ende of that lucky bygynnyge . . . But for asmoche as the loue and amyte of Chrysten folke sholde be rather goostly frendshyp then bodely, syth that all faythfyll people are rather spyrituall then carnall. For as thapostle seyth we be not now in flesshe but in spyryte yf Chryste abyde in us.[15]

Paradoxically, it was at this time also in the year 1505 that Thomas More, who commended her so highly for having chosen the religious life, realized that his own vocation was not that of a Carthusian praising God in the cloister, but in the arena of the world as a Christian layman. Nevertheless, he became a monk in spirit and received the palm of martyrdom just two months after five of his beloved Carthusian Fathers had strengthened and edified him with their heroic example. By dedicating the life of a layman, whose example he proposes to emulate, to this young girl who had just dedicated her life to God as a Poor Clare nun, he wishes to strengthen her in the beautiful and noble vocation she has deliberately chosen. He assures her of his prayers for her perseverance. The following excerpt from his dedicatory epistle to Joyeuce Leigh shows the true import of his motives:

> The werkes are suche, that truely, good syster, I suppose of the quantyte there cometh none in your hande more profitable, neyther to thachyuynge of temperaunce in prosperite, nor to the purchasynge of pacience in aduersite, nor to the dyspysyrge of worldly vanyte, nor to the desyrynge of heuenly felycyte, whiche werkes I wolde you gladly to receyue, ne were hit that they be suche that for the goodly mater (how so euer they be translated) may delyte and please ony persone that hathe ony meane desyre and loue to God. And that your selfe is suche one as for your vertue and feruent zele to God can not but ioyiously receyue ony thynge that meanely sowneth eyther to the reproche of vyce, commendacyon of vertue or honoure and laude of God, who preserue you.[16]

The fact that Thomas More dedicated this work to Joyeuce Leigh is also tangible proof of his interest and zeal in fostering the education of women and of his open-mindedness in admitting that their intellect also possesses depth and acumen. He admirably suits his subject matter to the recipient of this scholarly work, for the omissions he makes in Pico's *Life* are adventitious to the spiritual impact of the work as a whole, while the selections he makes are well-chosen and felicitous. He begins the *Life of John Picus Erle of Myrandula* with a description of his noble lineage and then gives an original discourse on 'Honour and Virtue [which] Come not by Inheritance'.[17] The style is elegant, forceful, and perspicuous, and the marginal notes aid the reader in comprehending the text. Organized in this manner, the book could have been used for community spiritual reading; and hence, not only one novice aspiring to perfection in the religious life, but all the nuns in the House of the Minoresses in Aldgate could benefit from it. After describing the death of John Picus and including excerpts from Savonarola's bizarre sermon in which he reveals a 'secret thing'[18] from Picus' past life to his large Florentine congregation, More adds an original exhortation to pray for the deceased. In view of the last paragraph, in which Thomas More solicits prayer for the departed soul of Picus, Earl of Mirandula, one finds a plausible key to the translating of this work and the dedicating of it to a Poor Clare nun. He evidently wanted the good nuns to pray for the soul of Giovanni Pico della Mirandola so that as soon as possible his soul could taste of the sweetness of the Lord and experience an eternity of blissful joy. Giving at least some credence to Savonarola's vision in which the stern Friar Preacher of Ferrara saw Pico's soul 'all compassed in fire',[19] More beseeches all Christians to speed him to an enjoyment of the Beatific Vision in the concluding words of the *Life of John Picus Erle of Myrandula*:

> Now syth hit is so that he is adjudged to y^t fyre from which he shal undoubtedly depart unto glory & no man is sure how longe hit shalbe fyrst: & may be ye shorter tyme for our intercessyons: let every chrysten body shewe theyr charite upon hym to helpe to spede hym thyder where after the longe habitacion with ye darke fyre of purgatory (in whiche venyall offences be clensed) he may shortly (yf he be not all redy) entre y^e in accessible & infinite light of heven; where he may in ye presence of ye soveraygne Godhed so pray for us y^t we may ye rather by his intercession be perteyners of y^t inspecable joy which we have prayed to bryng hym spedely to.[20]

Thomas More follows the *Life of John Picus* with three epistles, of which the first and the third are addressed to his nephew, Giovanni Francesco Pico, while the recipient of the second one is a nobleman of Italy, Andreas Corneus of Urbino. These letters discuss the specious pleasures of this life, the wretchedness of the court, the way of sin as being more painful than the way of virtue, evil company, and the brevity of this life. Thomas More further renders into the vulgar tongue John Picus' interpretation of Psalm XV, 'Conserva Me Domine', in which both the writer and the translator are of one mind and spirit when they consider the felicity of the heavenly Jerusalem and contrast it with the misery of this world. The sections of Picus' life and the selection of the epistles he had written are suited admirably to the contemplative exercises of meditation and spiritual reading the Poor Clare Sisters engaged in. The subject matter of the fourteen pages of poetry that follow the Psalm is also based on edifying themes concerning man's twelve weapons in overcoming temptation, the twelve characteristics of a lover of God, and a translation from the Latin of 'A Prayer of Picus Mirandula unto God'.

Besides the spiritual motive which prompted Thomas More to undertake this literary work, one notices an obvious preoccupation with style and form, and an emphasis on the mother tongue as a fit vehicle for poetic expression. The very fact that he rendered into poetry 'Twelue rules of John Picus Erle of Myrandula, partely exciting, partely directing a man in spiritual bataile'. which were written in prose, and added to it another original poem 'The twelue weapons', consisting of twelve rhyme royal stanzas on the same theme, is indicative of a highly literary and creative approach to this work. Likewise, the eighteen stanzas on 'The twelue propertees or condicyons of a louer' are original with the exception of the last two stanzas. These verses are a paraphrase of a short Latin excerpt, which has for its thesis three principal considerations exhorting us to the service of God. The only literal translation of a poem is Pico's 'Deprecatoria', a hymn to God written after his conversion, which More rendered into felicitous poetical expression in the English language.

This English humanist's poetical approach to the translation of Pico's life may be a tribute to the Italian scholar's early poetical achievements, both in Latin elegiacs and in Italian, his vulgar tongue. Of the five books of poetry that Pico himself burned, only two Latin elegies survive: (1) a hymn to God and (2) an encomiastic poem on his friend, Girolamo Benivieni. His nephew, Giovanni Francesco, tells us that his uncle destroyed the voluminous early love poems 'religionis causa',[21] fearing that they might bring shame to him and scandal to others.

Angelus Politianus, to whom Pico sent his five books of amatory effusions for a critical estimate thereof, calls them 'terse, melodius, and poetical'.[22] Pico, however, was subtly and humbly aware of his own deficiencies not only in poetry but also in the field of learning in general. An indefatigable and inquiring scholar, he says of himself with a tone of sincerity and conviction:

> I am a novice, a tiro, and have advanced but a step, no more, from the darkness of ignorance. It is a compliment to place me in the rank of a student . . . Meantime I will follow your example, Angelo, who excuse yourself to the Greeks by the fact that you are a Latin, and to the Latins on the ground that you grecize. I too will have recourse to a similar subterfuge, and claim the indulgence of the poets and rhetoricians because I am said to philosophize, of the philosophers because I play the rhetorician and cultivate the Muses; though my case is very different from yours. For in sooth while I desire to sit, as they say, on two chairs, I fall between them, and it turns out at last (to be brief) that I am neither a poet, nor a rhetorician, nor a philosopher.[23]

Since a poem is a structure of norms and since a structure is an aggregate of elements set up by the relationship among them, the emphasis in the analysis of this poem is placed on its construction as a speech product. Since the speech process is a human act, the cognitive, affective, and volitive ends are directly related to it. The agent who is Thomas More, produces a deviation of the speech process, which is the poem and through which he communicates a delimited type of experience[24] to a select group in society that has been like him enlightened, affected, and moved by the magnetic attractions of love.

221

The agent, the means, and the end of this speech construct are determined by the basic denominator of voice and address and the pervasive element of structure which includes both sound and meaning. The qualitative and quantitative features of the sound structural pattern result in the rhyme scheme and the rhythm employed in the poem, while the first person, second person, and third person references strengthen and clarify its meaning pattern.

The first poem, 'Twelue rules of John Picus Erle of Mirandula, partely exciting, partely directing a man in spiritual bataile', is based on the Latin prose work of the Italian humanist. More's twenty-three rhyme royal stanzas comprising this poem are paraphrases rather than translations of Picus' treatment of this theme. In the ensuing analysis of this poem the writer would like to refute the opinion held by a few irresponsible individuals, that because a poem is theological or religious in context, it is by that very fact devoid of literary merit. Mr. J. M. Rigg gives testimony to this unscientific conclusion when he says that 'the attempt to give poetical expression to the mysteries of Christian theology is nearly always unsuccessful, and Pico's "Deprecatoria" forms no exception to the rule'.[25]

Imbued with the techniques and principles of medieval rhetoric, More follows the three main divisions of: (1) arrangement or organization, (2) amplification and abbreviation, and (3) style and its ornaments. Just as Chaucer begins the 'Parlement of Foules' with a *sententia*, namely: 'The lyf so short, the craft so long to lerne', so too, Thomas More opens his one hundred and sixty-one line poem with the following provocative statement: 'If we refuse the Way of Vertue for that it is painful for the like cause oughte wee to refuse the way of sin'.

'These rules, of which More's verses are rather a paraphrase than a translation, were written by Pico in prose . . .' says Rigg.[26] In view of this fact, the marginal notes may have been taken from Pico's prose work.

The first two stanzas explicate the theme that whether one chooses the way of virtue or the way of sin one must endure hardship and suffering, with the exception that the reward in each case is infinitely different:

> Whoso to vertue estemeth hard the way,
> Because we must haue warre continuall
> Against the worlde, the fleshe, the devill that aye
> Enforce themselfe to make us bonde and thrall,
> Let him remember, that chese what way he shall.
> Euen after the worlde, yet must he nede sustain
> Sorowe, Aduersitee, labour, grief, and payne.[27]

More looks at these two ways of life realistically, i.e., the deliberate pursuance of a life of virtue or the willing immersion in this world's false pleasures. He shows perspicuously, however, that the results of the second are more painful and disastrous both in this present life and in the next:

Thinke in this wretched worldes besy wo,
The battaile more sharpe, and lenger is ywis,
With more labour and lesse fruite also,
In whiche the ende of labour: labour is:
And when the worlde hath left us after this
Voide of all vertue: the rewarde when we die
Is nought but fire and paine perpetually.[28]

The ensuing eighteen stanzas are amplifications of the opening *sententia*, while the last three are built around *exempla* which exhort the readers to follow the glorious example of St. Paul and to consider the sublime example of Christ Himself. Sententious proverbs give the poem a colloquial flavor as can be seen in the following examples:

1. He that loueth peril shall perish therein.
2. Grete aduenturers oft curse the dice.
3. Too late cometh the medicine if thou let the sore
   By long continuance increase more and more.
4. Of virtue more ioy the conscience hath within,
   Then outwarde the body of all his filthy sinne.
5. Vainglory maketh many a man blind.
6. Perilous is the canker that catcheth the bone.

A. W. Reed favourably comments on the second and sixth statements, which are More's 'original lines in expansion of the Latin'.[29]

Thomas More handles a difficult spiritual theme with dexterity. By associating himself with the reader in the person of 'we', he avoids becoming pedantic or moralistic. The predominating voice asserts itself in the second line of the first stanza when the poet says: 'Because *we* must haue warre continuall / Against the worlde, the fleshe, the deuill . . .' Speaking in this facile vein, he seems to take the reader into his own mental meanderings as he urges his fellow-companion to think and consider these problems for himself. Hence, there is no dogmatic asserting of irrevocable truths and practices, but simply a challenge to weigh the assets and liabilities of both ways of life particularly, in view of their last end. With pronounced conviction in his voice the author pleads with his reader to contemplate the wretchedness of this earthly exile as his Second Rule:

Thinke in this wretched worldes besy wo,
The battaile more sharpe, and lenger is *ywis*,
With more labour and lesse fruite also,
In whiche the ende of labour: *labour is*.[30]

In the third stanza, which gives the principle for the Third Rule of life, Thomas More enunciates a conviction upon which he loved to meditate often and which

223

he impressed on his wife and children. William Roper records the fact, that to incite them to desire heavenly things, he used to say:

> We may not look at our pleasure to go to heaven in featherbeds; it is not the way! For our Lord Himself went thither with great pain, and by many tribulations, which was the path wherein he walked thither; the servant may not look to be in better case than his master.[31]

Then, as if preparing his family for his irrevocable decision concerning Henry VIII's mandate on the supremacy question and the martyrdom which it precipitated, he would say:

> It is now no mastery for you children to go to heaven, for everybody giveth you good counsel, everybody giveth you good example; you see virtue rewarded and vice punished; so that you are carried up to heaven even by the chins. But if you live the time that no man will give you good counsel, nor no man will give you good example – when you shall see virtue punished and vice rewarded – if you will then stand fast and firmly stick to God, upon pain of my life, though you be but half good, God will allow you for whole good![32]

The poet addresses the reader directly and manifests thereby a personal interest in him and respect for his opinion when he says in the fifth verse of the Third Rule:

> . . . . then wer it no right,
> That any seruant, *ye* will *your selfe* recorde,
> Should stande in better condicion than his lorde.[33]

The Fourth Rule, unlike the First, Second and Third Rules which have one stanza apiece, is composed of five rhyme royal stanzas, which have for their thesis the imitation of Christ and the patient endurance of pain and woe. In these thirty-five verses More exhorts his addressee, whom he has taken into his confidence, to consider the joyful consequences of this struggle and the many salutary benefits that accrue therefrom. The greatest benefit, however, that results from this close imitation of our model is:

> To be conformed and like in some behaviour,
> To Jesu Christ our blessed lorde and saviour.[34]

Thomas More gives the receptor of his oral or verbal meditations some specific methods for combating temptation, and he puts these principles of behaviour on an empathetic level when he addresses him as 'thou' or 'thee'. Although it is difficult to veil a moralistic poem with pleasing diction and subtle persuasion, More does this successfully in the following stanza:

> If thou withdrawe thine handes, and forbere,
> The rauen of anything: remember than,
> How his innocent handes nailed were,

If thou be tempt with pride: thinke how that whan
He was in forme of God: yet of a bond man,
He toke the shape and humbled himself for thee
To the most odious and vyle death of a tree.[35]

The above lines are devoid of moralizing or wrathful calling down of God's vengeance upon sinful man; further, one perceives in them an emotion that is tender without femininity and a virility that is characterized by virtue and sacrifice.

Similarly in the next stanza the poet holds up to the eyes of his sympathetic addressee a picture of Christ

. . . . scorned and scourged both,
And as a thefe betwene two theues threst,
With all rebuke and shame.[36]

If his words do not carry force of conviction, surely the sublime example of the forgiving Saviour will melt the reader's heart and sway his will:

. . . . yet from his brest
Came neuer signe of wrath or disdain,
But paciently endured all the pain.[37]

The speaker implies that he and his address have achieved mutual empathy, for in the Fifth Rule he says:

Remember wel, that *we* in no wise must
Neither in the foresaid esperitual armour,
Nor any other remedy put our trust.[38]

Without the nominative plural 'we', the 'Remember' would be harsh and dogmatic and, instead of gaining the confidence of the reader, the poet would antagonize him and arouse his resentment. Furthermore, More does not place himself on a pedestal as an example of virtue to him, but points to the virtue and patience of the Saviour whom they both should strive to emulate:

For he it is, by whose mighty powre,
The worlde was vainquished and his prince cast out,
Whiche raygned before in all the earth about.[39]

The following stanza, i.e., the second in the Fifth Rule, is particularly interesting in regard to the voice-addressee relationship, for Thomas More merges his reader and himself in the first person objective plural 'us'. He uses the imperative mood of the verb 'let us' but he does so in a manner that is not repelling, for he does not command his reader as an inferior, but tactfully exhorts him as an equal in these stirring lines:

> In him let us trust to ouercome all euill,
> In him let us put our hope and confidence,
> To subdue the fleshe and maister the deuil,
> To him be al honour and lowly reuerence.[40]

He reverts to the nominative plural 'we' as convinced of his own helplessness, he incites himself and his recipient to invoke the aid of Christ:

> Oft should we require with al our diligence,
> With praier, with teares, and lamentable plaintes,
> The aid of his grace and his holy saintes.[41]

One notices a close and consistent affinity between the voice-addressee reference and the moods of the verbs. For example, when using the subjunctive mood, Thomas More addresses his reader as 'thou': 'For if thou be ready, the deuil wil thee feare'.[42] Likewise, he employs the same second person reference in the imperative moods, which without gentleness and tactfulness on the part of the author, could convey a supercilious point of view. With respect he uses the second person reference three times in two lines, the first time in both the nominative and accusative cases following each other: 'Wherefore in any wise so euen *thou thee* beare / That *thou* remember and haue euer in memorie . . .'[43]

To palliate the grating effect of the imperative mood, which always implies a tone of command no matter how subtly stated, More embodies his exhortation in a series of examples and proverbs, and thereby gives the following stanza, which elucidates the Tenth Rule, literary value:

> In all temptacion withstande the beginning,
> The cursed infantes of wretched Babilon,
> To suffer them waxe is a iepardous thing,
> Beate out their braynes therefore at the stone,
> Perilous is the canker, that catcheth the bone,
> To late commeth the medicine, if thou let the sore,
> By long continuaunce encrease more and more.[44]

The use of the infinitive mood in the third line, 'To suffer them waxe is a iepardous thing', adroitly sets off the imperative mood 'withstande'. It presents a picture to the mind, which is a recapitulation of past events involving suffering and distress. The application of this incident to the proverbial statements makes the exhortation to overcome temptation more justifiable and expedient.

In trying to prove this point that a virtuous life is less painful than a life of indulgence in sin, More uses an example of an unlocalized third person reference in the Eleventh Rule:

226

And yet alas he that oft hath knowne,
What griefe it is by long experience,
Of his cruel enemy to be ouerthrowne.[45]

Such a person, says Thomas More in a paraphrase of the ensuing lines, ought to point out to others and endeavour to prove to them

What pleasure there is, what honour peace and rest,
In glorious victory triumphe and conquest.[46]

The Twelfth Rule, which is composed of three stanzas, is cast in the form of *exempla* in which the poet holds up the example of 'the glorious apostle Saint Paul' and of Jesus Christ who 'Humbled himself for us unto the crosse' to the eyes and mind of his reader.

The voice-address relationship throughout the whole poem is versatile in its use of a combination of references, namely: the first person plural, in which the author identifies himself with the reader and which is the sustaining voice in the poem; the second person reference, which is handled with discrimination and skill and is usually identified with the imperative mood; and the third person reference, which is employed in giving examples of Christ or of the saints or objective reality identified, for the most part, with the indicative mood. The author ends this twenty-three-stanza poem with the first person plural voice reference, thus making it consistent with its beginning, the only exception being that the nominative 'we' in the second verse: 'Because we must haue warre continuall' changes to the objective 'us' in the twenty-third stanza: 'Shal us bereue wealth, riches and honowre / And bring us downe full lowe bothe small and great'.[47]

Alliteration used sparingly enhances the sound pattern of the poem and produces the desired effect of artless art and pleasing euphony. Most of the alliterated words begin with the lingual *th* spirant, the palatal semi-vowel *w*, and the lingual sibilant *s*. Examples of these lines follow:

*Th*inke in *th*is *w*retched *w*orldes besy *w*o	Stanza two	– line 1
And when the *w*orlde ha*th* left us after *th*is		
Voide of all *v*ertue: the re*w*arde when *w*e die	Stanza two	– ll. 5-7
Is nought but fire and *p*aine *p*erpetually.		
*H*ow *h*is innocent *h*andes nailed were	Stanza six	– line 3
*S*eyng him*s*elf *s*corned and *s*courged bo*th*	Stanza seven	– line 3
And as a *th*efe betwene two *th*eues *th*rest	Stanza seven	– line 4
If *th*ou *th*inke *th*y*s*elfe *w*ell fensed and *s*ure	Stanza sixteen	– line 1
*Th*ough *th*ou be tempted, dispaire *th*ee no*th*ing.	Stanza twenty-one	– line 1

Assonance combined with alliteration results in euphonious tone color, which gives pleasure to both the ear and the eye of the reader. The recurrence of the short sound of *e* in the following verse makes it particularly effective:

For he that loueth peril shall perish therein.[48]

A pleasing contrast is achieved by the recurrence of the long sound of *e* and the slightly different sounds of *o* in the following line which contains fifteen vowels:

And here take hede that he whom god did loue.[49]

The vowel sound pattern in the first rhyme royal stanza of the Eleventh Rule emphasizes the short *o*'s and *i*'s:

Of vertue more ioy the conscience hath within,
Then outwarde the body of all his filthy sinne.[50]

The vowel digraph *ai* blends effectively with the long sound of *a* and puts an emotional stress of intensity and colour on the words 'disdain' and 'pain'.

Thomas More deliberately strives after stylistic effects in this poem, and the tropes and schemes he uses, embellish it without making it ornate or pretentious. He employs the rhetorical scheme of accumulation which simultaneously amplifies the idea he wishes to stress and evokes a corresponding emotion from the reader. The five outstanding examples found in stanzas one, ten, twenty, and twenty-two are as follows:

Stanza one
ll. 6–7

Euen after the worlde, yet must he nede sustain
Sorowe, aduersitee, labour, grief, and *payne.*

Stanza ten
ll. 5–7

Oft should we require with al our diligence,
With *praier,* with *teares,* and lamentable *plaintes*
The aide of his grace and his holy saintes.

Stanza twenty
ll. 5–7

To proue and assay with manly defence,
What pleasure there is, what *honour peace* and *rest,*
In glorious *victory triumphe* and *conquest.*

Stanza twenty-
two   ll. 4-7

Well ought we then our heartes fence and close,
Against vainglory, the mother of reprief,
The very *crop* and *roote* of al mischief.

The fourth verse of the Second Rule contains an interesting rhetorical device which resembles an incomplete chiasmus, as is seen, for example, in this line:

In whiche the ende of *labour: labour* is.[51]

The anaphora in the second stanza of the Fifth Rule gives it sonorous quality and makes the object of the preposition receive the strong stress:

> In *him* let us trust to ouercome all euill
> In *him* let us put our hope and confidence.[52]

The simile in the third line of the Sixth Rule is made to appear more original by its association with the scheme hyperbaton, which rounds out its meaning:

> For *as a woode*[53] *Lion* the fende our aduersarie,
> Runneth about, seking whom he may deuoure,
> Wherefore continually *upon thy towre*
> Lest he thee unpurueid, and *unready catche*
> Thou must with the prophete stande and kepe watche.[54]

The unusual order of words, namely, 'upon thy towre / Lest he thee unpurueid,[55] and unready catche', not only gives emphasis to the idea of keeping guard, but also embellishes and strengthens the rhythm and rhyme scheme. The word 'towre' in the third line of the above stanza is a rhetorical trope which may be classified as metonymy. Taylor points out in his *Tudor Figures of Rhetoric* that this trope was used in the sense of 'an exchange of a name when one word comes in lieu of another, not for similitude but for other natural affinity and coherence, as 'I want silver' for money'.[56] In like manner, 'towre' is meant to connote the idea of keeping watch over one's lurking enemies. Thus, the participial modifier 'unpurueid' is in perfect keeping with this connotation, for it means that one is 'unprovided and unsupplied or unprepared to resist an attack.'[57]

Another striking example of hyperbaton is seen in the last three lines of the second stanza of the Seventh Rule:

> Thy good worke to *god let it be applide*
> Thinke it not thine, but a gift of his,
> *Of whose grace undoubtedly all goodness is.*[58]

The above verses are not made discordant by the use of this rhetorical scheme, which was so much in vogue during the Tudor period, but one notices the absence of a preposition in the next example in which hyperbaton, asyndeton, and accumulation merge in the following verses:

> And peraduenture death within one howre,
> *Shal us bereue, wealthe riches and honowre,*
> And *bring us downe full lowe bothe small and great.*[59]

Although the omitted word in the second line is not a conjunction but the preposition 'of', it achieves the same effect as asyndeton, for the words follow one another closely without necessary intervening words showing syntactical relationship. Nevertheless, although this technique does not make good, perspicuous prose, it gives force and pithiness to poetry. The placement of the comma after 'bereue' is indicative of Thomas More's knowledge of the rules of grammar, for the comma in this case logically takes the place of the pre-position in showing the relationship of the verb phrase to the following nouns.

The chiastic arrangement of the last verse in the second stanza of the Eighth Rule is particularly impressive in its terseness and pungency of thought. In Tudor rhetoric this trope was called antimetabole or commutation, and it was used by W. B. Yeats with precision and finesse. Thomas More encourages his reader to be ever ready for fresh onslaughts of the enemy of our soul, the devil, and to keep in mind:

> In *victory battle*, in *battle victory*.

Special features of the Ninth Rule are the effective use of prosopopoeia and a striking example of metonymy. The following revealing statement is More's original contribution to the 'expansion of the Latin':

> And great aduentures oft curse the dice.[60]

The prosopopoeia alluded to may be seen in the following two examples:

1. sottle suggestion of vice – attributing to an abstraction the characteristic of a human being.
2. fraile glasse may no distres endure – attributing a human characteristic to a concrete object.

An implied metaphor is seen in the word 'glasse', for it connotes the frailty of human nature which, upon succumbing to the occasions of sin, gives adequate proof of the syllogism: 'he that loueth peril shall perish therein'. Another metaphorical connotation is found in the verse: 'If thou thinke *thy self well fensed* and sure', and More uses it in the sense of feeling secure in the face of temptation.

The Tenth Rule contains a conspicuous allusion to the captivity at Babylon, which followed the conquest of Juda and the destruction of Jerusalem by Nebuchadnezzar in 586 B.C.:

> In all temtacion withstande the beginning,
> The cursed infantes of wretched Babilon,
> To suffer them waxe is a iepardous thing,
> Beate oute their braynes therefore at the stone.[61]

Verses 8 and 9 of Psalm 136 supplied More with the text he so skillfully incorporated into the above excerpt:

O daughter of Babylon, miserable: blessed shall he be who shall repay thee thy payment which thou hast paid us.

Blessed be he that shall take and dash thy little ones against the rock.[62] Just as it is 'a iepardous thinge, / To suffer them [the cursed infantes] waxe', so too, it is a perilous thing to permit temptation to overpower us and thus to make us slaves of sin and inheritors of misery. Colouring his counsel with metaphorical meaning structure, he makes the admonition plausible and effective:

> Perilous is the canker, that catcheth the bone,
> To late commeth the medicine, if thou let the sore,
> By long continuaunce encrease more and more.[63]

The two above injunctions are terse and provocative. The comparison to the devastating results which yielding to temptation causes is enlightening and convincing.

The simile in the second stanza of the Eleventh Rule is a conventional one, which in the context of a dissonant use of hyperbaton loses what little efficacy and claim to originality it had:

> But like rude beastes unaduisedly,
> Lacking discrecion thei compare and apply,
> Of their foule sinne the voluptuous delight
> To the laberous trauaile of the conflict and fight.[64]

A slightly better use of a combined trope and scheme is seen in the figurative presentation of the idea and the inverted arrangement of words. The metaphor and hyperbaton that follow are both found in the same verse:

> His *fleshe was suffred rebell* against the soule.[65]

The inverted syntax of the next two verses gives the rhythm smoothness and musical cadence:

> This did *almightie god of his goodnes prouide*,
> To preserue his seruaunt fro the daunger of pride.[66]

Even the apocope evident in 'fro', by means of which the last letter is omitted, tends to prove the fact that More was interested in rhythmical effect.

In the second stanza of the Twelfth Rule an impressive trope is found in the fifth verse:

> Well ought we then our *heartes fence* and *close*.[67]

Six stanzas above, Thomas More had used the word 'fensed' in an analogous connotation, and like the word 'wretched' it appears to be one of his favourite words. The three nouns used in apposition to 'vainglory' in the sixth verse are also coloured with metaphorical significance: 'the mother of reprief, / The very crop and root of all mischief'.

The metaphor, combined with alliteration in the first verse of the twenty-third and last stanza of the Twelfth Rule, forms an effective end-rhyme for the word 'cross'.

> Against this pompe and wretched worldes *glosse*,
>
> . . . .
>
> *H*umbled *h*imselfe for us unto the *crosse*.[68]

In spite of the pleasing effect of the two alliterated 'h's' and the perfect rhythm, this particular stanza fails in meaning structure since it does not sustain the inspiration it gradually builds up, but ends on a flat, adventitious note. Although these verses contain some noteworthy tropes and schemes, they are a poor clincher to the poem as a whole:

> And bring us downe full lowe bothe small and great,
> To vile carein and wretched wormes meate.[69]

The next poem, consisting of twelve stanzas also, is called 'The twelue weapons haue we more at length declared as foloweth'. The pun on 'we more' is an interesting but not uncommon one during the fifteenth and early sixteenth centuries, for writers would often adroitly annex their name to the title of the poem or subtly conceal it in its contents. J. M. Rigg emphasizes the fact that there is nothing in Pico's work that corresponds to the twelve rhyme royal stanzas Thomas More composed.[70] The Italian humanist, however, did write twelve short prose apothegms in the Latin language which More translated into the vulgar tongue. The title in its entirety is: 'The twelue weapons of spirituall battayle, which euery manne shoulde haue at hand when the pleasure of a sinnefull temptacion commeth to his minde'. Then follow twelve pithy aphorisms, which seem incongruous in length when compared with the long title. Since they are laconic, they are quoted here in full:

1. The pleasure litle and shorte
2. The folowers griefe and heauinesse
3. The loss of a better thyng
4. This life a dreame and a shadowe
5. The death at our hande and unware
6. The painefull crosse of Christ
7. The feare of impenitente departing
8. Eternal ioye, eternall payne
9. The nature and dignitie of man
10. The peace of a good minde
11. The great benefites of God
12. The witnes of martirs and exaumple of saintes

232

It is easy to reject a poem on the basis of its religious sentiment and to ostracize the writer as either an amateur without professional skill or an intruder who brings a theological theme into the secular domain of poetry. Oftentimes, a poem falling within this category is denounced without even being read. The shallow conviction, 'It deals with religion, ergo, it is no good', is a criterion which is applied by a few prejudiced individuals. Thomas More's poem on 'The Twelue Weapons' could likewise undergo an analogous censure, and the writer of this dissertation could peremptorily dismiss it on the basis of the above assertion. This poem is not good primarily because its theme is religious; that factor is not a contingency of its literary merit. It is very good in some of its stanzas, tolerably good in others, and cumbersome and strident in a few verses but, on the whole, the smooth rhythm, emotional intensity, and figurative devices make it a poem worth reading – perhaps even more than twice.

Since the stanzas have seven lines apiece and no apothegm has more than one stanza, they will be analysed separately and salient features determining their literary merit will be brought out according to the pattern of individual stanzaic structure, rather than the organic unity of the whole. One sees the rhetorician shining through these verses, for the beginning of each stanza differs considerably: verbs in the imperative mood are used three times, adverbs and conjunctions introducing complex clauses begin four stanzas, nouns preceded and followed by modifiers initiate four other stanzas, while an interrogative statement adds beauty and versatility to this rhetorical scheme of stanzaic structural beginnings.

Punctuation marks used meaningfully also reveal the careful grammarian; and the use of the colon, which is designated by the sense rather than the mark itself, is indicative of More's meticulous grammatical technique. The humanist-poet combines this knowledge with the art of rhetoric and metrics and produces a poem that has some literary merit.

Stanza one   The pleasure litle and shorte.

More's use of epitheton, a syntactical grammatical scheme which qualifies the subject with an appropriate adjective, is conspicuous in this stanza:

> Line two – *wanton* sight
> „   three – *vain* smell
> „   three – *licorous* taste
> „   five – *wretched* appetite

The inversion and substitutions in the fourth and fifth verses and the placement of the caesura give them sufficient flexibility to prevent ennui and to restrain them from degenerating into a horse-trot meter:

> Or fi / nal ly / in what / so e / ŭer de lite /
> Oc cu / pied is / thy wretch / ed ap / pe tite /

Alliteration joined with synathroismos or accumulation makes the last two verses notable:

> Thou shalt it finde, when thou hast al cast,
> Little, *s*imple, *sh*ort, and *s*odainly past.

Stanza two   The folowers griefe and heauiness.

This stanza deserves to be commended for its perfect craftsmanship, apparent especially in the intricate design of sound pattern and meaning structure. It is therefore quoted in full:

> Any *good worke* if thou with *labour* do,
> The *labour* goth, the *goodnes* doth remayne,
> If thou do *euill* with *pleasure* ioyned thereto,
> The *pleasure*, whiche thine *euill* worke doth contayne,
> Glideth his way, thou maist him not restraine,
> The euil then in thy brest cleaueth behynde,
> With grudge of heart, and heauines of minde.

Particularly impressive is the chiastic arrangement of the key words in this stanza: worke, labour, goodnes, euill, and pleasure. In Tudor rhetoric this scheme is more frequently referred to as antimetabole or commutation, in which the order of repeated words is inverted to contrast the idea they are meant to convey more forcefully. The first four lines quoted above have an almost perfect A B B A arrangement, which reminds one of a colourful tapestry and an artistic design. The only exception to the perfection of the chiastic structure is the fact that 'good worke' in line one and 'goodnes' in line two presuppose a synonymous connotation. This merging of the epithet 'good' into the abstract noun 'goodnes' is vital to the rhythm, the regularity of which augments its literary merit. Both techniques, the chiastic arrangement of words and the rhythmical pattern, are exemplified below:

A–B   A ny / good worke / if thou / with la / bour do /
B–A   The la / bour goth / the good / nes doth / re mayne /

The third and fourth verses follow the same pattern with the exception that the rhythm in the fourth verse is a little raucous:

A–B   If thou / do eu / ill with plea / sure ioyned / there to /
B–A   The plea / sure whiche / thine e / uill worke / doth con tayne /

The employment of prosopopoeia for 'The *pleasure . . . glideth* his way' is extremely felicitous and conforms propitiously with the sound structure, which

234

makes it even more enhancing. This trope evokes another figure in one's mind, namely, the comparison of 'pleasure' to a sly serpent that stealthily glides away and leaves his venomous poison in his unhappy victim. A penetrating thought is expressed in the last two verses, which veil a moralistic truth in a manner that would impress even the most prejudiced person. The regularity of the iambic pentameter is pleasingly set off by the third anapestic foot followed by a trochee in the first line of the following two verses:

> The̽ e̓ / uil the̓n / in̽ thy̽ bre̽st / cleá ueth / be̽ hyńde /
> With grudge / of heárt / and heáu / i ne̽s / of miǹde /

The last verse exhibits a salient characteristic of Thomas More's writing both in poetry and prose, namely, a rhetorical scheme which, in its broader sense, is termed isocolon.[71] This parallelism of structure is seen in sentences, clauses, or phrases which are made up of equal members and parallel one another. Thus, 'grudge of heart and heauiness of minde' achieves rhetorical emphasis through the use of this syntactical scheme.

Stanza three   The losse of a better thing.

The seven verses that form this stanza are onerous and ineffective. The use of hyperbaton in a cumbrous manner reveals an artificial employment for the sake of the rhyme scheme and, consequently, is a serious blemish in the sound and meaning structure of this stanza. The first four verses have a strained and vexing syntactical arrangement:

> When *thou laborest thy pleasure for to bye,*
> Upon the price *looke thou thee well aduice,*
> Thou sellest thy soule therefore euen by and by,
> To thy moste utter dispiteous enemies.[72]

In addition to the obvious stridency of these lines, the end-rhyme 'by and by' is meretricious. The only redeeming features of this stanza are found in verses five and six. Clothed with the figure of exclamation, or ecphonesis, as it is also called, the emotional intensity of these lines give it some merit:

> O madde marchaunt, O foolish marchaundise,
> To bye a tryfle, O childishe reckening.[73]

It is significant that Thomas More uses the word 'madde' in an age when this meaning was conveyed by the term 'wood' sometimes spelled 'wode'.[74] Hence, his contribution to the embellishment of English diction is noteworthy, occurring as it does in many analogous instances in his poetry. The last line ends the

235

poem on the same discordant note as it began, and the hyperbaton employed
therein is harassing:

> And paye therefore so dere a precious thing.[75]

Stanza four   This life a dreame and a shadowe.

In the first verse of the next stanza Thomas More uses one of his favourite
epithets, 'wretched', which he usually applies to this life or to the world with
its broad connotation of false glamour. It is used to begin a run-on line which is
thought-provoking:

> This wretched life, the trust and confidence
> Of whose continuaunce maketh us bolde to synne.[76]

The rhythm in the last two verses is pleasing to the ear, and one is prone to
repeat it for sheer enjoyment:

> But fãst / it rún / nĕth oñ / and pas̀ / sĕn shãll /
> As̃ doth / ã drearñe / ŏr shãd / ŏw oñ / thĕ wall /[77]

The particular merit of this rhyme royal stanza lies in the metaphorical application of life as a dream and a a shadow to the prosopopoeia that extends its
meaning, as is seen in verses five and six:

> It [life] holdeth on the course, and will not linne[78]
> But fast it runneth on, and passen shall[79]

As in stanza two, the word 'glide' spontaneously conjures the image of a
serpent ,so too the phrase, 'fast it runneth on', brings to mind the image of
an hourglass and the metaphorical sands of life slipping through it. Rigg calls
attention to the interesting fact that Spenser employs the word 'linne', which
means to 'cease' in the *Faerie Queene*:

> And Sisiphus an huge round stone did reele
> Against an hill, ne might from labour lin.[80]

Stanza five   Death at our hande and unware.

This stanza lays no special claim to poetic artistry, and in it one sees the
rhetorician excelling the poet. It begins with an imperative sentence in the first
line, and an adverbial complex clause is added in the second line. Dilation is
employed in lines three and four for rhetorical emphasis:

236

> Consider well that euer night and daye,
> While that we besily prouide and care
> For our disport reuill myrth and playe,
> For pleasaunt melody and daintie fare . . .

The climax which appears in the next line is trenchant and well-timed:

> Death stealeth on full slily and unware.

Betraying the careful rhetorician, More uses accumulation or synathroismos in a fourfold enumeration as the object of the preposition 'of' in line three of the above-quoted excerpt. Fortunately he does not overdo this technique, as the following line slows down the heightened tempo and its parallel structure adds balance and finality here. The epithets 'pleasaunt' prefixed to 'melody' and 'daintie' preceding 'fare' augment the auricular effect of the rhythm:

$$\text{Fo}\overset{x}{\text{r}}\text{ pl}\acute{\text{e}}\text{a / saunt m}\acute{\text{e}} \text{ / l}\overset{x}{\text{o}}\text{ d}\acute{\text{y}} \text{ / }\overset{x}{\text{a}}\text{nd dai}\acute{\text{n}} \text{ / ti}\overset{x}{\text{e}}\text{ fa}\acute{\text{r}}\text{e /}$$

Stanza six   Feare of impenitent departing.

The meaning structure in this stanza is more emphatic than its sound structure. Contiguous aspects of a sound theological truth are embodied in the framework of a rhyme royal stanza. In a laconic paraphrase, the gist of it is as follows: 'When we offend God, we deliberately risk our salvation'. Lines one and two form a run-on sentence while lines three, four, and five complete and round out the meaning:

> For happly thou shouldest not liue an howre more
> Thy sinne to clense, and though thou hadst space,
> Yet paraduenture shouldst thou lacke the grace.

In line one of the above excerpt 'happly' is used in the archaic sense of 'perchance' or 'by chance';[81] used otherwise, the thought conveyed would be paradoxical and anti-Christian. The precise syntactical and grammatical structure necessitates the use of the colon in lines two and five. The sentences that seem to demand the use of a colon are terminated at lines two and five:

> Thou were foorthwith in uery ieopardous case:

Both the 1557 and the 1931 edition have a colon at the end of the above line. It is missing, however, in the early edition at the end of the fifth line:

> Yet paraduenture shouldst thou lacke the grace [:]

where a comma is negligently put in its place.

In the 1557 blackletter edition one notices negligent and casual observances of the punctuation marks which the thought sequence of the lines nevertheless demands. Yet, William Rastell, More's nephew, who 'established himself as probably the best printer of his day',[82] was learned and conscientious. He is not to be blamed too much, however, since punctuation marks were not used accurately and consistently in the early stages of printing.

To offset the regularity of the iambic pentameter in this stanza, lines one and two contain three smooth anapests:

> Thŏu wére / foŏrth with / iñ ué / rў ieó / pǎr doŭs cáse /
> Fŏr háp / plў thoŭ shóuld / ĕst nŏt líue / ǎn hóu / rĕ móre /
> Yĕt pár / ad ueñ / tuře shoúldst / thoŭ lacke / thĕ gráce /

The inverted syntax in the seventh line does not appear discordant, since it completes the thought and fits neatly into the iambic mold:

> Wéll ŏught / wĕ thén / bĕ feárde / tŏ dóne / of feńce /
> Iṁ pé / ni teńt / lĕst wĕ / dĕ párt / ĕn heńce /

Stanza seven   Eternall rewarde eternall payne.

The ostensible merit in this stanza lies in the sustaining metaphor, which compares life to a thoroughfare and God, to man's host. The first verse is a reiteration of Chaucer's use of the word 'thorowefare' but with an amplification of meaning which is brought out by the use of the word 'host' in the second line:

Chaucer   This world nys but a thurghfare ful of wo,
And we been pilgrymes, passynge to and fro.[83]

More   Thou seest this worlde is but a thorowefare,
See thou behave thee wisely with thine hoost.[84]

Thomas More continues to apply this metaphor to life in the verses that follow:

> Hence must thou nedest departe naked and bare,
> And after thy desert looke to what coost
> Thou art conuaide at such time as thy goost
> From this wretched carcas shall disseuer
> Be it ioye or paine, endure it shall foreuer.

'Cost' or 'coost' in the above excerpt means state, condition, way or manner, according to the interpretation early sixteenth-century writers gave it.[85] Hence, it makes intelligible sense in this context and helps to round out the meaning. 'Wretched carcas' in the sixth line is a metaphor signifying the body's corrup-

238

tion, while the word 'disseuer' in the same line gives it a sense of finality. In keeping with this idea, so evocative of the irretrievable scale of justice concept, the last line conveys a Christian truth that the eternity we have merited, be it joy or pain, 'endure it shall forever'.

Stanza eight　　The nature and dignitie of man.

Here theology and dogma are compressed in an eloquent rhyme royal stanza. That man's dignity lies in the fact that he is made to the image of God and that the merits of Christ's passion are the heritage of men, not of angels, form the thought content in the first four lines. This is followed by a felicitous line synthesizing the above ideas in the form of an apostrophe:

Regard O man thine excellent nature.[86]

One hundred years later[87] William Shakespeare eulogized the nature of man as he regarded its excellency. Hamlet becomes the mouthpiece for this eulogy when he says in Act II, scene ii, lines 302–309:

What a piece of work is man! how noble in reason! how infinite in faculty! in form and moving how express and admirable! in action how like an angel! in apprehension how like a god![88]

The last two lines in More's stanza portray the angel, man, and devil, and stress the nobility of man's nature:

Thou that with angell art made to bene egall,
For uery shame be not the deuils thrall.

Stanza nine　　The peace of a good mind.

Euphonious sound structure, versatile adaptation of figurative devices, and felicitous meaning structure synchronize to make this stanza one of the best in the poem. Beginning with an ingenuous interrogation, the author establishes a direct voice-addressee relationship:

Why louest thou so this brotle worldes ioye?[89]

The reader, More's direct addressee, is taken into his confidence as he pleadingly presents reasons to him why the joys of this world are so 'brotle'.[90] He does not argue with or try to convince the reader against his will, but clothing his premises with the force of the rhetorical scheme, anaphora, he gently exhorts him to consider the following generalizations:

Take all the mirth, *take* all the fantasies,
Take euery game, *take* euery wanton toye,
Take euery sporte, that menne can thee deuise
And among them all on warrantise.[91]

The pleasing regularity of the rhythm, particularly of the first three above-quoted lines, joined with vowel assonance and the sincerity of the author's conviction, gives poetical quality to this stanza. The last line, including the word 'warrantise', echoes Thomas More's legal training as does also the very framework of this stanza. The conclusion is emphatic and reflects a prevalent and favourite Renaissance theme, the 'inwarde gladness of a virtuous mind'.[92]

> Thou shalt no pleasure comparable finde
> To thinwarde gladnes of a vertuous minde.

The use of apocope in 'the' for the purpose of joining the two words, as in 'th' inwarde', proves that Thomas More was capable of producing musical effects in his rhythm. The sound structure and the meaning structure in this couplet combine to give it artistic unity and poetic force. As a matter of fact, these verses have proverbial compactness and are adumbrative of the many lyrics and sonnets which extolled this felicitous theme in the late sixteenth century.

Stanza ten   The great benefites of God.

The ratiocination in this stanza has lyrical qualities which mitigate the didactic point of view of the speaking voice. The speaker assures the addressee of the many benefits he has received from God, namely, creation, the redemption of his soul, and the sustenance of his earthly life with a promise of eternal beatitude. The poet combines the art of rhetoric with the art of poetics and conveys his ideas in well-rounded sentences that begin with an introductory conjunction 'Beside' and an introductory adverb 'Though'. The hyperbaton in the second line is not inept or discordant, for it perfects the rhythm and forms an emphatic completion to the periodic sentence contained in lines one and two:

> Beside that God thee *bought* and fourmed both,
> Many a *benefite hast thou receiued of his.*[93]

The use of the word 'bought' to signify 'redeem' is highly reminiscent of Chaucer's line in the 'Pardoner's Tale', namely:

> And with his precious herte blood the *boghte.*[94]

On the other hand, the end-rhyme 'this' in line four is weak and ineffective and is used merely as a superfluous tag to rhyme with 'his' and 'blisse'.

The merit of the poem, however, lies in the last two lyrical verses, which are tender and lyrical:

> Hŏw maı́st / thŏṻ then̆ / tŏ hím / ŭn̆ ló / uın̆g bée /
> Thăt ĕ / uĕr hăth ben̆e / sŏ ló / uyn̆g un̆ / tŏ thée /

240

Again Chaucer is called to mind as one compares the pathos and gentle reproach in his following two verses with More's lines on the same subject of man's ingratitude to his Redeemer:

> That to thy Creatour, which that thee wroghte,
>
> . . . .
>
> Thow art so fals and so unkynde, allas![95]

Stanza eleven   The painefull crosse of Christ.

More's poetic innovations in diction are at times refreshing, but in this particular stanza his originality reaches the point of hyperbole. He uses the metaphor 'flame' consistently enough with the implied meaning of 'fire of temptation', but when he adds the word 'friest', the line becomes naive:

> When thou in flame of the temptacion friest.[96]

Nevertheless, could this line have been, perhaps, the inspiration for Robert Southwell's eloquent and appealing poem, 'The Burning Babe'? Southwell's art excells More's here, for he clothes his entire poem in the image of the flame of fire and artistically unites all the images in one central figure. The following verses of Southwell are among some of the finest in the English language:

> My faultless breast the furnace is, the fuel
> wounding thorns;
> Love is the fire and sighs the smoke, the
> ashes shame and scorns;
> The fuel Justice layeth on, and Mercy blows
> the coals;
> The metal in this furnace wrought are
> men's defiled souls . . .[97]

The initial anaphora in lines two, three, four, five, and six redeems some of this stanza's poetic quality as with its lilting rhythm it diverts the mind from concentration on a naively concocted trope. Beginning with a heavily-stressed syllable, lines two to six exhibit skillful prosodic structure and determine the mood of the stanza:

> Thinke on / the ve / ry la / men ta / ble paine /
> Thinke on / the pit / eous crosse / of wo / ful Christ /
> Thinke on / his bloode / bet out / at eu / e ry vaine /
> Thinke on / his pre / cious heart / car ued / in twayne /
> Thinke howe / for thy / re dem / ci on all / was wrought[98] /

241

The last verse is a forceful and fitting clincher to the meaning structure and has reference again to the trope 'bought' used in the previous stanza:

Lĕt hým / nŏt leése / thăt hé / sŏ dere / hăth bought /[99]

The fifth verse, 'Thinke on his precious heart carued in twayne', contains a beautiful image that impresses itself on one's heart and lingers hauntingly in one's memory.

The assonance, consisting of a recurrence of *ou*, *o*, and *e* in each line, helps to set the tonal pattern of the stanza and accentuates its quality of meditative speculation. Here, Thomas More makes ample and effective use of the epithets, which are so characteristic of his style: *lamentable* paine, *piteous* crosse, *woful* Christ, and *precious* heart.

Stanza twelve   The witnes of martirs and example of saintes.

The ponderous syntax which forms the hyperbaton in the two opening lines of this stanza mars its efficacy and detracts from the little poetical merit it possesses. Although the iambic rhythm suffers no blemish, the meaning structure is grossly impaired since the words are strained and twisted to provide the right accents and the exact number of syllables in each line:

Sinne tŏ / with stánde / saye nŏt / thoŭ láck / ĕst mýght /
Suche ál / lĕ gá / ciŏns fól / lў it is / tŏ usé /[100]

On the other hand, the hyperbaton in line four is effective, forming as it does the end of the periodic sentence begun in line three:

The witnes of saintes and martirs constaunt sight,
Shall thee of slouthfull cowardise accuse.[101]

'Eftsoon' in line six is a poor and strained end-rhyme for 'done' in line seven. This stanza is one of the ineffectual ones in the eighty-four line poem, and there is little by way of poetical merit to recommend it.

J. M. Rigg tells us that the stanzas on 'The twelue propertees or condicyons of a louer' are original except the last two, which are a paraphrase of a Latin sentence in which Pico explains the three principal considerations that ought to impel us to the service of God.[102] The poem consists of twenty-six rhyme royal stanzas which are based on twelve apothegms of John Picus, Earl of Mirandula. Since they form the framework of Thomas More's subsequent poem, they are enumerated here in full according to the English text of the 1931 edition:[103]

1. To love one alone and condemn all other for that one.
2. To think him unhappy that is not with his love.
3. To adorn himself for the pleasure of his love.

4. To suffer all thing, though it were death, to be with his love.
5. To desire also to suffer harm for his love, and to think that hurt sweet.
6. To be with his love ever as he may, if not in deed, yet in thought.
7. To love all thing that pertaineth, unto his love.
8. To covet the praise of his love, and not to suffer any dispraise.
9. To believe of his love all things excellent, and to desire that all folk should think the same.
10. To weep often with his love: in presence for joy, in absence for sorrow.
11. To languish ever, and ever to burn in the desire of his love.
12. To serve his love, nothing thinking of any reward or profit.

In his youth Pico della Mirandola had written love poetry, which was presumably more ardent than chaste, for, as Rigg informs us, he 'had wantoned with other ladies than the Muses'.[104] Throwing more light on these five books of erotic verses in Latin elegiacs, Ficino writes after Pico's death: 'Somewhat of love he had written in the heat of his youth, which in his riper judgment he condemned and determined altogether to destroy, nor could it have been published without damage to his reputation'.[105] Later, impressed with the discourses of Plato's 'Symposium' in which he viewed beauty as a reflection of the Divine countenance and spiritual love as 'the turning of the creature to God',[106] Pico wrote an extensive commentary in the vernacular on Girolamo Benivieni's 'Canzone della Amore secondo la mente e opinione de' Platonici', which describes the nature, source, properties, and effects of love. The commentary consists of two parts: the first is a philosophical dissertation on love in general and its place in the universal scheme of things; the second is a detailed analysis of Benivieni's *canzone* on 'Celestial Love'. How Pico's understanding had undergone maturity and his passion had become sublimated through grace can be seen in the following excerpt from the second book of his discourse:

> The more perfect human lovers are those that, remembering a more perfect Beauty than their souls saw of old, before they were fettered to the body, are kindled with an incredible desire of rebeholding that Beauty; and to the end that they may obtain this purpose, they sever themselves as much as they can from the body, in such fashion that the soul returneth to her pristine dignity, becometh entirely mistress of the body, and is no longer subject to it in any wise. And then is the soul in that love which is the image of celestial love, and this alone is the human love that can be called perfect.[107]

Applying Platonic principles to this celestial love, Pico further says of it: 'Its truest being is with the desire of Ideal Beauty in the first Minde, which God immediately adorns with Ideas'.[108] He defines celestial love as 'an intellectual desire of Ideal Beauty'.[109] Although his treatise is ambiguous and obscure, he shows the purifying influence of love which leads the soul through various stages and raises it from the preoccupation with sensuous beauty to the contemplation of ideal beauty, and thence to the knowledge and love of God.[110]

Thomas More expanded Picus' twelve apothegms on 'The twelue propertees or condicyons of a louer' into a one hundred-and-eighty-two line poem and appendixed to it the following title with an ingenious pun on his own name: 'The twelue propertees we have at length more openly expressed in Balade, as it followeth'. The poem is composed of thirteen units, each one consisting of two rhyme royal stanzas. In the first stanza of each unit Thomas More describes one of the twelve attributes of human love, while in the second, he compares it with divine love and shows the excellence and sublimity of the latter. Realizing that 'grace builds on nature', this Christian humanist views human love as a ladder one ascends in order to reach the pinnacle of spiritual love and divine union. In view of this fact, he does not despise the peculiar and exaggerated features of human love, as, for example, 'sighing, languishing, and weeping', but sublimates these manifestations of love into channels more noble and divine. These verses, then, are a canticle of love sung by a soul arduously in love with God Himself.

The agent or speaker in this poem is Thomas More, who assumes the disguise of an experienced Platonic lover in the first stanza of each of the twelve units of verse. In the second stanza he throws off his disguise and speaks to his addressee in his own voice, which is characterized by sincerity and conviction. The first rhyme royal stanza is a reiteration of the ways of love in the Petrarchan tradition; the following stanza applies these principles to the love and longing of the soul for God, the Supreme Good. The first seven lines are expository in form, and the author directs his message here to a plural addressee, whose interests, however, are so analogous to his that they are willing to hear him discourse on the attributes of this consuming passion. The next seven lines delimit this indefinite and plural 'you' in this specialized group bound together by a mutual proclivity, to an individual and distinct person designated by 'thou'. This second person reference shifts to the third person addressee, who in turn becomes crystallized in an individualized type of person, namely, the lover of God.

In this poem Thomas More communicates his ideas in the conventional language of love poetry. Hence, his diction is artificial and stereotyped in some places, but in perfect keeping with the particular love decorum and tradition of his age. The principle of organic unity is the languishing of the lover for his beloved, which is revealed by sighs, ecstasies, tears, and the desire of ultimate union with his love.

Only the salient aspects of the sound and meaning structure will be discussed here, and the poem will be treated as a whole in the subsequent analysis rather than in a discussion of each stanza's merits and demerits.

The following norms are conspicuous features of sound structure: (1) combination of sounds; (2) significations imposed upon these combinations; (3) formation of words constituted by this organization; (4) the presentation – the *Darstellung* or 'predication'[111] of meaning in the form of single signification.

Thus, the sound structure of a poem leads inevitably to the meaning structure with which it is inextricably related.

The combination of sounds is apparent in the rhyme scheme which follows the regular rhyme royal pattern. The stanza describing 'The VII propertee' is a good illustration of it:

There is no page or seruaunt moste or lest,	a
That doth upon his loue attende and waite,	b
There is no little worme no simple best,	a
Ne none so small a trifle or conceyte,	b
Lace, girdle, point, or proper gloue straite,	b
But that if to his loue it haue bene nere,	c
The louer hath it precious, lief, and dere.	c

Most of the rhymes are strong, masculine ones, and the few feminine end-rhymes which occur, particularly in the second stanza of the various units, are Latinized words, which fit the context of prose better than that of poetry. Examples of these rhymes are found in the second stanzas of units three and twelve:

> So thou that wilt with god geat into *fauour*,
> Garnish thy selfe up in as goodly wise,
> As comely be, as honest in behauiour,
> As it is possible for thee to deuise.

> So thou likewise, that hast thine hearte y sette
> Upwarde to God so well thy selfe *endeuer*,
> So studiouslye that nothing maie thee lette
> Not for his seruice any wise *desseuere*.

The vowel assonance, stressing various sounds of *o*, is particularly conspicuous in the opening stanza:

> The first point is t*o* l*o*ue but *o*ne al*o*ne,
> And f*o*r that *o*ne all *o*ther t*o* f*o*rsake,
> F*o*r wh*o*s*o* l*o*ueth many, l*o*ueth n*o*ne.

Then, to avoid monotony and turgidness, the poet changes his pattern in order to achieve a more euphonious effect with a harmonious balancing of the *a* and *e* vocalizations:

> The flo*o*de th*a*t is in m*a*ny ch*a*nnels t*a*ke,
> In *e*che of th*e*m sh*a*ll f*e*ble str*e*ames m*a*ke,
> The l*o*ue th*a*t is d*e*uided *a*mong m*a*ny,
> Unneth th*a*t *e*u*e*ry p*a*rt h*a*ue *a*ny.

Examples of consonance are sparse, not being necessary to the perfection of the rhyme scheme. One notable example occurs in the following word: *'regard – reward'*.

The first line of 'The XI propertee' is an excellent synthesis of the organic principle which forms the frame-work for the poem – namely, the languishing of the lover for union with his beloved. Since it is a pivotal stanza, its sound and meaning structure will be explained more fully, and it is hoped that its technical merits will justify this procedure. For this purpose the first and second stanza of 'The XI propertee' are quoted here in full:

> Diuersly passioned is the louers hart,
> Now pleasaunt hope, now dread and grieuous fere,
> Now perfit blisse, now bitter sorowe smart,
> And whither his loue be with him or elswhere,
> Oft from his eyes there falleth many a tere
> For uery ioy, when they together bee,
> When thei be sundred for aduersitee.

> Lyke affeccions feleth eke the brest
> Of gods louer in prayer and meditacion,
> Whan that his loue liketh in him rest,
> With inward gladnes of pleasaunt contemplacion,
> Out breake the teares for ioy and delectacion:
> And whan his loue list eft to parte him fro
> Out breake the teares againe for paine and woe.

The first sentence, 'Diuersly passioned is the louers heart', serves as a fine start for the development of the unit and is what one would call today 'the topic sentence of the paragraph'. Instead of a comma at the end of it, Thomas More, who was a meticulous writer, probably inserted a colon,[112] which leads logically to the enumeration of the passions that follow. He uses qualitative and quantitative sound structure in a pleasing and efficacious manner for this purpose:

> Now pleasaunt hope, now dread and grieuous fere,
> Now perfit blisse, now bitter sorowe smart.

One immediately notices a harmonious pattern of sound set up in these two lines; the repetition of the initial and medial word 'now' in four juxtaposed positions and the exact number of adjectival epithets for the four nouns: 'hope', as opposed to 'fear', and 'bliss' which is antithetical with 'sorrow' enhance not only the principle of difference in the sound structure but also add virility to its meaning structure. More has a tendency to round out his descriptions with a well-chosen epithet as the following brief diagram exemplifies:

Pleasaunt hope	*dread* and *grieuous* fere
perfit blisse	*bitter* sorowe

The group cadence in the first three lines quoted above follows a vigorously rhythmical pattern:

> Di uerse / lў pás / sioñed iš / thĕ ló / ueřs hárt /
> Nów plĕ / saŭnt hopĕ / nŏw dréad / añd grie / uoŭs feře /
> Nów pér / fit blisše / nŏw bit / teř só / roẘe smárt /

The virile masculine rhymes at the end of lines one and three give them periodic abruptness, while the tightly-knit combination of the grating *r* consonant and the clinching *t* consonant adds a note of finality to them. The words which are related inherently to the thought pattern of the poem are dynamic references to the emotions of the human heart: 'hope', 'dread', 'fere', 'blisse', and 'sorowe'.

The rhythm in the following line produces forced and discordant aural effects:

> Añd whi / theř his loŭe / bĕ with / hįm ŏr / els wheře /

The conjunction 'or' in the fourth foot constitutes a blemish in the sound structure and tends to end the verse on a prosaic note. The ending feminine rhyme 'elsewhere' is so vague that one feels it was used merely as a poetical tag to rhyme with 'fere' and 'tere'. The next verse, however, makes up for this deficiency by its rhythmical merit:

> Oft frŏm / his eўes / theře fa'l / lĕth má / nў ă teře /

The speech construct alluded to in the above verse lacks originality and impressiveness, but considering the fact that it was penned four hundred and fifty years ago, it is not as trite and stereotyped as appears at first glance. The harsh-sounding *w*'s and the explosive *wh*'s give way to the smooth and soothing *f* consonant which, followed by a short vowel as in 'from' and 'falleth', restores the delicacy and charm of the sound pattern in the first three lines. Taken out of its context, this line would undoubtedly be tagged as sentimental, and rightly so. In the context of this smooth-flowing verse, however, it loses its artificiality and fits in perfectly with the assonance pattern and strengthens the meaning rather than distorts it. The next three lines which clinch this sevenline stanza parallel the first three in their perfection of technique and musical quality:

> Főr uĕ / rў ioў / whĕn theў / tŏ gĕ / theř bĕe /
> Whĕn theў / bĕ suñ / drĕd főr / ăd uér / ši teĕ /

The hyperbaton seen in the first line above by no means detracts from the beauty of the stanza as a whole, but admirably strengthens its sound pattern and adds appeal to its meaning structure. The second line is masculine in its pithiness and powerful in its connotation of sorrow and suffering occasioned by separation from one's beloved.

The second stanza has the same basic idea as the preceding one, but sublimates the characteristic features of human love by placing them on a divine plane. The poet endeavours to be consistent in his treatment of this verse by embodying it in an analogous framework of sound and meaning structure. Hence, to achieve this end he follows the pattern of the same diction as above, which is predicated on affection and makes the following words, so indicative of the passion of love, his key words: 'affeccion', 'brest', 'loue', 'ioy', 'meditacion', and 'teares'. The sound structure includes more open vowels than the first stanza which, in turn, is characterized by the use of initial and medial consonants. In view of this fact, the vowel pattern composed of *a*'s, *i*'s and *o*'s makes the verse artless, but unfortunately loses the subtlety and restraint of the first stanza. The three final polysyllabic words: 'meditacion', 'contemplacion', and 'delectacion' in verses, two, four, and five, weaken the rhythm and give the lines a drawn-out and exasperating feature. Although the diction is not original and impressive in the first stanza either, it nevertheless does not contain as many archaic words (which probably appear so only to the modern reader) as the second stanza with a representation of words like 'eke', 'list', 'eft', and 'fro'.

The words in these seven lines, unlike the verses of the first stanza, are not taken from the conventional language of love poets in the early sixteenth century but from the newly-formed English language, with its many Latinized words indicative of the language of scholars. Herein lies the weakness of this particular stanza: a diction reflecting the embryonic growth of the vulgar tongue is adapted onerously to the tradition and technique of a Petrarchan love theme. For example, to illustrate this fact by way of contrast, the first verse in stanza one has a well-integrated and pleasing structure of sound which enhances its inherent meaning:

> Diuersly passioned is the louers hart.

The first line of the second stanza, on the other hand, is dull and prosaic:

> Lyke affeccions feleth eke the brest.

The last three lines of the second stanza lack the delicacy and charm of the first seven lines and end on a sentimental note:

> Out breake the teares for ioy and delectacion:
> And whan his loue list eft to parte him fro
> Out breake the teares againe for paine and woe.

The evocative word 'hart' is here changed to the prosaic word 'brest', and thus the poetical quality of the poem is lost. Seen in this light, the diction becomes comparable to a germ plasm being examined under a microscope and, instead of arousing emotion, it merely elicits speculation. Then, too, 'perfit blisse' is a more apt and felicitous poetical phrase than the two disyllabic words 'inward gladnes'. Followed by two more words of disyllabic and polysyllabic structure, 'pleasaunt contemplacion', the line becomes heavy and prosaic. It gives the impression of a literal translation, but in More's case, these verses are novel and intrepid applications of the fluid quality of the English language to the domain of poetry.

The outstanding tropes and schemes that colour Thomas More's *balade* on 'The XII Propertees' are a skillful use of hyperbaton, an effective manipulation of anaphora, and a rhetorical application of synathroismos or accumulation. Examples of these figures appear in the tabulation listed below:

Hyperbaton :	In thy remembraunce this emprint and graue.	line B. 2.
	Loue him therfore with all that he thee gaue.	line B. 5.
	Of his loue the sight and company	
	To the louer so gladde and pleasaunt is.	ll. B. 9–10.
	Where he of god maye haue the glorious sight.	line C. 9.
	The ioyfull presence of that parson get,	
	On whom he hath his heart and loue yset.	ll. B. 1–2.
Anaphora :	*For* him to suffer trouble paine and wo:	
	For whom if thou be neuer so wo bestad.	ll. C. 10-11.
	He fauoureth neither meate, wine, nor ale,	
	He mindeth not, what menne about him talke.	ll. B. 2–3.

In 'The VII propertee' anaphora, assonance, and accumulation combine to form one of the best stanzas in the poem:

> *There* is no *page* or *seruaunt* moste or lest,
> *That* doth upon his loue attende and waite,
> *There* is no little *worme* no simple *best*,
> Ne none so small a *trifle* or *conceyte*,
> *Lace, girdle, point*, or proper *gloue* straite,
> But that if to his loue it hath bene nere,
> The louer hath it *precious, lief*, and *dere*.

Thomas More uses accumulation with dexterity to accentuate the rhythm of the verses and to heighten the emotional impact of their meaning structure.

The following couplet from the second stanza of the first 'propertee' has an accelerated tempo which leads the reader swiftly to its conclusion:

> For body, soule, witte, cunnyng, minde and thought
> Parte will he none, but either all or nought.

Not only nouns are employed in this fashion of heightening accumulations, but adjectives also are used to achieve the same effect:

But all *well fashioned, proper, goodly, clene,*
That in his parsone there be nothing sene,
In speache, apparaile, gesture, looke, or pace,
That may offende or minish any grace.[113]

Beginning with a subjunctive, conditional clause, adjectives are again used effectively to achieve periodic abruptness and emotional intensity:

If loue be *strong, hote, mightie,* and *feruent,*
There maye no trouble, grief, or sorow fall.[114]

The abstract nouns in the second line 'trouble, grief, and sorow' complement the adjectives, and the verb 'fall' at the end of the line forms a fitting restraint to the climactic effect of adjectives and nouns. The young poet is so fond of this rhetorical device that he uses it also in verb formations, which in the following example are a perfect illustration of paratactic structure. The first stanza of 'The X propertee' is quoted in full:

The louer is of colour dead and pale,
There will no slepe in to his eyes stalke,
He fauoureth neither meate, wine, nor ale,
He mindeth not, what menne about hym talke,
But *eate* he, *drinke* he, *sitte, lye* downe, or *walke,*
He burneth euer as it were with a fire
In the feruent heat of his desire.

In the second stanza, which describes the same property of love as the above, namely, 'To weep often with his loue: in presence for ioy, in absence for sorow', verbal accumulations are balanced by nouns in lines four and five:

Here shoulde the louer of god ensaumple take
To haue him continually in remembraunce,
With him in prayer and meditacion wake,
Whyle other *playe, reuil, sing,* and *daunce,*
None earthly *ioye, disporte,* or vayne *pleasaunce*
Should him delite, or any thyng remoue
His ardent minde from god his heauenly loue.

Thomas More does not stress meaning to the exclusion of metrical cadence in the poem, but deliberately strives for the achievement of pleasing sound and sonorous effect as the following verses illustrate:

Nŏt ón / ĕly ă ló / ŭer cŏn teńt / ĭš iń / his hárt /
Bŭt có / ŭe teth eke / ańd lońg / ĕth tŏ / sŭs taine /
Sŏme lá / boŭr iń / cŏm mó / di teé / ŏr smárt /
Losśe / ăd uér / si tĕe tróu / ble grief / ŏr paine /[115]

The mellifluous substitutions and a strong headless line which is followed by an inversion, augment the felicity of the sound structure in this stanza:

Ańd óf / his só / rŏwe íoy / fúll is / ańd faíne /
Ańd háp / py thiňk / ĕth him sélf / thăt hé / măy take /
Sŏme mis / ăd uén / tŭre fŏr / his ló / uĕrs sake /[116]

Neither does the young poet sacrifice rhythm for the purpose of enunciating principles of religious truth, for he adroitly synthesizes cadence and diction to evoke the proper sentiments his poem is meant to convey:

Hĕre shoúlde / thĕ ló / uĕr ŏf gód / ĕn saúm / plĕ take /
Tŏ hăue him / cŏn ti / ňu ăl lý / in rĕ / mém braŭnce /
With him / iň prayèr / ańd mĕ / ďi tá / cion wake /
Whylĕ / ó thĕrs / playĕ rĕ / uil siňg / ańd daúnce /
Noňe eár / thly ioyĕ / dis porte / ŏr vayne / plĕa saúnce /
Shŏuld him / dĕ litĕ / or ă / nỹ thyňg / re moue /
His ăr / dĕnt miňde / frŏm gód / his heá / uĕn lỹ loúe /[117]

Likewise in these seven verses four substitutions, two inversions, a pyrrhic, spondee, and a headless line add flexibility and versatility to the meter.

The imagery in 'The XII propertees', as viewed in its entirety, is not profound, but it contains more rhetorical figures than meet the eye upon first glance. Since Thomas More wrote this poem during the Tudor Age, when poetry still resembled closely the art of rhetoric and was even considered a branch of it, he applied tropes and schemes which have little literary significance to the modern reader today. As a matter of fact, the entire poem with its twenty-three rhyme royal stanzas is an amplification of the passion of love that sways the human heart and moves it to languishing, sighing and weeping in the absence of its beloved. More's treatment of love is periphrastic, but he avoids ambiguous dilation and ornate phraseology. Apropos of this feature, his forte as a poet is his clarity of expression in an age which produced writing that was clouded with aureate and ink-horn terms. He wears his feather in his hat, figuratively speaking, not as an extraneous ornament but as an appropriate embellishment.

The merits and demerits of the poem as a whole may be summarized as follows:

1. The first stanzas of each unit on 'The XII propertees' appear to be more skillfully and artistically constructed than the second ones, which deal with the application of the properties of human love to divine love.

2. The amplification of the languishing love theme follows a paratactic structure which embellishes the poem with rhetorical schemes and tropes.

3. The juxtaposition of the monosyllabic and polysyllabic words accentuates the rhythm and prevents an over-emphasis on the 'sameness' principle of the sound pattern.

4. Although artificial and trite in some places, the poem, for the most part, maintains an elevated tone and sustained emotional intensity.

5. The diction in the first stanzas of the units is more consistent with the conventional treatment of love and attains a degree of verisimilitude, while the Latinized and polysyllabic words in the second stanzas make it better prose than poetry.

6. The elucidation of the poet's meaning is partially obscured by the turgid diction which palliates faults of the structure of sound and meaning alike. Particularly disconcerting is the 'breaking of the tears' in the second stanza of 'The XI propertee'.

7. The strained use of hyperbaton to produce felicity of rhythm mars the meaning of the poem and sometimes reaches the point of fatuity.

8. The hypotactic structure of some of the verses betrays a too strong resemblance to prosaic grammatical structure in a poem that has intensity of emotion for one of its chief characteristics. The use of the adverb 'when' and the conjunction 'and' exemplify this technique.

9. The principle of sameness enhances the sound pattern, while the principle of difference prevents it from becoming unduly repetitious or jejune.

10. All in all, the application of the twelve properties of human love to the spiritual level of divine love is made without didacticism or pedantry.

The above factors, being taken into due consideration, one can more readily appreciate Thomas More's contribution towards the creation of poetry in the vernacular.

Fitzroy Pyle highly praises More's translation of the 'Praier of Picus Mirandula unto God' from the Latin into the vulgar tongue. He says that

> More normally betrays no tendency to use syllabic variations wantonly and often employs them very artistically, and there can be no doubt at all that the rhythm of this passage (which surely, is worthy of a place among the loveliest there are) is the direct result of the fusion of emotion with a feeling for artistic fitness.[118]

The passages, in particular, upon which he lavishes so much deserving praise are the last two stanzas, which rise to a magnificent crescendo and then slowly die away, leaving the reader filled with emotions of sorrow and love.

This poem consists of twelve rhyme royal stanzas packed with emotional intensity and embodied in an artistic lyrical form. It is unfortunate that the title 'A praier of Picus Mirandula unto God' is so misleading, for like Donne's 'A Hymn to God the Father', it is a work of technical excellence and literary merit. The very word 'praier' included in the title is reprehensible to those who are alienated from everything that concerns religion and hence, it becomes, in their estimation, a valid criterion for denouncing the poem as pious propaganda. Nevertheless, stripping one's mind of such shallow conditioning, a careful reading of the poem will reveal its metrical versatility, emotional impact, and empathetic quality.

The speaker of these eighty-four verses is the immortal soul of human beings in general who direct their address to the God Who created them and through Whose love they were redeemed. In particular, the speaking voice belongs to one individual, Pico della Mirandola, who devoted the last years of his short life to prayer, contemplation, and good works. Pertinently, Symonds describes him as 'the prince [who became merged] in the philosopher, the man of letters in the mystic'.[119] The author bestows further praise upon him when he says: 'By no man was the sublime ideal of humanity, superior to physical enjoyments and dignified by intellectual energy, that triumph of the thought of the Renaissance, more completely realized'.[120] The voice in this poem, then, belongs to Giovanni Pico della Mirandola, who in his early thirties laments his youthful follies and, imbued with the burning love of God, says to his nephew, John Francis:

> Nephew, this will I show thee, I warn thee keep it secret; the substance I have left, after certain books of mine finished, I intend to give to poor folk, and fencing myself with the crucifix, barefoot walking about the world in every town and castle I purpose to preach of Christ.[121]

The attitude of the speaker is mingled with contrition, for the weight of his sins hangs heavily on his mind. Considering the sublime grandeur of God and His inexorable judgment, he addresses this august Supreme Being Whom he has offended:

> In straite balaunce of rigorous judgement
> If thou shouldest our sinne ponder and waye;
> Who able were to beare thy punishment:
> The whole engine of all this worlde I saie,
> The engine that enduren shall for aye,
> With suche examinacion might not stande,
> Space of a moment in thine angry hande.[122]

The rhetorical scheme 'engine' in lines four and five is here used with invigorating effectiveness, and its repetition in the form of an appositive reflects the poetical beauty of anaphora and the convincing appeal of epanodos. The meaning of the word 'engine' which, derived from the Latin 'ingenium', denotes 'to beget', signified native talent, mother wit, or genius in Chaucer's day, and More, apparently, uses it in the same sense. Thus in his *Astrolabe*, Chaucer uses the word in this sense when he says: 'I ne usurpe nat to haue fownde this werk of my labour or of myn engin'. (Prol. 2. line 1).

Scarcely one hundred years later, c. 1470, the meaning of the word expanded; and, in addition to the fifteenth-century interpretation of skill in contriving and ingenuity, the word 'engine' was also used in the deprecatory sense of artfulness, cunning, and trickery.[123]

A minor blemish in the foregoing stanza is the triteness of the end-rhymes 'saie' and 'aye', but one is inclined to overlook this fault in view of the lyrical qualities these lines possess:

> The whole engine of all this worlde *I saie*,
> The engine that enduren shall for *aye*.

The last two lines, on the other hand, have no defect to mar either the rhyme scheme or the rhythm. The sound and meaning structure blend harmoniously to form a perfect couplet:

> With such / ex a / mi na / cion might / not stande /
> Space of / a mo / ment in / thine an / gry hande /

The vowel assonance of the limpid sound of *a*'s, the firm intonation of *o*'s, and the tranquil *e*'s weave their way into the tapestry of the poem's workmanship with dexterity and deftness.

Beginning with the initial anaphora and ending with the impact of a rhetorical question makes the following third stanza rhythmical and impressive:

> Who is not borne in sinne originall?
> Who doth not actuall sinne in sundry wise?

Mindful of the fact that all mankind is burdened with the weight of original sin, the speaker reminds God of man's depravity as he appeals to His goodness and mercy:

> But thou good lorde art he that sparest all,
> With pitious mercy tempering justice.

Substitutions that are bit strident occur in the next three lines, but the beautiful and encouraging thought content is hardly impaired thereby:

> For as / thou dost / re ward / es us / de uise /
> A boue / our me / rite, so / dost thou / dis pence /
> Thy pu / nish ment / farre un / der our / of fence /

Thomas More adroitly begins the fourth rhyme royal stanza with a pun on his name. Thrice he uses the word 'more' in an ingenious manner, and what A. W. Reed calls 'a difficult stanza'[124] is one of the most clever and artistic stanzas in the poem. The anaphora at the beginning of lines one and three converge into epanodos in the middle of the third line, emphasizing thereby the playful pun on 'more' and forming an intricate but pleasing pattern of sound and meaning structure. In the fourth line, More manipulates the word 'worthy' in a dexterous manner, and linking to it the prefix *un*, forms a chiasmus with its A B B A pattern. Apropos of the stanza's meaning structure, 'more' is used in the sense of 'greater'; for, that God's mercy is greater than the sin of man is what Thomas More perspicuously implies in the first, second, and third verses. The use of the relative pronouns 'whom, which, and that' strengthens the skillful intricacy of the sound pattern and gives it forceful impact. The seventh line is a noteworthy example:

> Whom he unworthy findeth worthy maketh.

The entire stanza is an example of artistic craftsmanship and, as such, it is adumbrative of John Donne's 'A Hymne to God the Father'. In the following verses More implores God's mercy:

> More is thy mercy farre then all our sinne,
> To geve them also that unworthy bee,
> More godly is, and more mercy therein,
> Howbeit, worthy enough are thei pardee,
> Be thei never so unworthy: whom that hee
> List to accept, whiche where so ever he taketh,
> Whom he unworthy findeth worthy maketh.

More than a hundred years later, John Donne was to articulate an analogous theme imploring the mercy of God in a superbly dexterous fashion. In the first stanza of 'A Hymne to God the Father', he says poignantly:

> Wilt thou forgive that sinne where I begunne,
>   Which is my sin, though it were done before?
> Wilt thou forgive those sinnes through which I runne,
>   And doe them still: Though still I doe deplore?
>   When thou hast done, thou hast not done,
>   For, I have more.[125]

Deep emotions of the human heart find utterance in the fifth stanza, and these are aptly embodied in the framework of a fivestress line. The inversions that occur in lines one and six, however, are in all probability deliberate attempts at variation in the meter to avoid monotony:

> Where fore / good lorde / that aye / mer ci / full art /
> Fren dely / look on / us once / thine owne / we bee /

255

The first four verses contain caesuras, which enable the speaker to give vent to his emotions in these deliberate pauses, wherein even with his silence he invokes the mercy of God:

> Wherefore good lorde // that aye merciful art /
> Unto thy grace and soueraine // dignitee /
> We sely wretches / crye with hymble heart /
> Our sinne forgeat // and our malignitee /

The sound structure of the last line is consistent with the rhyme scheme, rhythm, and assonance of the previous lines, but the meaning is cumbersome and strained:

> Servauntes or sinners whither it liketh thee.

When it is followed by the successive enjambment of the next rhyme royal stanza, however, it takes on new significance and becomes a starting point for the lines that ensue:

> Sinners if thou our crime beholde certaine,
> Our crime the worke of our uncorteyse mynde,
> But if thy giftes thou beholde againe,
> Thy giftes noble wonderfull and kinde,
> Thou shalt us then the same parsones finde,
> Which are to thee and have be long space,
> Servauntes by nature, children by thy grace.

The paratactic structure in verses two, four, and seven knits this stanza into a forceful epigrammatic unit characterized by epanodos, which leads to the felicitous climax in the last line.

The originality of the second verse, seen in the striking epithet More uses to describe 'mynde', is an extremely propitious one:

> Our crime the worke of our uncorteyse mynde.

More begins the first and last lines of this stanza with a stressed syllable 'Sinners' – 'Servauntes' and ends this unit also with a heavily-stressed syllable 'grace'. How appropriate it is that 'grace' should be the word that successfully clinches these seven lines, which form the antithesis to the first word of the stanza, 'Sinners'. These seven verses are a periphrastic treatment of the last line of the preceding stanza, 'Servauntes or sinners whither it liketh thee', and the ambiguous hypothesis is finally resolved in the clinching statement, 'Servauntes by nature, children by thy grace'.

Stanza seven continues the meaning pattern of 'grace' and 'sin' and, clothed with the rhetorical scheme epanodos, it achieves effective results. The words are interwoven deftly into the pattern of the sound structure as skillfully as a *tapissier* weaves an intricate design on the warp of linen before him. Thomas

More exhibits a felicity of diction in this stanza, and his proficiency here proves that he is no longer an amateur in poetry. The fusion of meaning with sound in the following seven verses is so meritorious that it belies the fact that religious poetry is necessarily insipid and dull:

> But this thy goodness wringeth us alas,
> For we, whom grace had made thy children dere,
> Are made thy gilty folke by our trespace,
> Sinne hath us gilty made this many a yere,
> But let thy grace, thy grace that hath no pere,
> Of our offence surmounten all the preace,
> That in our sinne thine honour may encrease.

One can understand why Fitzroy Pyle, who made perhaps the first study of the rhythmical aspects of this poem, was so ecstatic over its many merits and considered it worthy of being compared with the best literary pieces of More's day. In a spirit of adulation he says:

> He [More] composed rhythms incomparably superior to those of the more 'regular' versifiers of the next generation. More's verse is the measure of what a man with a sensitive ear could do . . .[126]

Although this stanza has hypotactic structure so indicative of the skillful rhetorician, the repetition of words used in appositive contexts in medial and initial positions gives it poetical qualities. The last line in this stanza is structurally a result clause, but its compressed meaning and technical excellence are hardly questionable.

> That in our sinne thine honour may encrease.

Surely, the heart of God must be moved by such sincere and ingenious supplications of one who, with the verbal dexterity of a man of law, pleads his case in terms of the welfare that will accrue to the One offended. The paradoxical structure and virility of this line are indeed superb! The five-stress lines flow smoothly, and they parallel the smoothness of the penitent's supplication except in line four, which, being in a medial position, appears to be a pivotal one. Here the stress is on the first syllable and its context proves the justification of this inversion:

$$\text{Sínne háth / uš gíl / tỹ máde / this má / nỹ å yére /}$$

The prosopopoeia in the first line, 'goodness wringeth', is one of the salient tropes in the poem, and this example is a good indication of More's originality:

> But this thy goodness wringeth us alas,
> For we, whom grace had made thy children dere . . .

257

The parallelism of the sound pattern in the eighth stanza finds expression in the rhetorical schemes of epanodos and anaphora and makes the rhythm of these seven verses musical to the point of mellifluousness:

> For though / thy wise / dome though / thy soue / raigne powre /
> May o / ther wise / ap peare / suf fi / cient ly /
> As thin / ges whiche / thy crea / tures eue / ry howre /
> Al with / one voice / de clare / and tes / ti fie /
> Thy good / nes yet / thy sin / gu ler / mer cy /
> Thy pit / e ous heart / thy gra / cious in / dul gence /
> No thing / so clere / ly she / weth as our / of fence /[127]

Theology is here linked in a pleasing manner with poetry as the attributes of the Supreme Being are enumerated in an artistic manner. The author, in paratactic fashion, appeals to God by honouring Him for the attributes He possesses, namely:

1. thy wisedome
2. thy soueraigne powre
3. thy goodnes
4. thy singuler mercy
5. thy piteous heart
6. thy gracious indulgence

Then, in magnificent crescendo of penetrating acknowledgment of the heinousness of his guilt, he says with subtle but sincere verbal dexterity:

> Nothing so clerely sheweth as our offence.

The power and glory of God are made manifest through man's weakness, and his depravity provides an outlet for God's goodness and mercy. The poet hopefully reiterates the 'O felix culpa' theme – 'O happy fault' that opened for mankind both the gate of heaven and the heart of God.

The ninth stanza is interesting from the viewpoint of rhetorical effectiveness because it is one long sentence which ends in an emphatic interrogatory statement. The relative pronouns and conjunctions are indicative of hypotactic structure, and since they provide the necessary relationships and pauses in the movement of this sentence, they prevent it from becoming unduly cumbrous. This adroit amalgamating of rhetoric with poetics is characteristic of More's poetical craftsmanship. The following verses contain some effective run-on lines:

> What but our sinne hath shewed that mighty love,
> Whiche able was thy dreadfull magestee,
> To drawe downe into earth fro heauen above,
> And crucifie god, that we poore wretches wee,

Should from our filthy sinne yclensed bee,
With bloode and water of thine owne side,
That streamed from thy blessed woundes wide.[128]

Most of the lines are cast within the mould of the regular fivestress line, but a harmonious substitution exists in the fourth medial line:

$$\breve{A}nd \ cr\acute{u} \ / \ ci \ \overset{x \ x}{fie} \ g\acute{o}d \ / \ th\breve{a}t \ w\acute{e} \ / \ po\breve{o}re \ wr\acute{e}tch \ / \ \breve{e}s \ w\acute{e}e \ /$$

The repetition of 'we poore wretches wee', besides being effective epanodos, is a strong appeal to the emotions and a humble acknowledgment of one's guilt.

If Thomas More had been merely interested in translating a Latin prayer of John Picus, he would certainly not have taken the pains to make the next stanza so artistic in form and periphrastic in meaning. Because of its periphrasis it adds little to the theological tenets on which the poem is predicated, but because of its artistry of design and form it embellishes the poem and gives it poetical qualities. The seven verses are designed to elicit emotion on the part of the reader or the addressee, for they are built around three powerfully emotive words: 'Love, pitie, and goodness'. In the first verse the speaker appeals to the love, goodness, and pity of God and again reminds Him that it is man's miserable weakness that augments His mercy and makes it shine more gloriously:

Thy loue and pitie thus O heauenly king,
Our evill maketh matter of thy goodness.

Then, using the rhetorical scheme of anaphora and the rhetorical tropes apostrophe and prosopopoeia in one context, the poet goes on to say:

O loue, O pitie our wealth aie prouiding,
O goodnes serving thy servauntes in distres,
O loue, O pitie wel nigh now thankles
O goodnes mightie gracious and wise.

After this elevated tone and sustained emotional outburst the poet comes back to earth with a poignant realization of man's misery and, fully cognizant of man's ingratitude towards so merciful a God, he adds with chagrin and sorrow:

And yet almost vanquished with our vyce.

The rhythm of the two last stanzas in this poem is highly praised by Fitzroy Pyle. They contain artistic variations in the form of substitutions and inversions on More's part, and they testify to his proficiency in fusing emotional intensity with metrical skill. The eleventh stanza begins with what Pyle calls 'a beautiful

259

headless line',[129] and the initial stressed monosyllable is uttered in a prayerful and soliciting manner:

> Gráunt / I thĕe práie / sŭchĕ heát / iñ tŏ / miñe héart /
> Thăt tŏ / this loúe / ŏf thiñe / măy bĕ / é găl /

The vehement headless line in verse one is followed by a spondee in verse three which takes the form of a sincere and prayerful supplication:

> Gráunt mé / frŏ Sá / thă năs sér / uice tŏ / ă stárt /
> With whóm / mĕ rú / eth šo lóng / tŏ haúe / bĕ thráll /

The three stirring invocations do not follow one another in successive lines but appear in lines one, three, and five, thus making each one a separate and meaningful petition. The emotive element so conspicuous and effective in this stanza reaches a crescendo of emotional intensity in the last invocation:

> Graunt me good lorde, and creatour of all,
> The flame to quenche of all sinnefull desire,
> And in thy loue sette all mine heart a fire.

The imagery in the above stanza is highly consistent, for it begins with love being symbolized metaphorically as heat, then becomes a flame in line six and ends with the intensity of the phrase, 'sette all mine heart on fire'. More's originality in the use of figurative language foreshadows the conceits of Donne and other metaphysical poets. For example, More speaks of the soul of man as 'my sely goost' and the body as 'his fleshly wife' and, thus, shows the unity that exists between the two. He further compares the mercy and goodness of God to a 'well of indulgence', which metaphor he uses in line five in the form of an apostrophe. The metaphor 'iorney' as applied to life is not an unusual one, but four hundred and fifty years ago it was not as hackneyed as it is today. He applies the epithet 'deadly' to life, and this paradox is explainable in the light of the connotation of the word, which, in its theological sense, means pertaining to sin or entailing spiritual death and in its physical sense, subject to death, in danger of death.[130]

The last two verses of this final stanza are tender to the point of pathos, and, as such, they beautifully synthesize the effusion of emotions which make this poem so lyrical in quality and intensive in meaning:

> In thy lordeship not as a lorde: but rather
> As a very tender louing father.

In translating this poem from the Latin, Thomas More deliberately strove for artistic effect and, as a consequence, achieved a noteworthy poem that deserves to be read, studied, and included in anthologies. This beautiful twelve-stanza poem can rightfully be placed alongside of John Donne's 'A Hymn to God the Father'.

1. Christopher Hollis, *Thomas More* (Milwaukee, 1934), p. 15.
2. Reynolds, p. 51.
3. Stapleton, p. 10, cited in Reynolds, p. 51.
4. Algernon Cecil, *A Portrait of Thomas More* (London, 1937), pp. 50–51.
5. *Ibid.*, p. 50.
6. *Works*, I, 19.
7. *Ibid.*
8. *Ibid.*, p. 23, n.
9. Charles Butler, *The Life of Erasmus* (London, 1938), p. 69.
10. Alexander Dyce, *The Poetical Works of John Skelton* (London, 1843), II, 485.
11. Edwards, *Skelton: The Life and Times of an Early Tudor Poet* (London, 1949), p. 264, n. 8.
12. Elizabeth Frances Rogers, ed., *The Correspondence of Sir Thomas More* (Princeton, 1947), p. 100, Ep. 48.
13. *Ibid.*, p. 9, Ep. 4.
14. *Ibid.*, p. 9, Ep. 4.
15. *Ibid.*, pp. 9–10, Ep. 4.
16. *Ibid.*, p. 10, Ep. 4.
17. *Works*, I, 349.
18. J. M. Rigg, Esq. ed., *Giovanni Pico Della Mirandola*, translated from Latin by Sir Thomas More (London, 1890), p. 26.
19. *Ibid.*, p. 28.
20. *Ibid.*
21. *Ibid.*, Introduction, p. xxxii.
22. W. Parr Greswell, *Memoirs of Politianus, Picus Sannazarius et al.* (London, 1805), p. 175.
23. Rigg, Introduction, p. xxx.
24. Wilbur Marshall Urban, *Language and Reality* (London, 1939), p. 119.
25. Rigg, Introduction, pp. xxxii–xxxiii.
26. *Ibid.*, p. 89. n. 40.
27. 'Twelue rules' p. 21. A. 4–10.
28. *Ibid.*, B. 1–7.
29. *Works*, I, 201, G. 1.
30. 'Twelue rules', p. 21. B. 1–4.
31. Roper's *Lyfe*, ed. Cline, p. 31.
32. *Ibid.*
33. 'Twelue rules,' p. 21. C. 3–5.
34. *Ibid.*, C. 12. D. 1.
35. *Ibid.*, D. 9. p. 22. A. 1–6.
36. *Ibid.*, A. 9. B. 1–2.
37. *Ibid.*, B. 2–4.
38. *Ibid.*, C. 1–3.
39. *Ibid.*, C. 5–7.
40. *Ibid.*, C. 8–11.
41. *Ibid.*, D. 1–3.
42. *Ibid.*, P. 23. C. 6.
43. *Ibid.*, C. 7–8.
44. *Ibid.*, p. 23. D. 9–11., p. 24. A. 1–4.
45. *Ibid.*, p. 24. B. 8–9. C. 1.
46. *Ibid.*, p. 24. C. 4–5.
47. *Ibid.*, p. 25. A. 4–5.
48. *Ibid.*, D. 6.
49. *Ibid.*, p. 24. D. 2.
50. *Ibid.*, A. 11. B. 1.
51. *Ibid.*, p. 21. B. 4.
52. *Ibid.*, p. 22. C. 8–9.
53. *Woode*, mad.

54. 'Twelue rules,' p. 22. D. 7–10., p. 23. A. 1.
55. *OED*, X, 303: *unpurueid*, unprepared.
56. Taylor, p. 39.
57. *OED*, X, Part I, 303.
58. 'Twelue rules,' p. 23. B. 2–4.
59. *Ibid.*, p. 25. A. 2–4.
60. *Ibid.*, p. 23. D. 3.
61. *Ibid.*, D. 8–10. p. 24. A. 1.
62. *The Holy Bible Translated from the Latin Vulgate* (Maryland, 1914), p. 652.
63. 'Twelue rules,' p. 24. A. 2–4.
64. *Ibid.*, B. 4–7.
65. *Ibid.*, C. 10.
66. *Ibid.*, D. 1–2.
67. *Ibid.*, D. 6.
68. *Ibid.*, p. 24. D. 9., p. 25. A. 2.
69. *Ibid.*, p. 25. A. 5–6.
70. Rigg, p. 94.
71. Taylor, p. 36.
72. 'The twelue weapons,' p. 25. D. 6–9.
73. *Ibid.*, D. 10–11.
74. Rigg, p. 93, n. 42.
75. 'The twelue weapons,' p. 26, A. 1.
76. *Ibid.*, A. 3–4.
77. *Ibid.*, A. 8–9.
78. *OED*, 6, Part I, 304. linne, to cease.
79. 'The twelue weapons,' p. 26, A. 7–8.
80. Rigg, p. 94, n. 46, citing Spenser, *Faerie Queene* I. v. 35.
81. *OED*, V, 79.
82. *Works*, I, 11.
83. *OED*, IX, 336.
84. 'The twelue weapons,' p. 26, C. 4–5.
85. *OED*, II, 1034.
86. 'The twelue weapons,' p. 26, D. 4.
87. Although More's *Pico* was published in 1510, according to Reed, the date of composition may be placed as early as 1504–1505. See *Works*, I, 18.
88. Sidney Lee, ed., *The Complete Works of William Shakespeare: Hamlet* (New York, 1908), XXX, 69.
89. Here is evidence of the inaccuracy in printing referred to previously. The interrogative statement necessitates a question mark while in the 1557 edition a comma is used at the end of the line. The 1931 edition has a question mark. See *Works*, I, 388.
90. *Works*, I, 388: *brotle* is spelled *brittle* today.
91. 'The twelue weapons,' p. 26, D. 9–10, p. 27, A. 1–2.
92. This phrase is More's original expression and is found in line 7 of stanza 9.
93. 'The twelue weapons,' p. 27. A. 11–12.
94. Line 902, Geoffrey Chaucer, *Works*, ed. Fred Norris Robinson, 2nd ed. (Cambridge, Mass., 1957), p. 154.
95. *Ibid.*, 11. 901, 903.
96. 'The twelue weapons,' P. 27, B. 1.
97. Lines 15–21, Robert Southwell, *Poetical Works*, ed. William Barclay Turnbull (London, 1856), p. 98.
98. 'The twelue weapons,' P. 27, B. 2–6.
99. *Ibid.*, B. 7.
100. *Ibid.*, B. 9–10.
101. *Ibid.*, C. 1–2.
102. Rigg, p. 94.
103. *Works*, I, 389.
104. Rigg, Introduction, p. xxxii.
105. *Ibid.*
106. Edmund G. Gardner, ed., *A Platonic Discourse Upon Love by Pico della Mirandola* (Boston, 1914), Introduction, p. xvi.

107. *Ibid.*, P. xxiii.
108. *Ibid.*, p. 30.
109. *Ibid.*
110. Rigg, Introduction, p. xxv.
111. Urban, p. 68.
112. A colon is used in the 1931 edition. See *Works*, I, 393.
113. 'The XII propertees,' p. 28, D. 4–7.
114. *Ibid.*, p. 29. A. 9–10.
115. *Ibid.*, p. 29, C. 1–4.
116. *Ibid.*, C. 5–7.
117. *Ibid.*, p. 31, B. 9–10. C. 1–5.
118. Pyle, p. 76.
119. John Addington Symonds, *Renaissance in Italy* (New York, 1888), II, 331.
120. *Ibid.*, 330.
121. *Works*, I, 359.
122. 'A praier of Picus Mirandula unto God,' p. 32, D. 3–9.
123. *OED*, III, 176.
124. *Works*, I, 201, A. 8.
125. Helen Gardner, ed., *John Donne: The Divine Poems* (Oxford, 1952), p. 51.
126. Pyle, p. 76.
127. 'A Praier of Picus Mirandula Unto God,' p. 33, D. 5–9, p. 34, A. 1–2.
128. *Ibid.*
129. Pyle, p. 76.
130. *OED*, III, 62.

CHAPTER VII

CONCLUSION

THOMAS MORE'S STATUS AS A POET

Thomas More's place in literature was obscure in the eighteenth and nineteenth centuries because of a lack of texts; no editor was courageous enough to print his works. William Edward Campbell performed a praiseworthy and profitable task when he edited two volumes of *The English Works of Sir Thomas More* in 1927 and 1931. It will be a notable achievement indeed when some scholar presents to the public the remaining five volumes. A separate edition of More's English poems, too, would make them better known and appreciated, and thus his reputation as a poet would, perhaps, regain the distinction enjoyed during his lifetime.

Beatus Rhenanus, a man renowned for integrity and wisdom in the sixteenth century, praises More's verses, and Colet considers him a great poet 'even in his youth'.[1] In the *Theatrum Poetarum Anglicanorum: or, A Compleat Collection of the Poets, Especially the Most Eminent of All Ages*, this comment is found:

> His *Utopia* though not written in verse, yet in regard of the great fancy and invention thereof, may well pass for a poem; besides his Latin epigrams which have achieved a general esteem among learned men.[2]

Shebbeare, a twentieth-century Morean scholar, maintains that Thomas More, who was indubitably 'a leader of the English Renaissance',[3] was not a poet simply because 'he did not live in a generally poetic age'[4] and because of the fact that 'Poetry was reserved for the next generation'.[5] In view of the dearth of good poems during the Tudor period and the imperfection of prosodic techniques, Thomas More is to be commended for his efforts towards developing a poetical form, which, although by no means perfect, was nevertheless a definite step towards the development of the Spenserian stanza. One has only to glance through his 262 Latin epigrams, of which 160 are original, to observe the variety of forms and techniques he used, such as dactylic hexameter alternating with iambic strophes, hendecasyllabics, the elegiac couplet, iambic trimeter, and dactylic hexameter. The popularity of his poems is substantiated by the appearance of three editions within two years.[6]

T. S. Omond makes an interesting observation concerning More's experimentation with English meter. A group of young students, including Ascham, Cheke, and Smith, discussed 'the possibility of remodelling English metre . . .' and of devising 'other forms of verse'.[7] Omond adds that 'Sir Thomas More is said to have favoured the movement'.[8]

A general impression that needs to be corrected and that has done much to undermine More's status as a poet is the prevalent opinion that he wrote poems only in his youth. In their scholarly research Bradner and Lynch bring out the fact that with the exception of only one poem, written at the close of the fifteenth century, 'all the poems that can be dated by any historical subject matter or allusion fall within the period 1509–1519, that is, from More's thirty-first to his forty-first year'.[9] Having read all the epigrams carefully and compared them with other epigrams of the preceding age, particularly with the works of Marullus, Pontanus, and More's contemporary and fellow-humanist, Erasmus, these scholars claim that More's *Epigrammata* is 'incomparably the best book of Latin epigrams in the sixteenth century'.[10]

Perhaps these observations are irrelevant in an analysis of Thomas More's English poems, which were presumably written for the most part during his youth, but they add prestige to his status as a poet. The rhythm, emotion, and imagery he employs in the epigrams are not confined to one language only, for they come from the heart and soul of the man rather than from his pen. Consequently, if he is considered an adept versifier in Latin, there seems little reason to accept the view that his English poems are so inferior as to deserve oblivion.

In view of More's admirable capacity for friendship, one wonders whether the controversy with Brixius, which began with the publication of the French poet's *Chordigera* in 1513 and was climaxed by his *Antimorus* of 1519, could have had anything to do with More's apparent discontinuance of the writing of poetry.

Further, it is hardly any wonder that the works of Thomas More, still less his English poems, were not printed more often during the sixteenth and seventeenth centuries since the Catholic writer's martyrdom precipitated fear among his devoted clientele and antipathy among his enemies. In the 'History of the Reports of His Trial and Death', one reads:

> [More] was pursued even after death by cruel abuse and unrebuked attack . . . moreover [he] was depicted as a ferocious and cruel man, who had invented horrible tortures to chastize those whom he saw inclined towards the evangelical truth; he was represented as 'earthborn', as 'capriciously raised by fortune to a false position of wealth and dignity', 'as a tyrant, and in a manner hateful in the sight of God'.[11]

Apropos of the above facts, it is significant that More's *English Works* were published in London in a thick folio volume in the year 1557 by order of Queen Mary in whose reign, Cayley tells us, 'it was given out as an extraordinary circumstance that King Edward died and she succeeded to the crown on the anniversary of the knight's [More's] suffering on the scaffold'.[12]

In 1538 Robert Wyer printed More's verses on 'Fortune' separately and gave them the following title: *The Boke of the fayre Gentylwoman, that no man shulde put his trust, or confydence in: that is to say, Lady Fortune: flaterynge euery man that coueyteth to haue all, and specyally, them that truste in her, she deceyueth them at laste.*

The 'Lamentacion of quene Elisabeth' and the 'Certain meters' written for the *Boke of Fortune* are found in the *Commonplace Book* of Richard Hill, More's contemporary. To the 'Lamentacion' he adds a curious and interesting ten-line Latin and eighteen-line English epitaph on Queen Elizabeth attributed to More.

Doyle-Davidson mentions 'an interesting version [of the 'mery iest'], contemporary with More printed by Julian Notary and undated'.[13] Colonel Frank Isaac assigns it on typographical evidence to the period between 1515–1517. Three editions of the *Life of John Picus* exist: one by John Rastell, another by his son, William Rastell, and the third, a pirated edition, by Wynkyn de Worde.

The 'Nyne pageauntes' is apparently, the only poem that was not printed again during More's lifetime or within the next two centuries. Yet, it is surprising that excerpts from this poem, rather than from More's other eleven poems, are finding their way into modern biographies of More and into recent anthologies. 'Childhood', 'Manhood', and 'Age', and the two short ballettes, 'Lewys the lost louer', and 'Dauy the dicer', which More wrote in the Tower, are quoted in a modern anthology *Tudor Poetry and Prose*.[14]

Thomas More's metrical compositions have an integral bearing upon his life. They reveal the great interest and sympathy he had for the rising middle class and the leadership he exhibited therein. His knowledge of Latin and Greek, his oratorical ability, and his mastery of the vernacular enabled him to convey his ideas to the general public via the medium of poetry. He does this admirably in the first of 'These fowre things' – namely, in 'A mery iest how a sergeant would learne to playe the frere'. This humorous ballad throws much light on More's association with the Mercers, a leading London Company in the early sixteenth century, for whom he acted in the capacity of legal advisor and orator.

The 'Verses for nyne pageauntes deuysed in hys fathers house in London' reveal the influence of Oxford on the young humanist. In these nine stanzas Thomas More depicts the allegorical stages of man's life, and for this purpose he uses classical symbols with refreshing ingenuity. A preoccupation with form and style is apparent in these verses, and although some lines are amateurish and trite, most of them are good poetry.

The child playing with a top and whip who detests his books and wishes that they 'were in a fyre brent to pouder small'[15] does not represent the young More whose keen intellect manifested itself at an early age and who devoted himself to study with good-will and vigour. Thomas More's great-grandson, Cresacre More, quotes the statement of More's tutor, Nicholas Holt, in defense of this belief that 'he rather greedily devoured "than leisurely chewed" his grammar rules, and far surpassed all his school-fellows in understanding and diligence'.[16] Fifty years after Thomas More's death, John Stow informs us in his *Survey of London* that More attended the famous St. Anthony's school, which prized itself on having 'the best scholars':[17]

> Out of this school have sprung divers famous persons, whereof although time hath buried the names of many, yet in mine own remembrance may be numbered the following:
>
> Sir Thomas More, knight, lord chancellor of England, Dr. Nicholas

266

Heath, sometime Bishop of Rochester, and Doctor John Whitgift, Bishop of Worcester and after Bishop of Canterbury . . .[18]

The young man who delights in hunting and hawking and in 'bestryd[ing] a good and lusty stede'[19] is characteristic of the complacent and arrogant youth who scorns the simple pastimes of children. An interesting humanistic touch is evident in the last verse of this rhyme royal stanza when the young man perfunctorily dismisses the child and his love of play by asserting that 'his reason is no better'.[20] The whole poem, as a matter of fact, is an intriguing study in the exercise of giving substantial reasons to prove one's superiority in the personified abstractions of the stages of man's life.

It is apparent from the above discussion that this poem on the 'Nyne pageauntes' does not reflect any autobiographical glimpses from Thomas More's life as a child or as a young man, but it does show his attempt to use classical themes according to the norms of medieval treatment. Venus and 'her lytle sonne Cupyde',[21] Old Age 'with lokkes, thynne and hore',[22] Death, 'foule ugle lene and mysshape',[23] Fame 'with tongues . . . compassed all rounde',[24] Time 'with horyloge in hande',[25] Eternity who 'nedeth not to bost',[26] and the Poet who intrepidly enunciates More's own philosophy of life are classical delineations which the author brings to life with pen and brush as he portrays them on the 'goodly hangyng of fyne paynted clothe'[27] in his father's house in London.

Christopher Hollis alludes to the 'Nyne pageauntes' and shows how Thomas More in a certain sense adumbrates William Shakespeare in his delineation of the ages of man's life in this poem. He says:

But, while Shakespeare stops short at the old man in
    'second childishness and mere oblivion,
Sans teeth, sans eyes, sans taste, sans everything',
More leads the soul on past death to God. 'Qui', he says, breaking into
Latin as the language fit for the expression of the eternal verities,
    'Qui dabit aeternam nobis pro munere vitam,
In permansuro ponite vota Deo'.[28]

The third of 'These Fowre Thinges', namely, 'A ruful lamentacion . . . of the deth of quene Elizabeth', has great historical value and 'a wealth of allusion'[29] which, A. W. Reed maintains, 'must save it from neglect'.[30] The young humanist experiments here with the use of a refrain, which adds melody and charm to each of the twelve rhyme royal stanzas that comprise this felicitous poem. With the tenderness of a mother who sees her children for the last time and bids them farewell and the masculine stoicism of a monarch who must leave behind his splendid regalia, Thomas More makes a sympathetic appeal to the emotions of the reader. He combines sound structure with meaning structure so deftly and successfully that the fusion of the two results in a poem of remarkable literary excellence.

The last of 'These Fowre Thinges' are the verses entitled 'Certain meters' which were explicitly written for the *Boke of Fortune*. Besides the prologue and the epilogue, which are not included in the Rastell edition, this section of poetry contains three related poems with the following titles: (1) 'The wordes of Fortune to the people'; (2) 'Thomas More to them that trust in fortune'; (3) 'Thomas More to them that seke fortune'. It would be well for those who are sceptical about More's poetical ability to begin their examination of his metrical compositions by reading these poems. Clive S. Lewis, who is meticulous in his analysis and parsimonious in his praise of Tudor poets, highly commends these verses which Thomas More prefixed to the *Boke of Fortune*:

> Here, on a characteristically medieval theme, and in firmer metre, we have something like an anticipation of Spenser's court of Philotime in the underworld, and allegorical figures which are not much below Sackville's.[31]

Thomas Warton, who gives credit to More for being 'the restorer of literature'[32] in England, sees in this poem a deliberate 'attempt at personification and imagery'.[33] After briefly describing Fortune, who sits on a throne and dispenses her gifts to all mankind, he quotes the following two stanzas:

> Then, as a bayte, she bryngeth forth her ware,
> Silver and gold, riche perle and precious stone;
> On whiche the mased people gase and stare,
> And gape therefore, as dogges doe for the bone.
> FORTUNE at them laugheth: and in her trone
> Amyd her treasure and waueryng rychesse
> Prowdly she houeth as lady and empresse.
>
> Fast by her syde doth wery labour stand,
> Pale Fere also, and Sorow all bewept;
> Disdayn and Hatred, on that other hand,
> Eke restles Watche from slepe with trauayle kept:
> Before her standeth Daunger and Envy,
> Flattery, Dysceyt, Mischiefe, and Tiranny.[34]

Warton has perhaps unintentionally omitted the fifth verse from the last rhyme royal stanza quoted above and has thereby impaired its meaning content and rhyme structure. The omitted line reads as follows:

> His eyes drowsy and lokyng as he slept.[35]

The prologue and the epilogue which are appended to the 'Certain meters' give a clairvoyant picture of Lady Fortune, and characterize her as 'Inconstaunce, slypper, frayle, and full of treason'.[36] All his life Thomas More had a pronounced antipathy for the fickleness and deceit with which this treacherous Lady beguiled her sycophants, and he incessantly waged war against her. Although the vicissitudes in his life reflected the changing moods of this great Lady, he exults in his last days that he had never been her 'seruing man'.[37] In prison before his execution he wrote with charcoal a rhyme royal stanza on Fortune entitled 'Lewys the lost louer', in which he repudiates this false Queen and testifies that he had never entered her service. He had been cast from the top of the 'wheel of fortune' to the very ground which this wheel scorns to touch, but the Christian humanist sees in these vicissitudes not the fickle Lady's maneuverings but the omnipotent and omniscient providence of God.

The following seven-line stanza is a testimony of a dying man to the inconstancy and treachery of Lady Fortune who seeks admirers for herself by cajoling her subjects with gifts and then, assured of their devotion and service, treats them like puppets on a string:

> Ey flatering fortune, loke thou neuer so fayre,
> Or neuer so plesantly begin to smile,
> As though thou wouldst my ruine all repayre,
> During my life thou shalt me not begile.
> Trust shall I God, to enter in a while,
> Hys haven heauen sure and uniforme.
> Euer after thy calme, loke I for a storme.[38]

Unlike the other short ballette which was also written in the Tower, namely, 'Dauy the dicer', which More wrote as a pastime, the 'Certain meters' for the *Boke of Fortune* were not written merely to beguile a tedious moment or to amuse the reader, for they gave vent to a conviction that was deeply imbedded in his heart and mind. The humanist, who later turned apologist and staunchly defended Christian truths against the attacks of the heretics of his day, wielded the pen via the medium of poetry to enlighten the people whose minds were darkened and whose wills were weakened by superstitious, astrological beliefs and practices. With a beautiful respect for the free will of his readers, he says in the last stanza of this 329-line poem:

> All thynges in this boke that ye shall rede,
> Doe as ye lyst, there shall no manne you bynde,
> Them to beleve, as surely as your crede.
> But nothwithstandyng certes in my mynde,
> I durst well swere, as true ye shall them fynde,
> In euery poynt eche answere by and by,
> As are the judgementes of Astronomye.[39]

Viewed as a whole, 'These Fowre Thinges' that Thomas More wrote, fall into the following categories: (1) social-economic narrative, with an emphasis on the mercantile companies of early sixteenth-century London; (2) classical subject matter with medieval treatment of allegorical personifications of the stages of man's life; (3) a historical theme cast in the lyrical mode of a lamentation poem on the death of Queen Elizabeth, the mother of Henry VIII; (4) social-ethical poems denouncing the existence and power of Fortune in the vicissitudes of man's life.

The fourteen pages of verses appended to More's English *Lyfe of John Picus* consist of seventy-three rhyme royal stanzas and are not included in the introductory 'Fowre Thinges' designated by Rastell as More's youthful poems. Although the translation of Giovanni Francesco Pico's life of his uncle, the scholarly and renowned Earl of Mirandola, is dated in the table of contents of Rastell's *English Workes of Sir Thomas More* as belonging to the year 1510, A. W. Reed believes that 'this is probably the date of an edition by John Rastell'.[40] Chambers is also of the opinion that the actual date of the composition may have been 1504 or 1505,[41] when More was deciding whether to serve God in the cloister as a Carthusian monk, a Franciscan friar, or as a virtuous layman in the world.

It seems as if the opportune acquaintance with the life of this celebrated Italian humanist, who passed 'from extremely daring humanism to Christian humility, charity and discipline',[42] helped the young More reach a decision that was very difficult for him to make. In the year 1505, after the completion of the translation from the Latin into the vernacular of the *Lyfe of John Picus*, Thomas More at the age of twenty-seven settled down to family life and legal pursuits. He realized that God was not calling him to the cloister; therefore, he resolved to strive after perfection as a Christian layman. He chose Pico della Mirandola as his model, imitated his virtues, and bore a striking resemblance to him in his way of life.

The very fact that More incorporated 'a considerable body of verse not found in the original'[43] into his translation of Pico's Latin life written by his nephew is indicative of his interest and preoccupation with the medium of poetry. He expands Pico's 'Twelue rules of a Christian Lyfe', written in prose, into twenty-three rhyme royal stanzas.

It is interesting to note that Sir Thomas Elyot, author of the *Boke of the Governour*, translated Pico's 'Twelue rules . . .' into prose in the vernacular. Stapleton mentions the fact that 'both Elyot and his wife attended the school of More for literary studies',[44] and it may be that at this time Elyot also read the Earl of Mirandola's life.

Elyot was More's junior by twelve years and outlived him by eleven years. His association with Thomas More is readily deduced from his letter to Cromwell dated probably in 1536. In it he tries to vindicate himself of apparent charges that had been brought against him concerning his amity with More, who had been executed a year ago for refusing to take the oath of supremacy. He fearfully and apologetically says:

> I therefore beseche your goode lordship now to lay apart the remembraunce of the amity betwene me and sir Thomas More, which was but *usque ad aras*, as is the proverb, consyderyng that I was never so moche addict unto hym as I was unto truthe and fidelity toward my soveraigne lorde as godd is my juge.[45]

270

Thomas More moulded the pious sentiments of the Italian humanist, the Earl of Mirandula, into verse forms, and since the one hundred and sixty-one lines of verse are a paraphrase rather than a mere translation of the original, his concentration on poetry is apparent. In contrast to the short and unadorned title of Elyot's prose translation, 'The Rules of a Christian Lyfe Made by Johan Picus the Elder Erle of Mirandula',[46] Thomas More's title for the poem is more descriptive, original, and exact. He appends the following title to the body of the poem: 'Twelue rules of John Picus Earle of Mirandula, partly exciting, partly directing a man in spiritual bataile'.

The next metrical composition of More, which consists of twelve rhyme royal stanzas, is an elaboration of Pico's twelve short prose apothegms with the lengthy and descriptive title: 'The twelue weapons of spirituall battayle, which euery manne shoulde haue at hand when the pleasure of a sinnefull temptacion commeth to his minde'. With a touch of characteristic originality, More abridges the title for this body of poetry and inserts in it a clever pun on his own name: 'The twelue weapons haue *we more* at length declared as foloweth'.

In like manner Thomas More expands Pico's 'The twelue properties or condicions of a louer' into a twenty-six-stanza poem. He devotes two rhyme royal stanzas to each of the twelve properties and adds two more stanzas to clinch the poem. Beginning with the characteristics of human love, he compares it with divine love and effectively shows the superiority of the latter. The poem is a powerful and eloquent appeal to the intellect of man, to his emotions, and ultimately to his will, which is stirred to desire the 'summum bonum'.

An English verse translation of Pico's Latin poem 'Deprecatoria ad Deum' bears the title 'A praier of Picus Mirandula unto God' and admirably closes the life of this illustrious young scholar, poet, and humanist. It consists of twelve rhyme royal stanzas, which display metrical skill and lyrical movement that rise to a powerful crescendo of emotional impact.

It is significant that the prose life of John Picus, the Earl of Mirandola, consists of ten pages in the 1557 black-letter edition, while the four lengthy poems consisting of five hundred and eleven lines of verse take up fourteen pages. Consequently, Thomas More's approach to this work was literary and creative and, as such, it was a definite contribution to the humanistic study and culture of his age. Even in his prose translation one observes a preoccupation with style and a balancing of his phrases and sentences which conform to the rules of rhetoric. A. W. Reed comments on More's interesting approach to this work and commends its literary quality. He says succinctly:

> It is nevertheless distinguished as an essay by More's interest in the graces of style. There are instances in which his neat balancing of phrases anticipates his Richard III.[47]

Thomas More's poems have not been read and analysed sufficiently and unbiasedly, and hence, they have not been criticized objectively and appreciated for their true worth. Even reputable scholars reiterate platitudinous remarks about his English poetry and, merely assuming that 'none has found its way into anthologies'[48] they dismiss this English humanist as a negligible poet of the Tudor Age. Sidney Lee in his book, *Great Englishmen of the Sixteenth Century*, substantiates this point of view:

> Much English verse as well as much Latin verse came from More's active pen. Critics have usually ignored or scorned his English poetry. Its theme is mainly fickleness of fortune and voracity of time. But freshness and sincerity characterize his treatment of these well-worn topics ... and More at times achieves metrical effects which adumbrate the art of Edmund Spenser.[49]

Berdan mentions a curious fact that throws light on Thomas More's practice of writing poetry and his assiduous attempts to improve his proficiency in it. He quotes Erasmus's letter to Hutten:

> The history of his [More's] connection with me [Erasmus] was this. In his early life he was a versifier, and he came to me to improve his style. Since that time, he has written a good deal. He has written a dialogue defending Plato's community of wives. He has answered Lucian's 'Tyrannicida' ... Colet, a good judge on such points, says More has more genius than any man in England.[50]

More's epigrams were published in the leading anthologies of his day. *Totell's Miscellany* has a poem attributed to him,[51] besides having a reference to the 1557 printing of his works. In Warton's *History of English Poetry*, edited by Hazlitt, the latter remarks:

> Sir Thomas More was one of the best jokers of that age and there is some probability that this [poem] 'Of a New Married Student' might have fallen from his pen.[52]

'On Fortune and Fame'[53] in the section on 'Poems by Uncertain Authors' in *Totell's Miscellany* is also highly reminiscent of More's theme and treatment of this subject of Fortune, which so tantalized him during his life with its speciousness and chicanery.

In his *Life of Lord Chancellor Sir Thomas More*, Lord Campbell states an interesting fact which emphasizes More's predilection for the writing of poetry: 'At the University More distinguished himself very much by the composition of poems, both in Latin and in English'.[54] He adds an illuminating statement which implies that Thomas More wrote more poems than the ones printed in the *English Works*. In support of this theory the writer ventures to suggest that the interludes and poems, discussed briefly in the following paragraphs, come from More's creative pen rather than from his brother-in-law's, John Rastell, who is erroneously given credit for them. Even Thomas Warton, who exhibits vacillation in augmenting More's prestige as a poet, reluctantly supports this thesis when he says: 'If [Rastell was] the printer only, [the English verses in] *Necromantia* A Dialogue of Lucyan for his fantasy fayned for a mery pastime ... might come from the festive genius of his brother sir Thomas More'.[55]

Gabriel Harvey manifests more optimism and certitude when he says emphatically that 'some of Heywood's epigrams are supposed to be conceits and devices of pleasant sir Thomas More'.[56]

Thomas More is also reputed to have written interludes and to have acted in them. Subsequent study might prove that he composed the part he played as a twelve-year-old youngster in the household of Cardinal Morton in the play 'Fulgens and Lucres', which was written by Henry Medwall, chaplain to the Cardinal.[57] Frederick Boas sees in two Tudor plays attributed to Heywood the possible authorship of Thomas More. Speaking of the trilogy composed of the following popular plays: 'The Four PP', 'The Pardoner and the Frere', and 'Johan Johan', he says significantly:

> The 'Pardoner and the Frere' has also points of contact with an early poem of Sir Thomas More, 'A mery jest how a sergeant would learn to play the frere'. It has been suggested with good reason that Heywood may have written the trilogy when specially under the influence of More, and that it is even possible that the two anonymous plays were among the youthful comedies of Sir Thomas.[58]

The scene in 'The Pardoner and the Frere' where 'they gradually pass to personal abuse and thence to fisticuffs'[59] is analogous to the scene in 'A meri iest' in which the disguised friar and the merchant engage in a similar series of blows, and the dénouement in each also strikes a parallel note. The writer of this dissertation, however, does not believe that the third play of the trilogy 'Johan Johan' could possibly be by More because of its offensive theme and lack of a moral.

A. W. Reed in his 'Philological Notes' appended to Campbell's *English Works* refers to More's and Erasmus's translation of the 'Necromantia' of Lucian from the Greek into Latin in 1505 and attributes the English translation to More.[60] Since sixty-one verses of this translation are quoted in the 'Notes', only a brief excerpt will be given here to acquaint the reader with the nature of this work. The English poem is written in iambic pentameter and rhymes aa, bb, cc, dd, ee, etc. In this passage Menippus is relating his experience in the nether world to his friend:

> And as I on these thyngis dyd cast my syght
> Me thought mannys lyfe wel be lykenid might
> To a stage play wher it fortunyth alway
> That they that be the players shal be that day
> Apparelyd in dyuers straunge clothyng
> As rych aray for hym that playeth the kyng
> With a purpyll cap & a crown of gold thereon
> With a dyademe & knyghtis waytyng hym uppon.[61]

The writer ventures to suggest that Thomas More also wrote an English translation of Terence, called 'Terens in English', with a prologue in stanzas, tenuously attributed to John Rastell, More's brother-in-law. Many other pieces which probably came from More's pen were printed by Rastell and attributed to him. Among these is an interlude called 'Of Gentylness and Nobylyte ... With dyvers Toyes and Gestis addyd therto, to make mery pastyme and disport'. The latter part of the title savours of Thomas More's love of fun and drollery and reminds one of his humorous ballad 'A meri iest how a sergeant would learne to playe the frere'. The interlude spiritedly recounts the disputations of the merchant, the knight, and the plowman who are trying to assert themselves as 'the perfect gentleman' and who engage in a lively discussion of how man achieves authority over others. The fact that Thomas More wrote interludes and acted in them is finally substantiated by Erasmus, who wrote in one of his Latin epistles concerning More: '... adolescens COMOEDIOLAS et scripsit et egit'.[62]

Horace Walpole refers often to a curious statement attributing the verses under Holbein's paintings to Sir Thomas More. In *Anecdotes of Painting in England*, he says:

> ...however in Buckingham-house in St. James's Park, he [Vertue] found two such drawings, on one of which was an inscription attributing them to Holbein, and adding that they were the gift of Sir Thomas More who wrote verses under them.[63]

Hans Holbein, the renowned portrait painter whom Erasmus introduced to More, found hospitality in the English humanist's household in Chelsea; it is probable that he stayed there for a period of three years. More became very interested in the paintings of the German artist, while Holbein was eager to profit from the humanistic learning of the versatile scholar. Holbein artistically illustrated the Basle edition of More's *Utopia* and engraved his name HANS HOLB on its title page, besides designing two woodcuts prepared especially for this book.

In view of Thomas More's reputation as a humanist, the celebrated artist sought advice of him and probably asked him to write verses under his pictures according to the custom of the day. The pageant of 'The Triumph of Poverty' has a nine-line verse accompanying it, which is a perfect synthesis of More's philosophy concerning riches and contains his famous and oft-repeated allusion to the inconstancy of Fortune. An English translation is given below from Woltmann's book entitled *Holbein and His Time*:

> The desire of mortals is fleeting and wavering; they are moved and driven as a whirlpool in the storm. Thus we cannot trust in glory. He who is rich fears ignominious poverty; he fears constantly that the inconstant wheel of fate may turn, and so his life becomes a disappointment. He who is poor fears nothing; no loss threatens him, but joyful hope fills him; for he thinks to acquire, and he learns by virtue to serve God.[64]

The above paragraph closely parallels the theme and treatment More uses in the 'Nyne pageauntes', for the Poet enunciates ideas and convictions like the ones expressed in these verses. The delineation of Lady Fortune corresponds with More's characterization of her in the poems he wrote for the *Boke of Fortune*. One may conjecture that he not only wrote verses for Holbein's pictures, but perhaps, he also suggested themes and supplied the descriptions for allegorical personifications.

Another indication of Thomas More's active interest in the art of painting is his absorbing pre-occupation with the works of Lucian, whose mind and temperament 'perfectly suited the Renaissance epoch'.[65] Among the writers of antiquity Lucian is considered one of the most important judges of artistic matters; he frequently speaks of art, particularly in his 'Dialogue of the Gods' and in the 'Marine Dialogues'. Lucian gives such fine, distinct descriptions of paintings that he inspired Renaissance artists to delineate on canvas what he so admirably portrayed with his pen in writing.[66] 'The Panel of Cebes', an incident mentioned by Lucian, was designed accurately and painted realistically by Holbein. It too, suggests the influence of Thomas More, particularly, since it is doubtful whether Holbein read the Greek original or the Latin translation of Lucian's works.

To conclude this analysis on the English poems, 'A Godly Meditation' written by More while he was prisoner in the tower of London in the year 1534, is here quoted as a fitting finale. This fifty-one line poem, which resembles modern free verse, succinctly synthesizes the theory of life which led More to be 'the king's good servant, but God's first'.[67] It also exemplifies his felicity of expression and facility with rhythm:

> Give me thy grace, good Lord.
> To set the world at nought,
> To set my mind fast upon thee.
> And not to hang upon the blast of men's mouths.
> To be content to be solitary,
> Not to long for worldy company,
> Little and little utterly to cast off the world,
> And rid my mind of all the business thereof.
> Not to long to hear of any worldly things,
> But that the hearing of worldly phantasies may
>   be to me displeasant.
> Gladly to be thinking of God,
> Piteously to call for his help,
> To lean unto the comfort of God,
> Busily to labour to love him.
> To know my own vility and wretchedness,
> To humble and meeken myself under the mighty
>   hand of God,
> To bewail my sins passed,
> For the purging of them, patiently to suffer
>   adversity.

Gladly to bear my purgatory here,
To be joyful of tribulations,
To walk the narrow way that leadeth to life,
To bear the cross with Christ,
To have the last thing in remembrance,
To have ever afore mine eye my death that is
    ever at hand,
To make death no stranger to me,
To foresee and consider the everlasting fire of
    hell,
To pray for pardon before the judge come.
To have continually in mind the passion that
    Christ suffered for me,
For his benefits uncessantly to give him thanks.
To buy the time again that I before have lost.
To abstain from vain confabulations,
To eschew light foolish mirth and gladness,
Recreations not necessary to cut off.
Of worldly substance, friends, liberty, life
    and all, to set the loss at right nought, for the
    winning of Christ.
To think my most enemies my best friends,
    for the brethren of Joseph could never have
    done him so much good with their love and
    favour as they did him with their malice and
    hatred.
These minds are more to be desired of every
    man, than all the treasure of all the princes
    and kings, Christian and heathen, were it
    gathered and laid together all upon one heap.[68]

Thomas More's 'eloquent, dramatic, varied'[69] prose style is replete with
balanced sentences, and Chambers points out that many of these sentences
'can be scanned as rough alliterative lines'.[70] The following excerpt, for example,
in which More describes the covetous man in 'The Four Last Things', readily
falls into free verse form:

*H*is *h*ed *h*anging in *h*is bosom and *h*is body croked,
Walk *p*it *p*at . upon a *p*aire of *p*atens
Wyth the staffe in the tone hande . and the pater
    noster in the tother hande,
The tone fote almost . in the graue already,
And yet neuer the more hast . to part with
    anythynge,

Nor to restore . that he hathe euyl gotten,
But as gredy to geat a grote . by the begiling
   of his neybour
As if he had of certaynty . seuen score yere to liue.[71]

It is hoped that, with Thomas More's canonization accomplished and with prejudice against him mitigated, this Christian humanist will emerge as a necessary link not only in the 'continuity of English prose'[72] but also in the development of Tudor poetry, which bridged the gap between Medievalism and the Renaissance.

1. Crescare More, *The Life and Death of Sir Thomas More* (Printed for N.V., 1642), p. 41.
2. Edward Phillips (London, 1675), p. 80.
3. Claude Eustace Shebbeare, *Sir Thomas More: A Leader of the English Renaissance* (London, 1929), p. 12.
4. *Ibid.*
5. *Ibid.*
6. Bradner and Lynch, p. xxvii.
7. Thomas Stewart Omond, *English Metrists* (London, 1907), p. 2.
8. *Ibid.*, n.
9. Bradner and Lynch, Introduction, p. xii.
10. *Ibid.*, p. xxix.
11. *Acta Thomae Mori: History of the Reports of His Trial and Death with an Unedited Contemporary Narrative*, ed. Henry De Vocht (Louvain, 1947), pp. 30–31.
12. Cayley, p. 273.
13. *Works*, 'Notes on the Collations,' by W. A. G. Doyle-Davidson, I, 219.
14. J. W. Hebel, Hoyt H. Hudson, ed. al., eds., *Tudor Poetry and Prose* (New York, 1953), pp. 9–10.
15. *Works*, I, 'Nyne pageauntes,' C. iii[r] A. 8.
16. Cayley, p. 10.
17. (London, 1603), p. 28.
18. *Ibid.*, pp. 28–29.
19. 'Nyne pageauntes,' C. iii[r] B. 9.
20. *Ibid.*, C. 1.
21. *Ibid.*, C. 9.
22. *Ibid.*, D. 9.
23. *Ibid.*, C. iii[v] A. 10.
24. *Ibid.*, B. 10.
25. *Ibid.*, D. 1.
26. *Ibid.*, C. iiii[r] A. 5.
27. *Ibid.*, C. ii[v] H. 3.
28. Christopher Hollis, *Thomas More* (Milwaukee, 1934), p. 8.
29. *Works*, I, 16.
30. *Ibid.*
31. Lewis, p. 133.
32. Warton, III, 94.
33. *Ibid.*, p. 95.
34. *Ibid.*, p. 96.
35. *Works*, I, 'Certain meters,' Twelfth Page, A. 2.
36. *Works*, 'Notes on the Collations,' I, 226, 1. 18.
37. Line I, *Workes*, ed., Rastell, p. 1433.
38. *Ibid.*, p. 1432.
39. *Works*, I, 'Thomas More to them that seke fortune,' Sixteenth Page, C. 8–10. D. 1–4.
40. *Works*, Introduction by A. W. Reed, I, 18.
41. R. W. Chambers, p. 94.

42. *Works*, I, 19.
43. *Ibid.*, I, 19.
44. Berdan, p. 305, citing Stapleton's *Tres Thomae* which was published in 1588.
45. *Ibid.*
46. Rigg, p. 89.
47. *Works*, I, 19.
48. Reynolds, p. 48.
49. Lee, pp. 59–60.
50. Berdan, p. 276, citing Erasmus' letter to Hutten; abridged by Froude, p. 107.
51. Hyder Edward Rollins, *Totell's Miscellany, 1557–1587* (Cambridge, Mass., 1928), I, 150'
    no. 193.
52. *Ibid.*, II, p. 271, n. 150. 8, citing Warton's *History of English Poetry*, ed. Hazlitt, IV, 64.
53. *Ibid.*, p. 129. no. 176.
54. John Lord Campbell, *The Lives of the Lord Chancellors* . . . (London, 1846), I, 513.
55. Warton, II, 513, ng.
56. *Ibid.*, III, 86, n.
57. F. S. Boas and A. W. Reed, eds., *Fulgens & Lucres: A Fifteenth-Century Secular Play*,
    by Henry Medwall (Oxford, 1926), Introduction, [p. ix.].
58. Frederick S. Boas, *An Introduction to Tudor Drama* (Oxford, 1933), pp. 15–16.
59. *Ibid.*, p. 15.
60. *Works*, I, 209.
61. *Ibid.*
62. Warton, II, 530, n.^{r}, citing Erasmus's Epistle 447.
63. (Strawberry Hill, 1765), I, 87–88.
64. Woltmann, p. 353.
65. *Ibid.*, p. 208.
66. *Ibid.*
67. R. W. Chambers, p. 400.
68. Philip Edward Hallett, ed., *English Prayers and Treatise on the Holy Eucharist* (London
    1938), pp. 13–14.
69. Hitchcock, *Harpsfield's Life of More*, Introduction by Chambers, p. liii.
70. *Ibid.*, p. cxxiv.
71. *Works*, I, 491.
72. Hitchcock, Introduction by Chambers, 'On the Continuity of English Prose from Alfred
    to More and His School,' pp. xlv–clxxiv.

BIBLIOGRAPHY

1. PRIMARY SOURCES

A. THOMAS MORE

Acta Thomae Mori: *History of the Reports of His Trial and Death with an Un-edited Contemporary Narrative*, ed. Henry DeVocht. Louvain, 1947.

Harpsfield, Nicholas. *The Life and Death of Sr Thomas More, knight, sometymes Lord high Chancellor of England*, ed. Elsie Vaughan Hitchcock. With an Introduction on the Continuity of English Prose from Alfred to More and His School, a Life of Harpsfield, and Historical Notes by R. W. Chambers. London, 1932.

Hitchcock, Elsie Vaughan, and Rt. Rev. Msgr. Philip Hallett, eds. *The Lyfe of Syr Thomas More Sometymes Lord Chancellor of England by Ro: Ba:* With Additional Notes and Appendices by Professor A. W. Reed. London, 1950.

More, Thomas. *The Boke of the fayre Gentylwoman, that no man shulde put his truste, or confidence in: that is to say, Lady Fortune.* In Henry Huth's *Fugitive Poetical Tracts.* Introductory Notices by William Carew Hazlitt. London, 1875.

— *The Correspondence of Thomas More*, ed. Elizabeth Frances Rogers. Princeton, 1947.

English Prayers and Treatise on the Holy Eucharist. Edited with an Introduction by Msgr. Philip Edward Hallett. London, 1938.

— *The English Works*, ed. William Edward Campbell. Vols. I and II. London, 1927–31.

— *Epigrammata Thomae Mori Angli.* London, 1638.

— *Giovanni Pico Della Mirandola.* Edited with Introduction and Notes by J. M. Rigg, Esq., London, 1890.

— *The Workes of Sir Thomas More Knyght, Sometymes Lorde Chauncellour of England, Wrytten by Him in the Englysh Tonge*, ed. William Rastell. London, 1557.

Roper, William. *The Lyfe of Sir Thomas Moore, Knyght*, ed. Elsie Vaughan Hitchcock. London, 1935.

— *Life of Sir Thomas More*, ed. Israel Gollancz. London, 1902.

— *The Lyfe of Sir Thomas Moore, Knighte Written by William Roper*, ed. James Mason Cline. New York, 1950.

Stapleton, Thomas. *The Life and Illustrious Martyrdom of Sir Thomas More.* Part III of *Tres Thomae.* Douai, 1588. Translated for the first time into English by Philip E. Hallett. London, 1928.

B. LITERARY STUDIES

Aristotle. *Rhetoric.* Translated by Rhys Roberts. *Poetics.* Translated by Ingram Bywater. New York, 1954.

— *Theory of Poetry and Fine Art*, with a Critical Text and Translation of *The Poetics*, ed. Samuel Henry Butcher. With a Prefatory Essay by John Gassner. Fourth edition. New York, 1951.

Bradner, Leicester, and Charles Arthur Lynch, eds. *The Latin Epigrams of Thomas More.* Chicago, 1953.

Chaucer, Geoffrey. *Minor Poems*, ed. Frederick J. Furnivall. Chaucer Society [Publications]. First Series. London, 1871.

— *Works*, ed. Fred Norris Robinson, 2nd ed., Cambridge, Mass., 1957.

Daniel, Samuel. 'The Defence of Ryme,' in *A Panegyrike Congratulatorie to the Kings Maiestie*. London, 1603.

Davies, John. *Complete Poems*. London, 1876.

Donne, John. *The Divine Poems*, ed. Helen Gardner. Oxford, 1952.

Dunbar, William. *Poems*, ed. John Small. Introduction by A. J. G. Mackay. Vol. I. London, 1893.

Dyboski, Roman, ed. *Songs, Carols and other Miscellaneous Poems from the Baliol MS 354, Richard Hill's Commonplace Book*. London, 1907.

Erasmus, Desiderius. *In Praise of Folly*. London, 1930.

Fabyan, Robert. *Cronycle: Illustrates Different Fates of Prose and Verse*. [London] 1516.

Gollancz, Israel, ed. *The Parlement of the Thre Ages: An Alliterative Poem of the XIVth Century*. London, 1897.

Harrington, John. *The Metamorphosis of Ajax*. London, 1596.

Harvey, Gabriel. *Marginalia*, ed. G. C. Moore Smith. Stratford-Upon-Avon, 1913.

Haslewood, Joseph, ed. *Mirror for Magistrates*. Vol. I. London, 1815.

Hawes, Stephen. *The Pastime of Pleasure*. Early English Texts. Original Series 173, ed. William E. Mead. London, 1927.

Holbein, Hans. *The Dance of Death*. Illustrated with thirty-three plates, engraved by W. Hollar with Descriptions in English and French. London, 1816.

Holinshed, Raphael. *Chronicles*. 2 vols. London, 1587.

Hoskins, John. *Directions for Speech and Style*, ed. Hoyt Hopewell Hudson. Princeton, 1935.

Johnson, Samuel. *A Dictionary of the English Language*. London, 1775.

Jonson, Ben. *The English Grammar*. London, 1640.

Jordan, Thomas. *London's Triumphs: Illustrated with many Magnificent Structures and Pageants*. London, 1677.

Lydgate, John. *Fall of Princes*, ed. Henry Bergen. Vol. I, Washington, 1923.

— *The Court of Sapience*, ed. Robert Spindler, Leipzig, 1927.

Malone, Edmund. *Catalogue of Early English Poetry and Other Miscellaneous Works Illustrating the British Drama*. Oxford, 1836.

Meres, Francis. 'AComparative Discourse of Our English Poets,' in *Palladis Tamia*. London, 1598.

Peacham, Henry. *Gardens of Eloquence*, 1593. With an Introduction by William G. Crane. Florida, 1954.

Pecke, Thomas. *Parnassi Puerporium*. London, 1659.

Percy, Thomas. *Reliques of Ancient Poetry*. 2 vols. London, 1886.

Petrarch, Francis. *Sonnets, Triumphs and Other Poems*. Translated into English verse by various hands with a life of the poet by Thomas Campbell. London, 1901.

Phillips, Edward. *Theatrum Poetarum or Compleat Collection of the Poets*. London, 1675.

Pico, Giovanni della Mirandola. *A Platonick Discourse upon Love*, ed. Edmund G. Gardner. Boston, 1914.

Pico, Giovanni Francesco. *Giovanni Pico Della Mirandola: His Life by His Nephew*. London, 1890.

Puttenham, George. *The Arte of English Poesie*, ed. Edward Arber. London, 1869.

— *The Arte of English Poesie*, ed. Gladys Doidge Willcock and Alice Walker. London, 1869.

Rastell, John. *Hundred Merry Tales*. London, 1526.

— *Pastyme of People*. London, 1529.

Rollins, Hyder Edward, ed. *The Paradise of Dainty Devices*, 1576–1606. Cambridge, Mass., 1927.

A Handful of Pleasant Delights. Cambridge, Mass., 1924.

Scott, John, ed. *Arnold's Chronicle: The Names of the Baylifs Custas Mairs and Sherefs of the Cite of London*. Antwerp, 1503.

Skelton, John. *Poetical Works*, ed. Alexander Dyce. Vol. II. London, 1843.

Smith, George G. *Elizabethan Critical Essays*. Vol. II. Oxford, 1904.

Spenser, Edmund. *The Faerie Queene*, ed. A. A. Tunstall. New York, 1859.

Stow, John. *The Chronicles of England from Brute unto this present Yeare of Christ*, 1580. London, 1580.
— *Annales or a Generall Chronicle of England: Continued and Augmented . . .* by Edmund Hawes. London, 1631.
— *Survey of London*. London, 1598.
Tottel, Richard. *Miscellany* 1557–1587, ed. Hyder Edward Rollins. Vol. I. Cambridge, Mass., 1928.
Wood, Anthony. *Athenae Oxonienses: An Exact History of all the Writers and Bishops who have had their Education in the most Antient and Famous University of Oxford*. Vol. I. London, 1721.

II. SECONDARY SOURCES

A. THOMAS MORE

Adams, Maurice, ed. *More's Utopia with Roper's Life*. London, 1890.
Allen, Percy Stafford, and Helen Mary Allen. *Sir Thomas More: Selections from his English Works and from the Lives by Erasmus and Roper*. Oxford, 1924.
Ames, Russell. *Citizen Thomas More and his Utopia*. Princeton, 1949.
Brémond, Henri. *Sir Thomas More*. Translated by Harold Child. London, 1904.
Bridgett, Thomas Edward. *Life and Writings of Blessed Thomas More*. London, 1924.
— *The Wisdom and Wit of Blessed Thomas More*. London, 1892.
Campbell, Lord John. *The Lives of the Lord Chancellors and Keepers of the Great Seal of England*. Vol. I. London, 1846.
Cayley, Arthur, the Younger. *Memoirs of Sir Thomas More*. London, 1808.
Cecil, Algernon. *Portrait of Thomas More*. London, 1937.
Chambers, Raymond Wilson. *The Place of St. Thomas More in English Literature and History*. London, 1937.
— *Thomas More*. New York, 1935.
Delcourt, J. 'Some Aspects of Sir Thomas More's English,' *Essays and Studies*, XXI (Oxford, 1936), 7–31.
Hollis, Christopher. *Thomas More*. Milwaukee, 1934.
Hurdis, James. *Sir Thomas More: A Tragedy*. London, 1792.
Huth, Henry. *Fugitive Poetical Tracts*. First Series 1493–1600. Introductory Notices by William Carew Hazlitt. London, 1875.
Hutton, William Holden. *Sir Thomas More*. London, 1895.
Lee, Sidney. *Great Englishmen of the Sixteenth Century*. London, 1904.
Macdiarmid, John. *Lives of British Statesmen*. London, 1838.
Mackintosh, Sir James. *The Life of Sir Thomas More*. London, 1844.
— 'Sir Thomas More,' *Lives of Eminent British Statesmen* (London, 1831), I, 1–110.
Marsden, John H. *Philomorus: A Brief Examination of the Latin Poems of Sir Thomas More*. London, 1842.
Maynard, Theodore. *Humanist as Hero*. New York, 1947.
More, Cresacre. *The Life and Death of Sir Thomas More*. [London], 1642.
Nelson, William. 'Thomas More, Grammarian and Orator,' *Publication of Modern Language Association*, LVIII (June 1943), 337–352.
O'Connell, Sir John R. *Lyra Martyrum: The Poetry of the English Martyrs*, 1503–1681. London, 1934.
— *St. Thomas More*. London, 1935.
Paul, Leslie Allen. *Sir Thomas More*. London, 1953.
Phillimore, J. S. 'Blessed Thomas More and the Arrest of Humanism in England,' *Dublin Review*, CLIII (July 1913), 1–26.
Potter, George Richard. *Sir Thomas More*. London, 1925.

Pyle, Fitzroy, 'Sir Thomas More's Verse Rhythms,' *London Times Literary Supplement*, (January 30, 1937), p. 76.

Reynolds, Ernest Edwin. *Saint Thomas More*. London, 1953.

Rope, Henry. *Fisher and More*. London, 1935.

Shebbeare, Claude Eustace. *Sir Thomas More: A Leader of the English Renaissance*. London, 1929.

Sir Thomas More. Harley Ms 7368 in *The Shakespeare Apocrypha: Collection of Fourteen Plays Ascribed to Shakespeare*, ed. C. F. Tucker Brooke. Oxford, 1908.

Smith, Richard Lawrence. *John Fisher and Thomas More: Two English Saints*. London 1935.

Stewart, William. 'The Fortuna Concept in the English Writings of Sir Thomas More,' Unpublished Doctoral Dissertation. Johannes Gutenberg Universität, Mainz, 1953.

Sullivan, Sister Rosenda. *A Study of the Cursus in the Works of Sir Thomas More*. Doctoral Dissertation. Catholic University of America, Washington, D. C., 1943.

Walter, William J. *Sir Thomas More: His Life and Times*. Philadelphia, 1839.

Warner, Ferd[inand]. *Memoirs of the Life of Thomas More*. London, 1758.

Wordsworth, Christopher. *Ecclesiastical Biography or Lives of Eminent Men, Connected with the History of Religion in England*. Selected and Illustrated with Notes. 3rd ed. 4 vols. London, 1839.

B. LITERARY STUDIES

Allardyce, Nicoll. *The Theory of Drama*. London, 1931.

Allen, Percy Stafford. *The Age of Erasmus*. Oxford, 1914.

— *Erasmus*. Oxford, 1934.

Baldwin, Charles Sears. *Medieval Rhetoric and Poetic*. New York, 1928.

Barlow, Sir Thomas Dalmahag. *The Medieval World Picture and Albert Durer's Melancholia*. Cambridge, England, 1950.

Baugh, Albert C. *A Literary History of England*. New York, 1948.

Beaven, Alfred B. *The Aldermen of the City of London*. Vol. I. London, 1908.

Berdan, Johm H. *Early Tudor Poetry*. New York, 1928.

Besant, Sir Walter. *Medieval London*. 2 vols. London, 1906.

Blackham, Harold John. *The Human Tradition*. London, 1953.

Blackham, Robert J. *The Soul of the City London's Livery Companies*. London, [n.d.].

Boas, Frederick S. *An Introduction to Tudor Drama*. Oxford, 1933.

— and A. W. Reed, eds. *Fulgens and Lucres: A Fifteenth-Century Secular Play*, by Henry Medwall. Oxford, 1926.

Boase, Charles William, ed. *Register of the University of Oxford*. Vol. I. Oxford, 1885.

Bolgar, R. R. *The Classical Heritage*. Cambridge, Eng., 1954.

Chambers, Edmund Kerchever. *The Medieval Stage*. 2 vols. London, 1903.

Charpentièr, J. P. *Histoire de la Renaissance des Lettres en Europe au quinzième siècle*. Paris, 1843.

Clark, Donald Lemen. *Rhetoric and Poetry in the Renaissance*. New York, 1922.

Craig, Hardin. *English Religious Drama of the Middle Ages*. Oxford, 1955.

Day, William. *Punctuation Reduced to a System*. London, 1853.

Dugdale, William. *Origines Juridiciales or Historical Memorials of the English Laws, Courts of Justice, etc*. London, 1666.

Dunbar, Helen Flanders. *Symbolism in Medieval Thought*. New Haven, 1929.

Edwards, H. L. R. *Skelton: The Life and Times of an Early Tudor Poet*. London, 1949.

Ellison, Monroe Lee. *The Early Romantic Drama at the English Court*. Wisconsin, 1917.

Emerson, Thomas. *Courts of Law of City of London*. [London], 1795.

Faral, Edmond. *Les Arts Poétiques du XII et XIII Siècles*. Paris, 1924.

Gerould, Gordon Hall. *The Ballad of Tradition*. Oxford, 1932.

Greswell, W. Parr. *Memoirs of Angelus, Politianus, Joannes Picus of Mirandula et al.* London, 1805.

282

Grimm, Florence M. 'Astronomical Lore in Chaucer,' *Studies in Language, Literature anp Criticism*, No. 2 (Lincoln, 1919), 51,53, 54.

Harrison, David. *Tudor England*. Vol. I. London, 1953.

Hazlitt, William Carew. *A Hundred Merry Tales*. London, 1887.

— *The Livery Companies of the City of London*. New York, 1892.

Hazlitt, William Carew, ed. *Remains of the Early Popular Poetry of England*. Vol. II. London, 1866.

Hebel, William John. *Tudor Poetry and Prose*. New York, 1953.

— and Hoyt Hopewell Hudson. *Poetry of the English Renaissance 1509-1660*. New York, 1929.

Herbert, William. *Antiquities of the Inns of Court and Chancery*. London, 1804.

— *History of the twelve great livery Companies of London*. 2 vols. London, 1836.

Hodgetts, Frederick. *The English in the Middle Ages*. London, 1885.

Howell, Wilbur Samuel. *Logic and Rhetoric in England, 1500-1700*. Princeton, 1956.

Hunter, George Leland. *Tapestries, their Origin, History and Renaissance*. New York, 1912.

Hurst, Gerald Berkeley. *A Short History of Lincoln's Inn*. London, 1946.

Hyma, Albert. *Erasmus and the Humanists*. New York, 1930.

J. G. N. 'The Lord Mayor's Feast in 1529,' *Gentleman's Magazine*, *XVI* (November 1841), 500.

Jones, John Winter. 'Observations on the Origin of the Division of Man's Life into Stages,' *Archaeologia*, *XXXV* (London, 1853), 167-189.

Keddie, Henrietta. *Tudor Queens and Princesses*. London, 1896.

Ker, Walter Paton. *Essays on Medieval Literatnre*. London, 1905.

Kristeller, Paul Oskar. *The Classics and Renaissance Thought*. Cambridge, Mass., 1955.

Lanier, Sidney. *Forerunners of Shakespeare. Studies in Elizabethan Poetry and its Development from Early English*. Vol. II. New York, 1902.

Lee, Sidney. *The Complete Works of William Shakespeare*. New York, 1908.

Lemprière, John. *A Classical Dictionary*. London, 1930.

Lesley, John. *The History of Scotland*. Edinburgh, 1830.

Lewis, Clive Staples. *English Literature in the Sixteenth Century, Excluding Drama*. Oxford, 1954.

Lyte, Maxwell H. C. *History of the University of Oxford*. London, 1886.

Mackenzie, William Roy. *The English Moralities from the point of view of Allegory*. 2 vols. London, 1914.

Mallett, Charles Edward. *A History of the University of Oxford*. 2 vols. London, 1924-27.

Manly, John Matthews. *Chaucer and the Rhetoricians*. London, 1926.

Maynard, Theodore. *The Connection between the Ballade, Chaucer's Modification of it, Rime Royal, and the Spenserian Stanza*. Doctoral Dissertation. Catholic University of America. Washington, D.C., 1934.

Mohl, Ruth. *The Three Estates in Medieval and Renaissance Literature*. New York, 1933.

Nelson, William. *John Skelton, Laureate*. New York, 1939.

Northbrooke, John. *A Treatise Against Dicing, Dancing, Plays, and Interludes*. London, 1843.

Old, Walter Gorn. *Fortune Telling by Numbers by Sepharial*. Philadelphia, 1943.

Omond, Thomas Stewart. *English Metrists*. London, 1907.

Patch, Howard Rollin. 'Fortuna in Old French Literature,' *Smith College Studies in Modern Languages*, *IV* (July 1923), 1-32.

— *The Goddess Fortuna in Medieval Literature*. Cambridge, Mass., 1927.

Pound, Louise. *Poetic Origins of the Ballad*. New York, 1921.

Powell, Frederick York. *Some Words on Allegory in England*. London, 1910.

Robertson, Joseph. *An Essay on Punctuation*. London, 1796.

Rossiter, Arthur Percival. *English Drama from Early Times to the Elizabethans*. London, 1950.

Saintsbury, George Edward. *The Flourishing of Romance and the Rise of Allegory*. London, 1897.

— *History of English Prosody*. 3 vols. London, 1906-10.

Sandys, John Edwin. *Harvard Lectures on the Revival of Learning.* Cambridge, Eng., 1905.
Selden, John ed. *A Brief Discourse Touching the Office of Lord Chancellor of England by Sir William Dugdale.* London, 1677.
Seznec, Jean. *The Survival of the Pagan Gods,* trans. from French by Barbara F. Sessions. New York, 1953.
Shipley, Joseph Twadell, ed. *Dictionary of World Literature.* New York, 1953.
Snell, Frederick John. *The Fourteenth Century.* London, 1899.
— *The Age of Transition 1400–1580.* 2 vols. London, 1905.
Spencer, Lyle M. *Corpus Christi Pageants in England.* New York, 1911.
Swan, Charles, translator. *Gesta Romanorum or Entertaining Moral Stories.* Introduction by Thomas Wright, Vol. I. New York, 1871.
Symonds, John Addington. *Renaissance in Italy.* Vol. II. New York, 1888.
Taylor, Henry Osborn. *The Classical Heritage of the Middle Ages.* New York, 1901.
— *The Medieval Mind: A History of the Development of Thought and Emotion in the Middle Ages.* 3rd ed. 2 vols. New York, 1919.
Thomson, W. G. *A History of Tapestry.* London, 1906.
Tilley, Morris Palmer. *A Dictionary of the Proverbs in England in the Sixteenth and Seventeenth Centuries.* University of Ann Arbor, Michigan, 1950.
Tillyard, Eustace M. W. *The English Renaissance.* Baltimore. 1952.
Triggs, Oscar Lovell, ed. *The Assembly of Gods by John Lydgate.* Doctoral Dissertation. University of Chicago, Chicago, 1895.
Walpole, Horace, ed. *Anecdotes of Painting in England.* Vol. I. Strawberry Hill, 1765.
Warton, Thomas. *The History of English Poetry.* 2nd ed. Vols. II and III. London, 1840.
Ward, A. W. and A. R. Waller. *Cambridge History of English Literature 1907–27.* Vol. II. Cambridge, Eng., 1908.
Weiss, R. *Humanism in England. During the Fifteenth Century.* Oxford, 1941.
Williamson, James A. *The Tudor Age.* London, 1953.
Wilson, John. *A Treatise on English Punctuation.* New York, 1871.
Woltmann, Alfred. *Holbein and his Time.* Translated by F. E. Bunnett. London, 1872.
Wyld, H. C. *Studies in English Rhymes from Surrey to Pope.* London, 1923.
Wynne, William. *Observations Touching the Antiquity and Dignity of the Degree of Serjeant at Law.* London, 1765.
Young, Frances Berkeley. 'The Triumphs of Death. Translated out of Italian by the Countess Pembroke,' *Publication of Modern Language Association, XXVII* (March 1910), 47–75.

III. LITERARY ANALYSIS

Albright, Evelyn May. *The Short Story: Its Principles and Structure.* New York, 1907.
Alden, Raymond Macdonald. *English Verse Specimens illustrating its Principles and History.* New York, 1903.
— *An Introduction to Poetry.* New York, 1909.
Auden, W. H. *Making, Knowing, Judging.* An Inaugural Lecture Delivered before the University of Oxford on 11 June, 1956. Oxford, 1956.
Barry, Sister Mary Martin. 'An Analysis of the Prosodic Structure of Selected Poems of T. S. Eliot.' Unpublished Dissertation. Catholic University of America, Washington, D.C., 1948.
Boulton, Marjorie. *The Anatomy of Poetry.* London, 1953.
Brower, Reuben Arthur. *The Fields of Light.* New York, 1951.
Brooks, Cleanth. *Understanding Fiction.* New York, 1943.
Chapin, Elsa, and Thomas Russell. *A New Approach to Poetry.* Chicago, 1929.
Cowl, R. P. *The Theory of Poetry in England.* London, 1941.
Duffy, Rev. John, C.S.S.R. *A Philosophy of Poetry Based on Thomistic Principles.* Doctoral Dissertation. Catholic University of America, Washington, D.C., 1945.

284

Eaton, Ralph Monroe. *Symbolism and Truth*. Cambridge, Mass., 1925.

Eliot, Thomas Stearns. *The Three Voices*. New York, 1954.

Ellis, Oliver, Geoffrey Johnson, and Christabel Burniston. *Poetic Technique*. Altrincham, 1949.

Empson, William. *Seven Types of Ambiguity*. London, 1947.

Flygt, Sten G. '"Durwachte Nacht": A Structural Analysis of Annette Von Droste-Hulshoff's Poem," *Journal of English and Germanic Philology*, (April 1956), 257–274.

Goodman, Paul. *Structure of Literature*. Chicago, 1954.

Grabo, Carl H. *The Art of the Short Story*. Chicago, 1913.

Gruber, Charles Frederick. *A Concept of Poetry*. Doctoral Dissertation. University of Pennsylvania, Philadelphia, 1934.

Hart, Walter Morris. 'Ballad and Epic, A Study in the Development of the Narrative Art,' *Studies and Notes in Philology and Literature*, (Boston, 1907), XI, 1–315.

Kaln, Sholom J. 'Towards an Organic Criticism,' *The Journal of Aesthetics and Art Criticism, XV* (September 1956), 58–73.

Kent, Charles William. *Study of Poetry*. Charlottesville, 1895.

Ker, William Paton. *Form and Style in Poetry: Lectures and notes*, ed. Raymond Wilson Chambers. London, 1928.

Krieger, Murray. *The New Apologists for Poetry*. Minneapolis, 1956.

Langer, Mrs. 'Structural Methods in Four Quartets,' *Journal of English Literary History, XXII* (September 1955), 240.

Leavis, F. R. *New Bearings in English Poetry*. London, 1932.

Macdermott, Mary Marshall. *Vowel Sounds in Poetry: Their Music and Tone Colour*. London, 1940.

Masson, David, I. 'Word and Sound in Yeats' "Byzantium",' *Journal of English Literary History, XX*(June 1953), 136–160.

Millett, Fred Benjamin. *Reading Poetry: A Method of Analysis with Selections for Study*. New York, 1950.

Perry, Bliss. *Study of Poetry*. London, 1920.

Richards, Ivor Armstrong. *Principles of Literary Criticism*. London, 1924.

— *Practical Criticism*. New York, 1950.

Richardson, Charles F. *A Study of English Rhyme*. Hanover, N. H., 1909.

Roberts, Michael. *Critique of Poetry*. London, 1934.

Routh, James E. 'The Theory of Verse.' Unpublished Doctoral Dissertation. Johns Hopkins University, Maryland, 1948.

Sewell, Elizabeth. *The Structure of Poetry*, London, 1951.

Stauffer, Donald A. *The Nature of Poetry*. New York, 1946.

Taylor, Warren. 'Tudor Figures of Rhetoric,' Part of an Unpublished Dissertation. University of Chicago, Chicago, 1937.

Urban, Wilbur Marshall. *Language and Reality*. London, 1939.

Wellek, René and Austin Warren. *Theory of Literature*. New York, 1949.

Wells, Henry W. *Poetic Imagery*. New York, 1924.

Whalley, George. *Poetic Process*. London, 1953.

Wilson, Edmund. *Axel's Castle*. New York, 1931.

Winchester, Caleb Thomas. *Some Principles of Literary Criticism*. New York, 1950.